FIGHTING FOR PEACE IN SOMALIA

Fighting for Peace in Somalia

A History and Analysis of the African Union Mission (AMISOM), 2007–2017

PAUL D. WILLIAMS

OXFORD
UNIVERSITY PRESS

OXFORD

UNIVERSITY PRESS

Great Clarendon Street, Oxford, OX2 6DP,
United Kingdom

Oxford University Press is a department of the University of Oxford.
It furthers the University's objective of excellence in research, scholarship,
and education by publishing worldwide. Oxford is a registered trade mark of
Oxford University Press in the UK and in certain other countries

© Paul D. Williams 2018

The moral rights of the author have been asserted

First Edition published in 2018
Impression: 6

Published in the United States of America by Oxford University Press
198 Madison Avenue, New York, NY 10016, United States of America

British Library Cataloguing in Publication Data
Data available

Library of Congress Control Number: 2017962083

ISBN 978-0-19-872454-4

Printed and bound by
CPI Group (UK) Ltd, Croydon, CR0 4YY

Acknowledgements

This book has been nearly eleven years in the making and I have incurred many debts of gratitude along the way. I am pleased to acknowledge them here.

First and foremost, this book would not have been possible without the numerous individuals who took time out of their busy schedules to help me understand different aspects of AMISOM's activities and answer my many questions. Some of them did this many times over and also subsequently spent considerable additional time commenting on more of my draft publications than I could reasonably expect. Many of them worked (or are still working) in incredibly difficult jobs under testing and sometimes deadly circumstances trying to build a more secure, democratic, and prosperous Somalia, whether as citizens or journalists, in NGOs or in governments, or for international organizations including the African Union (AU), United Nations (UN), and European Union. Since most of them were serving officials, and as agreed at the time, they will remain anonymous. But this book is far better than it would have been without your constructive engagement and I am truly grateful.

I owe a particular debt of thanks to the African Union. This book could not have been completed without the AU granting my request to meet its personnel and access documentation and other material. In places, my work is critical of aspects of the AU's policies, but I gratefully acknowledge the constructive support that I received for more than a decade from numerous AU officials. They have my respect and admiration.

While in Somalia, thanks are especially due to the AU–UN Information Support Team for providing accommodation, flights, security, and facilitating access for interviews. They too were always supportive of my research, even when I criticized elements of their work. I also want to thank various Bancroft Global Development personnel for their hospitality and taking the time to discuss their operations in Somalia with me.

A special note of thanks is also due to Dr Timothy Rainey and the team at the US Department of State's Africa Contingency Operations Training and Assistance (ACOTA) programme for granting me full access to their unclassified documentation related to AMISOM. This was immensely helpful in completing this book and shedding important light on the complex challenges that ACOTA confronted and the important training and capacity-building work that their personnel provided to AMISOM and its contributing countries.

For financial assistance that facilitated my research and travel, I would once again like to thank Michael Brown, the former Dean of the Elliott School of International Affairs, for awarding me several SOAR grants. I am also grateful to the Elliott School for granting me sabbatical leave during academic year 2014–15. During that period I was awarded a fellowship to work on this book at the Woodrow Wilson International Center for Scholars. I am very grateful to the Wilson Center staff and especially the Africa Program team for providing such a welcoming and conducive setting for scholarship. Thanks are also due to Katharina Krause and Dan Morgan-Russell, research assistants that the Wilson Center arranged to help me during my fellowship. I also received helpful research assistance from Elliott School student Jianyi Nie during 2014.

Acknowledgement is also due to several journals and institutions that published earlier versions of some of my arguments about AMISOM, including 'Into the Mogadishu Maelstrom: The African Union Mission in Somalia', *International Peacekeeping*, 16:4 (2009), pp. 514–30; 'Fighting for Peace in Somalia: AMISOM's Seven Strategic Challenges', *Journal of International Peacekeeping*, 17:3–4 (2013), pp. 222–47; 'The African Union Mission in Somalia and Civilian Protection Challenges', *Stability: International Journal of Security & Development*, 2:2 (2013), p. 39. DOI: http://dx.doi.org/10.5334/sta.bz; 'Stabilising Somalia: The African Union Mission and the Next Stage in the War against Al-Shabaab', *RUSI Journal*, 159:2 (2014), pp. 52–60; B.E. Bruton and P.D. Williams, *Counter-Insurgency in Somalia: Lessons Learned from the African Union Mission in Somalia, 2007–2013* (Tampa, FL: United States Joint Special Operations University, 2014); 'After Westgate: Challenges and opportunities in the war against al-Shabaab', *International Affairs*, 90:4 (2014), pp. 907–23; P.D. Williams with A. Hashi, *Exit Strategy Challenges for the AU Mission in Somalia* (Mogadishu: Heritage Institute for Policy Studies, February 2016); 'AMISOM Under Review', *RUSI Journal*, 161:1 (2016), pp. 40–9; W. Lotze and P.D. Williams, *The Surge to Stabilize: Lessons for the UN from the AU's Experience in Somalia* (New York: International Peace Institute report, May 2016); *The Battle at El Adde: The Kenya Defence Forces, al-Shabaab, and Unanswered Questions* (New York: International Peace Institute, July 2016); *UN Support to Regional Peace Operations: Lessons from UNSOA* (New York: International Peace Institute, February 2017); 'Joining AMISOM: Why six African states contributed troops to the African Union Mission in Somalia', *Journal of Eastern African Studies*, 12:1 (2018), pp. 172–92; 'Strategic Communications for Peace Operations: The African Union's Information War against al-Shabaab', *Stability: Internatioanl Journal of Security & Development*, 7(1) (2018), p. 3. DOI http://doi.org/10.5334/sta.606. and my chapter on AMISOM in J.M. Okeke and P.D. Williams (eds.), *Protecting Civilians in African Union Peace Support Operations: Key Cases and Lessons Learned* (South Africa: ACCORD, 2017). I owe an especially large debt to my co-authors on some of these publications, namely, Arthur Boutellis, Bronwyn Bruton, Katharina Coleman, Solomon Dersso, Abdirashid Hashi, Walter Lotze, and Jide Okeke. I learned a great deal in the process and am grateful for their expertise and friendship. I also want to recognize other friends and colleagues who have given up considerable amounts of their time to help me complete this book, either through conversations or commenting on draft papers. Thank you Alex Bellamy, Eric Berman, Cedric de Coning, Jonathan Fisher, Linnéa Gelot, Marco Jowell, Robyn Kriel, Jair Van Der Lijn, Ty McCormick, Frank Reidy, Colin Robinson, Timo Smit, Thierry Tardy, Tres Thomas, and Nina Wilén. I am also grateful to Thong Nguyen of the International Peace Institute for drawing several of the figures that appear in this book.

My final debt of gratitude is to my family. Neither of my parents, Carole and David Williams, lived to see this book's completion, but I wouldn't be where I am today without the love and support they gave me. I miss you. Once again, my incredible wife, Ariela Blätter, has enabled me to do what I do and I could not do it without her. I love you. Finally, I want to thank my wonderful daughter Zoë for bringing us such joy. This time around, aged four, she voiced a clear opinion about my work. Flicking through a pile of books on my office floor, she declared, 'Daddy, your books are too serious and don't have enough pictures!' You're right Zoë, and soon I'll explain why.

Of course, I alone am responsible for any remaining errors.

PDW

Washington DC
October 2017

Contents

List of Figures, Tables, and Box

Figures

Tables

Box

List of Abbreviations

ACOTA	Africa Contingency Operations Training and Assistance (US)
AFRICOM	US Africa Command
AMIS	AU Mission in Sudan
AMISEC	AU Mission for Support to the Elections in the Comoros
AMISOM	African Union Mission in Somalia
APC	Armoured Personnel Carrier
APF	African Peace Facility (EU)
ARPCT	Alliance for the Restoration of Peace and Counterterrorism
ARS	Alliance for the Re-Liberation of Somalia
ASWJ	*Ahlu Sunna Wal Jamaa*
AU	African Union
BNDF	Burundi National Defence Force
BOI	Board of Inquiry
C-IED	Counter-Improvised Explosive Device
CAR	Central African Republic
CCTARC	Civilian casualty tracking analysis and response cell
CIA	US Central Intelligence Agency
CIMIC	Civil–Military Coordination
CONOPS	Concept of Operations
DDR	Disarmament, Demobilization, and Reintegration
DFS	UN Department of Field Support
DPKO	UN Department of Peacekeeping Operations
DRC	Democratic Republic of the Congo
EARF	East African Response Force (US)
EASF	Eastern Africa Standby Force
EDD	Explosive Detecting Dog
ENDF	Ethiopia National Defence Force
EOD	Explosive ordnance disposal
EPRDF	Ethiopian Peoples' Revolutionary Democratic Front
EU	European Union
FAD	*Forces Armées de Djiboutiennes*
FGS	Federal Government of Somalia

FOB	Forward Operating Base
FPU	Formed Police Unit
HRDDP	Human Rights Due Diligence Policy (UN)
IDP	Internally Displaced Person
IED	Improvised Explosive Device
IGAD	Intergovernmental Authority on Development
IGASOM	IGAD Peace Support Mission to Somalia
IHL	International humanitarian law
IMATT	International Military Advisory and Training Team
IPO	Individual Police Officer
IRA	Interim Regional Administration
ISF	International Stabilization Force
ISR	Intelligence, surveillance, and reconnaissance
IST	Information Support Team
ISTAR	Intelligence, surveillance, target acquisition, reconnaissance
JCM	Joint Coordination Mechanism
KDF	Kenyan Defence Force
MIA	Mogadishu International Airport
MOCC	Military Operations Coordination Committee
MONUSCO	UN Stabilization Mission in the Democratic Republic of the Congo
MRAP	Mine Resistant Ambush Protected
MSR	Main Supply Route
NATO	North Atlantic Treaty Organization
NGO	Non-Governmental Organization
NSC	National Security Council
NSSP	National Security and Stabilization Plan (Somalia)
OCHA	Office for the Coordination of Humanitarian Affairs (UN)
PIU	Public Information Unit
POC	Protection of Civilians
PSC	Peace and Security Council of the African Union
PSOD	Peace Support Operations Division (AU)
QIP	Quick Impact Project
QRF	Quick Reaction Force
RPG	Rocket-propelled grenade
ROE	Rules of Engagement
RSLAF	Republic of Sierra Leone Armed Forces
SCIC	Supreme Council of Islamic Courts

SEA	Sexual exploitation and abuse
SNA	Somali National Army
SNP	Somali National Police
SNSF	Somali National Security Forces
SPF	Somali Police Force
SRCC	Special Representative of the Chairperson of the AU Commission
SRSG	Special Representative of the UN Secretary-General
SSR	Security sector reform
TCC	Troop-Contributing Country
TFG	Transitional Federal Government
TFI	Transitional Federal Institutions
TNG	Transitional National Government
UAV	Unmanned aerial vehicle
UPDF	Uganda People's Defence Force
UN	United Nations
UNAMID	African Union–United Nations Mission in Darfur
UNMAS	UN Mine Action Service
UNMEE	UN Mission in Ethiopia and Eritrea
UNMIS	UN Mission in Sudan
UNMISS	UN Mission in South Sudan
UNOCI	UN Operation in Côte d'Ivoire
UNPOS	UN Political Office for Somalia
UNSOA	UN Support Office for AMISOM
UNSOM	UN Assistance Mission in Somalia
UNSOS	UN Support Office in Somalia
USC	United Somali Congress

Maps

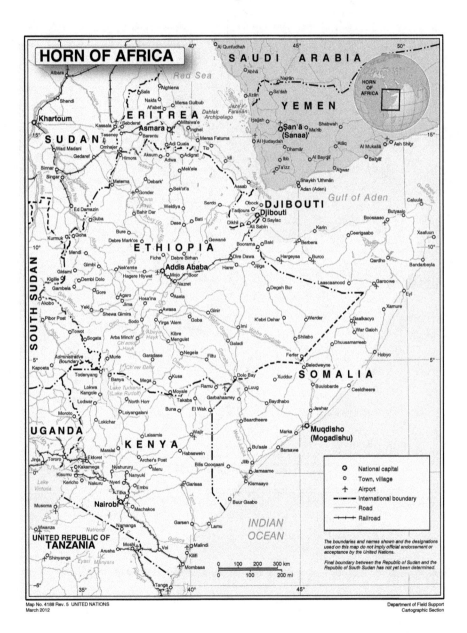

HORN OF AFRICA

◎	National capital
○	Town, village
✈	Airport
▬▪▬	International boundary
▬▬	Road
┼┼┼	Railroad

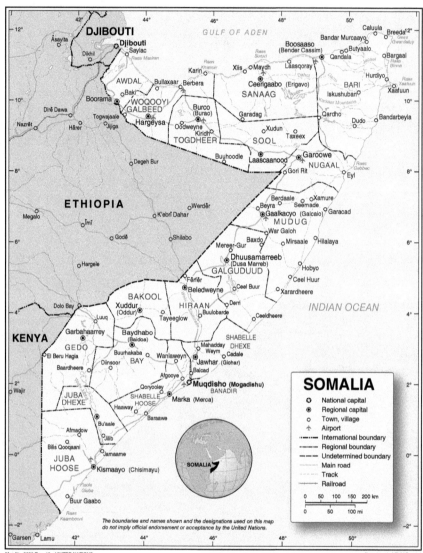

SOMALIA

- National capital
- Regional capital
- Town, village
- Airport
- International boundary
- Regional boundary
- Undetermined boundary
- Main road
- Track
- Railroad

0 50 100 150 200 km
0 50 100 mi

The boundaries and names shown and the designations used on this map do not imply official endorsement or acceptance by the United Nations.

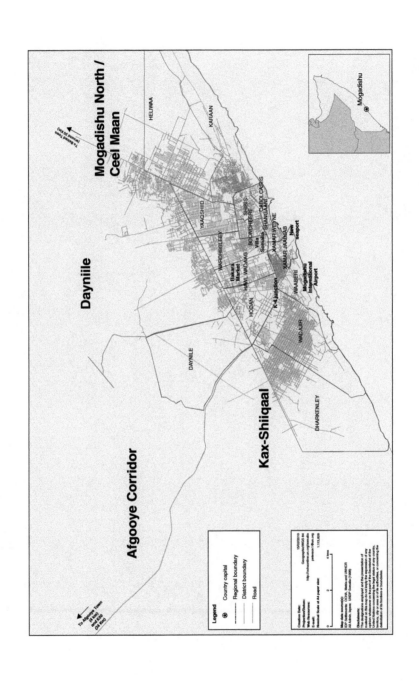

Afgooye Corridor

Daynille

Mogadishu North /
Ceel Maan

Kax-Shiiqaal

To Afgooye Town
(4 km)
and K50
(24 km)

To Balad Town
(14 km)

HELIWAA

KARAAN

YAAQSHIID

SHIBIS

WARDHIGLEY

BONDHEERE

Villa
Somalia

CABDLCASIS

SHANGAANI

XAMARWEYNE

New
Airport

Bakara
Market

HAWL WADAAG

XAMAR JAAB JAB

HODAN

K-4 Junction

WAABERI

Mogadishu
International
Airport

DAYNILE

WADAJIR

DHARKENLEY

Mogadishu

Legend

⊛ Country capital

— · — Regional boundary

—— District boundary

—— Road

Creation Date: 15/02/2010
Projection/Datum: Geographic/WGS 84
Web Resources: http://ochaonline.un.org/somalia
E-mail: pwteam1@un.org
Nominal Scale at A4 paper size: 1:153,836

0   2   4 Km

Map data source(s):
IDP Settlements: OCHA, Metta and UNHCR
All Admin. layers: UNDP Somalia (1998)

Disclaimers:
The designations employed and the presentation of
material on this map do not imply the expression of any
opinion whatsoever on the part of the Secretariat of the
United Nations concerning the legal status of any country,
territory, city or area or of its authorities, or concerning the
delimitation of its frontiers or boundaries.

Introduction

'Each morning the lion wakes up and knows that he must run faster than the antelope or he will starve. The antelope wakes up and knows that he must run faster than the lion in order to survive. So whether you are a lion or an antelope, when the morning arrives, you'd better be running.'

This version of a motivational African fable was displayed in the force headquarters of the African Union Mission in Somalia (AMISOM) in January 2013. Deployed to Mogadishu in March 2007, AMISOM's peacekeepers have been 'running' for more than ten years. They were tasked with stabilizing the country that had become the world's paradigmatic example of 'state failure', warlordism, and corruption for more than twenty years.[1] In practical terms, this meant AMISOM's personnel had to fight for peace in Somalia not just keep it. Their principal opponent was the *Harakat al-Shabaab al-Mujahideen* (hereafter, *al-Shabaab/*'the youth'), an adaptable and deadly organization that tried to destroy the successive sets of Somali authorities that AMISOM was mandated to protect.

The story of AMISOM's struggle in what became the deadliest peace operation in modern history is remarkable in its own right for many reasons that will be discussed in this book. But it is also important because it provides insights into how to address some of the most difficult challenges facing contemporary peace operations in other countries: How, for instance, can a peace operation help stabilize a country without a functional central government or a peace process? How can a peace operation combat a transnational, partly criminal organization that relies on asymmetric and terror tactics but also has deep roots in significant segments of the local population? How can multiple international organizations and states partner effectively to defeat such a foe? How can a peace operation succeed when there is a huge gap

---

[1] During this period, Somalia consistently ranked at or very near the bottom of governance and corruption indices such as the World Bank's *Governance Matters* database, http://info. worldbank.org/governance/wgi/#home; the Fund for Peace's Failed/Fragile States Index, http:// fundforpeace.org/fsi/; and Transparency International's Corruption Perceptions Index, www. transparency.org.

between its capabilities and its mandated tasks? And how should analysts and practitioners alike set expectations for such missions and evaluate success and failure? Understanding the case of Somalia over the last decade can shed important light on these and other questions at a time when more organizations than ever before are conducting military operations designed to bring peace to various war-torn territories, perhaps most notably in Afghanistan, Iraq, Democratic Republic of the Congo (DRC), Mali, Central African Republic (CAR), the Lake Chad Basin, central Africa, and the Sahel.

Initially comprising just one battle group of Ugandan soldiers who were airlifted into Mogadishu on 6 March 2007, AMISOM was the fifth peace support operation authorized by the African Union (AU), following earlier missions in Burundi, Sudan, and the Comoros. It was remarkable in several respects. First, it would become the AU's largest peace operation by a considerable margin. Indeed, by mid-2017, AMISOM was the largest deployment of uniformed peacekeepers in the world. Second, it became the longest running mission under AU command and control, outlasting the nearest contender—the AU Mission in Sudan—by over seven years. Unsurprisingly, therefore, AMISOM also became the AU's most expensive operation, at its peak costing approximately US$1 billion per year. As the only AU-led peace operation launched between 2007 and 2012, AMISOM also became a key barometer for the broader debates about how much progress was being made towards building the African Peace and Security Architecture. And, sadly, AMISOM became the AU's deadliest mission, although as discussed below the precise number of fatalities and wounded was not made public. AMISOM was also unusual in a doctrinal sense. Although it was often referred to as a peacekeeping operation, including at times on the mission's own website, AMISOM's mandated tasks went well beyond the realm of peacekeeping, including VIP protection, war-fighting, counterinsurgency, stabilization, and state-building as well as supporting electoral processes and facilitating humanitarian assistance.

This book has two central aims, which are reflected in its two parts. First, it aims to provide a detailed analysis of AMISOM's evolution from its genesis in an earlier, failed regional initiative in 2005 up to mid-2017. During that time, AMISOM evolved geographically, politically, and militarily. Geographically, the mission started out in the highly unusual position of having its military component deployed in one country, Somalia, but its civilian component, including the head of mission, deployed in another country, Kenya. Inside Somalia, AMISOM gradually evolved from occupying just a handful of strategic locations in Mogadishu to covering an area of operations that encompassed the whole of south-central Somalia, a region roughly the size of Iraq. Politically, having initially concluded that AMISOM's peacekeepers should not be drawn from Somalia's neighbouring countries, the AU and UN Security Council reversed this decision, and from 2012 Somalia's neighbours became an increasingly important part of the mission's military component (see Table I.1).

Table I.1. AMISOM TCCs army size, defence spending (US$), and contribution

Country	Joined AMISOM	Army Size	Defence Spending (deployment year)	AMISOM Contribution (est. maximum)
Uganda	2007	45,000	232m	6,200
Burundi	2007	35,000	78m	5,400
Djibouti	2011	8,000	Unknown (2010) 12m	1,800
Kenya	2012	20,000	942m	4,300
Sierra Leone	2013	10,500	14m	850
Ethiopia	2014	135,000	375m	4,400

Source: IISS, *The Military Balance* (London: Taylor & Francis, 2007, 2008, 2010, 2011, 2012, 2013, 2014, 2015).

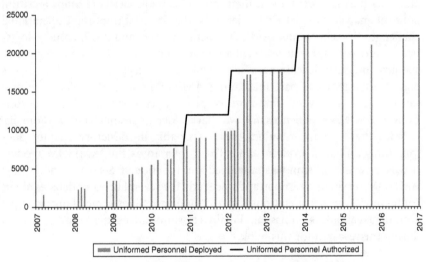

Fig. I.1. AMISOM Authorized and Deployed Strength, 2007–17

Source: Compiled by author from official AU and UN sources and interviews.

Militarily, AMISOM's initial authorized strength was 8,000, a ratio of approximately one peacekeeper for every 1,125 Somalis. This was subsequently increased to 12,000 uniformed personnel in December 2010, 17,731 in February 2012, and in November 2013 a temporary 'surge' raised that number to 22,126, which was still in operation by late 2017. However, as illustrated in Figure I.1, AMISOM's deployed strength increased irregularly.[2] Starting with approximately 1,600 Ugandan troops, it took AMISOM over three and a half years to

[2] In 2007, only ten of AMISOM's uniformed personnel were women. By 1 November 2017, AMISOM's military component had 741 women, while women represented 20 per cent of its police component. See AMISOM SRCC's Tweet at https://twitter.com/AmbFMadeira/status/925729141659521026

reach its initial authorized strength. The mission subsequently enlarged in two significant bursts in 2012 and early 2014.

The book's second aim is to understand how AMISOM and its key partners tried to overcome the major challenges confronting the mission, and what lessons should be learned from their experiences. As will become clear, the focus of my analysis is not the international and regional political debates that took place about AMISOM, principally between the members of the AU's Peace and Security Council in Addis Ababa, the Intergovernmental Authority on Development (IGAD) in Djibouti, the UN Security Council in New York, or the European Union (EU) in Brussels. Instead, my focus on the operational level is in keeping with the primary purpose of peace operations, to influence outcomes on the ground in their host country, and how AMISOM's personnel and their partners went about their jobs. This book therefore offers a critical political analysis of what I consider to be the six most important operational challenges that confronted AMISOM between 2007 and 2017, namely, logistics, security sector reform, civilian protection, strategic communications, stabilization, and developing a successful exit strategy. Each of these issues played an important part in shaping AMISOM's activities. They are also salient for most twenty-first-century peace operations and hence lessons from AMISOM's experiences may well have wider applicability beyond Somalia.

With these points in mind, the rest of this introductory chapter does four things. First, it explains what I will refer to as the 'AMISOM model', that is, how the mission was organized and functioned. Second, it notes how AMISOM serves as an important case study for several broader debates about contemporary peace operations. Third, it briefly outlines some of my principal arguments about the mission. Finally, it summarizes the sources utilized during the research for this book.

THE AMISOM 'MODEL'

I use the phrase the AMISOM 'model' as shorthand to describe how the mission was organized across the three dimensions of political authority, financing, and operations.[3] In brief, the AMISOM model became extremely

---

[3] References to AMISOM as a potential model for responding to other crises started appearing after late 2011 when the mission forced *al-Shabaab* to withdraw its main forces from Mogadishu and began to be viewed as a relative success. See, for example, Matt Freear and Cedric de Coning, 'Lessons from the African Union Mission for Somalia (AMISOM) for Peace Operations in Mali', *Stability*, 2:2 (2013), http://www.stabilityjournal.org/article/view/sta.bj/76; Cecilia Hull Wiklund, *The Role of the African Union Mission in Somalia* (Sweden: FOI, June 2013); and 'Letter dated 20 January 2013 from the Secretary-General addressed to the President of the Security Council', (S/2013/37, 21 January 2013).

complicated because it required significant coordination and cooperation between at least three international organizations and an array of bilateral partners. Specifically, for most of its duration, AMISOM required the AU to provide the troops, the EU to pay them (and provide other forms of support), the UN to provide logistics support, and key bilateral partners, notably the United States and United Kingdom, to provide equipment, training, and other forms of security assistance to the troop-contributing countries (TCCs).

As a consequence, while AMISOM's activities were principally conducted in Somalia, in order to understand how the mission was organized and made key decisions, the analysis must also explore political processes in Addis Ababa, New York, Nairobi, and Brussels, as well as in the capital cities of each of its major contributing countries and external partners. It must also take account of the activities of the mission's principal opponent, *al-Shabaab*, which also operated beyond Somalia.

Political Authority

AMISOM drew its authority from both the AU Peace and Security Council and the UN Security Council. At the UN, the mission was authorized by Security Council resolutions to help maintain international peace and security and respond to the particular threat posed by *al-Shabaab* militants. These resolutions also defined the details of AMISOM's mandate and specified the nature of UN support it could receive. At the AU, it was the Peace and Security Council that initially mandated AMISOM. Operational authority over the mission was subsequently vested in the Chairperson of the AU Commission, who delegated responsibility for all peace operations to the Commissioner for Peace and Security, with responsibility for the day-to-day strategic coordination issues falling to the Commission's Peace Support Operations Division (PSOD). Unlike the case of Darfur, where the AU Commission established the Integrated Task Force to oversee its peace operation there, no dedicated equivalent structure was created for AMISOM, although several ad hoc mechanisms were established from 2012 at the behest of AMISOM's TCCs and some of its external partners. With the approval of the AU Peace and Security Council, the Commission Chairperson appointed a Special Representative (SRCC) as head of the mission who exercised authority over AMISOM's military, police, and civilian components. The SRCC reported to the Chairperson through the Commissioner for Peace and Security. AMISOM's senior leadership appointments are listed in Appendix B, while an indicative snapshot of the mission's internal organization from 2012 is provided in Figure I.2. From 1995 until June 2013, the UN also operated a special political mission in Somalia, the UN Political Office for Somalia (UNPOS), which subsequently transitioned into a larger UN Assistance Mission (UNSOM). Both of these interacted with and

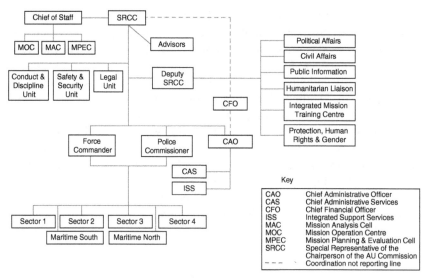

Fig. I.2. AMISOM's Organizational Structure, 2012

supported elements of AMISOM's mandate as well as pursuing their own. From 2009, the UN also established a novel mechanism, the UN Support Office for AMISOM (UNSOA), to provide the AU peacekeepers with logistical support and later support to some Somali security forces. UNSOA was financed from the UN-assessed peacekeeping contributions and was transitioned into the UN Support Office for Somalia (UNSOS) in late 2015.

Finance

AMISOM's financing was complicated, primarily because funds came from multiple sources, some of which were not designed to deal with the main challenges AMISOM faced. In addition, unlike most peace operations, AMISOM was unable to rely on many resources generated by the host state. Not only had Somalia's formal security sector collapsed since 1991, but the subsequent Somali federal authorities that were established since the early 2000s themselves lacked any major sources of sustainable revenue.

AMISOM's sources of funding included AU Member States, the AU Peace Fund, AMISOM partner countries and institutions, the UN Trust Fund for AMISOM (and, later, the Somali National Army), the UN Trust Fund for Somali Transitional Security Institutions, and from 2009, UN-assessed peacekeeping contributions.[4]

---

[4] Details of the donations to the AMISOM trust fund are provided in Chapter 8.

The non-AU sources were required because the AU's official system of financing peace operations did not work, owing to a lack of financial contributions from the Union's member states.[5] Even if it had worked, however, AMISOM's long duration and subsequent size would have made it impossible for the AU alone to fund. This was part of the reason why the AU made several attempts to find alternative sources of sustainable funding for its peace and security activities.[6] AMISOM's initial financial costs therefore fell directly on its first two TCCs, Uganda and Burundi (which joined at the end of 2007). They received considerable financial assistance from several external partners, notably the US, the UK, Italy, the EU, and a private firm, Bancroft Global Development.[7] The US, for instance, provided over $1.2 billion worth of bilateral security assistance to support the AMISOM forces fighting *al-Shabaab* between 2006 and mid-2015.[8]

While bilateral partners provided most training, equipment, and mentoring support for the TCCs, the EU provided the allowances for AMISOM's uniformed personnel, the mission's civilian component, as well as some other forms of support. The EU monies came from its African Peace Facility (APF), which is part of the European Development Fund and therefore had restrictions on paying for lethal equipment. By the end of 2017, the APF had dispersed more than €2 billion to support peace and security activities in Africa, with approximately €1.5 billion going to support AMISOM.

As noted above, the UN provided various forms of support. A UN Trust Fund for AMISOM and a UN Trust Fund for Somali Security Forces were established and received donations from various partner states and international organizations, some with caveats.[9] After UNSOA was established in 2009, AMISOM also received financial support for its logistics package from the UN's assessed contributions for peacekeeping.

Calculating the overall cost of AMISOM's activities would therefore involve the sum of bilateral support to all the TCCs, AMISOM's annual budget,

[5] As stated in the Protocol Relating to the Establishment of the Peace and Security Council of the African Union (2002), Member State TCCs bear the costs of any AU peace support operations during the first three months. The AU will then reimburse these countries within a maximum period of six months and then proceed to finance the operation.

[6] See, *Securing Predictable and Sustainable Financing for Peace in Africa* (African Union, August 2016), http://www.peaceau.org/uploads/auhr-progress-report-final-020916-with-annexes.pdf

[7] Smaller contributions were also made by Australia, Canada, China, Denmark, Japan, and Spain.

[8] Lauren Ploch Blanchard, testimony to US Senate, 4 June 2015, p. 2, https://www.foreign.senate.gov/imo/media/doc/060415_Blanchard_Testimony.pdf This figure does not include US contributions to UNSOA/UNSOS, which amounted to an additional $720 million between 2009 and 2016, or support to the Somali security forces.

[9] Reimbursement of lethal contingent-owned equipment was at times particularly challenging because donor caveats on the use of trust fund monies often restricted their use for reimbursement in this area.

additional donor support (through the UN trust funds) as well as UNSOA's budget (see Chapter 9). Between 2009 and 2016, these costs rose from approximately US$350 million per year to approximately US$1 billion per year.

Operations

AMISOM also had to rely on contributions from multiple actors at the operational level. These were the result of several interconnected levels of activity: political, strategic, operational, and tactical. As an AU peace support operation, at the political level, the AU claimed nominal control and authority over AMISOM. However, the UN Security Council claimed that it set the definitive mandates for the mission because it and the EU were providing the bulk of the financial resources. Following the end of Somalia's Transitional Federal Government (TFG) and its replacement with a permanent Federal Government in September 2012, Somalia's president also vied for a more significant say in AMISOM's political direction.

At the strategic level, things were relatively simple for AMISOM's first five years, when it functioned to all intents and purposes as a Ugandan-led coalition with Burundi as the junior partner. However, this changed in 2012 when various coordination mechanisms were established to give the AU Commission and AMISOM's partners a greater role in decision-making. Most notable were the mission's Force Headquarters, the Military Operations Coordination Committee (MOCC), the Joint Coordination Mechanism (JCM), the Joint Operations Centre, and the AMISOM/UNSOA Joint Support Operations Center, which also included personnel from the UN offices in Addis Ababa and New York.

The same was largely true at the operational level. During the mission's first five years, it was successive Ugandan Force Commanders that took most of the key decisions but these were then interpreted and implemented by the respective Contingent Commanders. Of course, official discussions took place between the AMISOM senior leadership team, including the SRCC, Deputy SRCC, Force Commander and Police Commissioner, but the reality was that the SRCC was based in Nairobi, and the Ugandan Force Commanders listened first and foremost to their long-time President Yoweri Museveni. The additional layers of bureaucratic complexity and coordination mechanisms that arrived from 2012 did little to change the reality that the TCC commanders looked primarily to their national capitals for direction. This was also reflected in the tactical level decision-making. Here, it was AMISOM's Contingent Commanders and later the Sector Commanders that really exercised control over AMISOM's operations in their respective areas.

As far as AMISOM's sectors were concerned, until early 2012, the organizational partitions of the mission's area of operations reflected the division of

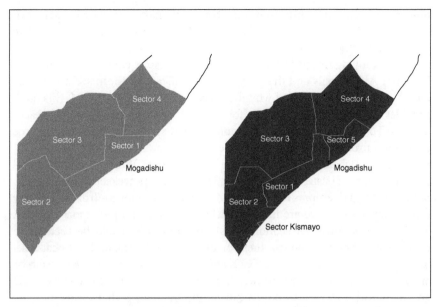

Fig. I.3. AMISOM's Sector Boundaries: 2012 (left) and 2014 (right)

labour between its Ugandan and Burundian contingents in the parts of Mogadishu under their control. From January 2012, however, AMISOM adopted a new force posture based around four land sectors and two maritime sectors (north and south of Mogadishu). From January 2014, AMISOM adopted a revised force posture, this time based around six land sectors and the maritime sectors. These are illustrated in Figure I.3.

In sum, the AMISOM 'model' was complicated and, I would argue, unrepeatable. Not only would it be extremely difficult to reassemble the model's constituent parts, as I discuss in the book's concluding chapter, there is a strong case to be made that it should not be repeated because parts of it were simply not fit for purpose.

PUZZLES, DEBATES, CONTROVERSIES

AMISOM's experiences serve as an important case study for several debates about contemporary peace operations. The first puzzle relates to the long-standing debate about why states provide peacekeepers.[10] Specifically, why did

---

[10] The literature on this topic has focused overwhelmingly on why states contribute to UN peacekeeping operations. See, for example, Jonah Victor, 'African peacekeeping in Africa: Warlord politics, defense economics, and state legitimacy', *Journal of Peace Research*, 47:2

only six of the AU's fifty-four members contribute troops to AMISOM: Uganda (2007), Burundi (2007), Djibouti (2011), Kenya (2012), Sierra Leone (2013), and Ethiopia (2014)?[11] Thirteen more African states reportedly considered deploying troops but decided against it, despite considerable lobbying by senior AU officials and the prospect of significant Western security assistance.[12] In telling the story of why those six states joined AMISOM, this book provides new empirical evidence for theories of why states provide peacekeepers. To my knowledge, it represents the first systematic study of the force generation process in an AU peace operation.

A second debate focuses on when and whether Western states should provide security assistance to countries that provide peacekeepers given some of the risks and dilemmas involved.[13] Since donors cannot control the military forces they assist, there are inherent risks, including an operational risk that TCCs underperform; an economic risk that resources could be used more effectively, either on other partners or on other activities; and political risks to the donor's reputation if the TCCs engage in misconduct in the mission or are used for oppression back home.[14] Such risks were widely debated by the AU and its partners at various points during the mission, perhaps most notably around the elections in Uganda (2011, 2016), Burundi (2015), and Ethiopia (2015). Indeed, several of AMISOM's partners including the United States and the EU suspended aspects of their security assistance and financial support to

---

(2010), pp. 217–29; Alex J. Bellamy and Paul D. Williams (eds.), *Providing Peacekeepers* (Oxford: Oxford University Press, 2013); Jacob D. Kathman and Molly M. Melin, 'Who Keeps the Peace? Understanding State Contributions to UN Peacekeeping Operations', *International Studies Quarterly*, 61:1 (2017), pp. 150–62. See also the roughly seventy peacekeeping country profiles compiled by the Providing for Peacekeeping project at www.providingforpeacekeeping.org

[11] There is also a related puzzle of why all but one of those TCCs maintained its commitment to AMISOM in the face of very high casualty levels and often incomplete financial reimbursement. As discussed in Chapter 6, Sierra Leone withdrew its battalion in December 2014 owing to the Ebola pandemic back home.

[12] These were Benin, Ghana, Malawi, Nigeria, Rwanda, and Tanzania during 2007. In 2010, Zambia and Senegal also studied the situation with an eye to deployment and Guinea pledged nearly 2,000 soldiers to AMISOM. And in a 2014 publication, the Kenyan government suggested that Gabon, Mali, Tunisia, and Swaziland had also 'promised to join' the AU mission. See, respectively, Milton Olupot, 'UPDF earn dollars in Somalia', *New Vision* (Kampala), 4 February 2007; 'Somalia: 'We'll fight back if attacked', AU troops say', *IRIN News*, 7 March 2007; and Wikileak Cable, 07ADDISABABA2185, 13 July 2007, §7; Mary Karugaba, '4 nations plan Somalia entry', *New Vision* (Kampala), 22 July 2010; Sarah Childress, 'Civilian Casualties Dog Troops in Somalia', *Wall Street Journal*, 29 July 2010; and KDF, *Operation Linda Nchi: Kenya's Military Experience in Somalia* (Nairobi: Ministry of Defence, 2014), pp. 257–8.

[13] For example, Danielle Beswick, 'The Risks of African Military Capacity Building: Lessons from Rwanda', *African Affairs*, 113:451 (2014), pp. 212–31; Jonathan Fisher, 'Managing Donor Perceptions: Contextualizing Uganda's 2007 intervention in Somalia', *African Affairs*, 111(444) (2012), pp. 404–23; Jonathan Fisher and David Anderson, 'Authoritarianism and the securitization of development in Africa', *International Affairs*, 91:1 (2015), pp. 131–51; Michael J. McNerney et al., *Defense Institution Building in Africa: An Assessment* (Santa Monica, CA: RAND, 2016).

[14] Beswick, 'The Risks'.

the Burundian government in 2015. The UN also shared some of these risks when it began providing logistical support to AMISOM and later some Somali forces. This prompted a debate about the application of the UN's Human Rights Due Diligence Policy, which is discussed in Chapter 10.

A third, and relatively under-studied issue for contemporary peace operations is how they can implement successful exit strategies.[15] Understanding why states joined AMISOM can shed some light on the circumstances under which they might ideally want to leave. But there are numerous other factors that shaped AMISOM's approach to implementing a successful exit strategy. These are analysed in detail in Chapter 13, but they hinge on AMISOM's ability to simultaneously reduce the threat posed by *al-Shabaab*, enhance the ability of local Somali forces to deal with that threat, and facilitate a political settlement that enables Somalia to build a legitimate, effective, and sustainable set of security services. Given AMISOM's expansive list of mandated tasks and the weak capacity of many Somali institutions, the prospects for the mission rapidly engineering a successful exit remain slim.

A fourth debate concerns how peace operations should deal with the unintended negative consequences of their deployment.[16] When large missions deploy into the complex social systems that characterize war-torn societies, they inevitably produce unintended consequences, that is, developments directly generated by the operation that were not intended by those who planned it.[17] Some unintended consequences can be foreseen and anticipated; others might be impossible to predict. They are not necessarily negative, but negative consequences—such as misconduct—have attracted most media headlines. In AMISOM's case, some positive unintended consequences— such as peacekeepers providing water and humanitarian assistance, or donating blood and medical supplies to local hospitals outside of the mission's formal mandate—were usually considered less newsworthy. Negative unintended consequences can be damaging in several ways, including causing civilian harm, weakening the ability of the peacekeepers to achieve their mandated tasks, and eroding the legitimacy of the authorizing organizations and peace operations as an appropriate tool of conflict management.

In AMISOM's case, the most widely debated negative unintended consequences were those where mission personnel engaged in corruption or caused harm to civilians, most notably through indiscriminate shellfire and instances

---

[15] For example, William J. Durch, 'Supporting Peace: The End', *Prism*, 2:1 (2010), pp. 43–56; Richard Caplan (ed.), *Exit Strategies and State Building* (Oxford: Oxford University Press, 2012).

[16] See Chiyuki Aoi, Cedric de Coning, and Ramesh Thakur (eds.), *Unintended Consequences of Peacekeeping Operations* (Tokyo: UN University Press, 2007).

[17] Chiyuki Aoi, Cedric de Coning, and Ramesh Thakur, 'Unintended consequences, complex peace operations and peacebuilding systems' in Chiyuki Aoi, Cedric de Coning, and Ramesh Thakur (eds.), *Unintended Consequences of Peacekeeping Operations* (Tokyo: UN University Press, 2007), p. 7.

of sexual exploitation and abuse (see Chapter 10). Corruption included cases of AMISOM personnel engaging in the illicit trade of goods and mission supplies, including rations, fuel, equipment, including HESCO defensive barriers and sandbags, and even ammunition. This eventually led to some AMISOM TCCs establishing courts martial in Somalia to try suspects. Arguably the most damaging set of allegations in this area revolved around claims that Kenyan forces were profiting from the illicit trade in charcoal and other commodities in southern Somalia. As discussed in Chapter 6, this was particularly controversial because the UN banned charcoal exports from Somalia in February 2012, in large part because the trade was known to support *al-Shabaab* activities in the region.[18]

Finally, AMISOM is a crucial case study in debates about assessing the risks to peacekeepers and developing effective force protection policies.[19] Once again, these debates have focused almost exclusively on UN peace operations. This book provides new information about the threats that AMISOM faced and how it sought to counter them, including *al-Shabaab* snipers, improvised explosive devices (IEDs), complex suicide/commando raids, ambushes of convoys, as well as more conventional large-scale attacks on AMISOM bases. Information about AMISOM's casualties proved to be a particularly controversial topic. Unlike for some other AU peace operations, there is no publicly available official total of how many AMISOM peacekeepers died or were wounded. This is because AU Commission policy for AMISOM was that the decision to release such information rested with the mission's contributing countries. The contributing countries chose not to release the full details and hence only bits and pieces of information appeared in the public realm. Appendix C provides a brief analysis of estimates of AMISOM's fatalities, which are probably more than 1,500. For now, suffice it to say that the comparatively large number of AMISOM casualties probably played a role in dissuading some countries from joining the mission. Uncertainty over casualty figures generated arguments back home within the TCCs, not least over whether AMISOM personnel killed in the line of duty should be publicly recognized, as is the case for all UN peacekeepers. The number of casualties also became tied up with the broader issue of financing AMISOM because it was the EU that paid the mission's death and disability compensation. Finally, uncertainty about casualties undermined AMISOM's credibility as a source of authentic information, stimulated considerable speculation in the media, and failed to effectively rebut *al-Shabaab* propaganda on the issue (see Chapter 11).

---

[18] S/RES/2036, 22 February 2012, §22.
[19] See, for example, Heidi Willmot, Scott Sheeran, and Lisa Sharland, *Safety and Security Challenges in UN Peace Operations* (New York: International Peace Institute, July 2015); Marina E. Henke, *Has UN Peacekeeping Become More Deadly? Analyzing Trends in UN Fatalities* (New York: International Peace Institute, December 2016).

PRINCIPAL ARGUMENTS IN BRIEF

Throughout the book, I make a number of arguments about AMISOM that are relevant to how we think about success and failure for such a complex mission.

First, AMISOM's relatively long duration and evolution through qualitatively different phases means it is usually unwise to draw blanket conclusions spanning the entire period. AMISOM was never a monolithic mission and as Part I of the book explains in considerable detail, it evolved in significant ways between 2007 and 2017. Indeed, it is probably more appropriate to think of AMISOM*s*—in the plural. Politically, AMISOM initially straddled three nodes in Mogadishu, Nairobi, and Addis Ababa. These reflected its military component, civilian component, and the AU Commission and some planning elements respectively. Officials operating in these locations did not always agree or even share all the same information. AMISOM's mandated tasks also evolved in significant ways and hence the mission was configured for different priorities at different times. These ranged from securing a foothold in Mogadishu to expelling *al-Shabaab*'s fighters from the entire city, and then shifting from urban warfare to undertake a range of expansion and stabilization operations across south-central Somalia. AMISOM also evolved in size. By January 2014, AMISOM had increased in size to nearly fourteen times its initial deployed strength, while its authorized strength of 8,000 was nearly tripled by November 2013. Similarly, AMISOM's area of operations expanded from roughly 100 square kilometres to more than 400,000 square kilometres from January 2012. Operationally, AMISOM's command and control structures and concomitant high degree of autonomy exercised by the TCCs in their respective sectors meant that it often functioned as separate missions. And as a multidimensional mission, its military, police, and civilian components did not always function in a coherent and coordinated manner. It is therefore sensible to limit most analytical conclusions to specific time periods or aspects of the mission's mandate.

That said, there were elements of continuity, and it is important to recognize that AMISOM achieved notable aspects of its mandate. At the strategic level, the mission successfully protected two iterations of the TFG and helped secure two electoral processes that produced new Federal Governments in September 2012 and January 2017. It is also reasonable to conclude that without AMISOM, *al-Shabaab* forces would have overrun the TFG after Ethiopian troops withdrew from Mogadishu in January 2009. Moreover, AMISOM's deployment was a precondition for enabling Ethiopia's withdrawal. The mission also weakened *al-Shabaab*, certainly from what one astute analyst called its 'golden age', during 2009 and 2010.[20] But its success pushed *al-Shabaab* to become more transnational and adopt more asymmetric tactics, which proved difficult for AMISOM to counter.

---

[20] The phrase is from Stig Jarle Hansen, *Al-Shabaab in Somalia* (London: Hurst, 2013), Chapter 6.

A third argument explains AMISOM's operational and tactical successes against *al-Shabaab*, most notably during the battle for Mogadishu in 2010 and 2011. As discussed in Chapter 4, these came about because of shifts in AMISOM's pre-deployment training regimes, the innovative use of urban warfare tactics including sniper teams, 'mouse holes', and breaching operations, and the sheer resilience of AMISOM's rank-and-file troops. Indeed, by late 2011, I submit that AMISOM's overall strategic success in protecting the TFG and weakening *al-Shabaab* was a direct result of these operational and tactical successes. And as detailed in Chapters 3 and 8, they came despite political and strategic problems in the design of the mission and the AU's weak political leadership, exemplified by successive heads of mission not being based in Somalia during this crucial period.

That decision stemmed from the dire security situation in Mogadishu. But it left AMISOM a military-heavy mission: most of its personnel were soldiers, and the Force Commander in Mogadishu became the principal interlocutor with the Somali authorities and visiting international officials. Later on, and especially after AMISOM expanded its operations across south-central Somalia during 2012 and was required to conduct stabilization operations, the military-heavy nature of the mission led to a mismatch between its capabilities and its mandated tasks. As demonstrated in Chapters 6, 7, and 12, not only were the mission's small police and tiny civilian components overwhelmed by the scope of the tasks, the lack of effective and legitimate Somali forces to fill in the gaps also presented an enormous challenge.

This relates to a fifth argument, namely, the difficulty of aligning the mission's progress on both the military and political tracks simultaneously. In sum, while AMISOM managed at various times to make significant progress on the military track, political progress usually lagged behind. And without genuine political progress on issues like power-sharing between the federal authorities and the regions or national reconciliation, military progress was likely to be unsustainable. During the period of the two TFG administrations, AMISOM's principal strategic challenge was to consistently win the support of the local population when it was mandated to support a political entity that was perceived as illegitimate, corrupt, and ineffective by many of those locals. Once a new Federal Government was established in September 2012, AMISOM's key local partner was considered more legitimate, but it still suffered from chronic levels of corruption, clan-based rivalries, and very limited capacity to deliver essential services to Somali citizens. As successive reports by the UN Monitoring Group pointed out, there was in essence a misalignment of political interests between AMISOM and key Somali political elites.[21] While AMISOM and its partners engaged in an essentially top-down exercise in state-building

---

[21] See, for example, *Report of the Monitoring Group on Somalia and Eritrea pursuant to Security Council resolution2182 (2014): Somalia* (S/2015/801, 19 October 2015), p. 6.

that usually prioritized the supply of resources to the central government rather than Somalia's regions, the political elites in the capital saw little incentive to take the tough decisions on power-sharing and reconciliation that would have enabled legitimate and effective state institutions to be built. As the Chairperson of the AU Commission had correctly pointed out shortly before AMISOM's deployment,

> The Somalis and their leaders have a central role to play. The issues confronting Somalia are first and foremost of a political and governance nature. A peace support operation is indeed needed to address them, but it cannot substitute a genuine commitment to dialogue and reconciliation among the Somalis, including addressing the grievances of groups that may feel left outside of the emerging political dispensation.[22]

It was Somalis, not foreign peacekeepers, who ultimately held the key to peace in Somalia. AMISOM was therefore caught in a difficult position in large part because no matter what military successes it achieved, sustainable peace in Somalia depended on political progress being made on the fundamental questions of governance. And when issues of governance were concerned, AMISOM, like every other external actor, also became caught up in the dynamics generated by clan/sub-clan politics and a war economy that continued to benefit some well-placed elites. This caused problems on a variety of issues but most notably over the role of Kenyan forces in the establishment of the Interim Jubaland Administration in 2013 (discussed in Chapter 6) and AMISOM's attempts to help build the Somali National Army (discussed in Chapter 9).

As will also become clear in the chapters that follow, throughout its first ten years AMISOM suffered from severe capability gaps across two dimensions. First, the capabilities for AMISOM authorized by the African Union and United Nations were insufficient to achieve its stated objectives. This was particularly apparent after 2012 when AMISOM was given a relatively small number of troops to stabilize the huge area of south-central Somalia.[23] As discussed in Chapter 5, this was largely because one of the planning assumptions for the mission's 2012 Concept of Operations was that the Somali security forces would be able to field an equivalent number of troops to support AMISOM. This turned out to be a faulty assumption. The second dimension was AMISOM's inability to generate some of the capabilities it was authorized to have. One problem was vacancy rates. Most peace operations suffer from some gaps between their authorized and deployed strength on the

---

[22] *Report of the Chairperson of the Commission on the Situation in Somalia* (PSC/PR/2(LXIX), 19 January 2007, §41.

[23] For some force-to-space and force density ratios applied to Somalia, all of which show AMISOM to fall well short of the advised numbers, see Noel Anderson, 'Peacekeepers fighting a Counterinsurgency Campaign: A Net Assessment of the African Union Mission in Somalia', *Studies in Conflict & Terrorism*, 37:11 (2014), pp. 945–7.

ground, but AMISOM was an extreme case: there was no agreed timetable for deploying troops and ultimately it took three and a half years to reach the mission's initial authorized strength of 8,000 troops. Even by March 2017, AMISOM's civilian component was missing one hundred staff out of the 240 approved posts.[24] But numbers were not the only problem. The mission's inability to generate a range of military enablers also presented major challenges. Specialist units such as logistics, heavy transportation, engineering, ISTAR, special forces, medial support, and, crucially, aviation were all in short supply. To take just two examples, AMISOM's early logistics support was so bad that between April 2009 and May 2010, approximately 250 peacekeepers contracted wet beriberi from lack of thiamine/vitamin B1. Over fifty of them were airlifted to hospitals in Kenya and Uganda, and four died.[25] It is also shocking that AMISOM did not acquire its first military helicopter as a mission asset until December 2016, despite being authorized an aviation component of twelve military helicopters in February 2012.[26]

The final argument to flag here relates to the many challenges AMISOM faced when trying to establish a unified system of command and control, admittedly a perennial problem for most multinational forces. When Uganda and Burundi were AMISOM's only TCCs, the mission's command structure was effectively a mini-coalition with Uganda assuming the lead role. But things became more complicated from 2012 when other countries joined the mission and a multinational Force Headquarters and other international coordination mechanisms were established. Being in essence a war-fighting operation, AMISOM's national contingent commanders in their respective sectors retained a considerable degree of autonomy and did not always coordinate their activities with the Force Commander. As one senior AMISOM official put it, 'National officers in AMISOM contingents will talk to their national headquarters before talking to the Force Commander.'[27] Another senior commander summed up the situation by saying that the AMISOM Force Commander had command but no real control of the national contingents, and hence trying to ensure coordination between them was the best that could be achieved in practice.[28] In some ways this was simply a recognition of the realities and national politics of fighting a war by coalition. As one informed

[24] Cedric de Coning, Irene Limo, James Machakaire, and Jide M Okeke, 'The Role of the Civilian Component in African Union Peace Support Operations' in Thomas Mandrup and Francois Vrey (eds.), *The African Standby Force: Quo Vadis?* (Stellenbosch: SunMedia, 2017), pp. 63–86.

[25] John T. Watson et al, 'Outbreak of Beriberi among African Union Troops in Mogadishu, Somalia', *PloS ONE* 6:12 (December 2011), e28345.

[26] S/RES/2036, 22 February 2012, Annex. From late 20009, AMISOM was able to call on the support of the two utility helicopters provided as part of UNSOA.

[27] Telephone interview, senior AMISOM official, 7 November 2015.

[28] Interview, senior AMISOM official, Nairobi, 9 April 2015.

analyst put it, the Force Headquarters 'was never designed to exercise command and control over the national contingents. It could only ever provide a coordinating function and facilitate positive interaction between the TCCs. This was war-fighting and troops were always going to respond to their national capitals.'[29] Nevertheless, these command and control arrangements had several important consequences. Most notably, they gave considerable power to the Contingent Commanders and hence the national capitals of the TCCs, and they made coordination across AMISOM's different sectors difficult. This, in turn, provided *al-Shabaab* with an opportunity to take advantage of the relatively sheltered areas along AMISOM's sector boundaries.

A NOTE ON SOURCES

My analysis of AMISOM has been informed by a wide range of primary and secondary sources, as well as data gathered from more than 200 interviews. Interviews were conducted with relevant experts since 2007 in Djibouti, Ethiopia, France, Germany, Kenya, Uganda, Somalia, the United Kingdom, and the United States, as well as by telephone or email. They included AMISOM personnel and representatives from the mission's main troop- and police-contributing countries, officials (civilian and military) from the AU, UN, IGAD, and the EU, analysts, journalists, academics, and members of NGOs, as well as Somali officials, intellectuals, journalists, and members of the public. Since many of them were serving officials of governments, international organizations, or NGOs, and as agreed at the time, all communications were conducted on a not-for-attribution basis and hence my interviewees remain anonymous. Where I reference their contributions directly, I have identified them by their most relevant generic affiliation or position.

In addition to communications with these interlocutors, primary sources included a wide range of official documents from the AU, IGAD, UN, EU, and Somali authorities. I also analysed several hundred WikiLeaks cables sent from US embassies and missions, mainly between 2006 and 2010, from AMISOM's troop-contributing countries as well as the AU and relevant EU member states.

During the course of my research, I also acquired several hundred unpublished documents, principally, but not exclusively, from the AU, UN, Somali authorities, and a variety of AMISOM's partners. These include concept of operations documents, rules of engagement, strategic directives, mission directives, operational directives, policy guidelines, annual reports, mission implementation

---

[29] Interview, US analyst, Washington DC, 20 January 2016.

plans, aide memoirs, concept papers, position papers, technical assessments, conference summaries, scoping studies, strategic reviews, strategic plans, road-maps, joint reviews, benchmarking reports, legal documents (including memorandums of understanding), planning assessments, lessons learned reports, briefing papers and presentations, letters, memorandums, special inquiries, presentations, work plans, equipment inventories, situation reports, trends analysis, operations orders, after action reviews, polling data (including surveys and reports), *notes verbale*, standard operating procedures, minutes of meetings, training documents, and financial records. Naturally, these unpublished primary sources form an important part of my analysis and they are referenced in the book when I draw on them directly.

Finally, I was also granted access to the relevant unclassified documentation of the US Department of State's Africa Contingency Operations Training and Assistance (ACOTA) programme. This included several hundred additional unpublished documents that shed important light on the training and capacity-building work conducted by and for AMISOM and its contributing countries. Throughout the book, unpublished documents that were accessed via ACOTA are designated with 'ACOTA files' after the reference.

During 2016 and early 2017, I participated in the joint AU–UN review of available mechanisms to finance and support AU peace support operations authorized by the UN Security Council and the AMISOM ten-year lessons learned process organized by the AU Commission. Hence I benefited from the participants' insights, particularly on the issue of AMISOM's exit strategy challenges (see Chapter 13).

STRUCTURE OF THE BOOK

The following chapters aim to substantiate the arguments sketched above. Part I, 'History', comprises seven chapters that trace AMISOM's evolution from its genesis in the international efforts to resurrect a central government in Somalia in the early 2000s until a few months after the London Security Pact was concluded in May 2017. Part II, 'Challenges', comprises six chapters that analyse how AMISOM tried to overcome its major operational challenges. These focus on logistical support, building and reforming the Somali security forces, civilian protection, stabilization, strategic communications, and developing a successful exit strategy. The concluding chapter reflects upon how we should assess this remarkable peace operation and the main lessons that emerge from it.

Part I
History

1

Genesis

October 2004 to March 2007

This chapter analyses AMISOM's genesis. It argues that the mission emerged as the major international response to four important developments in Somalia and the Horn of Africa in the aftermath of *al-Qa'ida*'s attack on the United States on 11 September 2001. First was the establishment, in Kenya, of a Transitional Federal Government (TFG) for Somalia in 2004, after more than a dozen failed attempts.[1] However, the TFG lacked local legitimacy and the ability to move into Somalia's capital without massive external assistance. Second, the African Union (AU) and Intergovernmental Authority on Development (IGAD) responded to the subsequent call by the new TFG president for a peacebuilding mission to help his regime establish itself inside Somalia. The third development came in June 2006 with the decisive victory of the Union of Islamic Courts over the various warlords that had previously run Mogadishu and much of south-central Somalia. Their collusion with elements of *al-Qa'ida* and *al-Shabaab* was used in both Washington DC and Addis Ababa to justify further Ethiopian military engagement. Finally, AMISOM emerged as an exit strategy for Ethiopia's troops after Prime Minister Meles Zenawi decided to intervene militarily to topple the Islamic Courts and install the TFG in Mogadishu in December 2006.

The decision to establish AMISOM was thus taken in light of the previous failure to deploy the IGAD operation. The mission's initial rationale was to protect Somalia's fledgling TFG and provide an exit strategy for the embattled Ethiopian forces that were defending it. The fact that Uganda was the sole TCC for the first nine months also requires some explanation.

---

[1] TFG, *Somalia National Security and Stabilization Plan (NSSP)* (Baidoa: 14 June 2006), p. 2. Hereafter, TFG, *NSSP* (2006).

ESTABLISHING SOMALIA'S TRANSITIONAL FEDERAL GOVERNMENT

By the late 1990s, the process of establishing a transitional federal government for Somalia was seen as desirable by a range of Somali and international actors. It was thought necessary because in January 1991 Somalia's central government collapsed after approximately three years of civil war.[2] Specifically, several Somali armed factions had cooperated to drive long-time dictator General Mohamed Siad Barre from the capital city, Mogadishu. Barre had taken power in a military coup in October 1969. He ran a highly personalized and corrupt regime that dispensed money, land, and favours to his most loyal supporters, including over fifty members of his family who occupied official positions as well as favoured members of the Marehan and related Darod clans. Once Barre's forces fled Mogadishu in early 1991, however, conflict erupted between his principal opponents, most notably the leaders of two factions of the United Somali Congress (USC), General Mohammed Farah Aidid and Ali Mahdi. Aidid, the Chairman of the USC, thought he should become Somalia's president but the USC leadership instead endorsed as Interim President Ali Mahdi, a wealthy businessman who supported the pro-reform Manifesto Group comprising over one hundred important moderates, intellectuals, community organizers, and merchants. The subsequent fighting between these two factions left Somalia without a federal government and displaced many thousands of people across the south-central region.

The state collapse and subsequent humanitarian crisis prompted the deployment of three separate peace operations between mid-1992 and mid-1995: the UN Operations in Somalia (UNOSOM I and II), and the Unified Task Force, a multinational force led by the United States. The latter two missions saw nearly 40,000 foreign troops and peacekeepers deploy into south-central Somalia, initially with a mandate to support peacemaking initiatives but which was later broadened to protecting humanitarian relief and an array of so-called 'nation'-building tasks.[3] After attempting to forcibly disarm the warring factions in Mogadishu, in June 1993 two-dozen Pakistani UN peacekeepers were killed by Aidid's forces. This prompted several US-led attempts to capture him, culminating in the infamous 'Black Hawk Down' battle in Mogadishu on 3–4 October 1993. This saw a botched unilateral US raid to capture some of Aidid's senior aides end in a lengthy battle that killed eighteen American soldiers, one UN peacekeeper, and several hundred Somalis. Shortly

---

[2] For background on the civil war and Somali politics more generally see I.M. Lewis, *A Modern History of the Somali* (Oxford: James Currey, 4th edition, 2002).

[3] See Paul D. Williams, 'UNOSOM I' and 'UNOSOM II' in Joachim Koops et al. (eds.), *The Oxford Handbook of United Nations Peacekeeping Operations* (Oxford: Oxford University Press, 2015), pp. 408–15 and 429–42.

thereafter, the United States withdrew its forces and the rest of the UN peacekeeping force followed suit by March 1995.

In essence, the foreign peacekeepers left behind much the same situation in Somalia as they had confronted at the start of their deployment: a country awash with weapons and riven by factionalism based on a mixture of allegiances to clans, sub-clans, and sub-sub-clans, as well as the so-called 'warlords' and powerful business elites. Noted academic Ken Menkhaus described the situation as 'governance without government', whereby a variety of non-state actors and informal systems of adaptation delivered services 'in the prolonged absence of a central government'.[4] This uncertain and often violent environment proved very difficult for international actors (including most NGOs) to operate in and effectively led to a period of international neglect. This changed somewhat after Ethiopian forces began to conduct cross-border raids against a radical militant organization called *al-Ittihad al-Islamiya*, and after the bombings carried out in August 1998 against the US embassies in Nairobi, Kenya, and Dar es Salaam, Tanzania, because US officials believed some of the perpetrators were hiding in Somalia. The prominence of the US counterterror lens for viewing events in Somalia increased again after the 9/11 attacks on the World Trade Center and Pentagon. In the early 2000s, therefore, these US interests as well as those of several regional states, notably Ethiopia and Kenya, prompted a major international effort to resurrect a central government for Somalia.

Somalia's TFG emerged in late 2004 as the successor of the Transitional National Government which was established in 2000 out of the Somali National Peace Conference (alternatively known as the 'Arta Process' named after the town in Djibouti where it was held). Little substantive process was made, however, until the aftermath of *al-Qa'ida*'s 9/11 attacks on the United States. This heightened fears that Somalia's anarchic territories might provide a safe haven for *al-Qa'ida* and stimulated renewed interest by some external actors in efforts to resurrect the Somali state.

In December 2001, negotiations were started in a new Somali National Reconciliation Conference or 'Mbagathi Process' (after the Kenyan town where discussions were eventually held).[5] They were led by the IGAD as part of the regional institution's efforts to take a more proactive role in conflict management in the region's two key cases of Somalia and Sudan.[6] The Mbagathi process started with two parallel sets of talks between the Transitional National Government and the Somali Restoration and Reconciliation

---

[4] Ken Menkhaus, 'Governance without Government in Somalia', *International Security*, 31:3 (2006/07), p. 74.

[5] Funding for the talks was provided by the European Commission with political support coming from the AU, the Arab League and the UN.

[6] For a discussion of IGAD's weaknesses in the field of conflict management see Sally Healy, *An Assessment of IGAD's Contribution to Regional Security in the Horn of Africa* (London: LSE Crisis States Working Paper No. 59, April 2009).

Council in Nakuru, Kenya and in Gode, Ethiopia. Like previous efforts, the process failed to immediately resolve the underlying drivers of the Somali conflict and aggravated the clan factions' feuding. Despite the best efforts of the Kenyan mediators, the process unfolded over three phases and several years. Nevertheless, it did eventually produce the TFG.

In October 2002, the parties were able to agree the Eldoret Declaration on Federal Government Structure and Cessation of Hostilities. In February 2003, phase two began when the talks were relocated to Mbagathi, outside Nairobi. After several months of wrangling, a draft charter was eventually produced on 15 September 2003, but in October the talks closed down. Phase three began in May 2004 when a new round of negotiations was launched and between August and October the constituent parts of what would become the TFG took shape: a Transitional Federal Charter was adopted and a unicameral, 275-member Transitional Federal Parliament was selected, composed primarily of faction leaders or 'warlords', many of whom were suspected of engaging in criminal activities and of committing atrocities following the civil war. The TFG was known amongst many locals by the derogatory Somali nickname *daba dhilif*, which translates roughly as a 'government set up for a foreign purpose' or a 'satellite government'.[7]

The Transitional Charter outlined a five-year mandate for the TFG that would, theoretically, lead to a new Somali constitution and a transition to a representative government following national elections envisaged for 2009. It called for a decentralized system of administration in Somalia that would be headed by the TFG but be inclusive of existing state governments and regional administrations, such as Somaliland and Puntland. Although the Transitional Charter established Islam as the national religion of Somalia and was based on *shari'a* law, it nevertheless established a quota requiring 12 per cent of parliamentary seats be filled by women.[8] The Transitional Charter also included the highly controversial '4.5 formula'. This was a quota system devised during a 1997 conference in Ethiopia that was designed to equally distribute power among Somalia's four majority clans (Dir, Darod, Hawiye, and Rahanweyn), while giving a half of one share to the historically disenfranchised minority clans (such as the Gaboye, Tumal, Yibir, Jaji, Yahar and the ethnic Bantus—the '0.5' in the formula).[9] The 4.5 formula had been applied to previous governments and, though donors saw this as a way to create a level playing field between the clans, it had proven ineffective at

---

[7] Mary Harper, *Getting Somalia Wrong?* (London: Zed, 2012), p. 177.
[8] The Transitional Federal Charter of the Somali Republic (February 2004), Article 29, https://peacemaker.un.org/somalia-transitionalcharter2004
[9] This was translated into sixty-one seats in parliament for each of the four major clans and thirty-one seats allocated for the remaining groups.

balancing clan interests and was widely despised in Somalia as an undemo-cratic ethnic quota system.[10]

A former warlord, Abdullahi Yusuf Ahmed, was elected by the new parlia-ment to serve as the transitional president of Somalia from October 2004 until 2009. Yusuf was at the time the president of the Puntland region of Somalia, and had played a significant role in attempts to defeat the radical *al-Ittihad al-Islamiya* movement during the 1990s.

In contrast to the earlier Transitional National Government (TNG), which had been dominated by the Mogadishu-centred Hawiye clan, the TFG's top leaders and security forces were dominated by members of a coalition between Yusuf's Majerteen/Darod clan (based in Puntland) and the Abgal/Hawiye clan. This group was predominantly pro-Ethiopian, pro-federalist, and anti-Islamist.[11] The TFG was inaugurated in December 2004 and immediately gained international recognition.

The 4.5 formula required Yusuf to select his prime minister from a rival clan, rather than his own Darod/Majerteen sub-clan. He chose a relatively unknown 'technocrat' (a veterinarian) from the Hawiye/Abgal subclan, Ali Mohamed Gedi. Yusuf and Gedi clashed from the beginning, and worse, Gedi's strong personal ties to the ruling regime in Addis Ababa cemented rumors within the Somali population that the TFG was an Ethiopian proxy regime. Gedi's attempt to mend fences by adopting a posture of inclusiveness also backfired when, attempting to satisfy a host of competing clan constitu-encies, he appointed an unwieldy ninety-member cabinet. This huge cabinet and the rancor between Yusuf and Gedi rendered the TFG utterly dysfunc-tional throughout Yusuf's entire five-year term in office. The situation was well summed up by Britain's minister for Africa, Chris Mullin, who described a meeting with Yusuf in Nairobi in 2004.

> Item One on today's long agenda: a call on Abdullahi Yusuf, the new 'President' of Somalia. At the moment, of course, he is nothing of the sort. Just a man in a hotel in Nairobi. Later, in another hotel, I addressed the new Somali 'parliament', which comprises some of the very people who have reduced Somalia to rubble.[12]

IGASOM: AUTHORIZED BUT NOT DEPLOYED

Created in Kenya with donor funding and populated primarily by faction leaders and many members of Somalia's diaspora, it was not surprising that

[10] See, for example, *Selection of the Next Somalia Parliament: The Citizens' View* (Mogadishu: Heritage Institute for Policy Studies, 2015), pp. 8–12.

[11] Ken Menkhaus, *Somalia: A National and Regional Disaster?* (UNHCR, April 2009), pp. 1–2.

[12] Cited in Harper, *Getting Somalia Wrong?*, p. 176.

the TFG generated little popular support in Somalia. Shortly after assuming office, therefore, President Yusuf visited Addis Ababa to ask the African Union to deploy 20,000 peacekeepers to help him consolidate his government and disarm Somalia's 55,000 clan and bandit militiamen.[13] This resulted in the regional powers that had helped established the TFG issuing a communiqué via IGAD calling on the AU and IGAD to 'explore practical and more affordable ways to support and sustain a peace restoration and protection force for Somalia'.[14]

Although the AU did not carry out Yusuf's request for a 20,000-strong force, in January 2005 IGAD proposed the deployment of a 10,500 strong Peace Support Mission to Somalia known as IGASOM, which would facilitate the entry of Somalia's new government into its capital city, Mogadishu.[15] In mid-February, the AU and IGAD sent an initial Fact-Finding and Reconnaissance Mission to determine the mandate, force size, structure and tasks of the proposed peace support mission. The IGASOM Deployment Plan was presented by the military experts from the IGAD states, refined by their Chiefs of Defence, and approved by the Ministers of Defence on 14 March 2005 meeting in Entebbe, Uganda. On 18 March, the IGAD Council of Ministers adopted the IGASOM Deployment Plan in Nairobi.[16]

It was not until 12 May, however, that the AU's Peace and Security Council (PSC) endorsed IGAD's proposal and authorized the deployment of IGASOM, requested the UN Security Council grant an exemption to the arms embargo imposed against Somalia to facilitate the deployment of the mission, and stressed the need for AU member states and the UN to provide IGASOM with political, financial, and logistical support.[17] Later that year, the PSC also made clear that it envisaged the deployment of an AU peace operation to take over from IGASOM.[18] However, the IGASOM proposal did not gain sufficient

---

[13] Sally Healy, *Lost Opportunities in the Horn of Africa* (London: Chatham House, Horn of Africa Group Report, 2008), p. 22. Interestingly, the first IGAD fact-finding mission went to Somalia in May–June 2003 and recommended the deployment of an eighty-one-strong AU observer mission, but the AU subsequently decided it would not be possible to deploy such a force. Cited in Opiyo Oloya, *Black Hawks Rising: The story of AMISOM's successful war against Somali insurgents, 2007–2014* (Solihull, UK: Helion, 2016), p. 44.

[14] Joint Communique of IGAD Special Summit on Somalia, 15 October 2004, §4(VIII).

[15] IGAD, 'Communique on Somalia', issued in Abuja, Nigeria, 31 January 2005. IGAD's charter did not explicitly include a provision for deploying such a peace operation, although advocates suggested that Article 7(g) could perhaps be used as the legal basis. Article 7 on IGAD's Aims and Objectives states that the institution will: 7(g) Promote peace and stability in the sub-region and create mechanisms within the sub-region for the prevention, management, and resolution of inter and intra-state conflicts through dialogue. Signed March 1996, http://www.ifrc.org/docs/idrl/N527EN.pdf

[16] IGAD leaders subsequently reaffirmed their decision to deploy IGASOM at summits on 20 March and 13 June 2006.

[17] AU doc. PSC/PR/Comm.(XXIX), 12 May 2005.

[18] AU doc. PSC/Min/Comm.(XXXIV)–(i), 3 July 2005.

political traction. Although it was initially meant to provide regional ownership of the crisis, neighbouring states were subsequently excluded from being troop-contributing countries because of the potentially negative political ramifications. At the UN Security Council, IGASOM also failed to generate support, with the United States stating: 'We do not plan to fund the deployment of IGAD troops in Somalia and are not yet prepared to support a UN Security Council mandate for IGAD deployment in Somalia'.[19] Critics of US policies also noted that IGASOM might well run counter to the ongoing US covert support for various Somali warlords in Mogadishu under the guise of fighting terrorism (see below).[20]

In its 2006 national security and stabilization plan, the TFG explicitly called for IGASOM to support the establishment of a 45,000-strong set of Somali security forces and implement a disarmament, demobilization, and reintegration programme.[21] It also explicitly reiterated the need to exclude 'Front Line States' from such a force.[22] This was unsurprising: most IGAD states had their own vested interests in Somalia's conflict and were therefore not regarded as neutral by most Somalis. This left only Sudan and Uganda as potential contributors and both countries were slated to deploy a battalion of troops.[23] While Uganda did conduct pre-deployment training for its designated contingent, Sudan did not. Furthermore, IGAD did not have the resources to support such an operation. As a consequence, IGASOM did not deploy.

Yusuf's efforts to send foreign troops onto Somali soil nevertheless caused an irreparable rift within the TFG parliament, which had voted against the deployment of an IGAD force.[24] Yusuf was derided in Somalia as an Ethiopian puppet and support for the transitional government plummeted still further. The parliament feared to set foot in Somalia, and was forced to remain a government-in-exile in Nairobi until June 2005, when it tentatively relocated to the Somali town of Jowhar, where it sought the protection of warlord Mohammed Dheere. In January 2006, a new agreement was concluded between President Yusuf and the parliament speaker, Sharif Hassan Sheikh Aden, in Aden, Yemen. This paved the way for the TFG parliament to relocate to Baidoa, where in February 2006, it was finally able to obtain its first quorum of just over 200 members on Somali soil, in a repurposed grain warehouse.[25]

The threat of a Darod-led government with foreign military backing sparked a violent reaction in the Hawiye territories of southern Somalia. In Mogadishu, leaders of the Hawiye clan formed an alliance of convenience with a network of long-standing and clan-oriented Islamic community courts. They

---

[19] Cited in Oloya, *Black Hawks Rising*, p. 47.   [20] *Ibid.*, p. 47.
[21] TFG, *NSSP* (2006), pp. 9, 15–16. The 45,000 personnel included 25,000 army (including marines and coast guard); 12,000 police; 5,000 custodial corps; and 3,000 National Intelligence Agency personnel.
[22] *Ibid.*, p. 13.   [23] Oloya, *Black Hawks Rising*, p. 46.   [24] *Ibid.*, p. 47.
[25] TFG, *NSSP* (2006), p. 4.

formed a unified and publicly popular opposition to a clique of Hawiye warlords who supported the TFG, and were already notorious for carving up Mogadishu into criminal fiefdoms and taxing the flow of goods and people at illegal roadblocks throughout the city. The US Central Intelligence Agency (CIA) also reportedly began to engage in covert operations against a small faction of the Islamic Courts: specifically, against a poorly organized but radical Islamist youth militia which had begun a campaign of assassinations of TFG sympathizers. The CIA had also enlisted a disreputable clique of Mogadishu warlords to assist in the capture of suspected *al-Qa'ida* operatives. In February 2006, these warlords announced their CIA connections and formed a public partnership: the Alliance for the Restoration of Peace and Counterterrorism (ARPCT).[26]

THE ISLAMIC COURTS TAKE MOGADISHU

Even without IGASOM, the TFG moved onto Somali soil, protected instead by Ethiopian soldiers. But the TFG was unable to establish a presence in the capital city. Approximately a year later, a major alteration of the political terrain occurred on 5 June 2006 when a union of Islamic Courts and their fighters took control of Mogadishu.[27] They did so by defeating the newly formed, US-supported ARPCT.

The Islamic Courts had started operating in Somalia in early 1994. The Courts were clan-based entities, and thus poorly networked, and they were largely funded by Somalia's business community as a means of providing law and order as well as a degree of security for commerce within certain zones. In this sense, there was a convergence of interest between a business community seeking stability and radical Islamists who were also seeking a particular

---

[26] The US CIA reportedly provided some $2 million in return for help tracking down those individuals responsible for the US embassy bombings in Nairobi and Dar es Salaam in 1998. See, for example, Wikileak Cable 06NAIROBI840, 24 February 2006, Mark Mazzetti, 'Efforts by CIA Fail in Somalia, Officials Charge', *New York Times*, 8 June 2006; Menkhaus, 'Governance without Government', p. 76; Bronwyn E. Bruton, *Somalia: A New Approach* (New York: Council on Foreign Relations, March 2010), p. 7; Shaul Shay, *Somalia: Between Jihad and Restoration* (New York: Transaction Publishers, 2011), p. 189. US government officials also denied Washington was funding warlords to fight terrorists in Mogadishu in pursuit of the GWOT. See Wikileak Cable 06NAIROBI2165, 17 May 2006.

[27] For details see Appendix A and Roland Marchal, 'Islamic Political Dynamics in the Somali Civil War' in Alex de Waal (ed.), *Islamism and Its Enemies in the Horn of Africa* (Bloomington: Indiana University Press, 2004), pp. 132–9; Cedric Barnes and Harun Hassan, 'The Rise and Fall of Mogadishu's Islamic Courts', *Journal of Eastern African Studies*, 1:2 (2007), pp. 151–60; Healy, *Lost Opportunities in the Horn of Africa*, pp. 23–4.

form of order.[28] Politically, the Courts represented a 'broad mosque', bringing together individuals from the moderate and fundamentalist ends of the Islamic spectrum. The Courts enjoyed a renaissance in 2003 under the leadership of Sheikh Sharif Sheikh Ahmed, a geography teacher who won Somali hearts and minds by negotiating the release of a young man whose life was threatened by one of the kidnap-for-ransom gangs then plaguing the countryside.

Shortly after taking control of Mogadishu, the court leaders announced the formation of a Supreme Council of Islamic Courts (SCIC), with an individual who was in contact with Osama bin Laden in early 2001, Hassan Dahir Aweys, as the head of its *shura* and Sheikh Sharif Sheikh Ahmed as the administrative head.[29] (Somalis speculated at the time that Sheikh Sharif was appointed primarily to appease Western officials, who were alarmed by Aweys' leadership role within the Courts.) The SCIC opposed the proposed IGAD operation as tantamount to a foreign invasion by Ethiopia, and hoped to position itself as a more attractive 'bottom-up' alternative to the struggling TFG. To that end, the SCIC quickly set out to demonstrate its credentials: the sea and airports in Mogadishu were reopened, rubbish and roadblocks were cleared from the streets, squatters were evicted from government buildings, and the city enjoyed a degree of stability unseen since 1991. The United States and the United Nations were impressed and urged the TFG to negotiate a power-sharing arrangement with the SCIC.[30] So too were many local Somalis, who in retrospect referred to the peaceful period between June and December 2006 as *lix bilood oo janaah* or *lixdii bilool ee janada ahayd*, the period of paradise.[31]

But the SCIC then attempted to strengthen its bargaining position by capturing as much of Somalia's territory as it could. It was an unwise political gambit that was perceived as military aggression by Somalia's neighbours.

While Mogadishu's residents may have enjoyed the newfound stability, other actors were distinctly worried about the SCIC's expansion. The United States led an initiative to establish an informal International Contact Group to coordinate its partners' responses to Somalia.[32] At the time, the Bush administration's only pressing security objectives in Somalia were to capture or kill

---

[28] For details, see Aisha Ahmad, 'The Security Bazaar: Business Interests and Islamist Power in Civil War Somalia', *International Security*, 39:3 (2014/15), pp.89–117.

[29] See Appendix A.

[30] Some US officials saw the SCIC's attempt to establish its authority over Mogadishu as working against the 22 June 2006 agreement between it and the Transitional Federal Institutions in Khartoum advocating continuing discussions on security, politics, and impediments to peace. Wikileak Cable 06NAIROBI2781, 27 June 2006.

[31] Oloya, *Black Hawks Rising*, p. 40.

[32] Its participants included Austria, Belgium, Canada, China, Denmark, Djibouti, Egypt, Ethiopia, Finland, France, Germany, Italy, Japan, Kenya, Republic of Korea, Malaysia, Netherlands, Norway, Qatar, Saudi Arabia, Somalia, South Africa, Spain, Sudan, Sweden, Switzerland, Turkey, Uganda, United Arab Emirates, United Kingdom, United States, African Development

those individuals involved in bombing the US embassies in Nairobi and Dar es Salaam in 1998, and to deny *al-Qa'ida* a safe haven. It was, however, deeply alarmed by the rise of a populist Islamist movement with Aweys at its head. Washington's key concern on the latter score was probably that Aweys' protégé, Aden Hashi Ayro, was a leading figure in *al-Shabaab*.[33] Since 2005, *al-Shabaab* had been broadcasting its links with *al-Qa'ida*, assassinating rivals, and kidnapping and murdering foreigners in Somalia.[34] The problem for the United States, however, was that despite the SCIC leadership's connections with *al-Qa'ida*, Washington's public denunciation of the Courts as being dominated by terrorists and its dismissal of their achievements, notably bringing a semblance of order to Mogadishu, outraged many Somalis.[35]

For their part, in early July 2006, the AU and IGAD were still attempting to work with both the SCIC and TFG, as well the business community, civil society, and traditional elders to finalize modalities for deployment of the IGASOM force to Somalia. It was reported that the envisaged AU plan to help stabilize the TFG was that IGAD should deploy troops initially to Baidoa.[36] This would need partial lifting of the UN arms embargo on Somalia (privately AU officials acknowledged that Ethiopia and Eritrea were both breaking it by supplying arms to the TFG and SCIC respectively).[37] Despite these issues, on 5 September, IGAD member states endorsed the IGASOM deployment plan and on 13 September it was approved by the PSC after a review conducted by the AU Military Staff Committee.[38]

At the UN, however, the IGASOM proposals were met with considerable scepticism. At briefings to the Security Council, both the head of the UN Political Office for Somalia (UNPOS), Francois Lonseny Fall, and representatives of the UN sanctions monitoring group on Somalia and Eritrea warned against the deployment because of its strong potential to destabilize the situation in Somalia. The UN Secretary-General also cautioned that any IGASOM role should only be in support of an agreed political process and enjoy the consent of all major parties. He also felt it unwise for key regional players to interfere. Fall emphasized that an IGASOM deployment might increase the TFG's fragmentation and collapse; that it should only deploy

---

Bank, African Union, European Union, Islamic Development Bank, IGAD, League of Arab States, Organization of Islamic Cooperation, NATO, United Nations, World Bank.

[33] Ayro was killed in a US air strike in Somalia on 1 May 2008.   [34] See Appendix A.

[35] See, for example, Abdi Ismail Samatar, 'Ethiopian Invasion of Somalia, US Warlordism and AU Shame', *Review of African Political Economy*, 34:111 (2007), p. 158, Healy, *Lost Opportunities in the Horn of Africa*, p. 25.

[36] It was reported that Uganda was also ready to send a battalion to protect the TFG in Baidoa. Oloya, *Black Hawks Rising*, p. 58.

[37] Wikileak Cable 06ADDISABABA2118, 2 August 2006.

[38] Although the review was reported to have identified several problems with the IGAD deployment plan. As outlined in Wikileak Cable 06ADDISABABA2410, 5 September 2006.

after a ceasefire had been agreed; that there was, as yet, no consensus among key players including IGAD itself; and the mandate, composition, funding (estimated at some $335 million for the first year) and logistics remained vague.[39]

ETHIOPIA INSTALLS THE TFG IN MOGADISHU

The other state that was seriously concerned by developments in Mogadishu was Ethiopia. Ethiopia and Somalia had long suffered from historical animosities and rivalries, particularly stemming from tensions over the Ogaden region in eastern Ethiopia (which contains a large ethnic Somali population) and suspicion borne of religious differences.[40] Since August 1996, Ethiopian troops had engaged in a series of military incursions aimed at degrading Islamist bases in Somalia, particularly those of *al-Ittihad al-Islamiya*, which Ethiopia's Prime Minister Meles Zenawi believed were fermenting trouble in eastern Ethiopia.[41]

During August 2006, more Ethiopian troops were deployed to Baidoa, ostensibly to support the TFG authorities but also to create a buffer zone in case more radical voices within the SCIC gained the upper hand and incited irredentist violence in eastern Ethiopia. Just over a month earlier, however, Ethiopia's political leaders had told US diplomats that they would prefer the Islamic Courts be dealt with and the TFG protected by IGASOM. They also noted that Ethiopian troops should not be part of such a force because it was thought unwise to deploy troops from any of Somalia's neighbouring states. This left only Uganda and Sudan among the IGAD member states. Nevertheless, Ethiopia's leaders told US officials that they would be willing to intervene militarily themselves if IGASOM did not materialize.[42] Ultimately, this is what happened.

Probably more than any other event, it was Meles Zenawi's decision to use his army to attack the SCIC and install the TFG in Mogadishu that has shaped

---

[39] Security Council Report, 'Somalia: Monthly Forecast', December 2006, http://www.securitycouncilreport.org/monthly-forecast/2006-12/lookup_c_glKWLeMTIsG_b_2266983.php

[40] Somalia's invasion of Ethiopia in 1976 sparked the long-feared Ogaden War, pitching the Somalis against the largest army in Africa. Ethiopia won the war but as one analysis put it, the Derg regime in Addis Ababa 'would never win the peace, being unable to master any of the several regional insurrections that continually challenged its rule'. David M. Anderson and Øystein H. Rolandsen, 'Violence as politics in eastern Africa, 1940–1990: legacy, agency, contingency', *Journal of Eastern African Studies*, 8:4 (2014), p. 542.

[41] Roland Marchal, 'Islamic Political Dynamics in the Somali Civil War' in Alex de Waal (ed.), *Islamism and Its Enemies in the Horn of Africa* (Bloomington: Indiana University Press, 2004), p.138.

[42] See Wikileak Cables 06ADDISABABA1783_a, 29 June 2006, §9 and 06ADDISABAB1780_a, 29 June 2006, §1, §6, §8.

both contemporary Somali politics and international efforts to stabilize the country. Shortly after the SCIC forces had taken Mogadishu from the various warlords, Meles articulated the logic behind his decision to oust them in the following manner:

> We are aware of course, that the Union of Islamic Courts is a union of desperate forces. There are those Somalis who have supported the establishment of such courts because of the desperation that came as a result of the absolute chaos and lawlessness in Mogadishu. So, in a sense, for many supporters of these courts, the issue is one of order and stability. We understand their desire and we have nothing against that desire.... As regards the implications of the resurgence of terrorist groups within Somalia, on the security and stability of Ethiopia, naturally, like any country, we reserve the right to defend ourselves against all attempts to destabilize our security and stability.[43]

Interestingly, noted analyst Alex de Waal later referred to Meles' decision as a major 'political blunder'.[44]

A year later, Meles argued that Ethiopia intervened in Somalia for a combination of reasons. The first was to combat the destabilizing mission of the Eritrean government from the north. The second was in response to the declaration of jihad by SCIC forces against Ethiopia. His third rationale was to combat the presence in Somalia of Ethiopian insurgents who were seeking to overthrow the government of Ethiopia by force. And fourth, he wanted to reduce the presence and continued influx of foreign terrorist groups who were bent on advancing the SCIC's extremist agenda. Combined, these factors created a state of 'clear and present danger' which Meles said triggered Ethiopia's lawful right to self-defence under international law.[45]

Others have suggested that different factors were also relevant in this decision.[46] First, following the highly controversial 2005 elections, Meles wanted to be seen to be in control. The intervention was part of demonstrating this to his military, party, and opponents. Taking Ethiopian National Defence Force (ENDF) troops all the way to Mogadishu was, after all, something not even Mengistu tried to do. It was therefore partly about using nationalism to deflect from domestic problems. Second, in October 2006 there was a serious string of killings of Christians in Jimma Zone in western Ethiopia by Muslims. As the SCIC was rising in Somalia, in Ethiopia, Muslims killed about a dozen Christians and burned several churches and forced many other Christians to

---

[43] *Ethiopian Herald*, 30 June 2006 cited in Haggai Erlich, *Islam and Christianity in the Horn of Africa* (Boulder, CO: Lynne Rienner, 2010), p. 168.

[44] 'Do or Die Political Liberalization', *Addis Fortune*, 16:829, 21 March 2016, http://addisfortune.net/interviews/do-or-die-of-political-liberalization/

[45] Meles Zenawi, press conference, Addis Ababa, 26 June 2007 cited in Awol K. Allo, 'Ethiopia's Armed Intervention in Somalia: The legality of self-defense in response to the threat of terrorism', *Denver Journal of International Law and Policy*, 39:1 (2010), p. 157.

[46] Interview, Ethiopian analyst, Addis Ababa, 16 October 2013.

flee. Some of the incidents were shown on DVDs circulated in Addis. This added to the perceived need to respond vigorously to the situation in Somalia.

Whatever the true reasons behind Meles' decision, and amidst all the anti-Islamist rhetoric, it is often forgotten that a political settlement might have been forged between the SCIC and TFG forces before Ethiopia intervened. However, the prospects for any deal were dealt a major blow when on 30 October 2006 talks between the parties were cancelled. According to Security Council Report, this was 'due to disagreement on co-mediation by Kenya and the Arab League and by UIC demands that Ethiopia withdraw from Somalia'.[47] Yet as late as December 2006, the SCIC were still engaged in talks with IGAD and sent several letters sent to the UN Security Council. In these letters, the SCIC expressed:

- commitment to dialogue with the Transitional Federal Institutions (TFIs);
- respect for the territorial integrity of neighbouring countries and the implementation of agreements reached in the context of the Khartoum peace talks;
- interest in the deployment of international monitors to verify the presence of Ethiopian troops, whose withdrawal is a precondition of the Islamic Courts for talks with the TFG and with Ethiopia; and
- willingness to consider the deployment of an international mechanism to monitor the implementation of agreements reached with the TFG.[48]

On the other hand, some senior members of the SCIC sent mixed signals by openly questioning the legitimacy of the TFIs.[49] Indeed, more than that, as Ken Menkhaus noted, some 'hardliners' within the SCIC 'seemed intent on provoking a war with Ethiopia'. This, he concluded, 'doomed what might otherwise have been an legitimate Islamist solution to the long-running Somali crisis, and instead ushered in a period of extraordinary violence'.[50]

AUTHORIZING AMISOM

It was in this turbulent political context that the idea of an African peace-keeping force was resurrected. Beyond Somalia, the international climate was

---

[47] Security Council Report, 'Somalia', December 2006.

[48] Security Council Report, 'Somalia: Monthly Forecast', January 2007, http://www.securitycouncilreport.org/monthly-forecast/2007-01/lookup_c_glKWLeMTIsG_b_2294419.php

[49] *Ibid.*

[50] Ken Menkhaus, 'Violent Islamic Extremism: Al-Shabaab Recruitment in America', testimony to US Government, 11 March 2009, p. 3, www.hsgac.senate.gov/download/031109menkhaus

marked by the AU's various attempts to play more of a leadership role in addressing peace and security challenges on the continent.[51] By late 2006, the United States was also pushing hard for an African mission to lead the international response in Somalia. Specifically, when UN Security Council resolution 1725 (6 December 2006) authorized IGAD and AU member states to 'establish a protection and training mission in Somalia'. It was reported that although resolution 1725 was adopted by consensus 'European members sought and achieved some amendments to the US draft to emphasise balance, restrict the mission's mandate, exclude participation by neighbouring states and encourage political dialogue'.[52] The African force was mandated to: monitor the progress of, and ensure the safe passage of those involved in, the political dialogue between the SCIC and the TFG authorities; maintain security in Baidoa; protect members of the TFG as well as their key infra-structure; and train the TFG's security forces and help re-establish the national security forces of Somalia.[53] Interestingly, the US ambassador to the UN, John Bolton, told the Security Council that the role of this force was 'not to engage in offensive actions against the Union of Islamic Courts'.[54]

Nevertheless, resolution 1725 was quickly overtaken by events on the ground in Somalia. Most importantly, the resolution did not envisage the Ethiopian-led occupation of Mogadishu and its consequences. Resolution 1725 authorized a force with a mandate to 'ensure free movement and safe passage of all those involved with the dialogue process', i.e. personnel from both the TFG and the SCIC.[55] It is therefore notable that when the PSC authorized AMISOM in January 2007, it was in a completely different political context—one in which the process of dialogue had been stopped by Ethiopia's campaign to forcibly insert the TFG into Mogadishu and where Ethiopian soldiers were seen as an occupying power by many local Somalis. In this sense, AMISOM was primarily an AU initiative that received post-facto endorse-ment from the UN Security Council one month later (in resolution 1744, see p. 42).

By 10 December 2006, negotiations between the SCIC and Somalia's tran-sitional government had all but collapsed. In addition, Sheikh Sharif made clear the SCIC's intention to capture Baidoa from the TFG.[56] Two days later,

---

[51] On the evolution of this process, see Paul D. Williams, 'From non-intervention to non-indifference: the origins and development of the African Union's security culture', *African Affairs*, 106: 423, pp. 253–79.

[52] Security Council Report, 'Somalia', January 2007.   [53] *Ibid.*

[54] Colum Lynch, 'Peacekeeping force for Somalia approved', *Washington Post*, 7 December 2006, p. A24.

[55] S/RES/1725, 6 December 2006, §3.

[56] Erlich, *Islam and Christianity in the Horn of Africa*, p. 166. In late June 2006, Meles had reportedly confided with US Assistant Secretary of State Jendayi Frazer that he would only intervene in Somalia if the SCIC attacked Baidoa. Oloya, *Black Hawks Rising*, p. 55.

the SCIC's military chief, Sheikh Indha'adde, and his (*al-Shabaab*) deputy, Sheikh Mukhtar Robow, issued an ultimatum to the Ethiopian troops to leave the country or face forcible expulsion, and began moving their forces towards Baidoa.[57] A brief war of (often confusing and contradictory) words followed and fighting broke out between the SCIC forces and Ethiopian troops near Baidoa on 20 December. Here, in a single battle, Ethiopian forces quickly killed hundreds of ill-prepared Somali youths who had been sent to stop them by the Islamic Courts' leadership. Public support for the SCIC crumbled, and by 29 December Ethiopian troops, tanks, and aircraft alongside TFG soldiers had installed the TFG in Mogadishu. They also brought with them several of the warlords who the SCIC had dislodged earlier in the year. For example, Mohammed Dheere, the notorious warlord who controlled Jowhar, was at the forefront of the Ethiopian and TFG forces as they closed in on Mogadishu.[58] During the combat, Meles claimed his troops had killed 2,000–3,000 Islamist militants.[59] But he was also clearly delusional about the conflict dynamics his actions had stirred up, claiming that 'We will not let Mogadishu burn', and that the fighting could be over 'in days; if not, a few weeks'.[60] In fact, by keeping his troops in Mogadishu, Meles enabled a now weak *al-Shabaab* to play the nationalist card to good effect, which produced a dramatic increase in their strength.

The SCIC's forces were thus routed and their leaders and militia scattered across the country. As they retreated, the US air force also attacked SCIC forces in an unsuccessful attempt to kill *al-Qa'ida* operatives thought to be working with them.[61] By mid-January 2007, the TFG and AU estimated there were about 3,000 SCIC fighters in hideouts in and around Mogadishu, Kismayo, Jamaame, Jilib, and Dhuusamarreeb, with undisclosed numbers scattered in other parts of the country, with a suspected strong presence on farms in the lower Shebelle/Juba Valley.[62]

It is unclear how many Ethiopian soldiers deployed as part of this campaign. Meles claimed that under 4,000 of his troops had 'broken the back' of the SCIC.[63]

---

[57] Barnes and Hassan, 'The Rise and Fall of Mogadishu's Islamic Courts', p. 156.

[58] Xan Rice, 'Ethiopian army nears Somali capital amid calls for peace', *The Guardian*, 28 December 2006, p. 22 and 'Return of warlords as Somali capital is captured', *The Guardian*, 29 December 2006, p. 20.

[59] Andrew England, 'Spectre of rival clans returns to Mogadishu', *Financial Times*, 29 December 2006, p. 5.

[60] Steve Bloomfield, 'Ethiopia-led forces seize Mogadishu', *Independent* (London), 29 December 2006, p. 28.

[61] Mark Bradbury and Sally Healy, 'Endless War' in *Whose peace is it anyway? Connecting Somali and international peacemaking* (Accord Issue 21, 2010), p. 14.

[62] *Report of the Chairperson of the Commission on the Situation in Somalia* (AU doc. PSC/PR/ 2(LXIX), 19 January 2007), §30.

[63] Andrew England, 'Islamist rebels pull back in Somalia', *Financial Times*, 27 December 2006, p. 6.

By early 2007, Somali sources[64] estimated that 18,000 Ethiopian troops had deployed, concentrated in Baidoa and Mogadishu.[65] A senior official from Ethiopia's ministry of foreign affairs divulged that 15,000 ENDF entered Somalia in 2006 and a division was withdrawn within a month, leaving about 8,000 troops in and around Mogadishu from 2007.[66] This was almost identical to the US government estimate that Ethiopia had originally deployed approximately 15,000 troops in Somalia concentrated in Baidoa and Mogadishu (but had reduced that number to about 7,000 by late March 2007).[67] An independent Ethiopian analyst suggested that it would be highly unlikely that the ENDF had deployed more than two divisions (*c.*10,000 troops) given that the entire eastern command comprised four divisions.[68] One of the most well-informed scholars of the war estimated that 5,000 ENDF troops remained.[69] Other sources put the numbers much higher. A Ugandan analyst with excellent contacts with the Ugandan leadership estimated there were 30,000 ENDF troops in Somalia in January 2007.[70] Similarly, SwissPeace estimated the deployment of some 40,000 Ethiopian troops inside Somalia in early 2007.[71]

Whatever the true numbers of Ethiopian troops, in New York, the UN Security Council failed to agree on a resolution calling for a withdrawal of 'foreign forces', which also included Eritrean troops reportedly working as trainers, mentors, and liaison officers inside Somalia. While the US and UK led the support for Ethiopia's position the chairperson of the AU Commission called for 'the withdrawal of Ethiopian troops without delay', as did the League of Arab States, Djibouti, and Kenya.[72] Ethiopia's position was most strongly supported by the US government. In mid-December, for example, the US Assistant Secretary of State, Jendayi Frazer, asserted that the Islamic Courts were 'controlled by al-Qa'ida cell individuals'.[73] The US government even issued media guidelines to State Department personnel to shift attention from Ethiopia's intervention.[74]

---

[64] See Bronwyn E. Bruton and Paul D. Williams, *Counterinsurgency in Somalia* (Tampa, FL: US Joint Special Operations University Press, 2014), p. 24.

[65] Using IISS figures, this would constitute roughly 12 percent of Ethiopia's 150,000 strong army. IISS, *The Military Balance 2007* (London: Routledge for the IISS, 2007), p. 274.

[66] Interview, Ethiopian MFA official, Addis Ababa, 31 July 2012.

[67] Wikileak Cable 07ADDISABABA918, 26 March 2007, §3.

[68] Interview, Ethiopian analyst, Addis Ababa, 16 October 2013.

[69] Stig Jarle Hansen, *Al-Shabaab in Somalia* (London: Hurst, 2013), p. 52.

[70] Oloya, *Black Hawks Rising*, p. 102.

[71] SwissPeace, *Fast Update: Somalia, No.1 February-March 2007*, p. 2, http://www.swisspeace. ch/fileadmin/user_upload/Media/Projects/FAST/Africa/Somalia/FAST_Update_Som_07_01.pdf

[72] Xan Rice, 'Ethiopian army nears Somali capital amid calls for peace', *The Guardian*, 28 December 2006, p. 22.

[73] Steve Bloomfield, 'Somali Islamists say they are "at war" with Ethiopia', *Independent*, 22 December 2006, p. 30.

[74] Mark Mazzetti, 'US signals backing for Ethiopian incursion into Somalia', *New York Times*, 27 December 2006, p. 6.

In New York, the US, and China were sympathetic to military support for the TFG and containment of the SCIC. The African members on the Council (Ghana, Congo, Tanzania) appear to have supported the military option reluctantly, largely because of the previous AU and IGAD commitment to IGASOM (at a time when it was assumed it would be operating in a permissive environment). The European members preferred an approach that recognized the practical power wielded by the SCIC but emphasized dialogue rather than reliance on military force.[75] The key issue dividing the UN Security Council members was how they perceived the SCIC: was it a radical, expansionist entity that needed to be tackled militarily, or was it an entity that could play a part in a power-sharing administration and peacemakers should therefore test the credibility of its promises? The Ethiopian and US governments clearly held the former interpretation (and yet ended up two years later working closely with one of the SCIC's leaders who subsequently became president of the TFG).

On 26 December, the UN Security Council held an emergency meeting where a Qatari-proposed presidential statement failed to generate consensus. The sticking point appears to have been a call for withdrawal of all unauthorized foreign forces from Somalia.[76] The very next day, the UN Secretary-General appealed for Somalia's neighbours to stay out of the country, while the AU Chairperson convened a consultative meeting on the situation in Somalia in Addis Ababa. The meeting appealed to all parties concerned to enact an immediate and unconditional ceasefire and for the TFG and the SCIC to resume their political dialogue in Khartoum, under the co-chairmanship of the League of Arab States and IGAD. The meeting called for the withdrawal of all foreign forces from Somalia, including Ethiopian troops. This did not happen.

Legally, Ethiopia justified its military operation and subsequent occupation of Mogadishu as an example of collective defence under Article 51 of the UN Charter, since it took place at the behest of the TFG, which was at the time the internationally recognized authority for Somalia.[77] Ethiopia's critics, on the other hand, claim that its government simply used the rhetoric of some Somali extremists as justification for destroying the SCIC, which was its real

---

[75] Security Council Report, 'Somalia', January 2007.

[76] Security Council Report, 'Somalia: Monthly Forecast', February 2007, http://www.securitycouncilreport.org/monthly-forecast/2007-02/lookup_c_glKWLeMTIsG_b_2461261.php

[77] For a discussion of the legal dimensions, see Zeray W. Yihdego, 'Ethiopia's military action against the Union of Islamic Courts and others in Somalia', *International and Comparative Law Quarterly*, 56:3 (2007), pp. 666–76. On the politics of the process of international recognition see Anonymous, 'Government recognition in Somalia and regional political stability in the Horn of Africa', *Journal of Modern African Studies*, 40:2 (2002), pp. 247–72.

objective.[78] It is important to recall that the jihadist and irredentist statements made by sections of the SCIC in late 2006 with regard to eastern Ethiopia certainly inflamed tensions with the authorities in Addis Ababa. And although the SCIC lacked a competent army with which to invade Ethiopia, its followers did have the ability to exacerbate tensions in Ethiopia's Ogaden region in particular.

Regardless of Ethiopia's legal justifications, Islamists around the world depicted its military campaign as a crusade. As one scholar put it, Ethiopia's intervention was 'the ultimate provocation'.[79] Meles Zenawi was depicted as the modern-day Abraha al-Ashram—an Ethiopian ruler of pre-Islamic Yemen who in AD 570 tried to demolish the Ka'ba shrine in Mecca—'the would-be Ethiopian destroyer of Islamic holiness'.[80] For many Somalis, the SCIC's faults were less important than its impressive achievements, notably bringing a semblance of order to Mogadishu. Ethiopia's decision to oust them in favour of a 'government' selected by foreigners in Kenya was widely seen as outrageous.[81] The result was, as Ken Menkhaus noted, 'the Ethiopian occupation inadvertently fueled a dramatic rise in radicalism and violent extremism in the country and among the diaspora'.[82] Even Somalis as far away as America cited their reasons for subsequently joining *al-Shabaab* as feeling 'compelled' to help repel the Ethiopian 'invaders'.[83]

The result was a torrent of anti-Ethiopian messages from a variety of sources. On 5 January 2007, for example, Osama Bin Laden's deputy Ayman al-Zawahiri issued a videotaped message entitled, 'Help Your Brothers in Somalia!' which called for jihadists to supply fighters, money, and expertise against Ethiopia.[84] The rampant human rights abuses perpetrated during Ethiopia's occupation of Mogadishu only deepened Muslim outrage.[85] Many of the civilian casualties were generated by the ENDF's use of heavy artillery, even in urban areas.[86]

---

[78] Abdi Ismail Samatar, 'The production of Somali conflict and the role of internal and external actors' in Redie Bereketeab (ed.), *The Horn of Africa* (London: Pluto, 2013), pp. 171–3.

[79] Erlich, *Islam and Christianity in the Horn of Africa*, p. 176.   [80] *Ibid.*, p. 7.

[81] See, for example, Samatar, 'Ethiopian Invasion of Somalia,' p. 158, Healy, *Lost Opportunities in the Horn of Africa*, p. 25.

[82] Menkhaus, 'Violent Islamic Extremism', p. 2.

[83] Dina Temple-Raston, 'Minnesota Trial Offers Window On Jihadi Pipeline'. *NPR*, 10 October 2012, http://www.npr.org/2012/10/10/162663573/court-minn-man-recruited-somalis-for-terrorism

[84] The subsequent number of foreign jihadist fighters who came to Somalia was the subject of much debate. Estimates of several hundred seem to be the most reliable.

[85] Human Rights Watch, *Shell Shocked: Civilians Under Siege in Mogadishu* (New York: Human Rights Watch, Vol.19 No.12(A), August 2007).

[86] Hansen, *Al-Shabaab in Somalia*, pp. 49–50.

Also, on 5 January 2007, the International Contact Group on Somalia concluded that, 'if international support is to be effective, it is essential that an inclusive process of political dialogue and reconciliation—embracing representative clan, religious, business, civil society, women's, and other political groups who reject violence and extremism—be launched without delay'.[87] The EU and US both pledged to support the proposed African peacekeeping force, but at this stage the EU made its funding conditional on the TFG holding talks with moderate elements of the SCIC. The EU released the promised funds only when TFG President Yusuf agreed on 30 January to call a broad conference of clan and religious leaders.[88]

Less than a week after the Contact Group's meeting, on 10 January, the AU Commission organized a consultative meeting bringing together military officers and other representatives from IGAD, the TFG, Ethiopia and Uganda. It was agreed that an AU technical assessment mission should urgently travel to Somalia to gather additional information that would form the basis of the proposals to be submitted to the PSC. The mission visited Mogadishu on 13–15 January 2007, consulting with the TFG and Ethiopian military officers. The AU team recommended establishing an AU peace support mission to Somalia as soon as possible for a period of six months to protect TFIs, assist in the implementation of the National Security and Stabilization Plan (NSSP), support disarmament and stabilization, and facilitate humanitarian operations.[89] The mission was to deploy 'with a clear understanding that [it] will evolve to a United Nations mission that will support the long term stabilization and post-conflict reconstruction of Somalia'.[90] The whole mission concept was based on the following assumption: 'the transition of the proposed mission to a UN multidimensional peacekeeping operation, immediately after the six month initial stabilization phase'.[91] This was highly significant because at this stage the UN Security Council had not authorized a UN peacekeeping operation for Somalia.

This led some UN diplomats to speculate that AU Commission Chairperson, former President of Mali Alpha Oumar Konare's arm had been twisted to deploy an AU operation into Somalia by Ethiopia, and perhaps also the US.[92] This view is not unfounded. Indeed, within the AU there was a common perception that Ethiopia had succeeded in shaping its position on the Somali conflict in an unhelpful manner. Although many African governments were probably untroubled by the demise of the SCIC, there was considerable scepticism that Ethiopia's actions were either entirely justified or likely to prove effective. Added to other concerns about funding, overstretch, logistics, and the conflict environment in Mogadishu, this dissuaded most African

---

[87] Available at http://2001-2009.state.gov/p/af/rls/78933.htm
[88] Security Council Report, 'Somalia', February 2007.
[89] PSC/PR/2(LXIX), 19 January 2007, §33.   [90] *Ibid.*, §33.   [91] *Ibid.*, §34.
[92] Interview, UN official, Addis Ababa, 2 August 2012.

countries from contributing troops to AMISOM. It was also widely noted that Ethiopia broke the PSC's internal procedures when it shepherded AMISOM's authorization through the Council. Despite being a key party to the conflict under discussion, the Ethiopian representative played a crucial role in the debate to establish AMISOM. Under Article 8.9 of the *Protocol Relating to the Establishment of the Peace and Security Council of the African Union* (9 July 2002) Ethiopia's representative should have withdrawn from the deliberations after the briefing session.[93] Article 8.9 states:

> Any Member of the Peace and Security Council which is party to a conflict under consideration by the Peace and Security Council shall not participate either in the discussion or the decision making process relating to that conflict or situation. Such Member shall be invited to present its case to the Peace and Security Council as appropriate, and shall, thereafter, withdraw from proceedings.

Instead, the Ethiopian representative even sought to chair the meeting, arguing that her country was not a party to the conflict. This statement was apparently greeted with open laughter within the meeting chamber and prompted one representative to ask what Protocol the Ethiopian representative had been reading. After an hour of argument, it was decided that the representative from Gabon would chair the final part of the meeting, but the Ethiopian representative continued to participate.[94]

And so it was that the African Union decided to deploy its fifth and largest ever peace operation into Mogadishu's war-torn landscape. On 19 January 2007, the PSC authorized AMISOM to deploy 8,000 troops 'supported by maritime coastal and air components, as well as an appropriate civilian component, including a police training team'.[95] Its initial mandate was '(i) to provide support to the TFIs in their efforts towards the stabilization of the situation in the country and the furtherance of dialogue and reconciliation, (ii) to facilitate the provision of humanitarian assistance, and (iii) to create conducive conditions for long-term stabilization, reconstruction and development in Somalia'.[96] To that end AMISOM was required to perform the following tasks:

> 1) support dialogue and reconciliation in Somalia, working with all stakeholders,
>
> 2) provide, as appropriate, protection to the TFIs and their key infrastructure, to enable them carry out their functions,
>
> 3) assist in the implementation of the National Security and Stabilization Plan of Somalia, particularly the effective reestablishment and training of all inclusive

---

[93] The *PSC Protocol* (9 July 2002) came into force on 26 December 2003 (after ratification by twenty-seven of the fifty-three AU members) and the PSC officially began work on 16 March 2004 at the ministerial level in the margins of the 4th Ordinary Session of the AU Executive Council.

[94] Interviews: AU official, Addis Ababa, May 2007; former Ethiopian official, Washington DC, March 2008.

[95] PSC/PR/Comm.(LXIX), 19 January 2007, §9.   [96] *Ibid.*, §8.

Somali security forces, bearing in mind the programs already being implemented by some of Somalia's bilateral and multilateral partners,

4) provide, within capabilities and as appropriate, technical and other support to the disarmament and stabilization efforts,

5) monitor, in areas of deployment of its forces, the security situation,

6) facilitate, as may be required and within capabilities, humanitarian operations, including the repatriation and reintegration of refugees and the resettlement of IDPs, and

7) protect its personnel, installations and equipment, including the right of self-defense.[97]

Conspicuously absent from the mandate was the need to protect local civilians (other than members of the TFG). The AU called on the UN to provide AMISOM with financial and other support.

AU leaders launched AMISOM despite lacking most of the capabilities necessary to sustain such a mission in the field. As the AU Commission Chairperson Konare put it:

> I am fully aware of the challenges facing our Organization. Indeed, unlike the United Nations, the AU does not have a system of assessed contributions to fund its peace support operations; we rely to a very large extent on the support of our partners. This means that the funding of our operations remains precarious. I am also aware of the limitations of the Commission with respect to its management capacity to oversee large-scale peace support operations, as clearly demonstrated by the AMIS operation [in Darfur, Sudan]. Finally, the challenges of an operation in Somalia, a country that has been without central Government for the past 16 years and where security remains precarious, cannot be underestimated. . . . Yet, the African Union cannot abdicate its responsibilities vis-à-vis Somalia and fail its people. The African Union is the only Organization the Somali people could readily turn to as they strive to recover from decades of violence and untold suffering. We have a duty and an obligation of solidarity towards Somalia.[98]

Hence, while political pressures convinced the AU to act, it decided to deploy AMISOM without having the requisite management and support capabilities in place.

Importantly, the AU did not at the time have an effective mission planning team. In February 2007, the AU planning cell had just two assigned personnel. The AU Commission therefore requested help from the UN Department of Peacekeeping Operations (DPKO) and donors to devise AMISOM's initial Strategic Directive, which was developed between 5 and 9 February by AU and UN planners.[99] Even as the number of AU planners slowly increased, most of

---

[97] *Ibid.*, §8.   [98] *Ibid.*, §36–7.
[99] Wikileak Cable 07ADDISABABA409, 8 February 2007.

their practical experience had come from serving in much more benign peace operations and most of them had not been to Mogadishu.[100]

Although the consensus within the UN DPKO was clear that Mogadishu was not a conducive environment for a UN peacekeeping mission, the Security Council endorsed the idea of an African force despite being well aware that the AU lacked the capabilities needed to carry out such a mission. Part of the explanation for the UN Security Council's decision was the sense that it had effectively abandoned Somalia for the previous decade and so needed to be seen to act.[101]

The result was Security Council resolution 1744, passed on 20 February 2007. Acting under Chapter VII of the UN Charter, this authorized AMISOM

> to take all necessary measures as appropriate to carry out the following mandate:
>
> (a) To support dialogue and reconciliation in Somalia by assisting with the free movement, safe passage and protection of all those involved with the process …
>
> (b) To provide, as appropriate, protection to the Transitional Federal Institutions to help them carry out their functions of government, and security for key infrastructure;
>
> (c) To assist, within its capabilities, and in coordination with other parties, with implementation of the National Security and Stabilization Plan, in particular the effective re-establishment and training of all-inclusive Somali security forces;
>
> (d) To contribute, as may be requested and within capabilities, to the creation of the necessary security conditions for the provision of humanitarian assistance;
>
> (e) To protect its personnel, facilities, installations, equipment and mission, and to ensure the security and freedom of movement of its personnel.[102]

However, resolution 1744 embodied a basic tension: on the one hand, it stressed the 'need for broad-based and representative institutions reached through an all-inclusive political process'; on the other, in practice AMISOM clearly supported one faction which lacked a strong local constituency, certainly in Mogadishu. This left some Security Council members well aware that the TFG's relative lack of legitimacy with local Somalis was a contributory

---

[100] To fill this gap, in April 2007 the EU and United States subsequently helped establish the Strategic Planning and Management Unit (SPMU) within the AU to plan and manage the organization's peace operations. This was a major step forward, but it only achieved initial operating capacity in September 2007, six months after the first AMISOM troops deployed to Mogadishu.

[101] The UN had been deeply engaged in Somali affairs between 1992 and March 1995 when its peacekeeping operation, UNOSOM II, departed. After that, the UN's presence in Somalia was almost entirely humanitarian (through various UN agencies). The minimal political engagement that occurred was via the UN Political Office for Somalia (UNPOS). Established in April 1995 UNPOS comprised a small team of civilians based in Nairobi because Somalia was thought to be too dangerous. UNPOS was overseen by the UN's Department of Political Affairs and only relocated to Mogadishu in January 2012.

[102] S/RES/1744, 20 February 2007, §4.

factor to the current violence. This, in turn, led to reports that the 'emerging consensus' in the Council was 'that the process should include all key players, especially moderate Islamic individuals'.[103]

By late February 2007, AMISOM had mandates from both the PSC and the UN Security Council. All it needed now was personnel and the means to deploy them. As it turned out, of the fifty-four AU member states, AMISOM's peacekeepers initially came from just one African country: Uganda.

ENTER UGANDA

AMISOM succeeded where IGASOM failed for two main reasons: the altered regional context and Uganda's willingness to deploy peacekeepers. In terms of regional concerns, although IGASOM failed to deploy, there was still a pressing need felt among several IGAD members to protect the TFG and to provide an exit strategy for Ethiopia's forces. AMISOM's establishment was thus 'based largely on efforts to convince Ethiopia to withdraw its forces from Somali territory'.[104] As noted above, this was not difficult because Meles was quickly looking for a way to avoid a potential Mogadishu quagmire. By February 2007, Ethiopia had already withdrawn one-third of its troops and was reportedly planning to withdraw another third.

This left Uganda's willingness to deploy. Although the AU reportedly received informal pledges to cover roughly 60 per cent of the authorized force strength of 8,000–1,800 soldiers from Uganda, 1,600 from Burundi, 850 from Nigeria, 350 from Ghana, and up to 1,000 from Malawi—only Uganda deployed at the start of the mission.[105] Aside from the obvious high level of risk, the most common explanation for the lack of other African TCCs was 'the danger of AMISOM being seen as a proxy for US strategic interests in the "War on Terrorism."' This 'made most PSC members reluctant to contribute troops'.[106]

Put simply, therefore, AMISOM would not have happened without Uganda, the mission's sole TCC from March until November 2007. The Ugandan People's Defence Force (UPDF) soldiers did not expect to remain

[103] Security Council Report, 'Somalia Monthly Forecast', March 2007, http://www. securitycouncilreport.org/monthly-forecast/2007-03/lookup_c_glKWLeMTIsG_b_2549831.php

[104] Walter Lotze and Yvonne Kasumba, 'AMISOM and the Protection of Civilians in Somalia', *Conflict Trends* 2 (2012), p. 17.

[105] 'Somalia: "We'll Fight Back if attacked," AU Troops Say', *IRIN News*, 7 March 2007.

[106] Kathryn Sturman and Aissatou Hayatou, 'The Peace and Security Council of the African Union: From Design to Reality' in Ulf Engel and Joao Gomes Porto (eds.), *Africa's New Peace and Security Architecture* (Farnham, UK: Ashgate, 2010), p. 71. The US ambassador to the AU agreed, noting in January 2007 that AMISOM was seen as a puppet of US government and US airstrikes were eroding African willingness to become TCCs. Wikileak Cable 07ADDISA-BABA263, 30 January 2007, §6.

alone for so long because several other AU states had expressed their willingness to deploy. But none came. Uganda was reasonably well prepared because
of the preparations it had undertaken for the abandoned IGASOM operation
(placing a battalion on standby and conducting relevant pre-deployment
training). In January 2007, the US government contracted DynCorp International to help equip, deploy, sustain, and train soldiers from the vanguard
Ugandan contingent.[107] Uganda's parliament approved the decision to deploy
into AMISOM on 13 February 2007 by a majority vote. Shortly afterwards,
President Museveni announced: 'We will not go to Somalia to impose peace
on the Somalis, because we shouldn't do that and we can't do it. What we
are going to do in Somalia is to empower our Somali brothers to rebuild
their state'.[108]

Uganda's first battle group of 1,605 troops arrived in Mogadishu on
6 March, flown in on Algerian planes. The battle group had been scheduled
to deploy to Mogadishu on 5 March, but the trip from Entebbe was aborted
after the small UPDF advance team that was already in Somalia discovered a
security breach.[109]

Official explanations for Uganda's decision to lead AMISOM emphasized
Pan-African solidarity and fighting terrorism in the region. First, as both
President Museveni and senior Ugandan officials regularly stated, Ugandan
troops were sent to Somalia as a concrete expression of Pan-African solidarity
and the idea of 'African solutions to African problems'. There were several
dimensions to this point. As Uganda's Defence Minister Crispus Kiyonga put
it in a February 2007 parliamentary debate, Uganda's main reasons for leading
AMISOM were 'for the good of the region' and to support 'the Somali
people'.[110] It was also thought to be important for Uganda to honour the
peacekeeping commitments that had been agreed earlier by IGAD and play its
role as a good regional citizen.[111]

Second, Ugandan officials emphasized that Somalia was the region's frontline in the US-led 'global war on terrorism'. Not only were some of the
architects of the 1998 US embassy bombings in Kenya and Tanzania thought
to be hiding in Somalia, but in the second half of 2006 there was growing talk
of a new threat in the form of *al-Shabaab*, which was thought to have extensive
links with *al-Qa'ida*. As Fisher argued, AMISOM provided President Yoweri

---

[107] See   http://www.dyn-intl.com/what-we-do/contingency-operations/somalia-case-study.
aspx. Accessed 1 June 2012.

[108] Cited in Oloya, *Black Hawks Rising*, p. 75.   [109] *Ibid.*, pp. 71–2.

[110] Cited in Jonathan Fisher, 'Managing Donor Perceptions: Contextualizing Uganda's 2007
intervention in Somalia', *African Affairs*, 111:444 (2012), p. 418. The strength of these stated
sentiments is undermined by Uganda's decision not to deploy troops in the AU Mission in
Sudan (AMIS, 2004–07).

[111] *Ibid.* and interviews, senior Ugandan officials, Washington DC, June 2009; Addis Ababa,
30 July 2012.

Museveni 'with an opportunity to bolster and develop his international image as a key' ally against terrorism, while simultaneously escaping 'significant censure' from Uganda's development partners.[112] In August 2006, for example, the Whitaker Group, then the Ugandan government's major Washington DC lobbyist, wrote to President Bush's National Security Council team assuring them that 'President Museveni shares President Bush's particular concern about Somalia and its potential as a writhing hotbed of terrorism'.[113] Of course, fighting 'terrorists' in Somalia had its risks and some Ugandan officials raised concerns about the dire security situation there. For example, one senior Ugandan diplomat recalled that in late 2006 he had initially advised his government not to send troops to Somalia because many of them were likely to be killed.[114]

A desire to counter other regional threats was part of the mix but not as prominent. For example, Somalia remained a source of arms proliferation and piracy, which would negatively impact the region's economy. As the Commander of Uganda's Land Forces Katumba Wamala put it, the Ugandan deployment was partly to prevent cross-border insecurity: 'we also suffer from the instability in Somalia. The guns in Karamoja come from Somalia. Disarming the Karimojong without tackling the source is like wiping water while the tap is still running'.[115] Another senior Ugandan official noted that regional insecurity had an economic impact too, including the rising cost of insurance for sea travel around the East African coast because of piracy which had affected businesses in Uganda.[116]

In addition, Uganda's highly centralized decision-making system on foreign policy meant that any deployment of the UPDF could only take place with Museveni's personal commitment.[117] Uganda's decision was therefore really Museveni's decision. His desire to enhance his reputation as a regional leader was hence also part of the equation. In the Somali case, Museveni saw AMISOM as an opportunity to exercise regional leadership more generally, especially given the absence of an AU presence on the ground. The AMISOM deployment would also contribute to Uganda's broader international reputation.

---

[112] Fisher, 'Managing Donor Perceptions', p. 405. That Museveni decided to deploy troops to Somalia in 2005 probably helped shield him from more powerful criticism of his controversial retention of power in the 2006 presidential elections.

[113] *Ibid.*, p. 417.   [114] Interview, Ugandan official, Addis Ababa, 30 July 2012.

[115] Els de Temmerman, '1,500 troops set for Somalia', *New Vision* (Kampala), 24 January 2007.

[116] Interview, Ugandan official, Addis Ababa, 30 July 2012.

[117] Museveni is well known for dominating Uganda's national security policy since he assumed power in 1986. See, for example, Sabiiti Mutengensa and Dylan Hendrickson, *State Responsiveness to Public Security Needs: The Politics of Security Decision-Making: Uganda Country Study* (University of London, CSDG Paper No. 16, June 2008) and Marco Jowell, 'Uganda: Country Profile' (Providing for Peacekeeping, version 13 February 2014), http://www.providingforpeacekeeping.org/2014/04/03/country-profile-uganda/

For instance, it was probably a contributing factor in Uganda's selection as a non-permanent member of the UN Security Council in January 2009. Museveni also apparently saw the deployment in AMISOM was a way to 'help out' his 'friend Meles'.[118] Finally, acting in Somalia also resonated with Museveni's personal dislike of militant Islamists, including concerns about a potential Islamic threat facing his government at home. Politically, this fed Museveni's desire to protect the Somali transitional government as a bulwark to more radical Islamists and provide an exit strategy for Ethiopia's forces.

Although they were not given pride of place in official explanations, institutional factors linked to supporting the UPDF were also an important part of the decision to join AMISOM.[119] First, the UPDF's leading role in Somalia provided an opportunity to repair its poor international reputation after widespread criticism of its interventions in Democratic Republic of the Congo (1998–2003) and Sudan/South Sudan (2002–2006).[120] At home, the UPDF's reputation had also been tarnished by its action in the controversial 2006 presidential elections and its activities in the Karamoja cluster.

Second, AMISOM also brought the UPDF significant training, military financing, and equipment options, especially from the United States. It also kept many troops busy outside Uganda, following the return of the large UPDF force that had deployed into DR Congo for nearly a decade.[121] The economic benefits of such assistance accrued primarily to the security forces and individual troops rather than the national economy or Ugandan firms. Uganda became an ACOTA partner in 1998 but was inactive between 2000 and 2006. The decision to spearhead AMISOM saw a rapid intensification of US security assistance to Uganda, but also that provided by the UK and France. From the outset, the UPDF was particularly concerned about the risks of urban warfare, including improvised explosive devices (IEDs), which went well beyond traditional peacekeeping tasks. It was therefore particularly keen to receive counter-IED training from its partners. This is why, from November 2007, Uganda hired Bancroft Global Development to provide mentors and assistance to its troops on the challenges of urban warfare.[122]

---

[118] IGAD officials, cited in Jonathan Fisher, *Mapping 'Regional Security' in the Greater Horn of Africa* (Friedrich Ebert Stiftung, April 2014), p. 23, http://library.fes.de/pdf-files/bueros/aethiopien/10855.pdf

[119] Training and support for the UPDF was one of the five reasons stated by Defence Minister Crispus Kiyonga.

[120] See, for example, UN, *Final report of the Panel of Experts on the Illegal Exploitation of Natural Resources and Other Forms of Wealth of the Democratic Republic of Congo* (S/2002/1146, 16 October 2002), esp. §97–131 and Mareike Schomerus, '"They forget what they came for": Uganda's army in Sudan', *Journal of Eastern African Studies*, 6:1 (2012), pp. 124–53.

[121] Fisher, 'Managing Donor Perceptions', p. 418.

[122] Interviews, Bancroft personnel, Washington DC, June 2013. Bancroft Global Development is a multinational, not-for-profit nongovernment organization headquartered in the United States that implements stabilization initiatives in conflict zones. It worked in partnership

Later, Uganda's deployment in AMISOM enabled the UPDF to access not just US peacekeeping support but also the much more lucrative support for counterterrorism and stabilization operations under Section 1206 of the US National Defense Authorization Act.

In sum, Museveni's decision to lead AMISOM was based principally on boosting his regional leadership credentials and his key international political relationships, notably the United States and Ethiopia. Although less prevalent in official explanations, the institutional benefits that accrued for the UPDF were the other crucial part of the equation. These were significant enough that they can correctly be understood as part of a broader trend of using external sources of finance to the UPDF to support Uganda's governance regime.[123]

CONCLUSION

AMISOM was the successor of IGAD's failed attempt to deploy a peace operation in Somalia during 2005. Despite alluding to the potential for a peace deal between the conflict parties, in practice, AMISOM's principal rationale was to support one side (the TFG) and provide an exit strategy for the Ethiopian forces that had brought it to Mogadishu. This was arguably the first significant evolution of AMISOM's mandate and the lack of impartiality would come to shape all the mission's activities. Initially, there was also a clear attempt to keep Somalia's neighbours out of the mission because of the potential for political conflicts of interest. This meant that the onus of responsibility within IGAD fell almost solely upon Uganda. It was therefore crucial for AMISOM that Ugandan President Yoweri Museveni was a strong supporter of the operation, with Ugandan troops shouldering the responsibility alone for nine months. In that initial entry phase, one Ugandan battle group was sent into a war zone, nominally as peacekeepers but in reality supporting one side in the conflict and operating alongside an occupying Ethiopian force. This was a morally dubious decision that would cost the lives of many AU peacekeepers. At the outset, it also looked like a politically naïve strategy: to prop up an unpopular local government.

with Bancroft Global Investments, a profit-making limited partnership that allocates capital to create or scale commercial enterprises in unstable environments.

[123] See Koen Vlassenroot, Sandrine Perrot, Jeroen Cuvelier, 'Doing business out of war. An analysis of the UPDF's presence in the Democratic Republic of Congo', *Journal of Eastern African Studies*, 6:1 (2012), pp. 2–21.

2

Entry

March 2007 to January 2009

In its strategic directive dated May 2008, AMISOM's leaders made a number of explicit assumptions about the conduct of the mission. The last one stated: 'A pre-condition for the initial deployment of AMISOM is contingent to the overall security situation in Somalia, which must be non-hostile, safe and secure, particularly with regard [sic.] the capital Mogadishu and its direct surroundings'.[1] Unfortunately, reality did not oblige. When the first Ugandan advance elements arrived in Somalia in early 2007 they found themselves entering a city at war. When the main elements of the first UPDF battle group started to arrive in Mogadishu on 6 March they came under fire from day one, with mortar fire interrupting the welcoming ceremony for the first contingent of 400 Ugandan troops.[2] On day two, unknown insurgents using rocket-propelled grenades (RPG)s and small arms attacked a Ugandan convoy in central Mogadishu in the vicinity of the K-4 traffic intersection, injuring two soldiers and resulting in an unknown number of dead and injured civilians caught in the crossfire. On day three, in a pre-recorded audio tape played on Mogadishu's Radio Koran, a man claiming to be a senior *al-Shabaab* leader, Aden Hashi Ayro, called on Somalis, and especially the youth, to resist Ethiopian and AMISOM troops.[3] That same day, an AMISOM cargo plane (sortie number 12) caught fire after being hit by a missile while landing at Mogadishu International Airport (MIA). AMISOM's Force Commander, later recalled, 'When the plane was hit, we thought, oh, this is mission impossible!'[4] In week three, another AMISOM supply plane was hit on arrival at MIA, this

---

[1] *Strategic Directive for the African Union Mission in Somalia (AMISOM)* (AU internal document, 20 May 2008), §23g. Hereafter, *AMISOM Strategic Directive* (May 2008).
[2] Wikileak Cable 07NAIROBI1127, 9 March 2007, §1.   [3] *Ibid*, §5.
[4] General Levi Karuhanga speaking in John Allan Namu, 'The Somalia Mission', broadcast by KTN Perspective, 7 August 2013.

time killing all eleven crew.[5] Within a month, AMISOM suffered its first fatality (on 31 March) when a Ugandan soldier was killed by mortar fire directed near his unit's location at Villa Somalia.[6]

This chapter analyses the major developments during AMISOM's first two years before the withdrawal of the Ethiopian troops that had brought the TFG to Mogadishu. It is the story of a badly under-resourced mission trying to consolidate its presence in a violent city, struggling to retain its impartiality while operating under the shadow of Ethiopia's occupying forces and clearly supporting one side in the armed conflict, and then having to deal with the opportunities and challenges presented by the Ethiopian's withdrawal in January 2009. By that stage, AMISOM had still only reached just over 40 per cent (3,450) of its authorized strength of 8,000 troops. Nevertheless, this period saw AMISOM shift from playing a supporting role in Mogadishu's political drama to becoming the crucial life support system for the TFG.

To discuss these issues the chapter proceeds in six parts. The first section analyses the initial deployment challenges facing AMISOM and the problems presented by operating in Ethiopia's shadow. The second section explains Burundi's arrival as AMISOM's second TCC, while the third analyses some of the ways in which AMISOM came to be seen by many local Somalis as a proxy force for nefarious foreign agendas. The fourth section then discusses the 2008 Djibouti peace process as the route by which Ethiopia managed to withdraw its forces. This opened up a number of opportunities for AMISOM and pushed it towards the political centre stage. The fifth section discusses the opportunities and challenges presented by the withdrawal of Ethiopian forces in January 2009, while the final section examines what this meant for AMISOM being left alone to take on the leading role of protecting Somalia's TFG from *al-Shabaab*.

DEPLOYING UNDER ETHIOPIA'S SHADOW

Getting troops to Mogadishu in early 2007 was not easy. The Ugandans initially self-deployed a small number of troops on Antonov planes used by the Algerian air force while Ethiopian helicopters based in Somalia provided sector security for the waterborne approaches to Mogadishu airport.[7]

Once disembarked, the UPDF's first battle group established their main base at the international airport, located along the city's southwest coast. Securing the airport was the UPDF's top priority because it was literally their lifeline for

---

[5] Oloya, *Black Hawks Rising*, p. 82.
[6] Wikileak Cable 07NAIROBI1463, 2 April 2007, §1; Oloya, *Black Hawks Rising*, p. 83.
[7] Wikileak Cable 07ADDISABABA774, 14 March 2007.

supplies that were being flown in from Entebbe.[8] After taking control of Mogadishu in 2006, the SCIC had initially established a training camp near the airport but apparently gave up on the idea because of the huge number of snakes in the bush areas. It was here that AMISOM's first soldiers had to crawl through dense undergrowth full of snakes and pitch their tents in the old SCIC training camp. This was just to the west of what was known locally as the 'White House'—a large white building that had survived the war and became the Ugandan contingent headquarters.[9] Apart from this structure, AMISOM's personnel would not enjoy hard-wall accommodation for years.

Over the next two years, AMISOM forces and equipment would either be flown into MIA or delivered by ship to the seaport. Several different actors provided the strategic lift required to deploy AMISOM forces. Most important for the initial battle groups were the flights provided by DynCorp International, contracted by the US government, and the Algerian air force. They operated IL-76 and C-130 aircraft.[10] AMISOM referred to the logistics effort as Operation Mango Ramp. After August 2007, at the AU's request, NATO also provided strategic airlift and sealift support to AMISOM, including escorting an AU ship that later carried Burundian military equipment for one of the battalions that it had airlifted into Mogadishu.[11] The bigger items of equipment, including T-55 battle tanks, required the Ugandan troops to gain control of the seaport, which they did on 19 March.[12] But the seaport was also considered important because the UPDF suspected arms were being smuggled in through it to *al-Shabaab*.[13] The Ugandans also established bases at Villa Somalia and the K-4 junction, a crucial roundabout that provided a route between Villa Somalia and the airport.

From these locations, AMISOM protected key members of the TFG and a number of strategic points in the city from armed opposition. At the K-4 junction, AMISOM troops observed passing traffic and reported suspicious vehicles back to headquarters. This outpost came under regular attack. At the seaport AMISOM supervised the security measures implemented by the TFG port authorities. At Villa Somalia, AMISOM shared the tasks of protecting the areas outside the walls and controlling access to the gates with the Ethiopian troops. TFG forces guarded the president within the walls. AMISOM was also

---

[8] Interview, senior UPDF official, Kampala, 14 August 2012.

[9] Interview, AMISOM official, Mogadishu, 6 January 2013.

[10] *Technical Assessment Mission to Somalia: 12–25 January 2009* (UN internal document, January 2009), Annex D. Hereafter, UN, *TAM* (12–25 January 2009).

[11] 'NATO Assistance to the African Union', http://www.nato.int/cps/en/natohq/topics_8191. htm

[12] Oloya, *Black Hawks Rising*, p. 80. Among other things, Operation Mango Ramp delivered twenty-one T-55 tanks, one tank retriever, nineteen five-tonne trucks, and three battle wagons. 'AMISOM Brief to Visiting US Delegation' (AU internal document, 25 February 2009).

[13] Interview, senior UPDF official, Kampala, 14 August 2012.

called upon to provide escort services for visiting VIPs.[14] In doing so, the mission had to interact with the Ethiopian and TFG forces. However, AMISOM remained separate from the ENDF. AMISOM-ENDF-TFG interaction and information sharing was thus officially coordinated through a weekly triangular meeting. Unlike the Ethiopians, AMISOM did not attempt to patrol widely across the city. AMISOM never attempted to patrol in such hotspots as the notorious Bakara market and in mid-May the UPDF decided to suspend patrols in Mogadishu more generally after losing four peacekeepers in an incident on 16 May.[15]

Politically, the Ugandans found themselves in a city that was a patchwork of competing armed groups, including several warlord militias, the TFG's forces supported by Ethiopian troops, and fighters loyal to the Alliance for the Re-liberation of Somalia (ARS), the successor movement of the SCIC.[16] Several warlord factions persisted around Mogadishu airport because the SCIC had been unable to dislodge them. And then there was *al-Shabaab*, which from small beginnings was becoming increasingly influential by appealing to anti-Ethiopian sentiments.[17]

The fighting between these various groups was frequent and brutal, and displaced about 700,000 people from Mogadishu alone.[18] The anti-Ethiopian sentiment it generated also provided *al-Shabaab* with a massive recruitment boost and the movement grew to become the dominant force in opposition to the TFG. The depth of local rage was apparent from the desecration of the bodies of Ethiopian and TFG soldiers, some of whom were dragged through streets of Mogadishu and set on fire.[19] One senior Ethiopian official estimated that about 840 ENDF personnel were killed during operations in Somalia from late 2006 until their withdrawal in January 2009, most coming after the initial 2006 intervention.[20]

The conflict also pioneered the use of deadly suicide attacks in Somalia. On 26 March 2007, for example, 'a car packed with explosives, drove onto the Ethiopian military installation at Eel-Irfiid (about 5 km from Mogadishu) and detonated it in the middle of the base, resulting in 63 soldiers killed and approximately 50 wounded'.[21] On 19 April, *al-Shabaab* packed a vehicle with

---

[14] Wikleak Cable 07NAIROBI2630, 26 June 2007.

[15] Abukar Sheikh Ahmed and Richard Kinyera, 'Ugandan peace-keepers limit patrols in Mogadishu', *New Vision* (Kampala), 15 July 2007.

[16] See Appendix A.

[17] *Al-Shabaab* began its organizational existence in 2005 with a core of just thirty-three members. Hansen, *Al-Shabaab*, p. 29. See Appendix A.

[18] This was out of the city's total population of about 1.3 million. Menkhaus, 'Violent Islamic Extremism', p. 3.

[19] 'Rebels Drag Soldiers' Bodies Through Mogadishu Streets', *The Guardian*, 21 March 2007, http://www.guardian.co.uk/world/2007/mar/21/1

[20] Interview, Ethiopian MFA official, Addis Ababa, 31 July 2012.

[21] *Report of the Monitoring Group on Somalia pursuant to Security Council resolution 1724 (2006)* (S/2007/436, 18 July 2007), §37. Hereafter, *SEMG Report*, 18 July 2007.

explosives and attacked another Ethiopian military base, Aslubta, resulting in thirty soldiers killed and approximately 200 wounded.[22] Between September 2006 and September 2017, one study counted 155 operations involving 216 individuals who detonated as *al-Shabaab* suicide bombers, which killed an estimated 595 to 2,218 people (see also Chapter 3).[23] For their part, the ENDF were accused of rape, torture, and resorting to indiscriminate fire from artillery and helicopters.[24] At one point they were even accused of using white phosphorous against *al-Shabaab* forces in the Shirkole area of Mogadishu, killing approximately fifteen fighters and thirty-five civilians.[25]

With only about 1,600 troops, the UPDF's first battle group was in no position to fight and sensibly protested its neutrality on arrival. In April 2007, for instance, Ugandan Defence Minister Crispus Kiyonga was at pains to stress that AMISOM's mandate did not involve 'directly fighting insurgents'.[26] Consequently, when AMISOM troops arrived they had to establish relations with all these competing groups. The mission concentrated on consolidating its positions and getting to know the TFG and the local population. As the UPDF's first contingent commander put it, 'The time has come for us to show a friendly face to the Somali people, we cannot hide behind the wire forever'.[27] The patrols that occurred thus became a way not of displaying force but of highlighting AMISOM's presence. The UPDF's initial plan was to focus their engagement on the Hawiye clan elders as they were seen as the dominant force in the city. To both the remaining warlords and the Hawiye, UPDF commanders said they were a weak force that had not come to fight a war, but instead to act as peacekeepers.[28]

AMISOM's efforts to engage the local population were severely hampered, however, by the widespread fear of retaliation from *al-Shabaab*. UN and nongovernmental humanitarian workers also avoided any visible association with the AU 'peacekeepers' fearing that this would endanger their lives and severely restrict the delivery of services.[29] Perhaps rather optimistically, AMISOM announced a voluntary disarmament policy, and persuaded the Somali President and Prime Minister to go on the radio and call on fighters

---

[22] *Ibid.*, §37.

[23] Jason Warner and Ellen Chapin, *Targeted Terror: The Suicide Bombers of al-Shabaab* (West Point, NY: Combating Terrorism Center, 2018).

[24] Human Rights Watch, *Shell-Shocked*.

[25] *SEMG Report*, 18 July 2007, §30. See also §33–34. The Monitoring Group claimed this was not an isolated incident, although the Ethiopian authorities denied all such reports.

[26] 'We are keeping peace in Somalia—Uganda', *New Vision* (Kampala), 8 April 2007.

[27] Oloya, *Black Hawks Rising*, p. 83.

[28] Interview, UPDF officer, Washington DC, 23 October 2013.

[29] See Mark Bradbury and Robert Maletta, 'When state-building fails' in Antonio Donini (ed.), *The Golden Fleece: Manipulation and Independence in Humanitarian Action* (Boulder, CO: Kumarian Press, 2012), pp. 109–35.

to surrender their guns to AMISOM.[30] By the first week of May, AMISOM had recovered over 2,000 mines,[31] 200 guns, and three mounted battle wagons.[32] But this had little discernable effect on conflict dynamics in the city. In July 2007 when the TFG had organized a 'reconciliation conference' in Mogadishu attended by about 1,000 delegates, there was no discussion of power-sharing and representatives of major opposition groups, including senior Hawiye and SCIC leaders, were absent.[33]

In these circumstances, it was not surprising that AMISOM suffered attacks from several groups. Some hostility came from local warlord factions vying for control of the airport and its environs, into which AMISOM had deployed. *Al-Shabaab* forces also targeted AMISOM, claiming they had joined the ENDF and were acting as proxies of the United States. AMISOM also angered some city residents because it allowed the Ethiopians to stage their helicopters from the airport.[34] In September 2008, AMISOM also clashed with Ras Kamboni fighters who had attacked the TFG presidential compound in Mogadishu.[35] There were even reports that a contingent of fighters from the Nigerian *Boko Haram* had arrived in Mogadishu to help train *al-Shabaab*.[36]

In these early days, the UPDF high command thus saw themselves as insurgents because they only occupied several small locations in Mogadishu whereas the ARS and *al-Shabaab* occupied most of the country.[37] Essentially, the UPDF built a string of guerrilla bases in Mogadishu and spread out from there. Nevertheless, the UPDF's arrival sent an important signal. As the chief of Uganda's land forces, General Katumba Wamala, remarked, 'We burst the myth that Somalia is a no-go area'.[38]

At the outset of the mission, Uganda's soldiers did not expect to remain alone for so long. First, they expected to be joined by other African contributing countries. By March 2007 the AU had received additional pledges of 1,600 soldiers from Burundi, 850 from Nigeria, 350 from Ghana, and up to 1,000 from Malawi.[39] A couple of months later, Benin reportedly offered two

---

[30] Emmy Allio, 'Katumba in Mogadishu', *New Vision* (Kampala), 29 April 2007.

[31] The UN Development Programme, which had conducted anti-mine activities, suspended its operations in late 2008 and passed the buck in south-central Somalia to the UN Mine Action Service (UNMAS). UNMAS then helped build AMISOM's capacity in the technical area of explosive ordnance disposal.

[32] 'Ugandan troops recover arms in Somalia', *New Vision* (Kampala), 6 May 2007.

[33] Security Council Report, 'Somalia', August 2007.

[34] Wikileak Cable 07NAIROBI1463, 2 April 2007, §4.

[35] *Report of the Monitoring Group on Somalia pursuant to Security Council resolution 1811 (2008)* (S/2008/769, 10 December 2008), §92. For details of Ras Kamboni see Appendix A and Chapter 5.

[36] UPDF Brigadier General Paul Lokech cited in James Fergusson, *The World's Most Dangerous Place* (Boston, MA: Da Capo, 2013), p. 39.

[37] Interview, senior UPDF official, Kampala, 14 August 2012.

[38] Alfred Wasike, 'Somalia is accessible—Wamala', *New Vision* (Kampala), 30 April 2008.

[39] 'Somalia: "We'll fight back if attacked," AU troops say', *IRIN News*, 7 March 2007.

battalions.[40] Second, AMISOM troops were also expecting to transition into a UN mission. Back in Addis Ababa, AU Peace and Security Commissioner Said Djinnit was telling the international diplomatic circuit that AMISOM would remain in Somalia for 'five, six or seven months, and it would be followed by a larger United Nations operation'.[41] That did not happen, but it was not for lack of diplomatic efforts by some of AMISOM's key African supporters. In early May 2007, for example, Uganda's Minister of Defence told US officials that the deployment of other African units and a transition from an AU to a UN force were critical for creating a secure environment in Mogadishu.[42] The following month, Somali Prime Minister Ali Mohamed Gedi told a private meeting of the UN Security Council that the TFG wanted AMISOM to transition into a UN operation.[43]

By this stage, however, promises of additional troops were vanishing fast. Ghana withdrew its offer, citing security concerns and lack of equipment and logistics assets.[44] Rwanda said it was heavily committed to the AU mission in Darfur, Sudan, while a Nigeria reconnaissance mission to Somalia decided against further deployment.[45] Much later, Kenya also declined to send troops citing the original prohibition on soldiers from 'front line states' contained in the October 2006 deployment plan for the IGAD peacekeeping mission.[46] But this prohibition was rescinded by UN Security Council resolution 1744 (20 February 2007).

Debate about a potential transition to a UN peacekeeping operation was ended, at least temporarily, in November 2007 when UN Secretary-General Ban Ki-moon concluded that deploying UN peacekeepers to Somalia was 'neither realistic nor viable'—the security situation was so bad that it was not even possible to send a UN technical assessment team.[47] The decision was denounced by some African leaders, particularly Kenya's President Mwai Kibaki, who bluntly criticized the UN's indifference to the sacrifice of African soldiers, saying 'The perceived reluctance of the United Nations Security Council to engage with Somalia has been a matter of great concern for those of us who suffer the greatest consequences of the conflict'.[48] But it was not just the UN that refused to support AMISOM on the ground. Burundi was the

---

[40] Wikileak Cable, 07ADDISABABA2185, 13 July 2007, §7.

[41] Security Council Report, 'Somalia Monthly Forecast', April 2007, http://www.securitycouncilreport. org/monthly-forecast/2007-04/lookup_c_glKWLeMTIsG_b_2620663.php

[42] Wikileak Cable 07KAMPALA854, 18 May 2007.

[43] Security Council Report, 'Somalia', August 2007.

[44] Security Council Report, 'Somalia Monthly Forecast', July 2007, http://www.securitycouncilreport.org/monthly-forecast/2007-07/lookup_c_glKWLeMTIsG_b_2876601.php

[45] Wikileak Cable 07KIGALI1085, 26 November 2007, §4.

[46] Wikileak Cable 08NAIROBI2701, 2 December 2008. Paragraph 4 of UN Security Council resolution 1725 (6 December 2006) endorsed 'the specification in the IGAD Deployment Plan that those States that border Somalia would not deploy troops to Somalia'.

[47] 'Somalia peacekeepers "not viable"', *BBC News*, 9 November 2007, http://news.bbc.co.uk/ go/pr/fr/-/2/hi/africa/7086367.stm

[48] 'Kenya demands UN engagement in Somalia', *Afrol News*, 23 September 2008, http://www. afrol.com/articles/36631

only other African country that stepped forward. Ten months into the mission, this prompted the AU Commission Chairperson Alpha Oumar Konaré to publicly criticize AU member states for failing to honor their pledges of troops.[49] This changed slightly in November 2007 when advanced elements of the Burundi National Defence Force (BNDF) arrived in Mogadishu.

ENTER BURUNDI

After being part of the early discussions about establishing AMISOM, by June 2007, Burundi's Chief of Staff declared his country was 'ready now' to deploy two battalions to Somalia contingent on receiving 'adequate equipment and logistics support'.[50] In November 2007, BNDF forces started to arrive in Mogadishu and the first battalion deployed during the early months of 2008. They were light infantry troops with almost no armour. They deployed to the university area and the old Siad Barre Military Academy. By late April 2008, this brought AMISOM's total strength to about 2,400.

As the most thorough analysis of Burundi's decision to join AMISOM concluded, the main drivers revolved around its national and international reputation, boosting professionalism and cohesion within a newly composed army, and financial benefits.[51] At the heart of Burundi's deployment was the desire to consolidate and strengthen the newly integrated BNDF as a key part of the country's post–civil war peace process. The BNDF was itself a product of military integration carried out after Burundi's civil war (1993–2006) as part of the peace process. This involved a peace agreement based on strict quotas of shared positions between the Hutu-dominated Front for Democracy (FRODEBU) and National Council for the Defence of Democracy-Forces for the Defence of Democracy (CNDD-FDD) on one side, and Union for National Progress (UPRONA), largely supported by the Tutsi-dominated ex-*Forces Armées Burundaises*, on the other.

Speaking to US diplomats, senior Burundi officials explained their desire to participate in AMISOM as a way for the country to express its gratitude for the external assistance it had received to end its civil war and enhance Burundi's status on the international stage, in part through increasing the professionalism of its military.[52] Because of its civil war, however, Burundi had been

---

[49] 'AU head wants extension for Somali peace force', *Mail & Guardian Online* (Johannesburg), 18 January 2008, www.mg.co.za/article/2008-01-18-au-head-wants-extension-for-somalia-peace-force

[50] Memorandum for the record, 5 June 2007. ACOTA files.

[51] Nina Wilén, David Ambrosetti, and Gérard Birantamije, 'Sending peacekeepers abroad, sharing power at home: Burundi in Somalia', *Journal of Eastern African Studies*, 9:2 (2015), pp. 307–25.

[52] Wikileak Cable 07BUJUMBURA215, 26 March 2007, §6.

blacklisted from several external peacekeeping training programmes between 1995 and 2006. As a consequence, when in March and April 2007, Burundian officials repeated their willingness to deploy about 2,000 soldiers to AMISOM, they emphasized that this was dependent on external logistical, training, and financial support.[53] To that end, the Burundian military began planning for the operation before parliamentary approval was secured.[54]

The Burundian leadership believed that the army's professionalism could be enhanced by receiving security assistance linked to peacekeeping, injecting new financial resources, and carrying out novel operational experiences in peace operations.

To underscore how important these institutional rationales were in Burundi's decision to join AMISOM, one need only look at the state of the new BNDF. Burundi was so strapped for resources that it was unable to send a thirty-man reconnaissance team to Somalia in February 2007.[55] The government in Bujumbura therefore compiled a twenty-page list of requests that it considered necessary to become an AMISOM TCC, including trucks and bulldozers, aircraft, and helicopters as well as office supplies, sleeping bags, personal equipment, and optical equipment such as night vision goggles.[56] These items would need to be compatible with those of the UPDF to ensure effective interoperability. Similarly, an AU-led assessment team that visited Burundi during 2007 to evaluate the state of its preparedness for deployment to Somalia concluded that because of its limited capacity BNDF troops should be restricted to carrying out static security functions, principally providing force protection at the airport, seaport, and other military installations. This would reduce the need for patrolling and equipment and hence reduce the amount of pre-deployment training required.

The majority of this security assistance was provided by the United States but the Netherlands, France, Belgium, and Germany also contributed.[57] In August 2008, Burundi also asked Bancroft Global Development to provide them with similar assistance to that given to Uganda.[58] Although Burundi only became an ACOTA partner in November 2008, ACOTA started providing a ten-week peacekeeping pre-deployment course to Burundi from January 2008. As part of its growing security partnership, the United States would subsequently start building Burundi's National Peacekeeping Training Center at Mudubugu in late 2009 while command and staff training was conducted at the Military Academy in Bujumbura. By then, Burundi's goal was to

---

[53] Wikileak Cable 07BUJUMBURA206, 22 March 2007; Wikileak Cable 07BUJUM-BURA215, 26 March 2007; Wikileak Cable 07BUJUMBURA244, 2 April 2007.

[54] Wikileak Cabke 07BUJUMBURA215, 26 March 2007.   [55] *Ibid.*, §3.

[56] A European military officer working with the Burundian government believed this list to be overly short and optimistic! Wikileak Cable 07BUJUMBURA244, 2 April 2007.

[57] Wilén et al., 'Sending peacekeepers abroad', p. 315.

[58] Interviews, Bancroft personnel, Washington DC, June 2013.

concurrently deploy four battalions in peace operations: three in AMISOM and one to a UN operation by the end of 2010.[59] Between FY2007 and 2011, ACOTA invested approximately $20.3m in Burundi's security sector.[60]

It is also important to recall that this security assistance came in the context of mounting political pressures on AMISOM's architects to ensure Uganda was not left as the mission's sole TCC. The importance of Burundi's participation was thus amplified because within the AU and several Western states it was thought to represent a crucial step to get more TCCs on the ground by encouraging other AU members to join the massively under-strength mission.[61] Politically, therefore, the arrival of the Burundi contingent was seen as a crucial step to get more TCCs on the ground by encouraging other AU members to join the mission.[62] The Burundian troops were stationed to the north of Mogadishu airport at the university and former military academy.

In terms of military cohesion and professionalism, deployment in AMISOM offered former enemies the chance to bond with one another by fighting *al-Shabaab* 'behind the same trenches'.[63] Some NGO observers suggested that an additional motivating factor was to deploy outside the country ex-rebel fighters that had supposedly been reintegrated into the army.[64] Burundi's decision to join AMISOM therefore had a temporary stabilizing effect on the internal political balance due to several factors, including professionalization, prestige, and financial opportunities.[65] In hindsight, the AMISOM deployment eased tensions within the army, promised professionalization and prestige through assistance programmes that brought training and equipment, and it facilitated other international deployments including some senior positions for Burundian personnel, which also helped the country's image move from a victim of war to a provider of security. As Wilén et al, put it, 'The deployment helped... reduce frustration within the new FDN as it made it possible to engage the "surplus" soldiers and to temporarily justify it to donors, which consequently reduced the pressure to demobilize'.[66]

With regard to economic issues, some analysts have argued that this was the main reason Burundi deployed to AMISOM.[67] This overlooks the institutional and political reasons noted above, but it is part of the story. It was clear from the outset that Burundi sought assistance to enable it to provide its troops with

---

[59] Memorandum for the record, 1 June 2009. ACOTA files.
[60] ACOTA Partner Summary: Burundi, 8 August 2012. ACOTA files.
[61] Wikileak Cable 07BUJUMBURA460, 15 June 2007.   [62] *Ibid.*
[63] Charles Ndayaziga, 'Enjeux autour de l'intervention du Burundi en Somalie', *Africa Policy Brief No.7*, Nov. 2013, p. 3. Author's translation.
[64] Communication with Western human rights NGO official, July 2012.
[65] Wilén et al., 'Sending peacekeepers abroad', p. 307.   [66] *Ibid.*, p. 313.
[67] Elizabeth Dickinson, 'For tiny Burundi, big returns in sending peacekeepers to Somalia', *Christian Science Monitor*, 22 December 2011, http://www.csmonitor.com/World/Africa/2011/1222/For-tiny-Burundi-big-returns-in-sending-peacekeepers-to-Somalia

salaries of $500 per month and a monthly per diem of $750 per capita.[68] In retrospect, these allowances eventually rose to $1,028 per soldier per month (minus the government's administrative slice of $200). The result was that an entire neighbourhood in Gitega was constructed by AMISOM veterans from their allowances and became known as 'AMISOM District'.[69] On the other hand, some analysts remained sceptical that the government actually invested the AMISOM funds back into the BNDF, noting the purchase of a new presidential jet plane was apparently bought with AMISOM funds.[70]

In sum, Burundi's government used its position as an AMISOM TCC both to solve internal political problems related to its peace process and the security sector, and to facilitate closer relationships with some key external donors.[71]

AMISOM AS PROXY

While the arrival of Burundian troops was helpful, it neither generated a flood of new TCCs nor significantly altered dynamics in Mogadishu. The vast majority of AU member states voted with their feet and refused to deploy troops to Somalia. Uganda and Burundi would be left alone until a handful of Djiboutian troops arrived in Mogadishu in December 2011.

Several factors were at work here. There was considerable international pessimism about AMISOM's prospects, in part because many countries felt Mogadishu in early 2007 was not an appropriate destination for a peacekeeping force. Others, including Ghana and Nigeria, were also put off by the lack of a reliable funding source for the mission. But arguably AMISOM's main challenge was being seen by many local Somalis as a proxy for other nefarious interests rather than an impartial force seeking only peace. For example, some Somalis—and not just *al-Shabaab*—referred to AMISOM as 'infidel invaders' supporting an unpopular government.[72]

According to the AU's own internal assessment, there were two principal narratives critical of AMISOM's role.[73] One view suggested AMISOM was in Mogadishu to support and protect the corrupt and illegitimate transitional government of President Abdullahi Yusuf and defend the airport for his regime and the Ethiopian army. American spies, the AU, the Ethiopians,

---

[68] Wikileak Cabke 07BUJUMBURA215, 26 March 2007, §3.

[69] Wilén et al., 'Sending peacekeepers abroad', p. 316 and Ndayaziga, 'Enjeux autour', p. 4.

[70] Wilén et al., 'Sending peacekeepers abroad', p. 316.   [71] *Ibid.*, p. 317.

[72] In June 2010, *al-Shabaab* and *al-Kataib* released a propaganda video that exemplified this line of attack. It was titled 'The African Crusaders: Fighting the West's War'. http://archive.org/details/The-African-Crusaders [no date, posted 27 June 2010].

[73] See *AMISOM Media/Communication Plan* (AU Strategic Planning and Management Unit, no date [2008]).

and TFG troops were thought to use Mogadishu airport to reinforce and support the occupation of Somalia by an anti-Islam coalition maintained by the United States for its own interests. In April 2008, for instance, the ARS leadership told US diplomats that AMISOM was not neutral and viewed by the people of Mogadishu as part of the same continuum as the Ethiopian forces. They argued that AMISOM should be replaced by a neutral UN force but questioned whether those resources would not be better spent on reconstruction and assistance for the Somali people.[74]

A second variant depicted AMISOM as a surrogate or 'Trojan Horse' for the US-led 'war on terror'—itself a synonym for the war on Islam.[75] Ethiopia's use of helicopters also engendered a widespread belief in Mogadishu that Washington was fully supporting the Ethiopian campaign with intelligence, materiel, and American combat helicopters.[76] The idea that AMISOM was part of the US-led 'war on terror' was not implausible, and was believed by some within the AU.[77] After all, in 2006, senior US officials had equated the SCIC with *al-Qa'ida* in east Africa and had supported, if not encouraged, the Ethiopian military campaign to install the TFG in Villa Somalia.[78] AMISOM was then deployed with considerable Ethiopian input to provide an exit strategy for the Ethiopian forces by protecting the TFG. Further evidence was also found by pointing to the increasing use of US security assistance packages to 'train and equip' AMISOM's two contributing countries: Uganda and Burundi. In addition, two private contractor firms run out of the United States began operating in Mogadishu, further fuelling such views: DynCorp International and Bancroft Global Development.

In January 2007, the US government contracted DynCorp International to help equip, deploy, sustain, and train soldiers from the vanguard Ugandan and Burundian contingents of AMISOM.[79] DynCorp provided AMISOM with rations, fuel (diesel and gasoline) and general supply items, including materials for AMISOM's camp facilities and medical support. To source some of these supplies locally, DynCorp had to maintain a list of alternative contractors so as not to appear politically biased towards one local group.[80] Many of the materials had to be flown into the MIA by DynCorp's air support

---

[74] Wikileak Cable 08NAIROBI902, 4 April 2008, §7.

[75] *AMISOM Media/Communication Plan* (no date [2008]), p. 11.

[76] Wikileak Cable 07NAIROBI1440, 30 March 2009, §3.

[77] See Sturman and Hayatou, 'The Peace and Security Council of the African Union', p. 71.

[78] In December 2006, US Assistant Secretary of State for Africa Jendayi Frazer claimed that the SCIC were 'now controlled by...East Africa al-Qaeda cell individuals'. Cited in Ken Menkhaus, 'There and Back Again in Somalia', *Middle East Research and Information*, 11 February 2007, http://www.merip.org/mero/mero021107

[79] See http://www.dyn-intl.com/what-we-do/contingency-operations/somalia-case-study.aspx. Accessed June 2012.

[80] The Ugandan troops also purchased some rations locally, including cows, fresh vegetables, and rice, through deals facilitated by Somali businessmen who lived in Uganda and had

operation based in Entebbe, Uganda, which flew up to ten sorties per month. This was not easy. The MIA had no emergency crash and rescue equipment and none of the usual airport equipment such as runway lights, off-loading gear, and aviation fuel. Because of the persistent likelihood of attack, DynCorp tried to ensure its planes spent no longer than 90 minutes at MIA and only dispatched an aircraft from its base in Entebbe upon confirmation by AMISIOM troops in Mogadishu that it would be safe for it to land.[81] The seaport also posed problems, being only capable of handling three to five medium vessels at a time due to various sunken vessels blocking some quays and lacking handling equipment. The UK government also contracted DynCorp to obtain and transport military and non-military materiel to the deployed UPDF contingent. Overall, DynCorp provided over 80 per cent of the initial AMISOM fleet, by delivering and managing over one hundred new and remanufactured commercial, military, and armored vehicles. According to DynCorp's website, it moved 'more than 12,000 AU peacekeepers' into or out of Somalia; 'more than 15 million pounds of cargo transported by air, rail and sea; and more than 280 air sorties flown into Mogadishu and the region on DI-operated aircraft'.[82] The commander of Uganda's land forces, General Katumba Wamala, went on record to say that DynCorp's 'services right from deployment up to now have enabled us to achieve what many critics looked at as a mission impossible. DynCorp International stood with us even during the most challenging time of the deployment and did not waver even when one of the aircraft was shot at'.[83]

The second US-based firm was Bancroft Global Development, which would go on to play a key role in AMISOM's evolution. Bancroft was first approached by Ugandan leadership and invited to work with the UPDF contingent in Mogadishu in November 2007 but did not take up a Cooperative Agreement with the US Department of State until early 2010.[84] Under this agreement Bancroft was given the leeway to come up with its own ideas and methods for achieving its agreed objectives and was also subsequently able to add additional resources from other donors. The Ugandans were well aware their Somali campaign would get them into unknown military territory, especially related to the challenges of urban warfare. This is where they initially sought Bancroft's expertise, but it subsequently expanded to cover mentors in categories including C-IED, medical support, and engineering.

connections with local businesses in Mogadishu. Interview, UPDF officer, Washington DC, 23 October 2013.

[81] UN, *TAM* (12–25 January 2009), Annex D.

[82] http://www.dyn-intl.com/what-we-do/case-studies/training/supporting-peacekeeping-efforts-in-africa/ Accessed 22 December 2017.

[83] http://www.dyn-intl.com/what-we-do/contingency-operations/somalia-case-study.aspx/ Accessed 20 August 2015.

[84] Interviews, Bancroft personnel, Washington DC, June 2013.

After a few reconnaissance trips, Bancroft deployed an initial team of four advisers into Mogadishu in early 2008. Within four months, their team had expanded to twelve. After being impressed with their work in the field, Burundi approached Bancroft in August 2008 to provide them with similar assistance. During these early operations, Bancroft self-funded its activities in Mogadishu through its investment arm, Bancroft Global Investments, as part of a risky but ultimately lucrative business plan to establish themselves as reliable partners of AMISOM. It appears that most of the confusion surrounding the US government's involvement with Bancroft stemmed from the fact that some of the funding coming from Uganda and Burundi was drawn from part of their broader bilateral assistance packages and Cooperative Agreements with the US government. Hence from November 2007 until early 2010, when Bancroft was awarded a Cooperative Agreement by the US Department of State, funding for its operations in Somalia came from a combination of Bancroft resources and the contributions from Uganda and Burundi.[85]

The net result of these negative opinions was that many supporters of, and sympathizers with, the SCIC willingly took up arms against AMISOM. They were encouraged to do so by the SCIC leadership. In May 2007, for instance, former SCIC leader Sheikh Sharif Sheikh Ahmed and former parliamentary speaker Sheikh Sharif Hassan Aden urged 'the Somali people' to become 'resistance fighters', adopt 'hit-and-run' tactics, and 'never to kneel down' in front of the Ethiopians and their AMISOM allies.[86]

AMISOM also drew fire from Eritrea, which saw the mission as a proxy for Ethiopian interests in Somalia. Indeed, shortly after AMISOM's deployment, Eritrea had warned that the AU troops should not enter Somalia and would only exacerbate the violence there.[87] In April 2007, regional tensions increased when Eritrea announced it was suspending its membership of IGAD in protest at Ethiopia's military presence in Somalia; specifically, an IGAD communiqué (13 April 2007) expressing appreciation for Ethiopia's actions.[88] Eritrea also hosted the ARS-Asmara faction led by Hassan Dahir Aweys. The UN Monitoring Group on Somalia and Eritrea subsequently concluded that over the next few years, 'the Government of Eritrea has provided significant and sustained political, financial and material support, including arms, ammunition and training to armed opposition groups in Somalia since at

---

[85] 'It is the understanding of the Monitoring Group that Bancroft's status as a contractor for AMISOM means that its activities are subject to the exemption to the arms embargo provided for in paragraph 11(a) of UNSCR 1772'. *Report of the Monitoring Group on Somalia and Eritrea pursuant to Security Council resolution 1916 (2010)* (S/2011/433, 18 July 2011), p. 259.

[86] Wikileak Cable 07NAIROBI1918, 3 May 2007, §4.

[87] Henry Mukasa, 'Eritrea insists on UPDF pullout', *New Vision* (Kampala), 20 March 2007.

[88] Security Council Report, 'Somalia Monthly Forecast', May 2007, http://www.securitycouncilreport.org/monthly-forecast/2007-05/lookup_c_glKWLeMTIsG_b_2701407.php

least 2007'.[89] This was done to undermine the TFG's legitimacy and expel the AMISOM forces based in Mogadishu that were protecting it.

AMISOM's reputation was also tarnished at this important time by accusations of misconduct by its troops. Specifically, the UN Monitoring Group on Somalia and Eritrea accused both Ethiopian and AMISOM troops of entering the Somali arms market 'as sellers of weapons and ammunition' in clear violation of the UN Security Council's arms embargo established by resolution 733 on 23 January 1992.[90] The Monitoring Group accused UPDF officers of 'selling stockpiles of weapons and ammunition originating from arms caches found in Mogadishu'.[91] Thought to total some $80,000, some materiel was said to have ended up in *al-Shabaab*'s possession. The Monitoring Group concluded: 'Sales by the Ethiopian military and the Ugandan contingent of AMISOM are further increasing insecurity and are detrimental to efforts by the international community to bring peace and stability to Somalia and the wider region. As a result, in the current war economy, military commanders are profiting from the conflict'.[92]

Finally, AMISOM could not escape the perception that it was primarily a mechanism to enable Ethiopia to withdraw its forces while simultaneously protecting its investment in the form of the TFG. Beyond the human toll, Ethiopia's campaign was becoming increasingly costly in financial terms. Within a few months, Ethiopia's Foreign Minister Seyoum Mesfin was complaining to potential donors that the ENDF operations in Somalia were prohibitively costly and his troops could only stay if they received external financial support, perhaps under an 'AMISOM Light' option.[93] In March 2008, a senior Ethiopian government official claimed that Ethiopia had already reduced its troops in Somalia to about 2,500 and that their operation was costing about $1 million per day. He was also reported as saying that 'no one

---

[89] *Report of the Monitoring Group on Somalia pursuant to Security Council resolution 1853 (2008)* (S/2010/91, 10 March 2010), §58.

[90] *SEMG Report*, 24 April 2008, §29.

[91] *Ibid.*, §140. 'The Monitoring Group was able, through multiple sources, to assemble the modus operandi used by the Ugandan soldiers involved in the sale of arms as follows: the soldiers have set up a network through their translators who are in contact with the arms dealers; when the arms dealer receives a "wish list" from a client, a representative of the arms dealer contacts a trusted member of the Ugandan battalion stationed at the Mogadishu seaport, where the arms (from Shabaab weapon caches) are stored; he gains access to the containers (during the night), chooses his weapons and makes sure that they are operational; he pays the Ugandan officer (payment is always made before delivery); a representative of the Ugandan officer transports the weapons in 4x4 pickup trucks to an isolated location, for example, at Xooga Korontada (near the electricity plant) or in the bush, to the waiting arms trader; the weapons are transported by donkey cart in order to avoid being stopped by other Ugandan soldiers who are not part of the network; the smaller arms, such as AK-47s, RPG-2/7s, and PKMs, find their way to the Shabaab; heavy weapons such as Zu-23s and B-10s find their way to Puntland and Somaliland authorities'. *Ibid.*, §141. See also §140–6.

[92] *Ibid.*, §248.   [93] Wikileak Cable 07ADDISABABA2535, 13 August 2007, §2.

had dared to add up the total cost for the operation since December 2006'.[94] The following month Ethiopian Prime Minister Meles Zenawi was also vague on the subject stating only that in monetary terms the campaign had cost 'substantial amounts'—but not 'hundreds of millions of dollars'—and that his regime had maintained its presence in Somalia 'without breaking our back economically'.[95] Whatever the true cost of the campaign, Ethiopia was clearly looking for an exit strategy. Although senior Ethiopian officials were sceptical that AMISOM could bring peace to Somalia, they were not prepared to keep their own forces in Mogadishu any longer.[96] Instead, they pinned their hopes on the Djibouti peace process.

THE DJIBOUTI PEACE PROCESS

With Ethiopia developing a plan to withdraw its troops from Somalia, AMI-SOM also had to plan for how it would reconfigure its operations accordingly. As if it wasn't struggling enough, in May 2008, the UN Security Council also called on AMISOM 'to protect shipping involved with the transportation and delivery of humanitarian aid to Somalia and United Nations-authorized activities'.[97] To that end, on 20 May 2008, AMISOM adopted a new strategic directive. This defined AMISOM's mission statement in the following terms: 'to stabilize the security situation, including the take over from Ethiopian Forces, and to create a safe and secure environment in preparation for the transition to the UN'.[98] The mission was to unfold in four phases: 1) Initial Deployment Phase; 2) Expansion of Deployment; 3) Consolidation; and 4) a Redeployment/Exit Phase. The directive continued to maintain that AMISOM should 'Handover successfully to the advance contingent of a UN led peace-keeping mission within six months'.[99]

By this stage, much of AMISOM's motivation to transition to the UN was financial: UN blue helmets were compensated at a higher rate than African Union troops, and the transition to a UN peacekeeping force would raise danger pay rates across the board. Like most things connected to AMISOM, donors paid the allowances for its uniformed personnel. During 2007 and 2008, AMISOM troops initially received monthly allowances of $500 per soldier, before rising to $750 per month. (From January 2011, AMISOM

---

[94] This estimate is made in Wikileak Cable 08ADDISABABA855, 31 March 2008, §4.
[95] 'Ethiopia's PM on U.S. Alliance', *Newsweek*, 9 April 2008, http://www.newsweek.com/ethiopias-pm-us-alliance-86085
[96] Wikileak Cable 08ADDISABABA855, 31 March 2008, §7.
[97] S/RES/1811, 15 May 2008, §11.   [98] *AMISOM Strategic Directive* (May 2008), §22.
[99] *Ibid.*, §24f.

troops received the standard UN peacekeeping rate of approximately $1,028 per month. See Figure 13.1.)

The AMISOM directive also noted that the AU's planning capacity was still seriously limited and required UN planners from DPKO to embed within the PSOD to bring the total to twenty-four (seven for the military component, three for civilian police, and fourteen for mission support).[100] Crucially, it recognized the continued presence of Ethiopian troops for the major problem that it was. 'As much as the actions of the Ethiopian troops helped the TFG to defeat the ICU forces', the directive concluded:

> their prolonged stay in the country is considered inappropriate to the stabiliza-tion process. The Somalis will be quick to see them as an occupational force and step up guerilla attacks against them.... On the other hand, the withdrawal of the Ethiopian troops from Somalia without a credible force replacing them would result in a return to chaos.[101]

The international plan to avoid such chaos was hatched in Djibouti from mid-2008. In short, it was intended to replace the existing TFG with a more legitimate set of authorities. The Djibouti peace process was facilitated by the UN Secretary-General's Special Representative, Ambassador Ould-Abdallah, and unfolded in four rounds of talks that officially began in May 2008. It culminated in a series of agreements signed between the TFG and the ARS–Djibouti faction led by Sheikh Sharif Sheikh Ahmed, former leader of the SCIC, on 9 June, 26 October, and 25 November respectively.[102]

The political impetus for the process came from Ethiopia, which was desperately seeking a way to withdraw its soldiers from Mogadishu, save face, and leave behind at least potentially stable (and non-irredentist) author-ities. To that end, Ethiopia 'placed heavy pressure on the Yusuf wing of the TFG to embrace the accord, and when this failed it pressured Yusuf to resign, clearing the way for the formation of a new government'.[103]

Among other things, the 9 June Agreement endorsed the territorial integrity of Somalia (§5), agreed on a ceasefire (§6), and established a Joint Security Committee and High-Level Committee to oversee security arrangements and political cooperation respectively (§8 and §9).[104] The Joint Security Committee comprised fifteen members each from the ARS and TFG to draw up a framework for monitoring and verifying the ceasefire agreement and the eventual withdrawal of the ENDF from Somalia with timelines. The plan

---

[100] *Ibid.*, §46.   [101] *Ibid.*, §17.

[102] For an overview, see Apuuli Phillip Kasaija, 'The UN-led Djibouti peace process for Somalia, 2008–2009', *Journal of Contemporary African Studies*, 28:3 (2010), pp. 269–74.

[103] Menkhaus, *Somalia: A National and Regional Disaster?*, p. 7.

[104] 'Agreement between the Transitional Federal Government of Somalia and the Alliance for the Re-Liberation of Somalia', Djibouti, 9 June 2008. Although the Agreement is dated the 9 June 2008 it was not actually signed until 19 August 2008.

was for the Ethiopian troops to be replaced by a UN international stabilization force (ISF), which was to deploy within 120 days (§7a). The stabilization force was to be made up of troops 'from countries that are friends of Somalia excluding neighbouring states' (§7a) and 'UN forces' (§7b). Naturally, the signatories also called for external actors to fund the plan and for an international conference to be held within six months aimed at addressing Somalia's reconstruction and development. The Joint Security Committee was to establish a joint TFG–ARS security force to observe and verify the agreement and facilitate humanitarian relief supplies as well as protect aid workers.[105]

These agreements were important for several reasons, but for AMISOM they brought some additional mandated tasks and helped change its relationship with the ARS. Even after the first agreement, the ARS was explicitly hostile to AMISOM. In September 2008, for example, the ARS used its special *Jugta Culus* (Heavy Strike Force) unit, equipped almost exclusively with heavy weapons, to attack AMISOM.[106] That same month, Sheikh Sharif Sheikh Ahmed wrote a letter to the international diplomatic community in which he accused AMISOM of committing war crimes against civilians (and ARS supporters):

> AMISOM has been using tanks and heavy artillery indiscriminately against the population of Mogadishu. As a result, according to the latest estimates, over 100 people, including children, women, and elderly have been killed; more than 300 others have been wounded, and about 3000 have fled their homes, where Ethiopian troops and the TFG militias have been looting their homes.... It is obvious that AMISOM had used unnecessary force and targeted heavily populated quarters and markets far away from the fighting area(s) which can only be taken as deliberate mass killing. Since AMISOM had not come with the consent of the Somali people, lately we have been spending a significant amount of time and efforts to convince our people to accept AMISOM as a peace keeping force, but the latest terror has seriously damaged the image of the mission of AMISOM in Somalia.... We consider this AMISOM action as a war crime; therefore we urgently request the UN as well as AU to send an impartial fact find [*sic*] mission at the earliest possible time to investigate these atrocities and swiftly bring the culprits to justice.[107]

It was progress in the Djibouti peace process that succeeded in changing the dynamics between the ARS, the TFG, and AMISOM.

Following the High-Level Committee's 26 October 2008 Joint Declaration, the parties set out the modalities for the implementation of a cessation of

---

[105] Joint Security Committee, Terms of Reference, 19 August 2008, §4.

[106] *SEMG Report*, 10 December 2008, §65.

[107] Sheikh Sharif Sheikh Ahmed, Chairman ARS, 'AMISOM Brutality in Somalia', unpublished letter addressed to the UN Secretary-General, the presidents of the AU, Uganda, and Burundi, officials from the League of Arab States, the Organization of Islamic Conference, and various human rights organizations, 29 September 2008. Copy in author's possession.

hostilities between the two sides. The Committee also noted that Ethiopian troops would start their withdrawal on 21 November (§5). Part of this involved establishing an initial contingent of 5,000 joint security forces, to be drawn equally from TFG and ARS, and 10,000 civilian police, to be recruited in line with international standards.[108] On 25 November, the parties also signed an agreement involving plans to reconfigure the TFG, including by doubling the size of its parliament to incorporate members of the ARS-Djibouti and to reserve additional seats for other elements that remained outside the Djibouti peace process, as well as members of the civil society.[109] This development was crucial in changing the negative perception and attitude of the ARS towards AMISOM. Having initially viewed AMISOM as an occupying force, the ARS gradually accepted AMISOM as impartial and let it play a key role in assisting the emerging joint security apparatus. This made AMISOM an indispensable partner in the TFG/ARS security strategy. On 22 December, the AU PSC authorized AMISOM to 'support the implemen-tation of the Djibouti Agreement, including aspects relating to the training of the envisaged 10,000 joint TFG-ARS security force to promote security in Mogadishu and its surroundings'.[110]

But this new role also brought greater international pressure on AMISOM to deliver tangible results on the ground, which, in turn, led to more scrutiny of the mission's shortcomings and its capability gaps. As noted above, the AU and several African governments had always envisaged that AMISOM would transition into a UN peacekeeping operation, but there were few external supporters for this idea. In late 2008, however, the AU and the George W. Bush administration in the United States led a renewed push to deploy a UN operation to Somalia. Washington's principal concern was fear that Ethiopia's withdrawal would create a security vacuum that AMISOM was not equipped to fill. The result was a flurry of diplomatic activity in New York that culminated in mid-November 2008 with the UN Secretary-General recommending that an ISF of 'approximately two brigades' be deployed to Mogadishu.[111] Intended to unfold in four phases, the ISF was supposed to support the implementation of the Djibouti Agreement and create conditions for the deployment of a multidimensional UN peacekeeping operation.[112] The

---

[108] As agreed at the Joint Security Committee meeting in Naivasha, Kenya, 20–4 November 2008.

[109] Modalities for the Implementation of the Cessation of Armed Confrontation, 26 October 2008, https://unpos.unmissions.org/sites/default/files/081026%20-%20Modalities%20for%20Implementation%20of%20Cessation%20of%20Armed%20Confrontation.pdf

[110] PSC/MIN/Comm.4(CLXIII), 22 December 2008, §13.

[111] Subsequent UN–AU planning cohered around an ISF of approximately 6,000 troops.

[112] *Report of the Secretary-General on the Situation in Somalia* (S/2008/709, 17 November 2008), §31–43. Phase 1 would involve deployment to Mogadishu while in Phase 2 the ISF would monitor and verify the withdrawal of Ethiopian forces from the city. These two phases were scheduled to take place 'within six months' (§44). In Phase 3, the force would conduct stabilization operations in

ISF was also strongly supported by AU Commissioner for Peace and Security Ramtane Lamamra and Chairperson of the AU Commission Jean Ping. They wrote letters to individual African heads of state appealing for support to AMISOM, tried to get financial support for AMISOM from the League of Arab States, and dispatched a force generation mission around the continent asking for support.[113] While some governments, including the UK, argued that further investment in AMISOM was a 'gamble', Ping argued that a UN peacekeeping operation was a 'necessity' in Somalia and that all efforts must be made to prevent the 'catastrophic scenario' that would unfold should ENDF and AMISOM forces both withdraw.[114]

By mid-December, however, the UN Secretary-General had to inform the Security Council that although he still believed only 'a multinational force' was 'the right tool for stabilizing Mogadishu', just fourteen of the fifty countries approached had responded to his request for contributions. Of these, only two offered funding (the United States and the Netherlands). None of them pledged any troops or offered to assume the lead nation role. He went on to note that this was particularly 'disappointing' since it stood 'in such sharp contrast to the exceptional political will and commitment of military assets which Member States have shown in respect of the fight against piracy'.[115] (Since late 2008 various coalition forces conducted an anti-piracy and maritime security operation across the Gulf of Aden. The central actors included the EU's *Operation Atalanta*, as well as units from NATO, the Combined Maritime Forces, and individual states such as China, Japan, Russia, India, and others.)

With the death of the ISF concept, the UN Secretary-General explored other options to prepare for the expected security vacuum. In addition to advising that the UN continue its contingency planning for a potential UN peacekeeping operation, he proposed three steps.[116] First, AMISOM should be reinforced through bilateral support to Uganda and Burundi; support at the mission-level in the area of logistical, medical, and engineering capabilities; and the transfer of some $7 million worth of assets from the UN peacekeeping mission in Eritrea and Ethiopia (UNMEE), including prefabricated accommodation, electricity generators, air-conditioning units, ablution units, and soft-skin vehicles.[117] He also suggested the UN should bolster its support for

---

Mogadishu in order to facilitate the consolidation of the TFG's authority. Phase 4 involved the transition to a UN multidimensional peacekeeping operation of '22,500 troops operating in five brigade-sized sectors throughout southern and central Somalia' (§47).

[113] Wikileak Cable 08ADDISABABA3337, 10 December 2008, §5.   [114] *Ibid.*, §7.

[115] 'Letter from the Secretary-General to the President of the Security Council' (S/2008/804, 19 December 2008).

[116] *Ibid.*, Annex.

[117] Unfortunately, most of these assets were worn out, unserviced, missing parts, and some were obsolete. Only some 10 per cent of the vehicles could be driven from the Mogadishu seaport to the airport. Interview with AMISOM official, June 2013.

AMISOM by providing an additional logistics support package and continu-ing to assist AU planning and deployment preparations through its planners team in Addis Ababa. Second, the UN should build the capacity of the Djibouti Agreement signatories to restore the security sector and the rule of law by training and equipping 5,000 joint TFG/ARS-Djibouti forces, a 10,000-strong Somali Police Force, and other justice and corrections personnel. The third step involved the Security Council establishing a maritime task force which could support AMISOM operations, host a quick-reaction force, and serve as an operational platform for any envisaged UN peacekeeping oper-ation. As it turned out, none of these initiatives materialized as planned.

ETHIOPIA'S WITHDRAWAL

Soon after its troops installed the TFG in Mogadishu in December 2006, Ethiopia's leaders recognized that their presence was problematic. As already noted, Addis Ababa played a major role in establishing AMISOM to provide Ethiopian troops with a way out of Mogadishu and then providing the AU with a way to hand the mission over to the UN. But the AU's failure to generate sufficient numbers of troops and contributing countries left Ethiopia stuck without an alternative security force to cover its withdrawal. In December 2007, Meles Zenawi publicly admitted as much, saying that the withdrawal of Ethiopian troops was taking 'a lot longer' than planned.[118] By late 2008, Meles was reportedly coming under increasing domestic pressure to leave Somalia because of the growing financial burden and criticism from within the Ethiopian Peoples' Revolutionary Democratic Front (EPRDF).[119] It was the Djibouti agreements during the second half of 2008 that finally catalysed concrete plans for Ethiopia's troops to withdraw, albeit with an AU force that was smaller than envisaged.

The prospect of the ENDF's withdrawal presented AMISOM with both opportunities and challenges. It also generated a flurry of diplomatic activity in Mogadishu, Addis Ababa, and New York. On the one hand, it prompted discussion within AMISOM's leadership about the modalities of withdrawal and whether an under-strength AU force alone could protect the TFG. Most fundamentally, if the ENDF withdrawal precipitated the collapse of the TFG

---

[118] 'Ethiopia PM attacks UN on Somali', *BBC News Online*, 12 December 2007, http://news.bbc.co.uk/go/pr/fr/-/2/hi/africa/7152997.stm. In some respects the main point of AMISOM was to facilitate Ethiopia's withdrawal. As the British Foreign Secretary, Margaret Beckett, told Parliament in mid-2007, AMISOM had 'a crucial role to play in creating the security conditions that would enable a fuller withdrawal of Ethiopian troops from Somalia'. *Hansard* (Commons), 15 June 2007, col.1377W.

[119] Wikileak Cable 08ADDISABABA3393, 19 December 2008.

then AMISOM would no longer have a valid reason for being in Mogadishu. According to the Ethiopian Special Envoy to Somalia, Abdetta Dribssa, AMISOM's Force Commander General Okello initially insisted that if the ENDF withdrew from Mogadishu, then his AMISOM force should leave in advance of the Ethiopians. General Okello also reportedly mused that Ethiopian troops might be brought into AMISOM.[120]

In late November 2008, Ethiopian Foreign Minister Seyoum wrote to the AU and UN announcing that his country's troops would withdraw completely by the end of the year.[121] This stimulated hasty announcements that three additional battalions from West Africa could deploy to reinforce AMISOM[122] and that Algeria would put ten aircraft (five Ilyushin-76s and five C-130s) at the AU's disposal to airlift the new AMISOM troops to Mogadishu. The United States also wanted to keep the ENDF in Somalia until AMISOM could be reinforced to its authorized strength of 8,000 and discussed financial packages to support the Ethiopian troops.[123]

By this stage, however, AMISOM's deployed strength was only approximately 3,450. The AU estimated that *al-Shabaab*'s strength 'could be around 2,000', operating 'in cells and units of about 300–400 militias'.[124] However, their numbers were thought to be growing; not least because *al-Shabaab* was thought to be offering TFG troops $50 a month to swap sides as well as a chance to participate in 'a jihad against Ethiopia'.[125] AMISOM's Force Commander told UN officials that his mission was trying to counter such offers by providing TFG troops with consistent food rations.[126] AMISOM even provided some ARS fighters with food and water.[127] By the end of December 2008, in most regions of south-central Somalia clan-based militias loyal to members of the TFG could no longer be accurately described as 'TFG forces' as they had been earlier in the year. Most had re-joined clan-based alliances.[128]

At the African Union, Commissioner Lamamra remained adamant that 'The withdrawal of AMISOM from Somalia is not an option. All our partners

---

[120] Wikileak Cable, 08ADDISABABA2941, 27 October 2008, §10. In private, AMISOM leadership and its partners discussed various scenarios for withdrawing AMISOM, including by air and sea evacuation. See, for example, 'AMISOM Brief to Visiting US Delegation' (AU internal document, 25 February 2009).

[121] Wikileak Cable, 08ADDISABABA3258, 2 December 2008, §2.

[122] Nigeria promised three battalions by the end of the first quarter of 2009. Wikileak Cable 08ADDISABABA3399, 19 December 2008, §9.

[123] Wikileak Cable, 08ADDISABABA3258, 2 December 2008.

[124] 'Strategic Force Enhancement Plan to Support Djibouti Agreement—Option 2 (Joint Command)', (AU internal document, Draft version 19 November 2008).

[125] Wikileak Cables 09ADDISABABA110, 16 January 2009, §9 and 08NAIROBI2755, 11 December 2008, §2. In 2007, Ugandan officials claimed that *al-Qa'ida* was recruiting fighters in Somalia for $50 per hour. Wikileak Cable 07KAMPALA854, 18 May 2007, §5.

[126] Wikileak Cable 09ADDISABABA110, 16 January 2009, §9.

[127] UN, *TAM* (12–25 January 2009), p. 9.

[128] Wikileak Cable 08NAIROBI2755, 11 December 2008.

see the disaster that would be created by such a security vacuum'.[129] However, AMISOM's Force Commander noted that there could be dire consequences for his mission after the ENDF withdrew if, for example, supply routes were compromised and intelligence capabilities lost.[130] On 22 December 2008, the AU PSC extended AMISOM's mandate for a further two months (16 January to 16 March 2009), called on the UN Security Council to deploy an ISF as well as a support package for AMISOM, and subsequently a UN peacekeeping operation to take over from AMISOM.[131] This message was re-emphasized to US officials by the head of the AU PSC secretariat, Dr Kambudzi, who said that a UN operation was 'the only way to save Somalia'.[132]

At the UN Security Council in New York, debates over what would become Security Council resolution 1863 were also heating up. In a clear departure from the Secretary-General's earlier recommendations, the United States circulated a draft resolution authorizing a UN multidimensional peacekeeping operation and including details such as specific troop ceilings and a six-month deadline for deployment. Within a few days the UK produced its own text endorsing the Secretary-General's previous recommendations. Although the United States was isolated in the Security Council, the resulting debate produced a compromise resolution (1863), which more closely resembled the UK draft, although some of the tasks outlined previously in the US draft remained.[133] With the arrival of the Obama administration, however, Washington's push for a UN peacekeeping operation stopped and instead it came to be viewed as one potentially useful contingency plan among several.

On 29 December 2008, a crucial development occurred in Somalia when TFG President Abdullahi Yusuf resigned, thus ending a months-long standoff with the Prime Minister. Yusuf's resignation also came after two months of IGAD and AU-endorsed sanctions against Yusuf and his associates, although given Yusuf's ill health, a travel ban preventing his medical care visits to Nairobi was probably instrumental in his decision to resign.[134] In Yusuf's place, parliament speaker Sheikh Aden 'Madobe' became the interim President, and was charged with arranging Yusuf's successor. A succession race promptly followed in which Ethiopia was said to play a key role. The winner turned out to be Sheikh Sharif Sheikh Ahmed, the former leader of the SCIC. Initially, this was quite a popular result because the Djibouti Peace Process was viewed locally as heavily manipulated by the UN while Sheikh

---

[129] Wikileak Cable 08ADDISABABA3399, 19 December 2008, §7–8.   [130] *Ibid.*, §7–8.

[131] PSC/MIN/Comm.4(CLXIII), 22 December 2008, §19.

[132] Wikileak Cable 09ADDISABABA49, 12 January 2009, §5.

[133] Interview, US official, Washington DC, June 2009. Note that in January 2009 Italy, South Africa and Panama, which had been relatively supportive of the US position were replaced on the Council by Japan, Mexico and Turkey, which were not convinced of the need for a UN peacekeeping operation.

[134] Kasaija, 'The UN-led Djibouti peace process', p. 273.

Sharif's rise to the presidency was seen as a local triumph and a tacit redemption of the SCIC.

Back in New York, on 31 December, the Prodi panel on the modalities of UN support for African Union peace operations released its report.[135] Among other things, it referred explicitly to AMISOM as an example where 'Weaker organizations have been drawn into complex and volatile missions without the necessary capacities to succeed'.[136] Importantly for AMISOM, the panel also recommended 'the use of United Nations-assessed contributions on a case-by-case basis to support United Nations Security Council-authorized African Union peacekeeping operations for a period up to six months'.[137] Shortly thereafter, UN Security Council resolution 1863 (16 January 2009) authorized the UN's new Support Office for AMISOM (UNSOA) to support AMISOM in the functional areas of supply (rations, fuel, and general supply); engineering, including construction, power generation and water supply; medical support; aviation; transportation; strategic movement support; equipment repair and maintenance; public information; strategic and tactical communications; and information and technology support. The Security Council also agreed that this support to a regional peace operation should be financed through the UN's assessed peacekeeping contributions (see Chapter 8).

On 4 January 2009, the Ethiopian Ministry of Foreign Affairs issued a press statement titled, 'Mission Accomplished' that declared Ethiopian troops had 'eliminate[d] the clear and present danger' that their country faced.[138] And on 13–14 January 2009, ENDF troops completed their withdrawal from Mogadishu. Residents of northern Mogadishu poured into the streets to celebrate an Ethiopian departure that few believed would occur.[139] The Ethiopian troops left behind a predictable vacuum that was quickly filled by various militias. Some of the TFG forces that had been receiving food and stipends from ENDF deserted. As one TFG representative put it, 'some forces previously trained by the Ethiopians had dispersed to various militia groups, because they had not received food or payment from the TFG'.[140] In late 2008, the Ethiopian government estimated that of the roughly 17,000 Somali security forces it had trained about 14,000 had defected or deserted, taking their uniforms and weapons with them.[141] Neither the ARS nor the TFG forces were able to deploy into all the areas vacated by Ethiopian forces as planned. In particular, the ARS acknowledged it did not have sufficient weapons, forces,

---

[135] *Report of the African Union-United Nations panel on modalities for support to African Union peacekeeping operations* (A/63/666-S/2008/813, 31 December 2008). Hereafter, *Prodi Report* (2008).

[136] *Ibid.*, §13.   [137] *Ibid.*, §64.

[138] At http://www.tigraionline.com/mfa_press_release.html

[139] Wikileak Cable 09NAIROBI107, 16 January 2009.

[140] UN, *TAM* (12–25 January 2009), p. 8.

[141] Cited in *SEMG Report*, 10 December 2008, §19.

or ammunition to occupy the areas designated to them. Instead, militias operating under different banners moved in swiftly and took over several locations, including the pasta factory in north Mogadishu.[142] Nor did AMISOM have the manpower to replace the ENDF. As a result, *al-Shabaab* simply took over many areas vacated by the ENDF without a fight. *Al-Shabaab* thus took control of most of Mogadishu by default when the ENDF withdrew.[143] On 26 January, ENDF troops also departed from Baidoa. *Al-Shabaab* forces quickly took over there too.[144]

AMISOM ALONE

When the Ethiopian troops departed Mogadishu, AMISOM comprised four battalions, two each from Uganda and Burundi—totaling roughly 3,450 troops. One UPDF battalion was deployed at the MIA, with one company at K-4 road junction, the seaport, and Villa Somalia. Burundi deployed one battalion at the former US embassy and one at the university area to the northwest of the K-4 junction.

When the UN Technical Assessment Mission visited Mogadishu in January 2009, they asked AMISOM's Force Commander, General Francis Okello, to list his principal requirements. His list included supplies, engineering capabilities (especially combat engineers to improve force protection measures), medical support, movement support, aviation assets, communications and information technology, public information, surface transport (especially armoured vehicles), and repair and maintenance capabilities.[145] Okello added that the mission also needed better counter-IED and explosive ordnance disposal (EOD) capabilities and his headquarters had a 50 per cent vacancy rate among staff officers.[146] He also emphasized that most of his troops lacked key personal equipment items, including protective ballistic vests and night observation devices. Back in Addis, although the AU had authorized thirty-three positions in the SPMU, only fifteen were deployed by February 2009 (nine UN planners, five AU planners, and two NATO planners).[147] To fill this

---

[142] UN, *TAM* (12–25 January 2009), p. 8.

[143] Interview, AU official, Nairobi, 7 August 2012.

[144] Wikileak Cable 09NAIROBI146, 27 January 2009.

[145] UN, *TAM* (12–25 January 2009), pp. 12–13.

[146] *Ibid.*, p. 14. In April 2008, the AU Commission had requested US financial assistance and logistical support to establish a temporary AMISOM mission headquarters in Mogadishu to replace the current headquarters located in Nairobi. Wikileak Cable 08ADDISABABA941, 7 April 2008.

[147] 'AMISOM Brief to Visiting US Delegation' (AU internal document, 25 February 2009).

long list of capability gaps, the UN's technical assessment mission estimated that AMISOM required a total funding requirement of US$800 million.[148]

One of AMISOM's most visible shortages was armoured vehicles. Commanders felt these were necessary for conducting patrols and other mobile operations outside the mission's bases. AMISOM units generally only moved between the force's bases (a roughly 35km round trip covered the full circuit of AMISOM-secured positions in Mogadishu). Soft-skin vehicles were of little use outside such protected locations. At this stage, AMISOM's two Ugandan battalions had twenty-nine instead of the recommended fifty-two armoured personnel carriers (APCs) for a generic infantry battalion, while the Burundian battalions had just twenty.[149] These were mostly South African defence industry equipment such as Casspirs, Mambas, and Samil trucks and some former Soviet BMP-2s. AMISOM's main offensive capability came through the twenty-five T-54/55 battle tanks provided by the UPDF. Up to this point, the tanks were used primarily in a defensive, deterrent posture.[150] A big part of the problem was not just the number of available vehicles but maintaining them in working order. Crucially, there was no specific maintenance support provided in DynCorp's contract and hence AMISOM units had to remain self-sufficient. As a result, many of the mission's vehicles remained inoperable after suffering damage. This proved to be a persistent problem for the mission (see Chapter 8).

AMISOM also had poor medical capabilities.[151] At the start of the mission, more than sixty Ugandan troops developed serious cases of diarrhoea and some also caught cholera from a bad local water source.[152] Initially, the UPDF had deployed with just one Level-1 medical facility.[153] By early 2009, Uganda had one Level-2 field hospital (which conducted primary surgery and operated a mortuary container) with an integrated Level-1 facility, while the Burundi contingent had just one Level-1 medical facility. All these facilities lacked staff, equipment, and surgical, emergency, and intensive care capabilities. Each battalion also had one ambulance, while the Level-2 hospital had an additional two ambulances. All of them were old vintage, soft skinned, prone to frequent breakdown and lack required vital resuscitation equipment. Level-3 medical care was provided in Nairobi, Kenya. But AMISOM had no air assets for casualty and medical evacuation to the Level-3 facility. Between 2007 and 2009, therefore, these flights were provided through bilateral arrangements with DynCorp. However, they were only available during daylight hours as

---

[148] UN, *TAM* (12–25 January 2009), p. 30.

[149] *Ibid.*, Annex H, p. 3. It was reported that AMISOM originally ordered sixty-eight MK III Casspirs that were modified for combat before their delivery in 2008. Oloya, *Black Hawks Rising*, p. 123.

[150] UN, *TAM* (12–25 January 2009), Annex H, p. 1.   [151] *Ibid.*, Annex C.

[152] Oloya, *Black Hawks Rising*, p. 79.

[153] Interview, senior UPDF official, Kampala, 14 August 2012.

Mogadishu airport had no capability to operate during night-time. DynCorp also provided a limited supply of drugs and pharmaceuticals, but there was no provision of regular supply of consumables, blood, or blood products. AMISOM troops had no pre-deployment medical clearance, nor any immunization programme. They were consequently at high risk of infectious diseases. This led the UN's technical assessment mission to warn that: 'Due to a lack of basic sanitation systems, personal and collective hygiene, and continuous contact of the troops with local population, there is a high risk for epidemics'.[154] Nevertheless, despite these problems, and without the blessing of the AU Commission, AMISOM regularly provided medical care to the local population at both of its facilities. Initially, the lack of fencing around the AMISOM MIA base meant that local Somali civilians had simply walked into the area and asked for medical assistance. AMISOM's response was to create an Outpatient Department to provide what care it could. By late 2009, AMISOM's Outpatient Department had three doctors and about forty nurses and medical assistants providing care.[155] Patients included TFG soldiers and even some suspected members of *al-Shabaab*.[156] At their base at the Mogadishu University, the Burundians put water vases around their camp and allowed local civilians to come and help themselves, which was very popular and generated useful information about pending attacks.[157] By mid-2010, the commander of Uganda's land forces claimed that AMISOM's hospitals were treating 'at least 5,000 people every day'.[158]

With regard to engineering, a crucial part of operating in a war-torn city, each AMISOM battalion probably had only a platoon size capacity for military engineering tasks. Consequently, AMISOM's camp facilities were poor, and they tended to have life expectancy of only six to eight months due to salt, sand, and strong winds.[159] All camps fell well below UN standards for its peacekeeping operations. They were also prone to pollution since they lacked the ability to dispose efficiently of human waste, sewerage water, and fuel waste. Moreover, given the regular attacks by *al-Shabaab*, all of AMISOM's bases should have been protected from mortar attack; but they were not. The mission also lacked equipment for airfield support and material handling.

AMISOM was also forced to operate without any significant strategic communications capabilities. It had only one mission spokesperson and a Military Public Information Officer, plus a civilian public information officer in Nairobi. This was certainly on the AU's radar screen, and in late 2008 it had drafted a communications plan for AMISOM.[160] This highlighted the urgent

---

[154] UN, *TAM* (12–25 January 2009), Annex C. [155] Oloya, *Black Hawks Rising*, p. 84.
[156] Communication, AMISOM official, 5 October 2013.
[157] Communication, EU official, Addis Ababa, 13 December 2012.
[158] Patrick Jaramogi, 'UPDF to leave Somalia when peace returns', *New Vision* (Kampala), 22 June 2010.
[159] UN, *TAM* (12–25 January 2009), Annex B. [160] *Ibid.*, Annex 10.

need for the mission to establish a local radio station that could engage the Somali public. Because the AU and AMISOM had no practical experience in such matters, it was decided that the mission would need some implementing agency to do this (see Chapter 11).

AMISOM was also supposed to have some in-shore maritime support capabilities, which were necessary to protect aircraft taking off or landing at Mogadishu airport from possible seaborne firing points.[161] And as noted above, AMISOM was now mandated 'to protect shipping involved with the transportation and delivery of humanitarian aid to Somalia and United Nations-authorized activities'.[162] In practice, AMISOM's naval assets consisted of three rigid inflatable boats, which were usually inoperable.[163] An off-shore capability was also needed to ensure safe passage for naval deliveries of supplies. AMISOM had no such capability and despite the presence, from late 2008 of an international anti-piracy coalition, by October 2009, each of the four vessels that had transported UNSOA goods to Mogadishu seaport were attacked: three by mortars in Mogadishu harbor and one (failed) attack by pirates.[164]

Finally, despite being envisaged as a multidimensional mission, at this point in time, AMISOM had not deployed its police component. In 2008, the AU authorized AMISOM to deploy 270 police officers to train, mentor, and monitor the Somali Police Force. However, insecurity in Mogadishu rendered it impossible for them to deploy. Instead, the plan was to deploy seven senior officers to Mogadishu in early 2009 and then a further 170 officers by June. This would require over 100 additional vehicles.[165] As it turned out, the first AU police were not deployed to Mogadishu until early 2011.[166]

CONCLUSION

AMISOM's entry into Mogadishu did not go smoothly. For twenty-two months, the mission operated alongside Ethiopian forces to perform its principal task of protecting the TFG. This brought it into violent conflict with *al-Shabaab* but also some other armed groups. Although the arrival of Burundian troops from November 2007 proved useful militarily it did not fundamentally alter dynamics in Mogadishu or generate a wave of additional

---

[161] *Ibid.*, p.14.   [162] S/RES/1811, 15 May 2008, §11.

[163] UN, *TAM* (12–25 January 2009), p. 11 and Annex H, p. 7.

[164] Craig Boyd presentation to UN Security Council, 8 October 2009, http://www.unmultimedia. org/avlibrary/asset/U091/U091008a/

[165] UN, *TAM* (12–25 January 2009), p. 19.

[166] *Police Commissioner's Concept of Operations for African Union Police* (internal AU document, December 2011), p. 2.

TCCs for the mission. Moreover, for this entire period, even with Burundi's arrival the mission never reached even half of its authorized strength and lacked enabling capabilities in every area. AMISOM also struggled to persuade many local Somalis of its impartiality. As a result, the mission suffered from widespread perceptions that it was a proxy force for nefarious foreign agendas to keep Somalia weak and divided, most notably those of Ethiopia and the United States.

Ethiopia's decision to withdraw its forces opened up opportunities and challenges for AMISOM. The subsequent Djibouti peace process during 2008 changed some important political dynamics in Somalia, including bringing about a better relationship between AMISOM and the ARS and paving the way for a new TFG, ironically headed by the former SCIC leader Sheikh Sharif. This agreement brought AMISOM centre stage politically, making it a pivotal part of the TFG–ARS security relationship. As the Ethiopian troops withdrew, AMISOM was forced to address some difficult worst-case scenarios and to reconfigure its operations accordingly. Removing *al-Shabaab*'s main recruiting tool—the presence of ENDF troops in Mogadishu—was clearly useful, but the question remained as to whether the AU force could fill the security vacuum left by the Ethiopian withdrawal and how well it would cooperate with the new TFG. As Chapter 3 discusses, AMISOM held its ground but had to endure the rather painful stalemate that ensued.

3

Stalemate

January 2009 to August 2010

The withdrawal of Ethiopian troops from Somalia presented *al-Shabaab* with its largest territorial gains.[1] In Mogadishu, although the Ethiopians had initially left behind TFG forces in some key locations such as the Ministry of Defence, sports stadium, and pasta factory, these troops quickly melted away and *al-Shabaab* fighters moved in, sometimes extremely close to AMISOM. As one AMISOM political affairs officer put it, *al-Shabaab* 'did not win Mogadishu through fighting but by default when the ENDF withdrew'.[2] Beyond Mogadishu, *al-Shabaab* also took over the towns of Jowhar, Beledweyne, and the TFG's former capital at Baidoa. Although some fighters left *al-Shabaab* after the Ethiopian withdrawal, claiming their job was done, the group's newly established *Amniyat* intelligence wing systematically targeted defectors and their families, which stemmed the tide. With its expanded presence, *al-Shabaab* had to engage in governing its new territories and, as a direct consequence, had to interact more regularly with Somalia's complex clan system. It also attracted various criminal elements whose main concern was to be on the winning side or protect their illicit activities. *Al-Shabaab* thus became a mélange of true believers, international jihadis, clan militias, and bandits. Nevertheless, it not only held together, it became emboldened. With the Ethiopians out of the picture, it turned its attention to a new enemy—the AU forces protecting the TFG in Mogadishu.

The Ethiopian withdrawal thus ushered in a period of bloody stalemate in Mogadishu with neither the TFG supported by AMISOM nor *al-Shabaab* able to decisively defeat the other. For the next twenty months, the two sides fought for control of Mogadishu's sixteen districts. Possession fluctuated regularly as the TFG/AMISOM and *al-Shabaab* both gained and then failed to hold newly captured areas of the city.

---

[1] Hansen, *Al-Shabaab in Somalia*, pp. 73–5.   [2] Interview, Nairobi, 7 August 2012.

This chapter analyses how AMISOM dealt with this uncomfortable new political terrain between January 2009 and August 2010. It does so in four parts. The first section summarizes some of the main characteristics and conflict dynamics of the Mogadishu stalemate. The second section then examines the state of AMISOM's main partners: the second iteration of the TFG under President Sheikh Sharif Sheikh Ahmed, a former leader of the SCIC. It focuses on the TFG's (failed) attempts to build an effective set of security forces and some of the challenges this posed for AMISOM. One of the main areas of weakness for AMISOM and the TFG was logistics. The third section therefore analyses the UN Security Council's decision to establish a novel Support Office for AMISOM (UNSOA) in 2009, in order to provide AMISOM with better logistical support. The final section discusses how during the second half of 2010 the political and military balance began to tilt in AMISOM's favour as a result of two major blunders made by *al-Shabaab*, namely, the decision to bomb civilian targets in Kampala, Uganda, and the failure of its 2010 Ramadan offensive in Mogadishu.

FIGHTING ON DEFENCE

Following the Ethiopian withdrawal, it was clear that *al-Shabaab* would intensify its attacks against AMISOM. This led some commentators to call for AMISOM's withdrawal. Writing in early March 2009, Gérard Prunier, for example, argued there were three reasons to pull out the AU force. First, AMISOM soldiers were 'under-equipped, under-trained, and have a low morale. They do not know why they are there, their mission is opaque and their cultural environment is hostile'. Second, as a result, the military situation they found themselves in was 'awful'. And, third, AMISOM should leave because they were foreigners and the Somali hate foreigners, particularly armed foreigners who did little other than boost *al-Shabaab*'s recruitment propaganda. In sum, Prunier argued, 'the AMISOM soldiers should go before more of them die uselessly and before they kill more Somali civilians'.[3] Prunier was correct that many more AMISOM personnel and Somali civilians would die, but the authorities in Addis Ababa and New York, and perhaps more importantly the presidents in Kampala and Bujumbura, held a different view. AMISOM was to stay.

But the mission was stuck in a difficult situation. With *al-Shabaab* forces now as little as 50 metres from some AMISOM positions, the AU force entered into a period of almost constant engagement with its principal enemy. Small-scale

[3] Gérard Prunier, 'Get the AMISOM soldiers out of Somalia!' *OUPblog*, 10 March 2009, http://blog.oup.com/2009/03/amisom-in-somalia/

potshots, sniping, grenade and mortar attacks were interspersed with offensives and counter-attacks conducted by larger military formations. The subsequent fighting displayed several notable characteristics that are summarized here.

The first point to make is that AMISOM's deployed strength in January 2009 was 3,450. This meant that going on the offence was unrealistic. Instead, AMISOM commanders considered it prudent to consolidate their positions and improve their working relationship with the new TFG's forces. Importantly, this choice was driven by AMISOM's lack of troops and resources and not, as some commentators have argued, because the mission's mandate was not forceful or flexible enough. As AMISOM's Force Commander General Okello pointed out, his mandate was sufficient to protect his forces and strike against any imminent threat. His primary concern in early 2009, however, was protecting his bases and supply lines.[4]

Second, with the withdrawal of the Ethiopian forces, *al-Shabaab* clearly saw an opportunity to step up its attacks on AMISOM. The majority of *al-Shabaab* strikes used asymmetric tactics, notably snipers, IEDs, and suicide bombings.[5] There was also a constant threat of assassinations. This was taken so seriously that in late July 2009, the AU Commission had requested that the US provide bodyguard training for about one hundred AMISOM and TFG forces for TFG leaders, many of whom lived outside Somalia.[6]

As noted in Chapter 2, *al-Shabaab* pioneered its use of suicide bombings against TFG and Ethiopian forces during 2006.[7] Its success encouraged more frequent usage and in mid-June 2009 an *al-Shabaab* suicide attack in Beledweyne even succeeded in killing the TFG's National Security Minister, Omar Hashi Aden. Suicide bombers also proved deadly against AMISOM, helped significantly by the fact that *al-Shabaab* operatives could easily move through the civilian population and the militants could coerce Somalis with access to AMISOM facilities.[8] Some *al-Shabaab* suicide bombers disguised themselves as TFG soldiers, women, or spectators at events, and they often used vehicles, including trucks, cars, and motorcycles.[9]

---

[4] Wikileak Cable, 09ADDISABABA717, 25 March 2009, §10. If anything needed revision it was AMISOM's ROE in order to allow preemptive military action in certain circumstances. See the discussion in Wikileak Cable 09ADDISABABA2642, 6 November 2009.

[5] AMISOM was also reportedly worried about more brazen and innovative *al-Shabaab* attacks, including a USS Cole type attack from the water (where *al-Shabaab* might load small boats with explosives to render the seaport unusable by large resupply vessels) and even a 9/11 style aircraft attack on the AMISOM force headquarters. Wikileak Cable 10ADDISABABA342, 19 February 2010.

[6] Wikileak Cable 09ADDISABABA1864, 4 August 2009.

[7] The earliest confirmed suicide attack was on 18 September 2006, which targeted the TFG President's convoy. Oloya, *Black Hawks Rising*, p. 107.

[8] *AMISOM Force Protection Review* (Bancroft, September 2011), p. 27. ACOTA files.

[9] Anneli Botha, *Practical guide to understanding and preventing suicide operations in Africa* (Pretoria: ISS, 2013), pp. 78, 84.

During 2009, two attacks in particular killed thirty AMISOM personnel. On 22 February, two suicide bombers attacked AMISOM's Burundian base at the former Somali National University compound. Eleven Burundian peace-keepers were killed and twenty-eight injured in the coordinated attack.[10] The attackers were employees of a Somali company contracted to supply food and fuel and had been working with the Burundians for nine months and used this relationship to gain entry to the camp.[11] In the aftermath of this attack, the AU PSC ordered an urgent reassessment of AMISOM's mandate and appealed for greater African and UN support. The AU also thought that better intelligence may have thwarted the attack and hence it made more requests for enhanced intelligence sharing/support from the United States, United Kingdom, and France.[12] In the field, General Prime Niyongabo, the Burundi contingent commander, responded to the attack by saying: 'We have understood that with the Somalis, there can be no friends. So now, not a single Somali enters the camp, not a single car'.[13]

On 17 September, *al-Shabaab* repeated this deadly tactic by executing another major twin suicide attack against AMISOM. This one came two days after *al-Shabaab* vowed revenge for a US helicopter assault which killed *al-Qa'ida*'s East Africa leader, Saleh Ali Saleh Nabhan.[14] The AU thought that foreign fighters were involved in the suicide attack.[15] This time the bombers gained access to AMISOM and DynCorp positions using previously stolen vehicles from UN humanitarian agencies (from around Baidoa). This attack killed nineteen AMISOM peacekeepers and wounded more than forty.[16] AMISOM's Burundian Deputy Force Commander, Major General Juvenal

---

[10] *Report of the Secretary-General on Somalia pursuant to Security Council resolution 1863 (2009)* (UN S/2009/210, 16 April 2009), §6.

[11] Wikileak Cable 09NAIROBI346, 23 February 2009.

[12] Wikileak Cable 09ADDISABABA465, 24 February 2009, §3. AMISOM consistently lacked reliable, credible, and actionable intelligence. Initially, the mission tended to rely for its intelligence on the TFG's forces and some partners operating in Mogadishu. Although AMISOM's intelligence gathering improved somewhat over time, sharing sensitive information proved difficult given the flows that were required between the Somali authorities and AMISOM, between the TCCs and AMISOM headquarters, and between partners in support of AMISOM operations.

[13] Henry Mukasa, 'Katumba decorate AU troops in Somalia', *New Vision* (Kampala), 31 May 2009.

[14] Wikileak Cable 09NAIROBI1955, 17 September 2009.

[15] Wikileak Cable 09ADDISABABA2323, 25 September 2009, §3. At this stage, the status of *al-Shabaab*'s relationship to *al-Qa'ida* was murky, but on 12 June 2009 it was reported that an *al-Shabaab* group in Kismayo pledged allegiance to Osama Bin Laden. Fred Ngoga Gateretse, Adviser to the AU Special Representative for Somalia, Amb. Nicholas Bwakira, Statement before the House Subcommittee on Africa and Global Health, Washington DC, 25 June 2009, p. 3.

[16] There were lower estimates of twelve Burundian dead in Wikileak Cable 09BUJUM-BURA508, 21 September 2009, and seventeen dead in *Somalia Security Sector Assessment* (AU, US, EU, TFG, World Bank and UN: 1 January 2010), §1e. The correct figure of nineteen dead was confirmed to the author by a senior AMISOM official, September 2009.

Niyoyunguruza, was among the dead. Following the attack, Burundian officials called for an expansion of AMISOM's mandate to permit offensive operations as well as an increase in personnel and equipment, including tanks.[17] The Burundian head of AMISOM, Ambassador Nicholas Bwakira, for instance, said: 'The time has come to re-examine AMISOM's mandate so that we can have the power to act when and as necessary. We call today for more equipment, more financial means, reinforcements, and a stronger mandate which gives our troops the right to pursue if necessary'.[18] As noted above, however, AMISOM's mandate was not the problem. Moreover, as one US official correctly observed, the 17 September attack resulted from a failure of AMISOM's security procedures not its equipment.[19]

At times *al-Shabaab* also used more conventional tactics. Sometimes this was due to the proximity of the opposing forces. AMISOM was occasionally forced to conduct vicious street fighting with *al-Shabaab* forces less than 50 metres away from its positions. *Al-Shabaab*'s fighters tended to traverse Mogadishu in small units of ten or so fighters, but its network of underground tunnels also meant that it could mass a significant force—of up to a hundred fighters—very quickly when AMISOM patrols were spotted in the city. AMISOM's indirect fire weapons were thus often used 'Danger Close', i.e., within the minimum safety distances for AMISOM troops as well as any present civilians. There were also times when AMISOM underestimated *al-Shabaab*, including when the UPDF lost numerous personnel as well as several battle tanks, Casspirs, and armoured front-end loaders during the March 2010 operation to recapture the Global Hotel.[20]

Tunnels and pit traps were also used by *al-Shabaab*, the latter to snare AMISOM tanks and armoured vehicles. On 3 June 2010, for example, a Ugandan T-55 tank was caught in one such *al-Shabaab* camouflaged ditch. The crew was killed and *al-Shabaab* also managed to seize an AMISOM bulldozer.[21] This offered *al-Shabaab* a significant propaganda victory out of proportion to its military effect on AMISOM's operations.

On other occasions, *al-Shabaab* engaged in larger-scale offensives. Between 7 and 14 May 2009, for example, *al-Shabaab* and Hizbul Islam fighters launched an offensive against the TFG, which AMISOM helped repel.[22]

[17] Wikileak Cable 09BUJUMBURA508, 21 September 2009.
[18] Oloya, *Black Hawks Rising*, p. 133.
[19] Wikileak Cable 09BUJUMBURA508, 21 September 2009, §8.
[20] *Dayniile After Action Review* (Bancroft, 8 November 2011), p. 10. ACOTA files.
[21] Oloya, *Black Hawks Rising*, p. 147. AMISOM's three armoured bulldozers were key to gaining ground. The bulldozers would move up taking fire; deploy HESCO barriers, which were filled rapidly; and then AMISOM troops could get behind them quickly. The bulldozer seized by *al-Shabaab* was recaptured by AMISOM in a later operation. Telephone interview, former senior AMISOM official, 4 March 2015.
[22] Paula C. Roque, 'The battle for Mogadishu', *African Security Review*, 18:3 (2009), p. 76. For more information about Hizbul Islam see Appendix A.

A similar set of operations over the next six weeks also failed to dislodge the government, largely thanks to AMISOM protection.[23] In another example in early October 2009, AMISOM positions come under attack from *al-Shabaab* fighters using, for the first time, Soviet-made Saxhorn type anti-tank guided missiles.[24]

Al-Shabaab also regularly and deliberately engaged in tactics designed to provoke AMISOM into causing civilian casualties. Unfortunately, AMISOM often played into their hands by responding with indiscriminate fire into civilian populated areas. In a typical scenario during much of 2009 and 2010, *al-Shabaab* forces would fire several mortar rounds at AMISOM positions from Bakara market or residential areas and then withdraw. In one example, on 11 July 2009, *al-Shabaab* launched four mortar rounds into Villa Somalia, killing three AMISOM soldiers and injuring several others. AMISOM would usually return fire with heavy weapons without being able to observe the fall of shot and without being able to rapidly locate *al-Shabaab*'s heavy weapons, which meant AMISOM's return of fire was likely automated at preset targets. In another case, the TFG's Minister for Defence reported to the Associated Press that he witnessed AMISOM forces fire sixty artillery shells, missiles, and mortars into Bakara market in response to three mortars fired by *al Shabaab*.[25] *Al-Shabaab* would then claim AMISOM's fire had caused civilian casualties while AMISOM would deny this or claim *al-Shabaab* had forcibly kept civilians in Bakara market for precisely this reason. Alternatively, much the same scenario unfolded after *al-Shabaab* used converted Toyota minibuses as mobile artillery launchers, which would fire at TFG/ AMISOM positions before departing the scene, leaving the area exposed to likely retaliatory fire.[26]

Both AMISOM and the UNPOS were sometimes painfully slow to respond to allegations of civilian harm (see Chapter 10). In February 2009, for instance, when local newspapers reported AMISOM's fire on civilian passenger buses, the UN's Special Representative for Somalia accused the local reporters of being 'genocidaires' and called for an international boycott of the Somali press.[27] Although this was an egregious case, AMISOM officials invariably

---

[23] *Report of the Monitoring Group on Somalia pursuant to Security Council resolution 1853 (2008)* (UN S/2010/91, 10 March 2010), §12.

[24] *Ibid.*, §158.

[25] Malkhadir M. Muhumed, 'African peacekeepers blamed for Somali civilian deaths', *Associated Press*, 21 July 2010, http://www.nbcnews.com/id/38349076/ns/world_news-africa/t/african-peacekeepers-blamed-somali-civilian-deaths/

[26] CIVIC, *Civilian Harm in Somalia: Creating an Appropriate Response* (Washington DC: CIVIC, December 2011), p. 19.

[27] Ould-Abdallah's comments originally appeared in a *Voice of America* interview. *Voice of America* subsequently removed the interview from its site, but Ould-Abdallah's comments were extensively condemned in reports by, among others, Human Rights Watch and CNN. See, for example, Anna Husarska, 'They kill journalists, don't they? Why is a U.N. diplomat comparing

denied reports of civilian casualties from their fire (see also Chapter 11). As late as July 2010, for example, AMISOM spokesman Gaffel Nkolokosa told the *Washington Post* that 'AMISOM has never shelled indiscriminately at civilians ... Peacekeepers have always avoided civilian shellings and observe international humanitarian laws'.[28] This did not go down well with local residents and AMISOM was subject to regular criticism for its indirect fire. In another case, in March 2009 a memorandum submitted by traditional leaders to the new Prime Minister recommended that because of such practices no additional AMISOM troops should be deployed, no UN troops should enter Somalia, and that AMISOM should depart within 120 days.[29] On another occasion, the Hawiye Traditional and Unity Council condemned AMISOM for indiscriminate shelling of residential areas of Mogadishu on 17 June 2009.[30]

At times, AMISOM also fired on civilians who were mistaken for enemy fighters. In one such incident in 2009, a passenger bus was accidentally fired upon by AMISOM troops after they were ambushed by a combination of a roadside bomb and machine gun fire.[31] Although *al-Shabaab* was clearly trying to goad AMISOM into this type of retaliation and deliberately operated among crowds to maximize the potential for civilian casualties, AMISOM was slow to adapt its tactics. After a few months, AMISOM said it would only return fire when its soldiers could visually identify the attackers, and would only use weapons that allowed for discriminate fire.[32] But this was not consistently implemented in practice and a new indirect fire policy was not adopted until 2011 (see Chapter 10).

By January 2010, the situation was so bad that in an opinion poll of 1,150 Somalis released by Mogadishu Media House (but really conducted by the AU–UN Information Support Team, see Chapter 11) almost one-third of all respondents thought AMISOM was in Somalia to cause harm.[33] Examples continued to mount. In July 2010, a local grocer in Bakara market lamented that ordinary citizens 'are like insects to Amisom'. She went on to say: 'They massacre us, and then deny it. Why don't they pursue al Shabaab instead of shelling us?'[34]

Somali journalists to Rwandan war criminals?' *Slate*, 17 February 2009, http://www.slate.com/articles/news_and_politics/foreigners/2009/02/they_kill_journalists_dont_they.html

[28] Sudarsan Raghavan, 'Rising Civilian Toll Ignites Anger at African Force', *Washington Post*, 18 July 2010.

[29] *Report of the Secretary-General on Somalia pursuant to Security Council resolution 1863 (2009)* (S/2009/210, 16 April 2009), §7.

[30] Wikileak Cable 09NAIROBI1236, 18 June 2009, §7.

[31] Communication, former senior AMISOM officer, May 2013. See also CIVIC, *Civilian Harm in Somalia*, p. 20.

[32] Refugees International, *Somalia: Political Progress, Humanitarian Stalemate* (Washington DC: Field Report, 3 April 2009), p. 4.

[33] Interview, AU–UN IST official, Nairobi, 18 December 2012.

[34] Sarah Childress, 'Civilian Casualties Dog Troops in Somalia', *Wall Street Journal*, 29 July 2010, http://online.wsj.com/article/SB10001424052748704895004575395111138942560.html

That same month, an internal African Union report recommended that it respond quickly and accurately to allegations that AMISOM was indiscriminately shelling residential areas, and that it should change its practices.[35]

Eventually, there was agreement throughout the AU, AMISOM, and various international partners that something needed to be done to reduce levels of civilian harm in Mogadishu, especially that caused by AMISOM. This was seen as important for moral and legal reasons, but also because not protecting civilians was inefficient for AMISOM strategically and a barrier to operational success. As discussed in more detail in Chapter 10, AMISOM eventually adopted a range of mitigation measures. They included arresting some of the offending individuals. In November 2010 and January 2011, three UPDF soldiers in AMISOM were arrested for shooting civilians. They were charged with carelessness contrary to section 125 of the UPDF Act 2005, tried in the Unit Disciplinary Court in Mogadishu, and in March 2011 sentenced to two years in prison.[36]

By this stage, the weight of evidence was clear that AMISOM's existing approach had neither defeated *al-Shabaab* nor destroyed its ability to launch mortar attacks. Among some local civilians this caused resentment, reduced cooperation, and probably aided *al-Shabaab*'s recruitment or at least turned people sympathetic to the insurgents.

WITH FRIENDS LIKE THESE

In March 2010, speaking at an AU consultative assessment workshop, the commander of Uganda's land forces, General Katumba Wamala called for a more holistic approach to the Somali problem. 'For those who think the solution to Somalia's problem is just guns', Wamala argued,

> they are mistaken. The problem is not the number of guns, the problem is the failed institutions and what is needed is a holistic approach to the problem.... We cannot think of sending more soldiers when other arms of government are not functional. We need to improve the arms of the state.[37]

Herein lay the second dimension of AMISOM's problem and the other reason it was stuck in a bloody stalemate. Not only was *al-Shabaab* proving a dedicated and adaptable enemy, but its ostensible partner—Sheikh Sharif Sheikh Ahmed's TFG that arrived in Mogadishu in late February 2009—was

---

[35] See *SEMG Report*, 18 July 2011, §221.

[36] Barbara Among, 'Soldiers jailed for shooting civilians', *New Vision* (Kampala), 16 March 2011.

[37] Steven Candia, 'Gen. Wamala advises on Somali crisis', *New Vision* (Kampala), 24 March 2010.

deeply corrupt, ineffective, and considered by many Somalis to be illegitimate. As a consequence, AMISOM faced a range of challenges to try and improve the TFG's performance as well as that of its so-called security forces.

The precarious position of Sheikh Sharif's TFG and the subsequent problems for AMISOM were well summed up by a US official:

> The fact that the TFG has constantly to purchase loyalty to motivate militias to fight in its defense suggests that there is a much deeper fundamental problem within the TFG that is beyond the international community's ability to address in the short-term, if at all.... In order to develop legitimacy, the TFG needs to provide basic services to the population, something they have thus far failed to do, partly because their priorities have been elsewhere, and partly because of a lack of resources.[38]

As if to exemplify this problem, an internal AMISOM study concluded that Sheikh Sharif controlled a private force of about 1,000 clan fighters, which probably took precedence over other TFG forces.[39] A major multi-stakeholder assessment of the Somali security sector (encompassing police, justice and corrections, military, intelligence, and financial mechanisms) conducted in 2009 came to a similar, dismal conclusion that: 'Security Sector Reform efforts will probably falter—and quite possibly even fail—without a broader political foundation that promotes good governance, transparency and accountability within the Transitional timeframe'.[40] This remained the TFG's basic problem for its subsequent three and a half years in power (see also Chapter 9).

Naturally, the TFG quickly came under attack from *al-Shabaab*. In mid-May, *al-Shabaab* mounted a sustained offensive, which was widely seen as an attempt to bring down the TFG. It failed. In response, in mid-July the TFG, aided by AMISOM about ten tanks and armoured vehicles, conducted its own offensive and captured significant territory in Mogadishu.[41] From this point on, *al-Shabaab* usually adopted hit and run strikes and avoided decisive set-piece battles.[42] The main exceptions were the so-called Ramadan offensives, when *al-Shabaab* believed that jihadi martyrs received extraordinary rewards (see p. 98). But *al-Shabaab* also attacked the regime's legitimacy. In late July, for example, it posted a forty-two-minute audio tape entitled 'Sharif Muslim, Sharif Murtad' (Sharif the Muslim, Sharif the Apostate), which cast the TFG President as leader of a heretical regime, AMISOM as infidel invaders, and

---

[38] Wikileak Cable 09ADDISABABA1409, 26 June 2009, §4, §6.

[39] *Post Election 2012 Scenarios facing Somalia* (AUUNIST Briefing Note 002, September 2012), p. 4.

[40] *Somalia Security Sector Assessment* (2010), §1i.

[41] Wikileak Cable 09NAIROBI1495, 13 July 2009, §4. The use of AMISOM's tanks in Mogadishu's streets apparently had a major psychological impact, boosting TFG morale and demoralizing the extremists. Wikileak Cable 09NAIROBI1798, 25 August 2009, §5.

[42] *Somalia Security Sector Assessment* (2010), §15c.

urged listeners to support jihad against them.[43] The following month, *al-Shabaab* also circulated a forty-seven-page religious ruling issued in Arabic against the outcome of the Djibouti peace process.[44]

But *al-Shabaab* was not the only group trying to bring down Sheikh Sharif's TFG. There were also rumours that Eritrea was providing support for these *al-Shabaab* operations because it saw the TFG as an Ethiopian-backed project.[45] Moreover, in early 2009, a group called Hizbul Islam emerged in opposition to the TFG.[46] This was principally a platform for the return of Hassan Dahir Aweys from Eritrea, where he had been based for more than a year, and to reinvigorate military opposition to the TFG.[47] A former leader of *al-Ittihad al-Islamiya*, Aweys, like Sheikh Sharif, had occupied a leadership role in the SCIC. After Ethiopia's intervention, he fled Mogadishu and played the leading role in the Alliance for the Re-Liberation of Somalia-Asmara faction. Hizbul Islam also wasted no time in attacking the TFG and AMISOM and just a few days after Sheikh Sharif arrived in Mogadishu, AMISOM's K-4 junction base came under mortar attack.[48] A couple of months later, Aweys declared that AMISOM were 'bacteria' and 'invaders' and called for 'all foreign troops to leave our country'.[49]

And then there were the so-called 'Moneylords'—a term applied to powerful individuals who benefitted economically from twenty years of chaos in Somalia for whom law and order would mean returning stolen property, paying taxes, or enduring government restrictions. They were widely believed to be funding insurgents to oppose the TFG and AMISOM.[50]

On the other hand, Sheikh Sharif's TFG made at least one attempt to build constructive alliances when in June 2009 it signed a cooperation agreement with the Ethiopian-backed *Ahlu Sunna Wal Jamaa* (ASWJ) in which the TFG agreed to provide military and logistical support to ASWJ and consult the group on administrative issues in areas under its control.[51] ASWJ reportedly had between 10,000 and 12,000 soldiers, including 3,000 in

---

[43] *SEMG Report*, 10 March 2010, §84.   [44] *Ibid.*, §86.

[45] Wikileak Cable 09NAIROBI967, 14 May 2009, §2. This speculation was fuelled when ARS-Asmara leader Hassan Dahir Aweys expressed his gratitude to Eritrea, stating to Reuters that 'Eritrea supports us and Ethiopia is our enemy—we once helped both countries but Ethiopia did not reward us'. *SEMG Report*, 10 March 2010, §59. On 21 May 2009, IGAD called for the UN Security Council to impose sanctions on Eritrea for financially and materially supporting *al-Shabaab* and encouraging the TFG's overthrow. It also called for a UN-led air and sea blockade of Islamist-controlled areas.

[46] See Appendix A.   [47] *SEMG Report*, 10 March 2010, §52.

[48] Wikileak Cable 09NAIROBI363, 25 February 2009, §2.

[49] 'Somali cleric demands AU leaves', *BBC News Online*, 24 April 2009, http://news.bbc.co.uk/2/hi/africa/8016985.stm

[50] Fred Ngoga Gateretse, Adviser to the AU Special Representative for Somalia, Amb. Nicholas Bwakira, Statement before the House Subcommittee on Africa and Global Health, Washington DC, 25 June 2009, p. 1.

[51] For more information about ASWJ see Appendix A.

Mogadishu.[52] Unfortunately, this agreement collapsed but was resurrected several times over the next few years.

AMISOM and the TFG thus clearly shared similar enemies. But AMISOM's other problem was that the TFG was a rather awkward partner. Given AMISOM's mandate to support the TFG, it was notable that in January 2009 the UN's technical assessment mission warned that security assistance should only be provided to Somali security forces if certain conditions were met. Specifically, '(i) existence of a recognized political and governance framework, providing for civilian oversight and control of armed forces and police; (ii) recruitment on an inclusive basis; (iii) mechanisms for assuring compliance with human rights and IHL; (iv) adequate and sustainable financial support, including for stipends'.[53] In practice, none of these conditions held. The TFG leaders had little oversight and control of their fighters, recruitment was generally based on clan identities, there were no effective accountability mechanisms, and the TFG's soldiers often went unpaid.

In theory, a high-level meeting of TFG, UNPOS, AMISOM, and IGAD technical experts and Ambassadors agreed the principal tasks of the Somali Army were to defeat anti-government extremists; protect the TFG and its institutions; secure key installations, facilities and terrain; facilitate movement of the TFG within Mogadishu; and facilitate delivery of humanitarian aid into Mogadishu.[54] It was estimated that a TFG force of 8,000 soldiers would be necessary to perform these tasks in and around Mogadishu, and a further 8,000 would be required to expand such operations to Lower and Middle Shabelle and across the country. But putting this into practice proved impossible for a variety of reasons. Not least was the fact that by November 2009, TFG armed forces were estimated to be only 2,900 strong (i.e., those active and on the government payroll).[55] An additional 3,500 unvetted, untrained, and unregistered fighters were thought to exist but consequently could not be considered for international support.[56] This was particularly worrying given that by early 2009, Ethiopia claimed it had trained some 4,000 TFG troops and Uganda had trained an additional battalion. The Ethiopians believed most of their trainees had quickly returned to their clans.[57] By January 2010 the Somali Police Force was estimated to be 5,000 strong out of the TFG's envisaged 10,000-strong force.[58] On top of these forces, the TFG President could also muster some *Darwish* (composite police/military) militia, which generally operated independent from the military.[59] By way of comparison, by late

---

[52] *Somalia Security Sector Assessment* (2010), §16a15.
[53] UN, *TAM* (12–25 January 2009), p. 16.
[54] *Somalia Security Sector Assessment* (2010), §16a8a.
[55] *SEMG Report*, 10 March 2010, §17.
[56] *Somalia Security Sector Assessment* (2010), §4ar.
[57] UN, *TAM* (12–25 January 2009), p. 17.
[58] *Somalia Security Sector Assessment* (2010), §6g.   [59] *Ibid.*, §16a9b12b.

2010, AMISOM estimated that *al-Shabaab* and Hizbul Islam had about 10,000 fighters, with their main hubs of operation in Mogadishu, Kismayo, Baidoa, Beledweyne, Jowhar, and Marka.[60]

AMISOM was thus presented with the major headache of figuring out how to effectively work with the TFG's troops and to encourage Sheikh Sharif to implement good governance reforms and pursue reconciliation with his rivals. While the latter goal was out of AMISOM's hands, the former was difficult for numerous reasons.

First of all, AMISOM had no clear picture of who the TFG forces were. This was particularly important given that the AU force was also unable to accurately identify fighters of its principal enemies: *al-Shabaab* and Hizbul Islam. AMISOM was mandated to help develop the joint force of TFG and former ARS fighters. However, Force Commander Okello noted that although both the TFG and ARS had submitted lists of names of soldiers to AMISOM to be placed into the Joint Security Force (TFG–ARS) they could not easily be verified, which was supposed to happen before AMISOM issued each individual with an identity card. By late March 2009, Okello said AMISOM had issued approximately 800 identity cards.[61] In operational terms, such confusion raised the risk of fratricide. Specifically, the inability of AMISOM commanders to communicate effectively with TFG units during operations, combined with their inability to distinguish some TFG forces and aligned militia from *al-Shabaab*, meant that there was a risk of casualties from 'friendly fire'.[62]

A second major problem was the initial mistrust between AMISOM and the TFG forces.[63] While the TFG forces were correct to grumble that they were generally treated as second-class citizens despite their local knowledge, the AU also had legitimate concerns with some AMISOM commanders often unsure about the real loyalties of many TFG troops.[64] Several factors contributed to this mistrust. One was the tendency of TFG soldiers to leak information.[65] In part, this was because senior UPDF commanders believed the TFG was heavily

[60] *Concept of Operations (CONOPS)* (AMISOM internal document, no date but *c.*October 2010), §13–14.

[61] Wikileak Cable, 09ADDISABABA717, 25 March 2009, §8.

[62] Sometimes, as in the operation to recapture the Global Hotel in March 2010, AMISOM and TFG commanders would coordinate in Bancroft's operations room owing to their lack of other channels for operational coordination and communication. *After Action Review for AMISOM* (Bancroft, 12 March 2010). ACOTA files.

[63] It should be emphasized that many local civilians did not trust the TFG forces either. A common view circulating amongst civil society at the time was: 'How can you trust today's police or military when they were militia yesterday?' *Somalia Security Sector Assessment* (2010), §18b10b.

[64] See, 'AU peacekeepers push back al Shabaab', *The New Vision*, 22 September 2010, http://allafrica.com/stories/201009230019.html

[65] Communication, senior UPDF officer, 12 February 2015.

infiltrated by *al-Shabaab* and the Ugandans could not easily tell who was who.[66] The issue of infiltration was exacerbated by the fact that TFG uniforms were easily available for sale and there were many family links across the Somali National Army (SNA)–*al-Shabaab* divide.[67] This issue would consistently bedevil efforts to build an effective set of Somali security forces, as discussed in Chapter 9.

Second, like many Somalis, their use of *khat* often rendered them largely ineffective by the early afternoon. This became such an issue that the failure of the TFG and AMISOM to ensure a supply of *khat* reached the frontlines meant that TFG forces routinely deserted their new positions by about 1100 hours.

A third element of mistrust was due to some of the TFG's new recruits. Under increasing pressure to generate effective fighting forces, the TFG reverted to using warlords to lead some of its troops, including Muse Sudi Yalahow, Abdi Qeybdid, and Mohammed Dheere, some of whom had been expelled from Mogadishu by the SCIC in 2006. While sometimes producing limited short-term gains, overall, this further 'eroded the government's already failing credibility and strengthened the status of the armed opposition'.[68] To take just one example, during the heavy fighting in August 2010 (see p. 98), UPDF commanders were particularly wary of whose side Indha'adde's approximately 300 men were fighting on.[69] One senior Ugandan intelligence officer summarized these concerns about the TFG troops in the following manner:

> Initially, we didn't trust the TFG security forces. TFG commanders were selling ammunition and weapons on the black market. We knew this because we traced the serial numbers of some ammunition and mortar shells which had been used against us back to the ones we gave the TFG from our own stores. We had initially started to cooperate with the TFG forces by sending them ahead of us to act as observers. But it soon became clear some of them would make deals with *al-Shabaab* and they would let them through to attack us. So after that we decided to advance together with the TFG forces to keep an eye on them and these attacks stopped. We also tried to find which TFG people were *al-Shabaab* agents. It was a big challenge to identify who was *al-Shabaab*.[70]

A third major problem was that the TFG was simply not an effective fighting force. This was not just a problem of split and shifting loyalties but stemmed from chronic levels of corruption among the political elites and senior commanders and the resultant lack of reasonable equipment, training, and support for the soldiers.[71] It was also, in part, a legacy of nearly twenty years of state

---

[66] Interview, senior UPDF officer, Kampala, 15 August 2012.
[67] Interview, UNPOS official, Mogadishu, 5 January 2013.
[68] Roque, 'The battle for Mogadishu', pp. 77–8.   [69] Oloya, *Black Hawks Rising*, p. 159.
[70] Interview, UPDF officer, Mogadishu, 4 January 2013.
[71] This point was made not just by AMISOM commanders but also relatively senior SNA officers. Interview, SNA officer, Mogadishu, 2 January 2013.

collapse (see Chapter 9). Corruption undermined not only the military chain of command but also the rudimentary procurement systems that existed. The result was that TFG forces lacked a whole host of basic equipment as well as force multipliers and enablers, including uncoordinated training, little infrastructure (notably barracks and medical facilities), as well as poor discipline.[72] Examples of bad practice were numerous as troops often lived among the population, had to barter medical assistance from friends and family, and usually had to communicate via commercial mobile phone networks because they lacked radios. This fragmented system also undermined the distribution of supplies to TFG forces, with a lack of food and water often being a reason for TFG troops to abandon their positions.[73] Limited control of TFG commanders over 'their' troops and aligned militia also inhibited their operational effectiveness.

The TFG also lacked a sustainable source of finance to pay its soldiers. As a consequence, in March 2009 it was reported that President Sharif took a $1 million loan from a Somali businessman to pay the salaries of TFG forces for one month.[74] Yet even when TFG troops were paid, their loyalty was often in doubt. As the Mayor of Mogadishu quipped in August 2009, there are 6,000–7,000 TFG soldiers on payday, yet only 2,000–3,000 when it is time to fight.[75] One persistent and not entirely unwarranted complaint from the TFG was that its forces were outgunned by their opponents because of the restrictions imposed by the UN arms embargo that was placed on the country in 1992. But the UN Security Council decided it would be foolish to fully lift the arms embargo while the TFG was unable to store and account for the weapons and ammunition it did receive. In early 2010, AMISOM began overseeing the storage and dispensation of the TFG's arms and ammunition as a way to stem corruption. Despite AMISOM oversight, ammunition continued to leak from the TFG and its aligned militia commanders to the illicit market.[76] Nevertheless, this situation also afforded AMISOM the opportunity to exercise some influence over TFG troops by strictly rationing supplies of ammunition to them, in part to prevent them from selling it on the black market.[77] AMISOM also sometimes used fuel in a similar manner.[78]

---

[72] See *Somalia Security Sector Assessment* (January 2010). Indeed, this assessment concluded that training the TFG forces without ensuring broader security sector reform and the regular payment of salaries was not only insufficient but likely to be counterproductive. In such circumstances, the risk of desertion and defection by trainees upon return to Somalia is high. *Ibid.*, §16a9b8j.

[73] *After Action Review for AMISOM* (Bancroft, 12 March 2010). ACOTA files.

[74] Wikileak Cable, 09ADDISABABA717, 25 March 2009, §2.

[75] Wikileak Cable 09NAIROBI1798, 25 August 2009, §5.

[76] *SEMG Report*, 18 July 2011, §133, §135.

[77] See, for example, Wikileak Cable 09NAIROBI1370, 2 July 2009, §6 and *SEMG Report*, 18 July 2011, §133, §135.

[78] *Somalia Security Sector Assessment* (2010), §16a9b10.

UNSOA BEGINS

While AMISOM was supposed to help support the TFG's troops, it also struggled to provide logistics for its own personnel. AMISOM's initial mission support strategy was based on the principle of initial self-sustainment by the TCCs with direct support from external partners, notably the United States, United Kingdom, and EU. Given the large number of AMISOM kinetic operations, logistics was a crucial component of mission support. With Uganda and Burundi unable to self-sustain their operations (i.e., transport, equip, and supply their own troops), various partners were required to provide them with direct logistical and other support. This rendered AMISOM's support systems complex and also susceptible to changing political priorities in partners. In 2008, the UN supplemented these efforts by providing AMISOM with approximately US$7 million worth of assets from the liquidated UN Mission in Ethiopia and Eritrea (UNMEE).[79] In 2009, however, the UN authorized the UN Support Office for AMISOM (UNSOA) to deliver a major logistical support package to AMISOM financed from UN assessed peacekeeping contributions (see also Chapter 8).

On 16 January 2009, UN Security Council resolution 1863 requested the Secretary-General to deliver a logistical support package to AMISOM. Shortly thereafter, UN Secretary-General Ban Ki-moon decided that the package should be delivered through a stand-alone support office overseen by the Department of Field Support (DFS).[80] UNSOA's initial package covered 'accommodation, rations, water, fuel, armoured vehicles [for AMISOM's police officers], helicopters, vehicle maintenance, communications, some enhancement of key logistics facilities, medical treatment and evacuation services'.[81] In order to deliver these services, DFS adopted a staffing model that deployed personnel to Mogadishu, Nairobi, and Entebbe (with some support staff in Addis Ababa).[82] The UNSOA logistics network initially consisted of the Mombasa Support Base from which supplies were transported by land and sea (every two weeks) to a Mogadishu Logistics Base. The network later expanded to include Sector Logistics Hubs and Battalion Logistic Locations.

---

[79] This included prefabricated accommodation, electricity generators, air-conditioning units, ablution units, and soft-skin vehicles. Unfortunately, most of these assets were worn out, unserviced, missing parts, and some were obsolete.

[80] For details, see UN document A/Res/64/287, 24 June 2010 and Report of the Secretary-General, *Support to African Union Peacekeeping Operations Authorized by the United Nations* (A/65/510-S/2010/514, 14 October 2010), §30.

[81] See *Letter Dated 19 December 2008 from the Secretary-General to the President of the Security Council* (S/2008/804, 19 December 2008), §8c; and *Letter Dated 30 January 2009 from the Secretary-General to the President of the Security Council* (S/2009/60, 30 January 2009).

[82] Initially, only third-party staff deployed through a UN contractor could deploy to Mogadishu because they were not subject to the security ruling issued by the UN Department of Safety and Security.

UNSOA's origins lie in an earlier and broader debate about how the UN should support AU efforts to increase its conflict management capabilities, including the deployment of peace operations. Since 2006, the UN's ten-year capacity-building programme for the AU had supported institution building and various capabilities for responding to peace and security challenges. The Somali case became particularly important. Although the UN Security Council decided that Mogadishu was not an appropriate place to deploy a UN peace-keeping operation—essentially because there was no peace to keep—it was willing to support AMISOM peacekeepers.

Almost immediately after AMISOM's deployment, the AU 'urged the United Nations to consider another vision of engagement, whereby troops might not be needed, but rather resources and management structures could be contributed by the Organization in support of African Union troops'.[83] Also during 2007, the UN sent about ten planning staff to Addis Ababa to help the AU support AMISOM and tasked a few staff in New York to help facilitate any potential transition of AMISOM into a UN peacekeeping operation. As discussed in Chapter 2, developments on the ground in Somalia, however, compelled additional UN action. But the failure of the ISF concept and the UN's unwillingness to deploy a peacekeeping operation meant that an alter-native mechanism was needed. It was the UN Secretary-General's job to develop other options to prepare for the expected security vacuum in Moga-dishu after the Ethiopian withdrawal. In mid-December 2008, he suggested the Security Council consider a logistical support package for AMISOM, including equipment and services normally provided to UN peacekeepers.[84]

The AU Commission, on the other hand, kept pushing for an ISF and, when that failed, a UN peacekeeping operation to take over from AMISOM.[85] The growing recognition that sustaining AU operations would likely require some form of UN support was also at the heart of the Prodi Report. Released in December 2008, this report focused on potential UN financial and logistical support mechanisms to the AU, although not in the form that UNSOA ultimately assumed.[86]

UNSOA thus emerged as a compromise deal struck between the UN Security Council and the African Union whereby the council would assist AU troops in Somalia but would not deploy a peacekeeping operation. The other crucial element of the overall bargain was that the European Union would pay the allowances for AMISOM's personnel. In this context, resolution 1863 expressed the Security Council's 'intent to establish a United Nations

---

[83] *Report of the Secretary-General on the Situation in Somalia* (S/2007/204, 20 April 2007), §34.

[84] *Letter Dated 19 December 2008 from the Secretary-General to the President of the Security Council*, Annex §8c.

[85] PSC/MIN/4(CLXIII), 22 December 2008.   [86] *Prodi Report* (2008).

Peacekeeping Operation in Somalia as a follow-on force to AMISOM, subject to a further decision of the Security Council by 1 June 2009'. It also requested that 'in order for AMISOM's forces to be incorporated into' such an operation, the UN should provide a 'logistical support package to AMISOM'.[87] UNSOA's initial goal was therefore to raise AMISOM's operational standards to enable its forces to be incorporated into a future UN peacekeeping operation.[88]

At this point, in mid-January 2009, a small UN team was dispatched to conduct a technical assessment of the situation. The team concluded that a future UN peacekeeping operation should only deploy if a variety of benchmarks were met.[89] It would also require 22,500 troops; a maritime and an aviation task force; up to 2,620 police officers (including FPUs); and an appropriate civilian component.[90] Given these conditions would not be met, the team recommended that the UN should establish a new field support headquarters in Nairobi, a small presence in Addis Ababa, and a forward element in Mogadishu, security permitting. Its strategic objectives should be to facilitate relocation of the peace process to Somalia, support the parties to create a minimum level of security to broaden participation in the peace process, and create conditions that would enable the deployment of a UN peacekeeping operation.[91]

Following this assessment, and as stipulated in resolution 1863, in April 2009 the UN Secretary-General submitted a report to the Security Council setting out four options to help achieve the UN's strategic objective of ending violent conflict and laying the foundations for sustainable peace and a return to 'normality' in Somalia.[92] On the political track the key was to support the peace process and foster national reconciliation by building capacity for local governance, drafting a constitution, and integrating human rights into all aspects of the process. On the security track the priorities were to create conditions in which the process of rebuilding state institutions could take root, especially 'a legitimate locally owned and developed national security apparatus'. On the recovery track, the key was to move beyond the current

---

[87] S/RES/1863, 16 January 2009, §4, §10.

[88] See *Letter Dated 7 October 2015 from the Secretary-General Addressed to the President of the Security Council* (S/2015/762, 7 October 2015), §7.

[89] Basic conditions to allow a UN peacekeeping mission to operate effectively should be in place before deployment. Important benchmarks would include: (i) formation of a Government of National Unity in Somalia; (ii) establishment and initial operation of JSF in Mogadishu; (iii) implementation of a credible ceasefire mechanism; (iv) lifting of illegal checkpoints; (v) active outreach by the parties to groups that remain outside the Djibouti process; (vi) consent to the deployment by all the major parties; and (vii) adequate pledges of troops and the required military capacities by Member States. UN, *TAM* (12–25 January 2009), Executive Summary and p. 32.

[90] *Ibid.*, Executive Summary.   [91] *Ibid.*

[92] *Report of the Secretary-General on Somalia pursuant to Security Council resolution 1863 (2009)* (S/2009/210, 16 April 2009), §48–80.

humanitarian emergency and provide basic services (including water, health, and education).[93]

With these issues in mind, the Secretary-General outlined four options for the Security Council. *Option A.* 'Transition from AMISOM to a UN peacekeeping operation', envisaged a 22,500-strong UN peacekeeping operation acting under Chapter VII of the UN Charter taking over from AMISOM. This was described as 'high risk'. Moreover, the Secretary-General noted that when in February 2009 the Department of Peacekeeping Operations had asked sixty member states whether they would be willing to contribute troops to such an operation, only ten responded, all negatively.[94] *Option B.* 'Staying the current course' envisaged a UN support package for AMISOM until the Somali National Security Force could secure Mogadishu on its own. This was described as a 'pragmatic' option. *Option C.* 'Staying the current course with a "light footprint" in Somalia', entailed the support package outlined in Option B as well as establishing a UN Political Office for Somalia and a UN Support Office for AMISOM in Mogadishu. This was described as the 'prudent' option. *Option D.* 'Engagement with no international security presence', was intended to serve as a contingency plan in case of an AMISOM withdrawal (intentional or forced).

The Secretary-General's preferred 'incremental approach' was for the UN to 'pursue its strategic objectives ... while continuing to work towards the deployment of a peacekeeping operation at the appropriate time'.[95] During what the Secretary-General called Phase 1, Option B would be carried out; during Phase 2, Option C would be practised. Only during Phase 3 would it be appropriate to enact Option A. Option D would remain the contingency plan in case of AMISOM withdrawal.

This approach resonated with some of the relevant advocacy groups. Refugees International, for instance, argued that 'Further, talk of deploying a UN peacekeeping operation should be put on hold [because it] would be a polarizing and destabilizing symbol of foreign meddling on Somali soil'.[96] At the other end of the spectrum, however, Gérard Prunier argued that insisting on a continued or increased AMISOM presence, 'would be a mistake' since AMISOM's impact was counterproductive: it was not strong enough 'to make a strategic difference' but was large enough to bolster *al-Shabaab*'s 'nationalist arguments', accusing 'the new president of betrayal'.[97]

And so it was that UNSOA's vanguard team of seven staff deployed into Mogadishu on 9 June 2009 after acquiring security clearance as part of Option B. Shortly thereafter, in August, UNSOA set up its logistical support

---

[93] *Ibid.*, §42.   [94] *Ibid.*, §55.   [95] *Ibid.*, §82.
[96] Refugees International, *Somalia*, p. 3.
[97] Gérard Prunier, 'Somalia: beyond the quagmire', *Open Democracy*, 25 February 2009, p. 6.

base in Mombasa by leasing storage space from a commercial provider for a year because the Kenyan government could not find a suitable site in time.[98]

As noted above, UNSOA was initially intended to raise AMISOM's standards so it could transition into a UN peacekeeping operation. However, things turned out rather differently. First, unlike the earlier UN support provided to the AU Mission in Sudan (AMIS) in 2007, with AMISOM there was no clear timetable to transition. UNSOA thus began without a clear exit strategy.[99] Second, the UN Department of Safety and Security ruled that because of security concerns, UNSOA personnel were only permitted to live in Mogadishu for short periods and had to be located in the same building as the AMISOM force commander.[100]

When the first UNSOA personnel arrived in Mogadishu in June 2009, they were shocked by what they found. About 4,000 AMISOM troops were living in the bush. The whole airport compound was trees and brush. Even two years into the mission, AMISOM personnel were still in tents with no 'hard' protected shelters, no mess hall, no purpose-built latrines, no conference rooms, only rudimentary medical facilities with an unrefrigerated tent as a mortuary, and no reliable medevac services. By this stage AMISOM had one (Ugandan) Level-2 hospital in the airport compound, and one (Burundian) Level-1 facility at the university base. The Level-2 facility had no hard wall accommodation except a containerized intensive care unit and operating theatre, it had two surgeons, one GP, one dentist, a radiographer, five health specialists and some nurses. The level-1 facility had no hard wall structures, no holding capacity and lacked basic lab facilities. It was also not secure from enemy fire. But it had three doctors and sixteen medical staff. Both facilities had insufficient medical equipment and drugs.[101] And yet between July 2008 and March 2009, these two medical facilities had conducted nearly 85,000 medical treatments, mostly to Somalis: 1,365 admissions and 50,753 outpatients at the Level-2, and 608 admissions and 32,190 outpatients at the Level-1.[102]

And the mission suffered considerable shortages of everything else from vehicles to flak jackets. AMISOM's base camp had no fixed perimeter, and various Somalis regularly came and went.[103] An internal study conducted for UNSOA described the situation as follows:

> With the help of DynCorp contractors, the Ugandans had sourced rice, meat, fruit and water locally. They brought in live cows for beef and cooked in huge pots over charcoal fires. Sourcing locally served a dual purpose. It meant they were not

[98] David Clarke, Unpublished UNSOA study, May 2014, p. 69.
[99] Telephone interview, DFS official, 21 October 2013.
[100] Interview, senior UNSOA official, Mogadishu, 3 January 2013.
[101] Communication, EU official, Addis Ababa, 20 April 2009.   [102] *Ibid.*
[103] Clarke, UNSOA study, pp. 21, 58, 62, 86–8.

solely dependent on flights from Entebbe to keep them alive, but they also wanted to ensure they were giving something back to the local community. "We never invested in concrete and walls. We invested in security through people being turned around to invest in peace. They were investing in their own protection," said [a member of] the first fact-finding mission.[104]

Cooking without refrigeration was risky. Soon after their arrival, UNSOA staff discovered that hundreds of AU troops had contracted a mystery disease.[105] Unsure what it was, the UNSOA team sent blood samples to doctors in the United States and United Kingdom, and by July the World Health Organization was alerted. It turned out that between April 2009 and May 2010, approximately 250 AMISOM soldiers had contracted lower limb oedema and symptoms compatible with wet beriberi from lack of thiamine/vitamin B1. Over fifty soldiers were airlifted to hospitals in Kenya and Uganda, and four died.[106] This episode, probably unique in the history of modern peace operations, illustrated the vital importance of logistical support and how badly AMISOM was struggling before UNSOA. As even a stoic Ugandan officer acknowledged, 'Before UNSOA came, it was bad, it was bad'.[107] A Western diplomat put it more vividly: 'We had a despicable situation. The field hospital was a cesspool'.[108]

By December 2009, UNSOA had made an impact but was struggling. For one thing, it proved difficult to recruit personnel, not least because the positions were not suitable for families, and the terms were not as attractive as those in some other UN missions. During 2009, 215 candidates were interviewed and twenty-five received job offers, but only fifteen accepted. By the end of 2009, less than half of the required positions had been filled, and the Mombasa operation was particularly stretched.[109] By May 2010, UNSOA had just fifty personnel.[110]

Nevertheless, by December 2009, UNSOA had shipped 1,200 tonnes of rations to Mogadishu, with ships sailing every fortnight.[111] Other services proved more difficult to provide and could take up to a year for the UN to process and deliver.[112] To deliver these services, UNSOA used a range of commercial vendors willing to take the risks involved, including Alpha Logistics (a Kenyan firm), American International Group (AIG), and RA International. Other big US firms, such as PAE and DynCorp, inquired about the project but declined, presumably because the financial rewards did not match the risk. Alpha Logistics regularly had its ships attacked by mortars

[104] Cited in *Ibid.*, p. 22.
[105] Interview, senior UNSOA official, Mogadishu, 3 January 2013.
[106] Watson et al., 'Outbreak of Beriberi among African Union Troops'.
[107] Cited in Clarke, UNSOA study, p. 58.   [108] Cited in *Ibid.*, p. 59.
[109] *Ibid.*, p. 71.   [110] Interview, senior UNSOA official, Mogadishu, 3 January 2013.
[111] Clarke, UNSOA study, p. 70.
[112] Interview, senior UNSOA official, Mogadishu, 3 January 2013.

when they arrived in Mogadishu. Among other things, these firms built a range of prefabricated structures, warehouses, and the compound fencing.

BREAKING THE STALEMATE

In July 2009, AMISOM appointed a new Force Commander, Major General Nathan Mugisha of the UPDF. Shortly after the September 2009 suicide attack, he emphasized that his forces were basically caught in a stalemate with *al-Shabaab*. By this stage AMISOM was deployed in six main locations: Mogadishu airport, the seaport, K-4 junction, Villa Somalia, Somalia University, and the Siad Barre Military Academy. To break the impasse, he argued, would require an additional 5,000 AMISOM troops as well as APCs, IED detection capability, fortified medical facilities, boats (AMISOM only had one small boat at this time),[113] and greater capabilities to train TFG forces, most of whom lacked even basic education. He also called for African Muslim countries to contribute forces to counter *al-Shabaab* propaganda about infidel troops in Somalia.[114] At a high-level stakeholders meeting on 14 December 2009, Mugisha outlined the key challenges facing AMISOM in the following manner:

1) inadequate troops numbers (for AMISOM and the TFG);
2) stakeholders did not understand the AMISOM mandate and had limitations on their assistance;
3) the TFG's lack of cohesion;
4) operational limitations, e.g., AMISOM's small maritime force;
5) lack of capability to track aircraft going in and out of Mogadishu;
6) difficulty deploying other components, e.g., humanitarian aid;
7) vulnerability to IEDs, suicide bombers, pirates, and spoilers; and
8) difficulty obtaining timely information.[115]

Despite these challenges, Mugisha believed that in order to secure Mogadishu, AMISOM required 12,000 troops supported by 20,000 Somali soldiers.[116]

In March 2010, the new head of AMISOM SRCC Ambassador Boubacar Diarra (from Mali), formerly director of the African Centre for the Study and

---

[113] General Mugisha believed AMISOM was particularly vulnerable at sea, along the approaches to Mogadishu airport, and in the immediate vicinity of the harbour. Wikileak Cable 09ADDISABABA2071, 26 August 2009.

[114] Wikileak Cable 09KAMPALA1095, 22 September 2009.

[115] Wikileak Cable 09ADDISABABA2946, 16 December 2009.

[116] Wikileak Cable 09ADDISABABA2959, 18 December 2009.

Research on Terrorism (ACSRT) in Algiers, also emphasized the need to 'take the fight to the enemy as opposed to turning into sitting ducks'.[117] In order to do so, he concluded that five strategic points in Mogadishu had to be secured: the Ministry of Defence, Stadium, Marine Base, and the air and sea ports.[118] In July 2010, with just over 6,000 troops deployed, AMISOM began to advance to additional positions across Mogadishu and by the end of 2010 it had nearly doubled its number of positions to more than two dozen.[119]

The explanation for how the balance of the war was tilted distinctly in AMISOM's favour lies with two events that took place during mid-2010: *al-Shabaab*'s bomb attacks in Kampala and the failure of its Ramadan offensive.

Probably in an attempt to weaken Uganda's resolve, in July 2010 *al-Shabaab* carried out two suicide bombings at a restaurant and rugby club in Kampala during the football World Cup. The day after the bombings, *al-Shabaab* spokesman Ali Dheere had gloated, 'We are sending a message to Uganda and Burundi, if they do not take out their AMISOM troops from Somalia, blasts will continue and it will happen in Bujumbura'.[120] But although the attacks killed over seventy people they did not have the desired effect: instead of pulling out, Uganda responded by deploying additional troops to Mogadishu and increasing its commitment to degrading *al-Shabaab*. So did Burundi.[121] Moreover, they reinvigorated IGAD's earlier call for AMISOM's troop levels to be raised to 20,000. As a result, the 15th AU Summit in Kampala (26–7 July 2010) authorized the increase of AMISOM troops strength from 8,000 to 20,000 and its police strength from 270 to 1,680 (560 police officers plus eight Formed Police Units of 140 personnel each). On 15 October 2010, this decision was endorsed by the PSC and the AU produced a revised Concept of Operations for AMISOM which provided an overview of the operational employment of the 20,000-strong force. As discussed in Chapter 4, the UN Security Council did not endorse these new numbers for the AU force.

The second key turning point was the failure of *al-Shabaab*'s major offensive against the TFG and AMISOM launched during Ramadan of 2010.[122] Known as *Nahayatu Muxtadiin* ('the end of the apostates') the offensive apparently took place at the insistence of *al-Shabaab*'s Amir, Ahmed Abdi Godane, despite considerable scepticism from other commanders, particularly those from the Rahanweyn clan who provided most of *al-Shabaab*'s foot soldiers

---

[117] *AMISOM Mission Implementation Plan January 2010–January 2011*, §51.
[118] *Ibid.*, §51.   [119] Mugisha, 'The Way Forward in Somalia', p. 28.
[120] Oloya, *Black Hawks Rising*, p. 152.
[121] Fifteenth Extra-Ordinary Session of the IGAD Assembly of Heads of State and Government, Addis Ababa, 5 July 2010, http://igad.int/attachments/222_Final_Communique_of_15th_IGAD.pdf
[122] This paragraph draws from Hansen, *Al-Shabaab in Somalia*, pp. 100–2.

who would spearhead the attack.[123] The plan was to isolate approximately 40 per cent of AMISOM's forces, i.e., those deployed in the Villa Somalia area. To help fund the war effort, *al-Shabaab* ordered traders in, amongst other places, Mogadishu, Afgoye, and Baidoa to make a special payment.[124] Unluckily for *al-Shabaab*, in the wake of the Kampala bombings new UPDF reinforcements began arriving in Mogadishu on 19 August.[125] These included an additional tank platoon.[126] By the end of August, AMISOM had, finally, nearly reached its authorized strength of 8,000 with some 7,650 troops deployed. On 23 August, *al-Shabaab*'s concentrated forces launched attacks across Hawalwadag, Hodan, Bondehere, and Whardigley districts of Mogadishu against AMISOM strongholds. But the attacks failed to dislodge AMISOM and the TFG. After two weeks of intense fighting, *al-Shabaab* forces had suffered a series of significant losses, with AMISOM intelligence estimating between 500 to 700 fatalities with an additional 2,000 wounded. On 13 September, the humiliating defeat was announced when a gathering of Hawiye elders publicly declared *al-Shabaab* had lost the campaign.

On the negative side, many TFG soldiers were reported to have abandoned their positions on the frontline during the fighting and tonnes of heavy weaponry was stolen from government armouries.[127]

On the positive side, and probably more important, as Colonel Sandy Wade, a former UK and EU security advisor recalled, *al-Shabaab* had made 'a serious tactical error as a guerrilla army—they attacked at a point of strength and got pushed back like a conventional force. They probably won't make that mistake again'.[128] It was after *al-Shabaab*'s failed Ramadan 2010 offensive that AMISOM decided to counter-attack and launch its own offensive.

CONCLUSION

For roughly twenty months after the Ethiopian troops withdrew from Mogadishu, AMISOM endured a bloody stalemate in Mogadishu. Ultimately, however, despite a range of challenges, the AU force endured this stalemate

---

[123] Rahanweyn clan members who had been farmers made up a considerable number of *al-Shabaab*'s rank and file, mostly under the direction of Mukhtar Robow. As one journalist summed it up, this was largely because Rahanweyn farmers had been among 'the greatest losers of Somali society' since the civil war began in 1988. Fergusson, *The World's Most Dangerous Place*, p. 60.

[124] Oloya, *Black Hawks Rising*, p. 156.   [125] *Ibid.*, p. 157.

[126] Interview, senior UPDF official, Kampala, 15 August 2012.

[127] Oloya, *Black Hawks Rising*, p. 161.

[128] Cited in Patrick Smith, 'African armies are better than you think', *The Africa Report*, 4 April 2013, http://www.theafricareport.com/North-Africa/african-armies-are-better-than-you-think.html

better than *al-Shabaab* and achieved its principal objective of protecting the TFG. As one long-time Somalia analyst put it, 'AMISOM managed to hold the line at a difficult time'.[129] As a result, the UN Monitoring Group on Somalia's 2010 report delivered an accurate conclusion when it stated: 'The government owes its survival to the small African Union peace support operation, AMISOM, rather than to its own troops'.[130]

The stalemate was produced by several main factors. First, AMISOM's low troop numbers made going on the offensive virtually impossible—and certainly there were too few AU soldiers to take the whole of Mogadishu. Second, AMISOM's principal partner, Sheikh Sharif's TFG was weak, corrupt, and largely incompetent, and so too were its security forces. Even when they did capture additional parts of Mogadishu, they usually proved unable to hold them. And, third, *al-Shabaab* was a cunning and adaptable foe that was well dug in in parts of the city and utilized various asymmetric tactics to its advantage. However, the balance of power was tipped in AMISOM's favour after mid-2010 when it received significant reinforcements after *al-Shabaab* made two important errors. First, its bombing of civilian targets in Kampala backfired inasmuch as President Museveni redoubled his efforts to support AMISOM rather than withdraw. Second, *al-Shabaab*'s Ramadan offensive in August 2010 caused it to suffer large numbers of casualties and failed to dislodge AMISOM and the TFG.

In addition to these factors, from late 2009, AMISOM also started receiving more and better logistics support thanks to UNSOA; an innovative mechanism developed by the UN Security Council that boosted AMISOM's morale, stopped diseases, and brought more resources. The AU troops were going to need it because, as Chapter 4 discusses, they were now about to launch their own counter-attack and series of offensive operations.

---

[129] Telephone interview, 12 June 2012.   [130] *SEMG Report*, 10 March 2010, p. 6.

4

Offensive

September 2010 to October 2011

With the military stalemate in Mogadishu tipped in AMISOM's favour, the mission prepared to go on the offensive. Over the next twelve months, AMISOM embarked on a series of often bloody operations that culminated in forcing *al-Shabaab* to withdraw its main forces from Mogadishu in August 2011. As preparation for the battle for Mogadishu, in December 2010 the UN Security Council authorized an additional 4,000 troops for AMISOM. Although this was well short of the additional 12,000 troops the AU had called for, the subsequent offensive operations saw AMISOM adopt innovative tactics that enabled them to prosecute a successful campaign of urban warfare. This was in spite of the mission suffering from many significant capability gaps. Crucial factors in their success included AMISOM's decision to stop using the city's main roads and instead cut 'mouse holes' through building walls to provide troops with cover; the effective use of engineering capabilities, especially bulldozers and front-end loaders, to conduct 'breaching operations' that enabled the AU forces to capture significant territory while under fire; and the deployment of sniper teams to counter not only *al-Shabaab*'s snipers but also the militants' efforts to plant IEDs. The use of drones by both the United States and AMISOM also helped with reconnaissance. Finally, AMISOM personnel also showed considerable resilience and tenacity in the face of many casualties.

These tactical successes not only pushed *al-Shabaab* forces out of central Mogadishu, they also turned significant pockets of international opinion from viewing the mission as a failure to a strategic success. This, in turn, helped encourage other countries to join the mission in late 2011. It also generated a renewed diplomatic push to create an effective set of federal authorities for Somalia as the only long-term antidote to *al-Shabaab* and other armed opposition groups.

This chapter analyses these issues in five parts. It starts by briefly summarizing the at times acrimonious debate about AMISOM's authorized strength before examining how the mission prepared for the upcoming offensive campaign with reference to its pre-deployment training programmes and some of their limitations. The third section then analyses how AMISOM took control of Mogadishu via a series of operations conducted during 2011. The fourth section briefly summarizes the challenges AMISOM faced in Mogadishu after *al-Shabaab* withdrew its main forces, while the final section discusses the problems involved in trying to end Somalia's transitional phase of government. This involved considerable international diplomacy to finally agree on the Roadmap on Ending the Transition, which was signed on 6 September 2011.

HOW MANY IS ENOUGH?

Having defeated *al-Shabaab*'s Ramadan offensive and having almost their full contingent of 8,000 troops, AMISOM's commanders were eager to take the fight to the militants. To that end, on 15 October 2010, the AU PSC endorsed an increased force strength for AMISOM of 20,000, with the requisite air and maritime capabilities, an enhanced police component of 1,680, and an enhanced civilian component.[1] The PSC also called on AMISOM's partners, 'in particular, the [UN] Security Council', to, among other things, impose 'a naval blockade and a no-fly zone over Somalia to prevent the entry of foreign elements into Somalia, as well as flights and shipments carrying weapons and ammunitions to armed groups inside Somalia which are carrying out attacks against the TFG, AMISOM and the Somali population'.[2]

Following on from the PSC meeting, the AU produced a revised Concept of Operations (CONOPS) for AMISOM, which provided an overview of the operational employment of 'a robust force of 20,000 troops with the requisite enablers and multipliers' (as set out in Table 4.1).[3] The new CONOPS defined the desired political end state of the mission as 'the creation of an enabling environment for the TFIs [Transitional Federal Institutions] to effectively implement their stipulated tasks as enshrined in the Transitional Federal Charter.... it is envisaged that the restoration of governmental authority and sovereignty would allow for long-term stabilization, reconstruction and development'.[4]

Crucially, the new CONOPS expanded AMISOM's geographical scope beyond Mogadishu to encompass 'the stabilisation of the extant security situation in South Central Somalia, and Mogadishu'.[5] It also called on AMISOM to 'place

---

[1] PSC/MIN/1(CCXXXXV), 15 October 2010, §13.   [2] *Ibid.*, §15.
[3] *Concept of Operations (CONOPS)* (AMISOM doc. [no date but c. October 2010]), §20.
[4] *Ibid.*, §9.   [5] *Ibid.*, §10.

Table 4.1. AMISOM's proposed force composition (2010)

Formation	Quantity	Strength
Infantry Battalions	20 (850 each)	17,000
Tank Regiment	1	395
Multirole Engineers Battalion	1	750
Multirole Logistics Unit	1	220
Multipurpose Transport Battalion	1	200
Signal Unit	1	195
Training Company	1	120
Military Police Unit	1	140
Aviation (Transport & Close Air Support)	1	150
Maritime Elements	1	150
MOVCON Platoon	1	35
Force Headquarters Guards Company	1	195
Level-II Hospitals	4	160
Artillery (Locating and Mortar Batteries)	6	195
Sector Headquarters	4	120
Force Headquarters	1	75
Total		**20,100**

Source: Concept of Operations (CONOPS) (AMISOM document no date [*c.*October 2010]).

more emphasis on the political strategy rather than an attritionist approach to warfare and therefore, pay more attention to civilian protection'.[6] The CONOPS envisaged a four-front push against the TFG's opponents: an eastern front in Mogadishu, a western front in Baidoa, a central front in Galgadud and Mudug, and a southern front in Kismayo.[7] The AU reinforcements would deploy in four phases up to the 20,000 maximum. Phase five was envisaged as the transition to a UN force. At the time, the AU estimated TFG forces at 8,000, a rather optimistic assessment that was based on the numbers of troops being paid stipends by the Italian and US governments (see Chapter 9).[8]

The main problem with this CONOPS was the UN Security Council proved unwilling to endorse it. This was because the AU's proposed 20,000-strong force was assessed by the UN's Military Staff Committee to be too high. First, the Military Staff Committee concluded that the new military strategy in the CONOPS was 'not framed by an overall political strategy, nor is it incorporated into an overall TFG strategy'. Second, the Military Staff Committee criticized the fact that the AU proposal lacked a troop-to-task assessment, was unclear on the timelines for the proposed phased operations, was unrealistic about the capacity of local forces, and failed to detail the assets required to establish and maintain a naval blockade and no-fly zone.[9] In sum, the UN did

---

[6] *Ibid.*, §11.   [7] *Ibid.*, §18.   [8] *Ibid.*, §21.
[9] *Military Staff Committee Non-Paper: Analysis of African Union Mission in Somalia Concept of Operations* (Unpublished document, December 2010) p. 1.

not feel that it should be expected to finance these troops if the AU did not show clearly what they were needed for.[10] As a result, in December 2010, the UN Security Council endorsed a troop increase for AMISOM from 8,000 to just 12,000.[11]

While this dispute caused some political acrimony, in one sense, the difference between an authorized AMISOM strength of 12,000 and 20,000 was moot because most AU members remained unwilling to send troops to Somalia. It was therefore left to Uganda and Burundi to increase their own troop levels. As it turned out, AMISOM fought most of the war for Mogadishu with under 9,000 troops, rising to about 9,600 by the time *al-Shabaab* withdrew most of its forces from the city in August 2011. With some TFG support, this proved to be enough.

The UN Security Council also rejected the AU's request for a no-fly zone and naval blockade. African leaders were once again disappointed by the Western response to the Somali crisis. One analyst offered the following explanation: the Western response to the AU's request was so different because for Western states 'the Kampala bombings were an embarrassment, not the crisis and shock that they were in East Africa'.[12]

PREPARING FOR URBAN WAR

Although AMISOM was often referred to as a peacekeeping operation, by this stage it was in reality a war-fighting mission with an admixture of VIP protection tasks. Consequently, its training needs went well beyond what was usually required for peacekeeping operations.

The theory behind pre-deployment training (PDT) for peace operations is that it should provide and hone the skillsets and utilize doctrine that troops use in field operations. It should also take account of the evolving tactics, techniques, and procedures used by armed opposition groups. There should be some validation of the PDT, based on regular monitoring and evaluation, to ensure that it is current and relevant to be able to meet the mission's objectives and immediate threats. PDT would be provided for individual peacekeepers in units (e.g. squads, platoons, companies etc.), multilateral trainings for command staffs, specialized trainings in areas such as medical, engineering, and communications, and 'train the trainer' activities designed to develop a cadre

[10] Interview, UN official, Addis Ababa, 9 May 2012.
[11] S/RES/1964, 22 December 2010.
[12] Michael Weinstein, 'Somalia: Washington's Response to the Kampala Bombings—Continued Procrastination', *Garowe Online*, 21 July 2010, http://www.garoweonline.com/ar tman2/publish/Somalia_27/Somalia_Washington_s_Response_to_the_Kampala_Bombings_-_Continued_Procrastination.shtml

of local instructors to enable the recipient country to become self-sustaining. PDT should always be supplemented by mission-specific induction training once personnel are deployed in theatre. In AMISOM's case, however, there were insufficient resources available to do these things and training materials and equipment did not always match that used in Somalia. To recount just one example, in 2013 PDT of Burundian bomb disposal teams in Bujumbura was based on use of the bomb suit. Following their deployment, however, they were combat ineffective until they had been retrained in the use of the new Casspir bomb arms, which UNMAS had recently fitted and deployed in the field for AMISOM's operations.[13]

With the AU possessing virtually zero capacity to run effective PDT programmes for its peacekeepers, and Uganda and Burundi also unable to provide all the necessary training themselves, multiple partners were engaged to fill the gap. They faced an array of challenges. The largest was the US Department of State's Africa Contingency Operations Training and Assistance (ACOTA) programme, but the United Kingdom, France, the Netherlands, Belgium and other countries were also involved. Over time, ACOTA provided training and some non-lethal equipment to four AMISOM TCCs: Burundi, Djibouti, Sierra Leone, and Uganda. The ACOTA trainings were conducted by State Department civilian contractors, including MPRI, Northrup Grumman, PAE, and FDR. Most of the vendors, however, were retired military personnel, although they sometimes received assistance from active duty US military, who served as mentors to the TCCs. Here, I briefly highlight four aspects of AMISOM's PDT that bore directly on the mission's ability to conduct successful urban warfare.

First, the UPDF and BNDF contingents were at very different levels of preparedness in terms of training and equipment. While the early Ugandan battle groups required some assistance, the Burundian contingents required considerably more, including large amounts of equipment and more training. As discussed in Chapter 2, in order for the Burundian battalions to deploy, the United States in particular had to supply a long list of items including vehicles, communications, medical equipment, general field items, office equipment and stationery, operational aids, defensive stores, mess utensils, accommodation, fire equipment, and recreational items. And for more sophisticated equipment, it takes time to learn how best to use it and, crucially, how to maintain it. Another source of inconsistency across the mission's contributing countries was that the AU and AMISOM Force Commander lacked training guidance, resulting in troops operating side-by-side in theatre with different types and levels of training.

---

[13] Communication, UK military adviser, 9 September 2014.

The second major issue was that AMISOM's training needs went well beyond those usually required for UN peacekeeping missions and other AU peace operations. In early 2011, top Ugandan General Katumba Wamala had remarked to a UK training programme audience that making the transition from operating in countryside to urban surroundings had been the key training objective for the UPDF deployed in AMISOM. 'The challenge we have on the military side', he said, 'is a new operational environment . . . What we are faced with in Mogadishu is urban terrorism operations'.[14]

In response, AMISOM became ACOTA's number one priority and it developed a refined PDT package that included more robust and better combat equipment, and focused on counterinsurgency tactics—including how to fight through buildings to tackle *al-Shabaab* sniper teams—and better force task organization (i.e. combat teams with armour and special forces).[15] For example, since neither the UPDF nor BNDF had much experience of urban warfare, two areas of particular importance during AMISOM's early years in general and the fight for Mogadishu in particular were infantry and medical 'Combat Life Saver First Aid' and 'Fighting in Built-up Areas'. To help with the latter, by December 2010 British personnel had built twenty-seven units at Uganda's Singo military training school that copied the plan and structures in Mogadishu. These were based on lessons learned by the UPDF in the last three years of its operations in Mogadishu. With regard to combat medical support, unlike more traditional peacekeeping operations, a high-risk mission like AMISOM had to ensure that every soldier received a first aid kit (with the right equipment) to care for the wounded, and training on how to care for an injured colleague. AMISOM forces also received more timely intelligence from their partners than ordinary peacekeeping missions and developed a better close combat supply arrangement. ACOTA also later developed a course designed to train AMISOM TCCs in how to establish and run an effective multinational force headquarters.

Third, even with considerable partner assistance, training gaps and challenges emerged. Training in International Humanitarian Law (IHL) and its relationship to civilian protection issues was a significant gap in AMISOM's early years, as was the issue of how peacekeepers should deal with child

[14] 'Training Ugandans for Somalia deployment', UK Ministry of Defence, 18 February 2011, https://www.gov.uk/government/news/training-ugandans-for-somalia-deployment

[15] This refined training package for AMISOM was made possible in part because the US government designated *al-Shabaab* a transnational terrorist organization and a significant threat to US national interests. The United States was therefore able to utilize Section 1206 counterterrorism and stabilization funds for AMISOM TCCs and expand the range of tasks usually associated with peace operations training programmes. See http://www.dsca.mil/programs/section-1206-train-and-equip. In December 2014 Section 1206 was replaced with Section 2282 and in FY2017 this was rolled into the programme 333 authority. The United Kingdom also provided the UPDF with an enhanced version of its Peacekeeping Training Team packages to include niche training in operational law and detention, CIMIC, information operations, and targeting. Interview, UK military official, Kampala, 13 August 2012.

soldiers.[16] Another limitation was that, compared to military PDT, civilian and police PDT was lacking or non-existent.[17] This was especially true in the area of stabilization (including how to use Quick Impact Projects (QIPs) to achieve immediate effects) and rule of law capacity-building which would come to occupy a more prominent place in AMISOM activities after 2012. Media training was also identified as a weakness, despite the importance of commanders and individual soldiers being able to understand and disseminate AMISOM's strategic narrative to help counter *al-Shabaab* propaganda (see Chapter 11). As AMISOM matured and expanded, it also became apparent that training for AMISOM Force Headquarters personnel raised particular challenges, including the fact that not all those who attended the numerous iterations of the ACOTA Force Headquarters training were subsequently assigned to the AMISOM Force Headquarters, or if they were, employed correctly in role (see Chapter 5). Female engagement training, especially related to providing all AMISOM personnel with an understanding of how to prevent sexual exploitation and abuse and operate within the cultural boundaries encountered in Somalia, was another area of identified weakness. Later in the mission, after AMISOM moved out of Mogadishu, PDT was also recommended to cover anti-ambush drills and vehicle recovery procedures.[18]

Finally, two of the most important initial gaps related to AMISOM's lack of capabilities to counter *al-Shabaab* snipers and IEDs. On the former, *al-Shabaab* snipers had long posed a deadly problem for AMISOM. Although it was impossible to determine how many snipers *al-Shabaab* possessed or whether they were trained locally or abroad, they often proved deadly, usually from distances of between 400m and 100m. This was brutally highlighted in an *al-Shabaab* propaganda video, 'Shoot, Oh Bani Ismail' released on 1 September 2011. This video appeared to show at least twenty-eight people being shot by snipers (it is impossible to verify how many were AMISOM personnel).[19] In one now infamous case, an *al-Shabaab* sniper is said to have put a round through the sight of an AMISOM sniper concealed in a sniper hide.[20] *Al-Shabaab* snipers would of course frequently move their positions, but by 2011

---

[16] In early 2011, for instance, eighty-nine TFG soldiers in Uganda for EU training were deemed children by a medical doctor. '1-9 April 2011 East Africa trip report', ACOTA files. Similarly, numerous reports of the UN Secretary-General identified children with the TFG security forces. For instance, the UN identified 179 cases where children were recruited and used by the SNA in 2012, 209 in 2013, 197 in 2014, 218 in 2015, and 117 during the first half of 2016. *Report of the Secretary-General on children and armed conflict in Somalia* (S/2016/1098, 22 December 2016), §23.

[17] See, for example, *IPSTC Mobile Evaluation and Training Needs Assessment in South Sudan and AMISOM* (Nairobi: IPSTC, 2014), pp. 15–16.

[18] *After Action Report: Qoryoley Offensive, 12–26 March 2014* (Bancroft, 2014). ACOTA files.

[19] At http://jihadology.net/2011/09/02/al-kataib-media-presents-a-new-video-message-from-ḥarakat-al-shabab-al-mujahidin-shoot-oh-bani-ismail/

[20] *AMISOM Force Headquarters Position Paper on Joint African Union/United Nations Benchmarking Exercise* (AU internal document, April 2015), Annex A, p. 6.

notable problem areas were the Juba Hotel and Fish Bar. Later, in early 2013, as AMISOM pushed out beyond Mogadishu, reports surfaced of *al-Shabaab* positioning snipers in treetops during ambushes to shoot at AMISOM top cover personnel in moving vehicles.[21]

In response to this problem, Bancroft Global Development was called upon to help AMISOM develop sniper teams, which it did from 2008. AMISOM used its sniper teams to great effect both to take out *al-Shabaab* snipers and also to defeat *al-Shabaab* operatives placing IEDs, all with little or no impact on the Somali civilian population. Nevertheless, *al-Shabaab*'s snipers became such a problem for AMISOM that an internal study in 2011 recommended 'that AMISOM marksmen and snipers should place al Shabaab snipers at the top of their priority target list with al Shabaab leadership being number two, and heavy weapons number three for eradication'.[22] It also recommended that AMISOM's snipers and marksmen be formed into a unit under the control of the Force Commander, in part because of the tactical intelligence and battlefield communications they could provide.[23]

With regard to IEDs, this too was a new threat to many of the AMISOM troops. It became more salient as *al-Shabaab* increasingly turned to IEDs as one of their preferred weapons. Between 2007 and 2014, AMISOM recorded 871 IED incidents. The numbers escalated dramatically in 2011, aided by an influx of specialists from Afghanistan, Yemen, and Saudi Arabia, among other countries. It became particularly important as AMISOM embarked on its campaign of urban warfare against *al-Shabaab* in 2011, which saw a large rise in the number of IED incidents AMISOM faced (see Table 4.2). Apart from human casualties, IEDs struck many AMISOM vehicles, and the subsequent service delays had at one stage rendered about 50 per cent of the mission's vehicles unserviceable, awaiting repairs.[24]

C-IED training, largely offered via UNMAS and some ACOTA programmes, was meant to enable AMISOM personnel to predict, detect, prevent, avoid, neutralize, deter, and defeat *al-Shabaab*'s IED networks. But gaps in technical equipment, particularly electronic counter-measures, were apparent. It also proved difficult to keep up-to-date with *al-Shabaab* IED techniques, which adapted to AMISOM's responses. Nevertheless, improvements were made through such measures as widening roads and enhancing the detection capacity of foot patrols, including by utilizing canine teams (first used in 2009) and providing better cartography and orientation capacity.[25] The overriding lesson from AMISOM was that C-IED activities must target the production

---

[21] *Operations Order 01/2015—Operation Juba Corridor* (AU internal document, November 2014), Annex B, p. 8.

[22] *AMISOM Force Protection Review* (Bancroft, September 2011), p. 17. ACOTA files.

[23] *Ibid.*, p. 19.　　　[24] Communication, former AMISOM official, 22 October 2017.

[25] One internal study assessed that from September 2009 to September 2010, forty-three IED attacks that targeted AMISOM resulted in twenty killed and thirteen wounded. In comparison,

Table 4.2. IED incidents in Somalia, 2007–14

Year	IED Incidents
2007	23
2008	10
2009	57
2010	36
2011	122
2012	225
2013	225
2014	173
Total	**871**

Source: *Operations Order 08/2014: Operation Ocean Build* (AU internal document, November 2014), p. 17.

and emplacement of IEDs and minimize the tactical value of such attacks. They should also be intelligence-driven and based on consistent information-sharing and should empower individual AMISOM and Somali troops who were often the first line of defence against IEDs. In addition, consent-winning activities with the local population were critical to help mitigate risk of IEDs. For example, one Ugandan CIMIC programme that involved opening AMISOM medical facilities to locals led to significant increase in information flows and tip-offs about IEDs from civilians.[26] An AMISOM internal review suggested 99 per cent of IEDs recovered in theatre were through information received from the local populace. Unfortunately, AMISOM's internal communications gaps meant that at times the development of successful countermeasures to *al-Shabaab* IED threats in one part of the theatre were not communicated to all other parts. In the worst cases, however, C-IED PDT was either insufficiently absorbed by AMISOM personnel or the learned techniques were not implemented and integrated into daily procedures.[27] Moreover, at some point, no amount of training could substitute for appropriate equipment such as

during the same period in 2010 and 2011, thrity-six IED attacks targeting AMISOM resulted in nine killed and ten wounded. *Ibid.*, p. 4.

[26] *Report of the AMISOM Lessons Learned Conference* (Unpublished document, Nairobi, 28–30 August 2012).

[27] Hence, the infamous case where *al-Shabaab* planted IEDs in the same pothole on one main supply route on three separate occasions, and AMISOM missed it each time—all three incidents were noted on hostile activity lists in the Operations Centre yet no pre-emptive measures were taken to avert similar incidents. Paul E. Roitsch, 'The next step in Somalia', *African Security Review*, 23:1 (2014), p. 6. More generally, many IED strikes against the UPDF have taken place in the same place IED strikes have occurred previously. The problem being that UPDF troops often patrolled by mounting their APCs and deciding what route they will take at the last minute without conducting route analysis or engaging UNMAS. Casualties were even sustained from known IEDs! Communication between US officials, 7 November 2015. ACOTA files.

mine-resistant vehicles (e.g. Casspirs and Mambas) and individual equipment such as Kevlar helmets, Level IV protective vests, and mine detectors. In Mogadishu, the use of Explosive Detecting Dog (EDD) teams also proved successful, with one internal study noting that 'no AMISOM or TFG facility guarded by EDD has been attacked since Bancroft introduced the first canine teams to Mogadishu in 2009'.[28]

TAKING MOGADISHU

By the end of 2010, therefore, AMISOM had the benefit of both a new Concept of Operations to guide the mission and various enhanced programmes of pre-deployment training for its two troop-contributing countries. But in Mogadishu, the situation was still extremely difficult and the mission suffered from a variety of significant capability gaps.

By December 2010, AMISOM had doubled its presence across the city from eight to sixteen combat outposts, which among other things helped with countering *al-Shabaab*'s IED emplacement. Along with the TFG forces, AMISOM now operated in ten of Mogadishu's sixteen districts but could not consolidate control of them all.[29] This was in part because of the mission's limited troop numbers, but it was also linked to the AU's ability to support its troops. This was unsurprising given that by the end of 2010 AMISOM had just fifty-three civilian staff, most of whom were not even in Somalia.[30] By the same time, of the 270 authorized AMISOM police only forty were deployed on mission and only seven of them were deployed in Mogadishu.[31]

AMISOM was also still facing some criticism from NGOs about the militarization of humanitarian assistance in the city. In response, AMISOM argued that its mandate was limited to the facilitation of humanitarian

[28] *AMISOM Force Protection Review* (Bancroft, September 2011), p. 10. ACOTA files.

[29] For a full list of the areas in Mogadishu captured by AMISOM between February 2010 and 16 February 2011, see *Mission Implementation Plan (MIP) March–December 2011* (AU internal document, no date), Annex A-2. Hereafter, *AMISOM MIP 2011*.

[30] *African Union Mission for Somalia (AMISOM): Annual Report 2010* (AU internal document, 2011), p.23. By May 2011, only 14 AMISOM civilian international staff were deployed to Mogadishu.

[31] *AMISOM MIP 2011*, p. 14. These were the Police Commissioner, five senior leadership staff and thirty-four police officers: seven from Ghana, Nigeria, Sierra Leone, and Uganda were deployed to Mogadishu, while twenty-seven from Ghana, Nigeria, Sierra Leone, and Uganda were deployed at Kenya Wildlife Service Field Training School at Manyani, Kenya. There were sixty-eight AU-screened Kenyan Police Officers, as well as 570 AU-screened Police Officers in Ghana, Nigeria, Sierra Leone, and Uganda who were also ready for deployment to AMISOM once the necessary infrastructure was prepared. *Police-Strategic Concept of Operations for the African Union Mission in Somalia (AMISOM)* (AU internal document, 2010), §5.

assistance rather than its direct provision. But in practice it was clearly directly engaged. As the UN Monitoring Group noted, 'Despite limited resources, AMISOM has played a de facto role in providing humanitarian assistance— most notably medical care—to civilians around Mogadishu'.[32] Indeed, AMISOM's provision of medical assistance to Somalis proved so effective that in late 2010, Sheikh Ali Mohamed Hussein, *al-Shabaab*'s governor for Banadir region, tried to prevent the stream of Somalis seeking AMISOM's assistance by declaring that medicine and drugs from AMISOM were infected with the HIV virus.[33]

In mid-2011, however, some of the focus was taken off AMISOM's humanitarian activities when a major famine struck south-central Somalia. Not only did *al-Shabaab* manage the situation terribly, contributing to many deaths, but it also generated serious internal divisions within the organization. The famine resulted from a rare combination of several developments.[34] First, Somalia suffered its worst drought in sixty years caused by two successive rain failures of the *deyr* rains in late 2010 and the *gu* rains in March–June 2011. The drought led to higher food prices locally and lower demand for labour and livestock but, combined with the increase in global food prices, this decimated terms of trade for food and fuel. Third, the war in Somalia had produced some 1.4 million displaced people who were particularly vulnerable. And then there was the suspension of food aid to *al-Shabaab*-controlled areas of southern Somalia. As Ken Menkhaus noted, this had been going on for about two years and was down to three issues: some aid groups had pulled out due to insecurity; the US government suspended its aid on the grounds that allowing relief supplies to reach *al-Shabaab*-controlled areas would violate the Patriot Act's counter-terrorism provisions; and, finally, *al-Shabaab* banned most international agencies from working in territory under its control, saying they were spies or trying to put Somali farmers out of business.[35] The result was that an estimated 260,000 people died from the famine, including 17 per cent of children in Mogadishu and 18 per cent of children in certain *al-Shabaab* territories.[36] For *al-Shabaab*, the famine also had internal reper- cussions that reopened some of the same splits which had been apparent after its failed 2010 Ramadan offensive. Specifically, arguments arose between its leaders with clan and other familial ties to the region's worst affected, who wanted to allow international relief agencies to operate, and *al-Shabaab*'s

---

[32] *SEMG Report*, 18 July 2011, p. 343.   [33] Oloya, *Black Hawks Rising*, p. 163.

[34] Daniel Maxwell and Nisar Majid, *Another Humanitarian Crisis in Somalia?* (Somerville, USA: Rift Valley Institute and Tufts University, 2014).

[35] Cited in Laura Heaton, 'Somalia Famine', *Christian Science Monitor*, 9 August 2011, https://www.csmonitor.com/World/Africa/Africa-Monitor/2011/0809/Somalia-famine-Lessons- we-can-take-away

[36] 'Somali famine "killed 260,000 people"', *BBC News*, 2 May 2013, http://www.bbc.co.uk/ news/world-africa-22380352

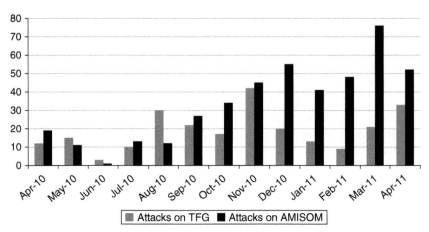

Fig. 4.1. Mogadishu Incident Review (April 2010 to April 2011)
Source: SEMG Report, 18 July 2011, p. 121.

Emir Ahmed Godane, an Isaaq clan member from Somaliland, who decided to ban them.

There were other developments on *al-Shabaab*'s side too. Even after the failure of its Ramadan offensive, *al-Shabaab* kept up smaller attacks on AMISOM and the TFG forces, and these significantly increased in number during late 2010 (see Figure 4.1). The militants were also still practising their usual techniques to damage AMISOM's reputation, including dressing their fighters in civilian clothes so that when they were killed their weapons could be removed and their bodies posed as 'innocent civilians' killed by AMISOM.[37] It was notable that a December 2010 AMISOM lessons learned workshop acknowledged that *al-Shabaab* was winning the propaganda war, in large part because the AU had no political presence in Mogadishu to counter it.[38] Moreover, the TFG remained untrustworthy for many locals and some blamed AMISOM for propping up an illegitimate government. Locals thus risked retaliation if they were seen contacting AMISOM, or even listening to Radio Mogadishu. The net result of which was that AMISOM could not trust the local populace during its operations.

In mid-December, *al-Shabaab* received an infusion of support when Hassan Aweys surrendered his Hizbul Islam forces to them.[39] *Al-Shabaab* was also still making good use of its snipers, with AMISOM peacekeepers coming under regular fire from the top of Juba Hotel and bank buildings, which enabled the militants to fire at the airport, seaport, and Base Camp.[40] Mogadishu thus

[37] UPDF AMISOM Lessons Learned Workshop Preliminary Notes, 21 December 2010. ACOTA files.
[38] *Ibid.*   [39] Oloya, *Black Hawks Rising*, p. 164.
[40] Barbara Among, '1,800 more UPDF sent to Somalia', *New Vision* (Kampala), 22 December 2010.

remained a very difficult operational environment. As one British military adviser deployed to Somalia recalled, 'My first trip to Mogadishu in late 2010 was characterized by driving through the streets in Casspirs at about 60 mph and taking bullet fire regularly along the way—this was just between the airport, K-4 and Villa Somalia!'[41]

Not surprisingly, therefore, AMISOM did not do a great deal of foot patrolling since the risks generally outweighed the benefits. Any patrols were therefore mounted to heighten force protection. However, this made it much more difficult for AMISOM to engage the local civilian population. AMISOM patrols also tended to be national affairs with no joint patrols between the UPDF and BNDF taking place due to command and control challenges.

By early 2011, therefore, AMISOM may have held the strategic upper hand, but it still faced a range of practical challenges. These were neatly captured by one internal study that suggested the mission would have to 'breach its way out of the obstacle belt that al Shabaab placed around it to negate the advantage of AMISOM armored vehicles'.[42] The obstacles included sniper positions, tunnels, tank traps, as well as *al-Shabaab*'s fighters and heavy weapons. As if that wasn't enough, AMISOM was also struggling against the elements: the harsh sea salt, for instance, required weapons and equipment to be cleaned daily or they could face rust problems overnight![43]

To break *al-Shabaab*'s grip on Mogadishu, during 2011 AMISOM embarked on three major offensives conducted in February, July, and October. In February, Operation *Panua Eneo* ('expand space' in Swahili) saw the Burundian contingent capture the *al-Shabaab* stronghold at the Ministry of Defence (*Gashandiga*, meaning 'Drop Your Weapons'), as well as the milk factory and cigarette factory. In July, the Ugandan contingent pushed *al-Shabaab* out of Hodon, Howlwadaag, and Wardhigley and Bondhere districts by capturing Kasapopulare, African Village, Red Mosque, Wadnaha Street, Florenza junction, stadium, Afrik radio station, the Ministry of Interior, and the sieging of Bakara market. This forced *al-Shabaab* to withdraw the majority of its fighters and heavy weapons from central Mogadishu on 6 August 2011 (although it retained a covert capability in the city which operates to this day). In October, the Ugandan contingent expanded its area of control northeastwards by capturing Ballad, pasta factory, Coca Cola factory, and Arafat Hospital in the Heriwa and Karan districts. Burundian troops moved into the Dayniile district areas of Tiida, Digmale, and Bangala. By the end of 2011, 98 per cent of Mogadishu was under AMISOM/TFG control.[44]

---

[41] Interview, Nairobi, 6 August 2012.

[42] *AMISOM Force Protection Review* (Bancroft, September 2011), p. 20. ACOTA files.

[43] UPDF AMISOM Lessons Learned Workshop Preliminary Notes, 21 December 2010. ACOTA files.

[44] *AMISOM Annual Report 2011*, p. 17.

These operations were successful, but some came at a significant cost. In part, the costs were exacerbated by some of AMISOM's own capability gaps. As the mission was launching its initial offensive, its leadership acknowledged five major challenges affecting its military component: there was inadequate provision of appropriate operational equipment for AMISOM troops; a lack of capabilities to repair and maintain equipment in theatre; no VSAT satellite connectivity between AMISOM Nairobi headquarters, Force headquarters, and the AU in Addis Ababa; inadequate coordination between AMISOM military and other forces; and there were no funds for reimbursement of contingent owned equipment to TCCs.[45] As noted above, AMISOM was also hampered by significant shortages of civilian staff, especially in its mission support elements.[46]

The operations turned out to be successful in large part because of the tenacity of the AU and some TFG forces combined with the adoption of some new techniques, tactics and procedures. That said, it is important to recall that at this stage, the idea that there existed a Somali National Army under TFG command was a myth. In reality, as the UN Monitoring Group pointed out, 'the most effective local allies of AMISOM are clan-based militias with loyalties to individual commanders and who look to the African Union rather than the Government for leadership and support'.[47]

Moreover, as previously noted, this form of urban warfare posed some new challenges for both the UPDF and BNDF. To help his troops overcome these challenges, the Ugandan contingent commander who orchestrated the crucial offensives, Brigadier Paul Lokech, had posted a sign around several of AMISOM's bases in Mogadishu (see Figure 4.2). In person, he frequently added to the sign's list, 'in an urban area "never move light". Always take your armor with you. They are hard to move but you need them to protect your force'.[48]

The first of the operations, *Panua-Eneo*, conducted during mid-February and early March 2011, saw AMISOM and TFG forces extend their areas of influence across Mogadishu. The UN Monitoring Group summarized this campaign in the following manner:

> Although the offensive entailed high casualties on the part of AMISOM forces, Transitional Federal Government and affiliated militias, it succeeded in expanding the AMISOM area of control, from five districts of the capital to seven, shifted the front line further away from Villa Somalia and placed al-Shabaab forces in Bakaara market and Dayniile under pressure.[49]

---

[45] *AMISOM MIP 2011*, p. 10.

[46] There was an immediate shortfall of 51 AMISOM personnel: 3 in Finance, 17 in Administration, 3 in Political, 3 in Civil Affairs, 7 in Police, 6 in Humanitarian, 4 in Mission Analysis Cell, 6 in Security and Safety, and 3 in Public Information. *AMISOM MIP 2011*, Annex O.

[47] *SEMG Report*, 18 July 2011, p.11.

[48] Telephone interview, senior UPDF officer, 4 March 2015.

[49] *SEMG Report*, 18 July 2011, §24.

LESSONS FOR ~~MISSION~~ OPS IN URBAN WARFARE
First study the people: One must understand the enemy in details, not from a military and political sense, but also from a cultural sense. **Second know the territory:** Key terrain in a city is at the micro level. Do not rely on street signs and most buildings as a reference points, use prominent buildings and monuments instead as they usually remain intact. **Third study the opposition weapon and equipment:** One need to know how this equipment can be employed in an urban environment. <div align="right">Brig Paul Lokech</div>

Fig. 4.2. AMISOM and Urban Warfare

Source: Photo by Susan Schulman of a notice displayed in AMISOM base Saad Stadium, Mogadishu, April 2012.

On the negative side, the Monitoring Group concluded that the offensive 'was followed by an increase in physical threats by Al-Shabaab against aid workers across southern Somalia'.[50]

The most intense battle during this period came at the Ministry of Defence (*Gashandiga*) complex, which along with the stadium was one of *al-Shabaab*'s main strongholds. Each of these locations was thought to house about 700 fighters. As it turned out, in late July/early August *al-Shabaab* deserted the stadium without a fight after they lost the nearby K-4 area.[51] However, at the Ministry of Defence complex AMISOM was not so lucky.

The battle began on 23 February 2011 and fighting raged for six days.[52] Initially, it involved an offensive by Burundian and TFG troops, but Ugandan troops and tanks would later join the battle.[53] Faced with a range of obstacles planted by *al-Shabaab* along the Industrial Road leading to the ministry complex, the Burundian commander chose instead to bypass them by launching an infantry assault involving multiple battalions over semi-open terrain. However, the undergrowth in this area was so dense and *al-Shabaab* had dug numerous trenches and laid tank traps that the BNDF were initially unable to use vehicles and so had to advance on foot. Although the assault had supporting fire from the roof of the nearby Military Academy, it exposed the attacking forces and the subsequent resupply efforts to *al-Shabaab* direct fire. The Burundian troops eventually closed with the enemy and defeated them in close combat but at considerable cost. A Canadian medic assisting at one of AMISOM's field hospitals recalled that many of the BNDF wounded suffered from knife/panga slashes and even blows from rocks.[54] This battle saw several hundred *al-Shabaab* fighters killed as well as the involvement of several

---

[50] *Ibid.*, §199.   [51] Interview, UPDF intelligence officer, Mogadishu, 3 January 2013.

[52] See Oloya, *Black Hawks Rising*, pp. 168–70.

[53] Interview, senior UPDF official, Kampala, 15 August 2012.

[54] Fergusson, *The World's Most Dangerous Place*, p. 109.

hundred TFG forces. At one stage, some Burundi troops coming from their base at the military camp got lost and ended up in the *al-Shabaab* training camp area in Shirkole where they were cut off and sustained numerous casualties. After that, the Burundians and TFG forces worked more closely together to avoid a repeat and utilize the Somalis' better knowledge of the area.[55] It was estimated that overall the BNDF suffered around sixty fatalities and during one thirty-six-hour period had to evacuate about 280 casualties from the area.[56]

While the Burundians led the way at the Ministry of Defence, the Ugandans concentrated on pushing forward on the other fronts on the approach to Bakara market. Here, AMISOM's plan was to try and avoid a large battle but instead close in on the market from three sides and leave *al-Shabaab* fighters with a single exit route. This involved a series of operations over the next few months. They too proved effective but costly in terms of casualties and equipment.

One of the principal problems facing AMISOM was that its reliance on moving via Mogadishu's roads played into *al-Shabaab*'s hands. The militants effectively let AMISOM use the main roads but hid in buildings and used their network of tunnels to move and mass their forces as necessary. AMISOM's commanders therefore decided to counter by dismounting from their armoured vehicles and moving to an infantry approach to take on *al-Shabaab* directly and force them out of the buildings. As the Ugandan contingent commander Michael Ondoga put it, 'mobility does not help us'.[57] This meant AMISOM had to move street-by-street and house-by-house. The Ugandan commanders called it 'creeping operations', which involved drilling 'mouse holes' through the walls of buildings and moving AMISOM troops surreptitiously through them.[58] This enabled AMISOM soldiers to largely avoid *al-Shabaab*'s snipers and then engage the militants in close quarter combat to take out their sniper teams.[59]

This method was effective, but when the new Ugandan contingent commander, Paul Lokech, arrived in March 2011 he pointed out it took a lot of time and resources. To give just one example, by this stage the UPDF reported that their forces and the TFG use approximately one million rounds per month.[60] Ultimately, Lokech adopted the idea of 'phase out' operations,

[55]   Interview, SNA officer, Mogadishu, 2 January 2013.
[56]   Interviews, UK military adviser, Nairobi, 6 August 2012; Bancroft official, Washington DC, 20 January 2016; *AMISOM Force Protection Review* (Bancroft, September 2011), p.20. ACOTA files.
[57]   John Allan Namu, 'The Somalia Mission', broadcast by KTN Perspective (Kenya), 7 August 2013.
[58]   Interview, senior UPDF officer, Mogadishu, 3 January 2013.
[59]   Interview, UPDF intelligence officer, Mogadishu, 3 January 2013.
[60]   '1-9 April 2011 East Africa trip report'. ACOTA files.

aimed at the capture of particular areas. These revolved around the idea of expanding AMISOM's territory by once again moving on the roads but creating fortifications as it went. This required armored bulldozers and front-end loaders to operate with the support of the UPDF's tanks and infantry. With cover from the tanks but still taking fire, the bulldozers would move up, deploy HESCO barriers, which were filled quickly, and then infantry were deployed behind them.[61] This process would then be repeated. As noted in Chapter 3, the UPDF had lost some of its armoured vehicles in the March 2010 operation at the Global Hotel, but it learned from its mistakes and ultimately this technique proved effective. Indeed, AMISOM's bulldozers proved so important that one of the *al-Shabaab*-controlled radio stations in Mogadishu announced that their drivers should be targeted as particular enemies of Islam.[62]

By late May 2011, TFG and AMISOM forces had taken control of Wadnaha Road, including the symbolic Red Mosque, the former military camp, Bondhere district headquarters, the former Italian Embassy, the former Interior Ministry building and Alimo Hotel.[63] While AMISOM was on the offensive, *al-Shabaab* kept up its suicide attacks, including two sophisticated incidents on 9 June at the Mogadishu seaport and 1 August at Sana'a Junction, which demonstrated their ability to gather detailed intelligence about AMISOM operations. On the other hand, AMISOM had a bit of good fortune on 7 June 2011 when *al-Qa'ida*'s leader in East Africa, Fazul Abdallah Mohammed, was killed when TFG police manning a checkpoint at Ex-Control Afgoye stopped his vehicle after his driver apparently made a wrong turn.

By this stage of the campaign, AMISOM's sole Level-2 hospital was dealing with a regular stream of casualties and using about 250 bags of blood every month (see Chapter 3). In comparison, a standard scale of blood for use in UN peacekeeping operations stipulates supplies of about 10 bags per month. To generate enough blood for transfusion, AMISOM had to establish a blood donor scheme among its personnel.[64] To supplement the mission's insufficient field medical facilities, the AU signed memorandums of understanding with Nairobi Hospital, Aga Khan Hospital Nairobi, Aga Khan Hospital Mombasa and Nakasero Hospital Kampala Uganda to act as Level-3 Hospitals for AMISOM. During mass casualty situations a number of critical casualties were taken for treatment in Level-4 military hospitals in France, Djibouti, and South Africa, under bilateral arrangements.[65] During this period, casualty evacuation was performed using armoured ambulances in the Mogadishu

---

[61] Telephone interview, senior UPDF officer, 4 March 2015.

[62] Fergusson, *The World's Most Dangerous Place*, p. 31.

[63] *Report of the Chairperson of the Commission on the Situation in Somalia* (PSC/PR/2 (CCXCIII), 13 September 2011), §17.

[64] Interview, UK military adviser, Nairobi, 6 August 2012.

[65] Communication, AMISOM medical officer, 5 October 2013.

operation area and UNSOA/AMISOM supporting Air MEDEVAC with Flying Doctor/AMREF, a company operating from Jomo Kenyatta International Airport/Nairobi (see also Chapter 8).[66]

By the end of July, AMISOM was ready to make the final push towards Bakara market.[67] The previous month it was reported that AMISOM had acquired four Raven drones as part of a US counterterrorism package for fighting *al-Shabaab*.[68] Combined with US-operated UAVs, these significantly improved AMISOM's surveillance capabilities. Forcing *al-Shabaab* out of Bakara market was crucial for several reasons. First, it provided the militants with their most important economic hub in Mogadishu, generating an estimated $30–60 million per year in taxes on sales and protection fees.[69] The hope was that loss of the market would leave *al-Shabaab* unable to pay wages to some of its fighters, resulting in defections.[70] But capturing the market also had an important psychological and symbolic value as far as the Mogadishu population was concerned. Capturing it would send a message to the population that *al-Shabaab* was weak after all and could be defeated. In sum, AMISOM needed this victory in order to gain the confidence of the local population.[71]

But because Bakara was such an important economic hub not just for *al-Shabaab* but for the wider population and because it housed a considerable civilian population, engaging in combat there would be disastrous. (Indeed, AMISOM had designated the area a no-fire zone.[72]) As a result, AMISOM commanders wanted to approach from three sides, leaving an escape route out of Bakara market towards a small airstrip going northeast for the estimated 2,000–3,000 *al-Shabaab* fighters in the city. AMISOM commanders also talked to the business community to get them to put pressure on *al-Shabaab* to leave.[73]

From 30 July, therefore, the plan was for the UPDF and its TFG allies to capture Mogadishu stadium because this was *al-Shabaab*'s tactical headquarters. Ideally, once the stadium was captured then Bakara would fall by itself. A secondary target was the so-called German Factory where *al-Shabaab* was manufacturing their IEDs. The Ugandans would then link up with the BNDF forces that were approaching via the Ministry of Defence.[74] The operation

---

[66] *Ibid.*

[67] This section relies heavily on telephone interview, senior UPDF officer, 4 March 2015.

[68] 'US taps $45m in gear for terror fight in Somalia', *Associated Press*, 26 June 2011, at http://somaliamediamonitoring.org/27-jun-2011-daily-monitoring-report/

[69] *AMISOM Force Headquarters Position Paper on Joint African Union/United Nations Benchmarking Exercise* (AU internal document, April 2015), Annex A, p. 11.

[70] To that end, AMISOM and its international partners had been working on developing a policy framework within which the TFG could deal with fighters defecting from *al-Shabaab* and other armed groups. See Communique of the Joint Security Committee, Djibouti, 20 January 2011, §4.

[71] Communication, senior UPDF officer, 24 February 2015.

[72] Interview, senior UPDF officer, Mogadishu, 3 January 2013.

[73] Brigadier Paul Lokech speaking in Namu, 'The Somalia Mission'.

[74] Telephone interview, senior UPDF officer, 4 March 2015.

involved a tough six days in complex built-up areas before the stadium was captured. To put pressure on *al-Shabaab* operations in Bakara, AMISOM wanted to dominate the area by putting its sniper teams onto the surrounding tall buildings. This was also a way to try and encircle any *al-Shabaab* snipers who remained in the city.

During these operations, AMISOM tried to ensure that all allied and TFG forces wore blue or yellow scarves. Indeed, Brigadier Lokech decided to issue different colour scarves to the TFG soldiers just three to six hours before the operation started because if left with the same colour scarf for more than one day they ended up in the hands of *al-Shabaab* due to infiltration and corruption problems. Nevertheless, some TFG soldiers proved very useful in the subsequent fighting.[75] This was a sign of progress given that in early 2011 a two-week assessment of the TFG security forces undertaken by former senior officials of the Somali Army and Police and three independent Somali researchers from Europe, the United States, and Canada concluded there was 'limited coordination' between AMISOM and the TFG forces 'which makes it difficult to conduct joint planning and operations to contain insurgent groups fighting against the TFG'.[76]

And then, on 6 August 2011, *al-Shabaab*'s leader, Ahmed Abdi Godane, decided to withdraw his main forces, heavy weapons, and remaining foreign fighters from central Mogadishu. The precise timing of *al-Shabaab*'s overnight withdrawal came as a surprise to AMISOM, but overall, their plan had worked, and Bakara market was captured without a fight.

In retrospect, AMISOM's success in forcing *al-Shabaab* out of central Mogadishu was due in significant part to the initial success of its creeping operations followed by breaching operations. These were successful because AMISOM changed its tactics in responding to the various obstacles placed in its way by *al-Shabaab*; the deployment of more engineering equipment, notably armoured bulldozers and front-end loaders; and the creativity and tenacity of AMISOM troops.[77]

SECURING MOGADISHU AFTER *AL-SHABAAB*

Initially, *al-Shabaab* fighters retreated only as far as settlements just outside Mogadishu, such as Afgoye, Balaad, and Marka. AMISOM and TFG forces did

---

[75] Interview, senior UPDF officer, Mogadishu, 3 January 2013.

[76] *Report of a Security Sector Assessment Scoping Mission in Somalia* (Prepared by former Somalia Senior Security and Military Officials, Mogadishu, June 2011), p. 6. Hereafter, *Security Sector Assessment* (June 2011).

[77] *AMISOM Force Protection Review* (Bancroft, September 2011), pp. 25–6. ACOTA files.

not take advantage and pursue them before they regrouped.[78] Instead, AMISOM largely transitioned from offensive to defensive mode and put its emphasis on security operations to consolidate the newly won territorial gains.[79] As a result, it would not be until mid-2012 that *al-Shabaab* forces were pushed out of these satellite settlements. From here, they often intermingled with the large displaced population to launch various guerrilla-style attacks and assassinations as well as suicide bombings against targets in the city centre. But central Mogadishu was now undoubtedly a different city. As one UN official put it, freed from *al-Shabaab* control, 'Mogadishu became deployable'.[80] It was certainly not without its challenges, however.

One challenge was to protect the mission's civilian staff. To that end, about a month after *al-Shabaab*'s withdrawal, the AU PSC requested the UN 'Security Council to authorize the enhancement of the support package provided by the United Nations' that would include the

> creation, as part of AMISOM and under its command, of a guard force of a battalion size (850), to provide security for civilian staff and protection for the AU, the UN and the TFIs in Mogadishu, it being clearly understood that this force should be in addition to the 12,000 strength already authorized by the UN Security Council under resolution 1964 (2010).[81]

However, the UN Security Council did not authorize this request. Instead, on 30 September, it encouraged AMISOM 'to develop a guard force of an appropriate size, within AMISOM's mandated troop levels, to provide security, escort and protection services to personnel from the international community, including the United Nations'.[82] AMISOM refused to do this and after a long diplomatic tussle, by mid-2014 the AU position eventually prevailed. A Guard Force of about 410 Ugandan troops was deployed as part of UNSOM, and hence was in addition to AMISOM's authorized strength and reimbursed by the UN.

Beyond the Guard Force issue, perhaps the three most immediate challenges for AMISOM were how to deal with the major humanitarian troubles *al-Shabaab* left behind in their former parts of the city; how to disarm the remaining armed youth without much violence; and how to reign in the warlords and clan militias who saw an opportunity to re-emerge. The warlords and clan militias, some under the command of politicians, quickly took advantage of the vacuum created by *al-Shabaab*'s withdrawal and set up illegal checkpoints in some districts to extort money from the public and in

---

[78] *Brief Report on the Situation of Somalia's Security Forces* (Former Senior TFG Military Official [name withheld], October 2011). Hereafter, *Brief Report* (October 2011).

[79] *Hand/Takeover Report for Sector One Commander* (AMISOM internal document, September 2012), p. 7.

[80] Interview, UNPOS official, Nairobi, 8 August 2012.

[81] PSC/PR/COMM(CCXCIII), 13 September 2011, §14.

[82] S/RES/2010, 30 September 2011, §5.

some cases steal humanitarian relief and even attack TFG/AMISOM forces attempting to extend the TFG's authority.[83] A leaked UN report documented the existence of seventeen such militias who were setting up roadblocks and engaging in extortion of passers-by, including some run by TFG members.[84] In part, therefore, AMISOM's job in Mogadishu involved trying to take down these roadblocks and integrating these clan forces into a national army. In Bakara market itself, a special police unit was created whose main task was to ensure the security of the area.

One senior AMISOM commander described the situation in the following manner:

> After acquiring the city we faced a big influx of IDPs. This generated several challenges: 1) al-Shabaab could infiltrate the city by coming in with the IDPs; 2) al-Shabaab could massacre IDPs and use this as propaganda to prove to the people that AMISOM could not protect them. Then when we realized al-Shabaab had remained just on the perimeter of Mogadishu we set up a safe zone perimeter. Inside this perimeter, we hoped this would put pressure on the TFG to deliver something positive to the locals. It gave them an opportunity to establish administrative structures. But unfortunately this did not happen. We have to win the hearts and minds of the people not just territory! But the TFG didn't get this.[85]

Once again, therefore, AMISOM faced a gap between its progress on the military track and the lack of progress on the political track. To genuinely stabilize Mogadishu, the TFG would need to start performing as a legitimate and effective government. But that was so unlikely that international diplomatic attention turned to thinking about how to end the 'transitional' government and replace it with something better.

TRANSITIONING A TRANSITIONAL GOVERNMENT

For the previous seven years, the focus of international diplomacy on Somalia was to support the TFG. Even so, everyone was well aware that the 'T' in TFG stood for 'transitional'. At some point the transition had to end and a permanent government be established. The TFG's original mandate had been five years (until August 2009). But Sheikh Sharif's TFG had essentially granted itself a stay of execution for an additional two years. This was the context that had produced a memorandum of understanding between AMISOM, IGAD, and UNPOS on 28 April 2010 wherein they agreed that the TFG

---

[83] PSC/PR/2(CCXCIII), 13 September 2011, §20.
[84] Telephone interview, Somalia analyst, 2 June 2012.
[85] Interview, senior UPDF official, Kampala, 14 August 2012.

had to give way to a permanent government structure. In practice, however, nothing happened until mid-2011 when the TFG recognized the need to do something about their transitional status.

The TFG's first response was simply to extend its own tenure. In the Kampala Accord, facilitated by President Museveni, and signed between the President of the TFG and the Speaker of the Transitional Federal Parliament on 9 June 2011, they agreed to defer elections of the President and Speaker for twelve months after August 2011. The Prime Minister would then resign within thirty days and the President would subsequently appoint a new Prime Minister who would, in turn, then appoint a new cabinet which reflected the 4.5 formula for power sharing.

President Museveni's facilitation and endorsement of this decision was criticized by many Somalis, who saw it as a major act of Ugandan interference in Somalia's domestic politics. Unsurprisingly, many of the international actors supporting the TFG were also furious, not just with Museveni but also because they had little to show for their investment and now the prospect of an additional twelve months stuck with a corrupt, incompetent, and still largely illegitimate government. The prevailing mood was captured succinctly in the July 2011 report of the UN Monitoring Group on Eritrea and Somalia. It set out its damning verdict on the TFG in the following manner:

> The principal impediments to security and stabilization in southern Somalia are the Transitional Federal Government leadership's lack of vision or cohesion, its endemic corruption and its failure to advance the political process. Arguably even more damaging is the Government's active resistance to engagement with or the empowerment of local, de facto political and military forces elsewhere in the country. Instead, attempts by the Government's leadership to monopolize power and resources have aggravated frictions within the transitional federal institutions, obstructed the transitional process and crippled the war against Al-Shabaab, while diverting attention and assistance away from positive developments elsewhere in the country.[86]

This assessment was accurate. After AMISOM had pushed *al-Shabaab*'s main forces out of Mogadishu, pressure from external donors encouraged the TFG to finally set out a Roadmap on Ending the Transition, which was signed on 6 September 2011.

The delegates included members of the TFIs, Puntland State of Somalia, Galmudug State of Somalia, and *Ahlu Sunna Wal Jamaa*. The authorities in Somaliland were notably absent. The Roadmap sought a definitive end to the transitional period in Somali politics before 20 August 2012. It did so by focusing on four priority tasks of security, the constitution, reconciliation, and

---

[86] *SEMG Report*, 18 July 2011, p. 12.

good governance. It also granted the TFG an additional year because it would have been politically unrealistic to completely tear-up the earlier Kampala Accord. The principles for the Roadmap's implementation were defined as:

(1) Somali ownership: the process would be led by the TFG and the preference would be to hold all meetings inside Somalia;

(2) inclusivity and participation: the process would involve all sectors of society (elders, women, youth), regional entities, civil society organizations as well as religious and business leaders;

(3) the meetings must be well-resourced: this was to be done by following a Resource Mobilization Plan which made international financial support contingent on seeing results related to the four priority tasks; and

(4) the roadmap would be monitored on a regular basis to ensure compliance.

While the TFG pushed the roadmap as a diplomatic success, its critics were not impressed with what looked like yet another deferral of the issues. One critic dubbed it a 'roadmap to nowhere'.[87]

From AMISOM's perspective, the most immediate concern was whether the new roadmap would bring any practical improvements to the TFG's security forces. In practice, this hinged on whether any progress could be made on combating corruption but also on Somalia's National Security and Stabilization Plan (NSSP), the principal Somali framework for security assistance. First adopted by the TFG in June 2006, the NSSP underwent a review process in mid-August 2011 when the TFG, AMISOM, UN, and Bancroft personnel participated in a strategic planning retreat in Naivasha, Kenya to iron out the delayed NSSP 2011–14.

The NSSP was intended 'to serve as the main conduit for supporting collaboration between the TFG and its international partners for sustained, coherent, harmonized and complimentary security sector stabilization in Somalia'.[88] The rationale for revising the 2009 NSSP was threefold. First, it had only been written with the transitional period in mind (i.e. ending in 2012) and hence needed updating. Second, a new NSSP was needed to take onboard the recommendations that came out of the Somali security sector assessment reports conducted in 2009 and 2011.[89] And third, a new

---

[87] Michael A. Weinstein, 'Somalia: A Roadmap to Nowhere', 22 September 2011, http://allafrica.com/stories/201109230675.html

[88] Cited in TFG, *National Security and Stabilization Plan* (TFG, 2011), p. 3.

[89] The 2009 report was compiled outside Somalia based on interviews with key actors and involved at one stage a team of over fifty people. But it was limited to south-central Somalia for political reasons. The 2011 report was compiled in Somalia. The 2009 report was led by US, EU, and other donors and started out with the impulse to address the principal donor concerns about the TFG forces, while the 2011 report was more Somali driven and linked to the idea of a revised

NSSP would give other international actors a structure for supporting the security efforts of the TFIs. For example, UN Security Council resolution 1964 (December 2010) demonstrated that the UN wanted to help, but there was no good document spelling out how best to structure that engagement.[90] The draft NSSP was prepared under the auspices of AMISOM with support of UNPOS and a team from Bancroft who acted as strategic advisers to the TFG. The NSSP was finalized with input from regional stakeholders (Puntland, Galmudug, and *Ahlu Sunna Wal Jamaa*) and debated and approved by the Council of Ministers at an emergency meeting on 26 October 2011.[91] It was submitted to Parliament on 29 October for discussion and adoption when Parliament resumed after the Islamic Holiday (Eid) break.

In sum, international partners pushed for a way to end the TFG and the TFG eventually agreed to a roadmap charting its own demise. The problem was that most practical incentives pushed in the opposite direction. As one European diplomat correctly concluded, life as a Somali MP was in some respects 'the perfect political job'. 'More than half of the MPs are in Kenya and still receiving salaries', he argued, and yet 'they have no real constituencies, they have no accountability to constituents as a result and they have no voters/elections to deal with. As a consequence, they have a vested interest in maintaining the status quo'.[92]

CONCLUSION

After nearly four and a half years, in August 2011, AMISOM's under-resourced troops achieved the immediate goal of their offensive campaign: to push *al-Shabaab*'s main forces out of Mogadishu. This victory came at a considerable cost, but it significantly altered the context of the city, which began to rehabilitate itself, and also earned AMISOM a more positive reputation internationally. It took another three months to make serious headway on the political track with the signing of a roadmap to end the TFG and a new NSSP. For AMISOM, this signalled the beginning of a qualitatively different phase of activities as the mission started expanding its

---

NSSP and was supported by UNPOS, the EU and AMISOM, and the Somali Embassy in Kenya. Communication, consultant on NSSP process, 31 July 2012.

[90] Interview, Western diplomat, Addis Ababa, 31 July 2012.

[91] This was considerably behind schedule given that the Joint Security Committee had recommended that the TFG adopt and implement the NSSP by April 2011. Communique of the Joint Security Committee, Djibouti, 20 January 2011, §4.

[92] Interview, senior EU official, Addis Ababa, 2 May 2012.

operations beyond Mogadishu. Nevertheless, as the Ugandan contingent commander warned, 'the security of Mogadishu still remains paramount and should not be compromised at any cost'.[93] The story of AMISOM's subsequent expansion and its attempts to maintain security in Mogadishu is the subject of Chapter 5.

---

[93] *Hand/Takeover Report for Sector One Commander* (AMISOM internal document, September 2012), p. 5.

5

Expansion

October 2011 to September 2012

Having fought its way out of Mogadishu, AMISOM underwent what the Ugandan contingent commander described as a metamorphosis from 'urban counter offensive to mounted operations'.[1] Those mounted operations would see the Ugandan and Burundian troops and their Somali allies push out from Mogadishu in three main directions. In mid-October 2011, AMISOM's situation changed considerably when Kenya decided to intervene militarily and unilaterally in Somalia, opening up a new front against *al-Shabaab* in the southwest of the country that would subsequently push north up to the port city of Kismayo. The following month, Ethiopian troops returned to central Somalia and they and their Somali allies pushed towards the strategic towns of Beledweyne and Baidoa. The entry of two of Somalia's neighbours into the war also encouraged the Djiboutian president to provide forces to AMISOM. Thus by 2012, AMISOM had doubled its TCCs and was once again working alongside separate Ethiopian forces. These developments, in turn, prompted a revision of the mission's concept of operations, which was endorsed by the AU Peace and Security Council and the UN Security Council in January and February 2012 respectively. From this point on, AMISOM was tasked to operate across the whole of south-central Somalia and it engaged in a series of expansion operations that dislodged *al-Shabaab* forces from many towns. It also prompted the new Ugandan Force Commander General Andrew Gutti to boast 'our mission is unstoppable'.[2] Although this turned out to be incorrect, AMISOM certainly made considerable military progress and attracted more international supporters.

In order to analyse these developments, this chapter proceeds in six parts. It starts by analysing Kenya's decision to launch Operation *Linda Nchi* into Somalia in October 2011 and why it subsequently integrated nearly 4,500

---

[1] *Hand/Takeover Report for Sector One Commander* (September 2012), pp. 3–4.
[2] Pamela Ankunda, 'AMISOM mission unstoppable', *New Vision* (Kampala), 1 June 2012.

troops into AMISOM in 2012. Less than a week after Kenya's intervention, Burundian forces fighting to expand the territory under their control endured an operation that went badly wrong. Tasked with capturing critical terrain in the Dayniile region outside Mogadishu, the BNDF suffered the deadliest day of fighting since AMISOM arrived in Somalia. The second section therefore discusses the major factors behind this bloody battle. The third section examines the return of Ethiopian troops to Somalia from November 2011, once again operating outside of AMISOM. In December 2011, AMISOM got its third TCC. The fourth section therefore explains why Djibouti took this decision yet also took nearly a year to deploy a single battalion of troops to Beledweyne. The penultimate section provides an analysis of AMISOM's new Concept of Operations that was developed in the wake of the Kenyan and Ethiopian interventions. It focuses on some of the new decision-making mechanisms that were developed for the mission as well as some of the problems of command and control issues that were generated as a result of AMISOM's expansion across the whole of south-central Somalia. It also briefly discusses the first ever deployment of Formed Police Units in an AU peace operation. The final section then summarizes some of the main expansion operations conducted by AMISOM, Kenyan, Ethiopian, and TFG forces during 2012 and some of the challenges they raised.

ENTER KENYA

A major shift in Somalia's strategic terrain occurred on 16 October 2011 when Kenyan forces launched Operation *Linda Nchi* (Swahili for 'Protect the Nation').[3] Although Kenya had long been a significant player in Somalia's politics and economy this was the first time it openly deployed troops across the border.[4] This was also the first time the Kenyan Defence Forces (KDF) had engaged in an expeditionary warfare campaign. Until then, Kenya's approach to stabilizing southern Somalia revolved around its Jubaland Initiative— basically, an attempt to dislodge *al-Shabaab* from the Juba and Gedo regions

---

[3] The official KDF history of the operation can be found in KDF, *Operation Linda Nchi: Kenya's Military Experience in Somalia* (Nairobi: Ministry of Defence, 2014). For a better analysis, see David M. Anderson and Jacob McKnight, 'Kenya at War', *African Affairs*, 114:454 (2015), pp. 1–27.

[4] On 29 December 2006, the KDF embarked on Operation *Linda Mpaka* 'to deter any incursion into Kenya by Al Shabaab and Islamic Courts Union'. This transitioned into Operation *Linda Mpaka II* in November 2007 to identify and deter extremist activities and prevent the infiltration of *al-Shabaab* sympathizers into Kenya. On 8 November 2010 Operation *Mamba* was conducted, which aimed to deter piracy along the Kenyan coastline and Exclusive Economic Zone. KDF, *Operation Linda Nchi*, p. 57.

by supporting local clan militias with funding and weapons. Specifically, Kenya recruited some 2,000 Somali Ogadenis in 2009, many of whom were registered refugees and whose illegal recruitment directly out of the Kenyan refugee camps sparked widespread criticism from human rights groups.

The Kenyan decision to intervene and increase fortifications along the Somali border followed the famine-induced mass exodus of refugees streaming into Kenya during 2011 (see Chapter 4) and the kidnapping of several foreign nationals along the same frontier. While the precise timing of Kenya's operation took some states by surprise, the authorities in Nairobi claimed it took place with the concurrence of the TFG and had the support of the Kenyan Parliament. (Initially, the former claim was contradicted by the TFG President, Sheikh Sharif Sheikh Ahmed, who complained to reporters that Kenya had not informed him of the invasion plans and that their transgression 'would not be allowed'.[5]) The operation may have been planned as early as June 2011.[6] Either way, Operation *Linda Nchi* was in line with a strategy that AMISOM's military planners had been working on for the previous year: a new offensive three-pronged push for putting *al-Shabaab* on the back foot. This envisaged coordinating increased AU troops and assets in Mogadishu to clear the city; Ethiopian troops moving in from the centre around Baidoa and Beledweyne; and Kenyan forces moving east towards Kismayo.[7]

One of Kenya's stated aims in launching the operation was to prevent crippling *al-Shabaab* attacks inside Kenya by creating a buffer zone up to the settlement of Afmadow, an *al-Shabaab* stronghold. Kenya's Ambassador to the UN, Macharia Kamau, presented the official explanation for Operation *Linda Nchi* in the following manner:

> Kenya, with the concurrence of the Transitional Federal Government of Somalia, has been compelled to take robust, targeted measures to protect and preserve the integrity of Kenya and the efficacy of the national economy and to secure peace and security in the face of the Al-Shabaab terrorist militia attacks emanating from Somalia. . . . The situation has worsened of late, following the unprecedented escalation of threats to the country's national security. Kenya has suffered dozens of incursions that were repulsed by its military and police forces. Scores of Kenyans have lost their lives over the past 36 months in border towns and communities owing to terrorist actions and incursions from Al-Shabaab militants. The violent and incessant infringement and violation of Kenya's territory, which has been reported over a long period of time by the international media, can no longer go unchecked. In the light of the foregoing, Kenya, in

---

[5] Mike Pflanz, 'Somalia's president questions Kenya's al-Shabaab mission', *The Daily Telegraph*, 25 October 2011.

[6] Kenyan military intelligence document cited in *Report of the Monitoring Group on Somalia and Eritrea pursuant to Security Council resolution 2002 (2011)* (S/2012/544, 13 July 2012), p. 226.

[7] Communications, AMISOM planner, January 2012.

direct consultations and liaison with the Transitional Federal Government in Mogadishu, ... decided to undertake remedial and pre-emptive action.[8]

The KDF later clarified that it entered Somalia in self-defence in accordance with Article 51 of the UN Charter.[9] The UN Monitoring Group, on the other hand, declared Kenyan operations between 16 October 2011 and 2 June 2012 to be a breach of the general arms embargo on Somalia because they were not part of AMISOM and only after 5 January 2012 did AMISOM's area of operations include Sector 2 where the Kenyan forces were operating.[10] The Kenyan government also mentioned that safeguarding the country's tourism industry was an important factor in the decision.[11] In addition, concerns about whether the threat of *al-Shabaab* terrorism would negatively affect the plans for the massive LAPSSET (Lamu Port, South Sudan, Ethiopia Transport) Corridor infrastructure programme were also part of the Kenyan government's equation. Overall, however, the official accounts emphasize that national security concerns drove Kenya's intervention. Notably, Kenya did not initially choose to address the *al-Shabaab* threat by working through AMISOM.

The precise numbers of KDF troops involved in Operation *Linda Nchi* are unclear, but the International Crisis Group estimated that for the first few months there may have been fewer than 2,000.[12] While France said it provided some logistical support for the operation, the United States stated it was not involved but continued to help Kenya enhance its counterterrorism capabilities and remained 'in close contact with them as they go forward with this operation'.[13] Nevertheless, the fact that US drone attacks in Somalia increased at the same time as Kenya's operation led many locals to interpret Kenya's operation as a US project.[14] The impression was confirmed in their eyes when the United States later agreed to provide financial support for the Kenyan troops.[15]

The Kenyan operation unfolded along three primary axes: a push towards Kismayo; from the border crossing at Liboi through the Somali border town of

---

[8] *Letter dated 17 October 2011 from the Permanent Representative of Kenya to the United Nations addressed to the President of the Security Council* (S/2011/646, 18 October 2011).

[9] KDF, *Operation Linda Nchi*, p. 253.   [10] *SEMG Report*, 13 July 2012, p. 229.

[11] *Ibid.*, p. 253.

[12] International Crisis Group, *The Kenyan Military Intervention in Somalia* (ICG Africa Report No. 184, 15 February 2012), p. 5.

[13] Comments by State Department Spokesperson Victoria Nuland at daily news briefing, Washington DC, 1 November 2011.

[14] Harper, *Getting Somalia Wrong?*, p. 179.

[15] In reality, neither the United States nor the United Kingdom received advance notice of the Kenyan intervention, although the basic concept of such an operation had been discussed. Interviews, US officials, Addis Ababa, 30 July 2012; UK official, Nairobi, 6 August 2012. See also Jeffrey Gettleman and Josh Kron, 'Kenya reportedly didn't warn US of Somalia incursion', *New York Times*, 20 October 2011.

Dhobley, toward Afmadow; and from the northern Kenyan border town of Elwaq into Somalia's Gedo region. The advance was reportedly preceded by air strikes and on 20 October Kenyan forces seized the town of Ras Kamboni. After that, Kenyan forces met somewhat stiffer local resistance and for two months the troops became literally stuck in the mud produced by the region's seasonal *deyr* rains (which usually last from October to December). By February 2012, one long-time external observer estimated that the deployment cost approximately $180 million and fifty deaths per month, though Kenya did not provide a public record of its fatalities.[16]

Naturally, *al-Shabaab* was disrupted by the Kenyan operation and in January 2012 its media wing, *al-Kataib* Foundation, released a video where Sheikh Ahmed Iman Ali, *al-Shabaab*'s newly appointed leader for Kenya, urged Kenyans to participate in jihad either locally or in Somalia.[17] The following month, *al-Shabaab* declared its allegiance to *al-Qa'ida*. It is unclear if these events are related.

The Kenyan intervention, like the Jubaland initiative before it, also generated tensions with Ethiopia's government because it empowered the Ogaden clan, which had powerful connections among Nairobi's political elite. The Ethiopian authorities were worried that the intervention would strengthen ex-TFG minister Mohamed Abdi Gandhi who was believed to support the Ogaden National Liberation Front, a long-standing rebel group waging armed conflict against the Ethiopian government.[18] The Kenyan intervention also worried significant swathes of the Somali population who viewed it as an illicit effort to help the Ogaden clan regain its hold on the lucrative port of Kismayo. Long the focus of interclan conflicts, some AMISOM officials nicknamed Kismayo the 'Jerusalem of Somalia' because of all the fights over who should govern it.[19] Assuming the KDF and their allied forces could eject *al-Shabaab* from Kismayo, this was sure to stir up old local rivalries.

In contrast to official accounts which stress defending Kenya's national security and its economy in the northeast, external observers suggest more

---

[16] See David W. Throup, 'Kenya's Intervention in Somalia', CSIS, 16 February 2012, http://csis.org/publication/kenyas-intervention-somalia. In March 2012, General Karangi told Kenya's Defence and Foreign Relations Committee of Parliament that twelve KDF soldiers had been killed thus far. 'AMISOM to pay KDF soldiers Sh84,296 monthly allowance', *Business Daily Africa*, 13 March 2012. The official KDF account of the operation lists only 10 fatalities. KDF, *Operation Linda Nchi*, pp. 282–92. A recent documentary claimed that Kenya had suffered 118 fatalities between October 2011 and December 2015. *The Jubaland Frontier*, NTV Investigates, Kenya, broadcast 13 December 2015.

[17] *SEMG Report*, 13 July 2012, p. 228.

[18] Since the mid-1990s, the Ethiopian government has waged a low-intensity armed conflict against the Ogaden National Liberation Front. In 2012, attempts to initiate a formal peace process and talks between the two parties broke down. Telephone interview, Ethiopian analyst, 16 October 2013.

[19] Interview, AMISOM official, Nairobi, 6 August 2012.

compelling explanations lie with Kenya's desire to be seen as a reliable partner in the US-led 'global war on terrorism', institutional interests within the KDF, and key political elites within the Kenyan government, notably Minister for Internal Security George Saitoti, the Defence Minister Yusuf Haji and several senior security chiefs, who advocated for intervention to advance their own economic and political interests.[20]

The importance of institutional and political rationales for intervening in Somalia become clear when we recall that in 2010 Kenya had embarked on a major modernization plan for its armed forces. Key to this process was persuading the United States in particular to help develop Kenya's ability to 'fight international terrorism and effectively secure our borders'.[21] Among other things, the plan, which resulted in a White Paper on cooperation between Kenya and the US, called for expanding the infantry by an additional brigade; equipping six infantry battalions with APCs; providing body armour and night vision devices; acquiring predator unmanned aerial vehicles (UAVs) and mobile radar stations; creating two special force battalions (one Ranger, one Special Forces); acquiring twelve medium lift helicopters to deploy up to two infantry companies, as well as an eight-strong squadron of attack helicopters; and new long-range patrol craft and upgraded naval communications equipment. Such reforms, the White Paper noted, would be dependent on the national economy improving.[22] The US role in this plan was considerable. Specifically, the United States was to equip six infantry battalions with APCs; equip six infantry units with body armour and night vision devises; provide six medium lift helicopters; two predator UAVs; mine detectors and mobile radars; three long-range patrol boats; and three-dimensional high-resolution coastal radars.[23]

Kenya's earlier unilateral intervention means that its subsequent decision to join AMISOM revolved around the benefits of rehatting some of its forces that were already deployed in Somalia rather than the choice of whether or not to send them there in the first place. This suggests that Kenya's decision to join AMISOM was a distinctly secondary choice, its initial preference being to address the *al-Shabaab* threat unilaterally. More than a month into Operation *Linda Nchi*, on 25 November 2011, IGAD Heads of State called upon Kenya to consider integrating its forces into AMISOM.[24] Kenya's cabinet approved the

---

[20] International Crisis Group, *The Kenyan Military Intervention*, p. 3.

[21] Government of the Republic of Kenya and the United States of America, White Paper on Military Cooperation, *A Multidimensional Approach to Security: Kenya's National Military Strategy for the period 2011–2016* (4 June 2010). Kenya became an ACOTA partner in April 2000 and subsequently hosted ACOTA's AMISOM Force Headquarters training programme at the International Peace Support Training Centre in Nairobi.

[22] *Ibid.*   [23] *Ibid.*

[24] The full communiqué is at https://igad.int/attachments/375_Final_Comminuque_of_the_19th_Extra-ordinary_session_of_the_IGAD_HoS.pdf

decision on 5 December and this was unanimously endorsed by the Kenya Parliament two days later.[25]

The question to consider is thus why Operation *Linda Nchi* was terminated and why some KDF forces were subsequently integrated into AMISOM. This decision appears to have been taken for two principal reasons: to gain the mantle of multilateral legitimacy for continued operations, and to ease the Kenyan government's financial burden.

First, Kenyan authorities concluded that they would gain greater international legitimacy by being part of a multinational force rather than a unilateral mission. In this case, Kenya's integration of the majority of its forces into AMISOM provided Kenya with an exit strategy for its unilateral military operation.[26] As the Chief of Kenya's Defence Forces General Karangi wrote in 2014, the KDF had integrated into AMISOM 'because of Kenya's belief and adherence to multilateralism'.[27] Kenyan authorities would subsequently supplement their forces in AMISOM with additional air and maritime assets that were not put under AMISOM command and control. Integration into AMISOM would also bring the additional benefit that Kenya could influence the mission from within, which was significant given Nairobi's concerns about Ethiopia spreading its influence in Jubaland.[28]

However, financial concerns were arguably paramount. In March 2012, for example, General Karangi had told the Defence and Foreign relations committee of Parliament, 'We entered Somalia with the full cost to taxpayers but with Amisom, Kenyans will no longer be required to pay for our stay in Somalia'.[29] Moreover, he continued that Kenya was also seeking UN reimbursement 'for our naval vessels wear and tear' which were not part of AMISOM. Kenya also secured sixteen slots in the new eighty-five-member AMISOM Force Headquarters in Mogadishu (see p. 145).[30] The KDF's official account of its experiences in Somalia was even more blunt when it concluded, 'The cost of the [unilateral] deployment was enormous' and joining AMISOM was a way 'to secure the operation at no cost to the Kenyan Government from then on'.[31]

These concerns about reducing its financial burden were also evident in the Kenyan Government's attempts to backdate its compensation payments from the African Union. Despite agreeing to join AMISOM in December 2011, Kenya's authorities took until 2 June 2012 to sign the technical memorandum of understanding with the African Union. The delay was caused by arguments over several issues: the precise number of troops in the Kenyan contingent and operational details remained unclear; there were problems with integrating

---

[25] KDF, *Operation Linda Nchi*, p. 260.   [26] As explicitly stated in *ibid.*, pp. 260 and 266.
[27] *Ibid.*, p. viii.   [28] Communication, former AMISOM official, 22 October 2017.
[29] 'AMISOM to pay KDF soldiers', *Business Daily Africa*.   [30] *Ibid.*
[31] KDF, *Operation Linda Nchi*, p. 263.

Kenyan air and maritime assets into AMISOM; there were ugly arguments about who should acquire key senior positions in the new force headquarters; and the issue of payment of troop allowances caused major arguments with the European Union because it was the EU that paid them on behalf of the AU.[32] Article 20.2 of the Kenyan memorandum of understanding stated that for the purposes of reimbursement for personnel and Contingent-Owned Equipment it shall be deemed to have entered into force on 22 February 2012 (the date of UN Security Council Resolution 2036). According to one EU official, the first draft of the Kenyan memorandum of understanding listed the entry into force date as 5 January 2012, the date when the AU PSC endorsed the new AMISOM CONOPS. In light of criticism from the EU, this date was shifted to 22 February 2012 and signed into the Kenya–AU memorandum of understanding without the EU's agreement.[33] The EU position, however, was that its payments of allowances for Kenyan troops should begin on the date that the memorandum of understanding was signed (2 June 2012), prompting a dispute over the provision of payment for the intervening months. In the end, Kenya refused to supply the EU with precise names, numbers, and locations of KDF troops in Somalia, which meant the EU refused to pay reimbursements before 2 June 2012.[34]

In sum, Kenya initially sought to address the security and economic problems raised by *al-Shabaab* without joining AMISOM. To do so, its security partnership with the United States was particularly important. However, after several months of unilateral operations, the Kenyan government sought to acquire greater legitimacy for its continued operations by joining AMISOM, but probably more importantly, to access the financial and technical support that came with it.

AMISOM'S DEADLIEST DAY

Less than one week after Kenyan troops intervened in Somalia, AMISOM suffered its most deadly day thus far. On 20 October 2011, three battalions of BNDF troops supported by a detachment of three Ugandan T-55 battle tanks and two brigades of SNA forces were tasked to seize and occupy the ground north of Mogadishu's suburbs and south of the Dayniile area.[35] This was an

---

[32] Interviews, EU officials, Addis Ababa, 2 and 5 May 2012; AMISOM official, Nairobi, 6 August 2012.

[33] Communication, EU official, 1 September 2012.

[34] Interview, EU official, Addis Ababa, 31 July 2012.

[35] This section draws heavily from *Dayniile After Action Review* (Bancroft, 8 November 2011). ACOTA files. It should be noted that SNA 'brigades' could range considerably in numbers and rarely comprised more than several hundred fighters.

important mission because not only was the area known to contain several hundred *al-Shabaab* fighters but the road from Dayniile via the cigarette factory into central Mogadishu remained a crucial conduit for *al-Shabaab* to smuggle IED components into the city.

The BNDF and Somali Army ultimately secured the key high-ground terrain as intended. During the course of the operation, however, an element of the Burundian force was ambushed by *al-Shabaab* and became cut off from the other forces and suffered a large number of casualties.

To achieve his objective, the Burundian commander split his forces to approach the target area in two columns. Six hours after the operation started, as they were entering the town of Digmale, soldiers from the BNDF 12th Battalion in the western column saw what they believed were friendly Somali troops approaching from their left flank. The approaching troops were moving rapidly towards them, but since they seemed to be wearing SNA uniforms, the BNDF held their fire, assuming they were friendly. Because it was common for SNA uniforms to end up in other hands, TFG soldiers had taken to wearing coloured ribbons to distinguish themselves from other militias and *al-Shabaab* forces. In fact, the advancing column was *al-Shabaab* troops launching a counter-attack from the Afgoye corridor, which leads south into Mogadishu. These *al-Shabaab* forces were able to open fire on the Burundians at close range with heavy machine guns, causing massive damage.

It is also believed that *al-Shabaab* had left some forces to blend in with the local population in this area. This was plausible because the Dayniile region was thought to contain many *al-Shabaab* sympathizers, in part because there had been no significant attempt by the TFG to reach out to the Murasade (a subclan of the Hawiye) who live in the area. These intermingled *al-Shabaab* fighters allowed the BNDF to pass by their positions before striking from the rear. This cut off the BNDF element, which was subsequently defeated.

A Burundian soldier wounded in the battle gave the following account to reporters from his hospital bed in Nairobi: 'It started off easy, too easy', said Cpl. Arcade Arakaza. They met little resistance, with only a few al-Shabaab fighters fleeing in front of them. Civilians they encountered along the route appeared friendly, saying things like, 'Don't worry, Shabab finished'. But the situation changed rapidly and the Burundians found themselves under fire from all sides with assault rifles, belt-fed machine guns, and RPGs. Corporal Arakaza said his unit was attacked by 'women, kids, everyone'.[36]

During and immediately after the battle, *al-Shabaab* collected dozens of dead (and probably wounded) BNDF soldiers and transported them north for subsequent exploitation in propaganda photographs and videos. According to one account, many of the BNDF casualties were captured when *al-Shabaab*

---

[36] Jeffrey Gettleman, 'African Union force makes strides inside Somalia', *New York Times*, 24 November 2011.

hijacked a truck being used to evacuate Burundian wounded. They were subsequently killed and their bodies posed in *al-Shabaab*'s propaganda releases.[37]

While this was going on, the remainder of the BNDF force in the eastern column encountered heavy *al-Shabaab* resistance at Bangala, which resulted in the destruction of one of AMISOM's armoured vehicles. The resistance was overcome and *al-Shabaab* retreated after suffering considerable losses.

Casualty numbers for the battle are unclear. The *New York Times* reported that 'more than 70 [Burundian soldiers were] killed in the span of a few minutes'.[38] Some local reports from Burundi suggested the military had compiled a list naming fifty-one deceased soldiers.[39] An internal AMISOM study suggests the BNDF suffered around sixty fatalities and an additional forty wounded.[40] In what is probably the most reliable estimate, financial records from the European Union suggest that on 20 October 2011 the African Union applied for compensation for thirteen Burundian soldiers killed with an additional fifty-five missing in action, and another sixty-three injured.[41]

As usual, *al-Shabaab* made contradictory claims about the battle. In their video 'The Burundian Bloodbath: Battle of Dayniile' (produced by *al-Kataib*), *al-Shabaab* claimed 101 Burundian soldiers had been killed, but they could collect only seventy-six of the bodies. Other media reported interviews with *al-Shabaab* spokesmen who claimed they had killed approximately 150 Burundian troops in the battle but had only seventy-six bodies in their possession.[42] Subsequent photographs and video released by *al-Shabaab* did not clarify that number of bodies.

The Burundian government did not publicly release the numbers of dead and wounded for the battle, presumably out of a fear of negative reactions back home. It was also alleged that the Burundian authorities threatened to withdraw their contingent from AMISOM if the deaths were officially confirmed.[43] Whatever the true figures, this was the largest loss of AMISOM soldiers in a single day and presented *al-Shabaab* with a propaganda victory of sorts.[44]

The combination of several factors explains the destruction of this BNDF unit. First, it became clear that the Burundian troops were not sufficiently

[37] Interview, Burundian AMISOM official, Nairobi, 6 August 2012.

[38] Gettleman, 'African Union force'.

[39] Onesime Nyungeko, 'Burundi anxious over 51 dead soldiers in Somalia', *Associated Press*, 28 October 2011, https://www.deseretnews.com/article/700192385/Burundi-anxious-over-51-dead-soldiers-in-Somalia.html

[40] *Dayniile After Action Review* (Bancroft, 8 November 2011). p. 8. ACOTA files.

[41] Confidential AU financial records. Copy in author's possession.

[42] 'Al-Shabab claims peacekeepers' killings', *Al Jazeera*, 21 October 2011, http://www.aljazeera.com/news/africa/2011/10/20111102141422988953.html

[43] Clarke, UNSOA study, p. 132.

[44] This would be surpassed by the *al-Shabaab* attack on the Kenyan base at El Adde in January 2016, discussed in Chapter 7.

aware of their surroundings and the locations of their allied forces. This was partly due to language differences, which rendered accurate communication difficult between some BNDF and Somalis and some of the Ugandan troops. This seemed to have exacerbated the problems at Dayniile inasmuch as the trapped BNDF could not talk clearly to the SNA forces and UPDF.[45] The BNDF also struggled to make quick and decisive decisions following the loss of several critical commanders.

Second, *al-Shabaab* probably employed deception to good effect, assuming they used SNA uniforms deliberately to sow confusion. *Al-Shabaab* also had excellent knowledge of the terrain and blended a number of fighters into the local population, which enabled them to launch a surprise attack on the BNDF forces from the rear, cutting them off.

A third problem alleged by some observers suggested the BNDF made basic tactical errors, such as dismounting from their vehicles, ignoring their flanking procedures by relying on the SNA and not covering their own flanks, and only calling for help after it was too late.[46] On the latter point, a senior Ugandan officer claimed that the UPDF had spoken with the Burundian commander under attack and were initially advised that his contingent did not require additional help.[47] This problem was exacerbated by the fact that once the BNDF called for help, some officers miscommunicated their exact where-abouts, which made reinforcement and support difficult.

A fourth factor concerned the lack of accurate real-time intelligence about the area the Burundians were moving into. The operational plans were based on satellite imagery of the area rather than real-time observation because AMISOM had no air assets to conduct such reconnaissance and the mission's human intelligence capabilities were poor. Presumably, AMISOM's Raven drones were not deployed for this operation. This issue may also have been exacerbated by the visit of the Burundian Minister of Defence to the forward areas during the planning period immediately before the operation. The subsequent delay may have left the operation without the most up-to-date intelligence of *al-Shabaab* positions.

Finally, although not a decisive factor, it is worth noting the persistently poor state of the BNDF's vehicles. Since its initial deployment in late 2007, Burundi's contingent had been largely dependent on bilateral US assistance for its equipment and had received some additional vehicles from the UPDF. Nevertheless, by the time of this battle many of the vehicles used by the Burundians were out of service: fifteen out of thirty-nine Casspirs, all six of

[45] Interview, UK military official, Kampala, 13 August 2012.
[46] Interview, UNOAU official, Addis Ababa, 3 August 2012; communication, senior former AMISOM official, 24 February 2015.
[47] Interview, senior AMISOM official, Mogadishu, 2 January 2013.

their Mamba armoured vehicles, seven of their eleven ambulances, and four of their eleven water trucks.[48]

ETHIOPIA RETURNS

At their summit on 25 November 2011 in response to Kenya's Operation *Linda Nchi*, IGAD Heads of State called upon Ethiopia 'to support the Kenya-TFG and AMISOM operation' against *al-Shabaab*.[49] Ethiopian troops thus returned to Somali territory in the wake of Kenya's unilateral campaign. According to the UN Monitoring Group, this was also a violation of the general UN arms embargo on Somalia.[50] Regardless, Ethiopia's top general, Samora Yunis, was reported to have said that Operation *Linda Nchi* opened up a possibility of Ethiopia acting decisively against *al-Shabaab* in Somalia, and hence it was an opportunity not to be missed.[51]

For the most part, the ENDF's initial operations went smoothly. With some support from *Ahlu Sunna Wal Jamaa* and Shabelle Valley State fighters, Ethiopian troops captured the strategic town of Beledweyne in December 2011 and Baidoa, the capital of southwest region, in February 2012. In Baidoa, *al-Shabaab* ceded without a fight. With a population of about 70,000, Baidoa was important as a trading hub for livestock (camel, cattle, sheep, goats) and for Somalia's sorghum belt. *Al-Shabaab* occupied Baidoa in January 2009 after a siege that started in July 2008. The defeated subclans then fled to Ethiopia where they trained for three years. When the ENDF recaptured the town, they handed political control to Abdifatah Mohamed Ibrahim 'Geesey'—the Governor of Bay region and an Ethiopian ally.[52]

It appears that most of the ENDF's operations went well, in part because *al-Shabaab* forces rarely chose to stand and fight but instead withdrew from towns before ENDF, TFG, and allied troops arrived. Despite controlling the major towns, however, the ENDF and allied forces struggled to secure the routes between them, which afforded *al-Shabaab* an opportunity to frequently attack ENDF and TFG supply routes.[53] Less frequently, *al-Shabaab*

---

[48] Clarke, UNSOA study, p. 91.

[49] At https://igad.int/attachments/375_Final_Comminuque_of_the_19th_Extra-ordinary_session_of_the_IGAD_HoS.pdf

[50] *SEMG Report*, 13 July 2012, pp. 229, 231.

[51] Interviews, Ethiopian official, Addis Ababa, 31 July 2012; UN official, Addis Ababa, 3 August 2012.

[52] *Baidoa Situational Awareness Brief* (AUUNIST Briefing Note 003, 2012).

[53] *Report of the Chairperson of the Commission pursuant to paragraph 21 of United Nations Security Council resolution 2036 (2012) on United Nations support to the African Union Mission in Somalia* (S/2012/176, 20 March 2012), §5.

also attacked the larger towns themselves. In one major incident on 9 March 2012, a landmine was reported to have killed twelve ENDF soldiers traveling in a convoy in Beledweyne.[54]

By opening up another front against *al-Shabaab*, the ENDF operations helped facilitate AMISOM's expansion beyond Mogadishu. Moreover, Ethiopia's announcement that it was going to take on *al-Shabaab* sent a helpful message of solidarity for AMISOM. Although Ethiopia did not release official figures, educated estimates suggested that the ENDF maintained about 4,000 troops in Somalia, including elite Agazi commandos.[55] Ethiopia's strategic goal seems to have been the stabilization of the territory that would become AMISOM Sectors 3 and 4 (see p. 143 and Figure I.3). It achieved this in tandem with AMISOM forces that later deployed to Baidoa and Beledweyne and, from December 2012, as part of the IGAD Grand Stabilization Plan for south-central Somalia.

But while the ENDF forces were clearly effective militarily, they were a potentially highly toxic political force for many Somalis. Indeed, the ENDF occupation of Baidoa and Mogadishu between 2006 and 2009 had been hugely unpopular with many local Somalis and spurred the rise of *al-Shabaab*. Yet the ENDF's re-occupation of Baidoa in late February 2012 and their removal of *al-Shabaab* was tolerated if not intensely welcomed by most locals. *Al-Shabaab* had become unpopular for banning external humanitarian assistance and apparently the locals were unconcerned about any prospects of Ethiopian neo-imperialism since ENDF troops had, as one local put it, 'been in Baidoa many times before'.[56] As one UN official subsequently observed, this time around, the ENDF managed to operate in Baidoa without disrupting the local flow of business and people. In contrast to the AMISOM contingents that would follow them there, the ENDF set up a much looser system without secure perimeters and moved around in pick-up trucks rather than AMISOM's favoured armoured vehicles. They also patrolled regularly on foot, including at night. On the other hand, the Ethiopians would ruthlessly deal with (i.e. arrest or shoot) anyone they suspected of being *al-Shabaab*.[57] After complaining at the length of time it took sufficient numbers of AMISOM troops to deploy to Baidoa, the ENDF forces withdrew from the town in July 2013.[58]

---

[54] 'Landmine explosion kills 12 Ethiopian soldiers in Beledweyne town', *Keydmedia*, 10 March 2012, http://www.keydmedia.net/en/news/article/landmine_explosion_kills_12_ethiopian_soldiers_in_beledweyne_town/

[55] Interview, EU official, Addis Ababa, 2 May 2012.

[56] Laura Heaton, 'Somalia: On Scene in Baidoa after Ethiopia's Rout of Al-Shabab', *Newsweek*, 12 March 2012, http://www.newsweek.com/somalia-scene-baidoa-after-ethiopias-rout-al-shabab-63659

[57] Interview, UN official, Nairobi, 7 August 2012.

[58] See Aaron Maasho, 'Ethiopian troops quit Somali city, but no full withdrawal planned', *Reuters*, 22 July 2013; S/2013/521, 3 September 2013, §12.

The net result was that although Ethiopian troops did not integrate into AMISOM, their return to Somalia facilitated the deployment of AU troops to towns like Baidoa and Beledweyne which would have been unthinkable to AMISOM commanders whose sights were still focused on Mogadishu's outskirts. While Ugandan and Burundian troops would subsequently join the ENDF in Baidoa, it was to Djibouti that the AU looked to become AMISOM's third TCC and deploy into Beledweyne and its surrounding areas.

ENTER DJIBOUTI

In early 2010, Djibouti's President Ismail Guelleh promised to contribute troops to AMISOM. In contrast, several of his senior military and political leaders did not like the idea of such a comparatively large deployment while the *Forces Armées de Djiboutiennes* (FAD) was still recovering from its 2008 border conflict with Eritrea.[59] The generals were overruled. The first Djiboutian troops arrived in Mogadishu in December 2011 when a company of FAD soldiers were flown in on an aircraft chartered by the UNSOA. However, they did not stay long and Djibouti's deployment turned into a protracted fiasco. The fiasco revealed that while President Guelleh wanted to join AMISOM to enhance his regime's political relationships with its key regional partners and external donors, Djibouti's military were motivated almost entirely by gaining new funds, equipment, infrastructure, and training.

After the initial FAD deployment in December 2011, it was not until July 2012 that Djibouti signed a memorandum of understanding with the AU to join AMISOM and the FAD's Battalion Hiil One did not fully deploy to AMISOM until November 2012.[60] When the initial company of FAD troops arrived in Mogadishu, its commander refused to deploy outside the airport to the designated area of operations (near Beledweyne in AMISOM Sector 4) and demanded that UNSOA build them new barracks there.[61] UNSOA refused and the FAD soldiers remained in the international airport compound until they and their equipment were sent back to Djibouti by sea. The Djiboutian government then sent UNSOA a bill for 'wear and tear' on their equipment during the process.[62] The protracted arguments with the AU over the memorandum of understanding for deployment into AMISOM took so long that

---

[59] Interviews, Western diplomat, Addis Ababa, 30 April 2012; US official, Djibouti, 22 November 2014.

[60] Battalion Hiil One, or *Hiil Walaal* as it was also known, is Somali for a 'helpful brother'. In comparison, the subsequent deployments of Battalions Hiil Two and Three went more smoothly.

[61] Interview, UNSOA official, Nairobi, 12 August 2012.

[62] Interview, UNSOA official, Nairobi, 13 December 2012.

Battalion Hiil One was required to redo its pre-deployment training programme. Moreover, UNSOA was forced to fly the battalion's troops into AMISOM Sector 4 in batches of roughly 40 per day in Dash 8 planes because they refused to be bussed to their sector through Ethiopia.[63] Ten tanks loaned from Ethiopia, ten APCs from the United Kingdom and various troop transports and cargo trucks arrived in Beledweyne by ground convoy in late September 2012.[64] Even after Battalion Hiil One's initial deployment, the FAD regularly argued with UNSOA over back payments for equipment and other costs. Overall, it cost UNSOA over $3 million to get the initial forty FAD troops to Beledweyne nearly a year later than planned.[65]

The FAD's official rationales for deploying to AMISOM revolved around enhancing their reputation by contributing to the 'global war on terrorism' and helping their Somali brothers.[66] This was partly correct: Djibouti became an ACOTA partner in November 2009 and several Western states thought it would be helpful to have a Muslim TCC join AMISOM. Moreover, the local knowledge and linguistic skills of some FAD soldiers would be useful on the ground (Djibouti's two main ethnic groups are the Afar, of Ethiopian origin, and Issa, of Somali origin).[67] Reflective of these connections, some local Somalis would affectionately refer to Djiboutian troops as '*Hiil Walaal*' (helpful brother).[68] But the most important driver was securing funds to modernize the armed forces.

The importance attached to these institutional and economic concerns were clearly paramount for Djibouti's military leaders. By early 2010, the FAD requested the United States provide pre-deployment training for a 663-strong battalion; construct a national peacekeeping training centre; supply individual soldier equipment for the battalion; and deploy equipment to be given to that battalion upon its arrival in Mogadishu.[69] The FAD said it would be ready to train by September 2010 and deploy to Somalia in January 2011. This did not happen.

In April 2010, the FAD gave the United States a draft memorandum of understanding but did not sign it. Nevertheless, ACOTA delivered training, constructed the requested peacekeeping training facility, and provided individual and deployment equipment. At this point, Djibouti said its strategic

---

[63] Interview, UNSOA official, Mogadishu, 3 January 2013.

[64] Communication, US official, Djibouti, 28 September 2015.

[65] Interview, UNSOA official, Mogadishu, 3 January 2013.

[66] Interview, FAD officer in AMISOM, Mogadishu, 4 January 2013.

[67] On the negative side, some non-Hawiye Somalis tended to see the Djibouti forces as basically part of the Hawiye clan lineage and were therefore critical of their activities. Telephone interview, Somali analyst, 25 October 2013.

[68] *Citizens' Perception of Peace and Stabilization Initiatives in Somalia* (Ipsos, Draft Summary Report, 2015), p. 11.

[69] ACOTA Partner Summary: Djibouti, 8 May 2011. ACOTA files.

objectives were to deploy a battalion in AMISOM by January 2011 and achieve full self-sufficiency in peacekeeping training by 2014. In May 2010, the FAD submitted its first equipment list to the United States valued at $58 million. In July, the United States countered with a $13.8 million equipment list (modelled after similar equipment provided to the Ugandan and Burundian AMISOM battalions). No agreement was reached and in January 2011 the FAD offered to deploy a company rather than a battalion but insisted on the company receiving the $13.8 million equipment list items offered by the United States for the original battalion. Meanwhile, the FAD sent three reconnaissance missions to Mogadishu, negotiating with various donors and the African Union. By April 2011, the FAD had still not committed in writing to deploying in AMISOM.[70] Moreover, when ACOTA started providing the FAD with pre-deployment training between September 2010 and March 2011, never more than 300 trainees turned up. Combined with the cost of building a new peacekeeper training camp at Ali Ouney (20 km south of Djibouti City) in FY2010, ACOTA invested $6.3 million in Djibouti.[71] Other support provided by the United States included over one hundred vehicles, English language lab and training, machine guns, and Harris radios.

As if to further emphasize the importance of external security assistance, during 2014, President Guelleh lobbied the AU to expand the FAD's deployment in AMISOM from one to two battalions.[72] AMISOM TCCs agreed in July 2014 and another 900 FAD arrived in Somalia in March 2015, having received a reimbursement of roughly US$1 million from UNSOA.

The FAD also suffered from rather significant inhibitors before its deployment into AMISOM. There were certainly concerns about insecurity, with the FAD arguing their forces would be best suited to training and helping to reorganize the Somali security forces rather than fighting *al-Shabaab* under AMISOM command.[73] As one Ugandan analyst noted, 'Within AMISOM, it was no secret that the Djibouti contingent continued to use every excuse to stay in Mogadishu, at one time offering the argument that it spoke the same language as the Somali people and was robust enough to provide better protection for the presidency at Villa Somalia'.[74]

---

[70] '1-9 April 2011 East Africa trip report'. ACOTA files.

[71] ACOTA Partner Summary: Djibouti, 8 May 2011. ACOTA files. The FAD subsequently removed all tents and equipment from Camp Ali Ouney to Camp Miriam and established their peacekeeping centre in Arta.

[72] Communication, US official, Djibouti, 28 September 2015. This decision may also have been partly related to the difficult situation the FAD experienced in Bulo Burto during late 2013 and early 2014 when approximately half its forces in Somalia were besieged by *al-Shabaab* and required UNSOA to provide an air bridge to sustain them. Communication, former AMISOM official, 22 October 2017.

[73] '1-9 April 2011 East Africa trip report'. ACOTA files.

[74] Oloya, *Black Hawks Rising*, p. 194.

Despite this reluctance to operate under AMISOM command, the FAD understood they must be part of AMISOM in order to receive logistics support from UNSOA and maintain US assistance. This was crucial to overcome the FAD's biggest inhibitor: its lack of capabilities. Part of the initial resistance to the deployment came from senior commanders who were unable to plan such a major deployment and did not want to disrupt their existing force structure. Moreover, in order to deploy an 850-strong battalion to AMISOM, the FAD had to recruit an additional 1,000 troops, increasing the army's total size from about 5,000 to about 6,000, i.e., the FAD had to expand by about 15 per cent in order to deploy a single battalion abroad.[75] Because it was such a large commitment, Djibouti was offered the Chief of Staff post for AMISOM, which they failed to fill because they fielded such a poor candidate.[76]

In sum, Djibouti's decision to join AMISOM can be summarized as stemming from a political judgement by the President to enhance his key regional and donor relationships. Initially, some senior FAD officers resisted this decision. But once it became inevitable, their principal concern was to extract as much security assistance as possible in return for joining AMISOM.

AMISOM EXPANDS

The arrival of soldiers from Somalia's three neighbouring states in late 2011 (Djibouti, Ethiopia, and Kenya) and AMISOM's continued push beyond Mogadishu set the stage for a major revision of the mission's strategic and military concept of operations (CONOPS). This took place in late 2011 and early 2012 and involved representatives from the AU, UN, IGAD, the TFG, Uganda, Burundi, Ethiopia, Kenya, the United States and the United Kingdom. The new strategic concept of operations adopted a new force posture based around four land sectors and involving nearly 18,000 troops.[77]

AMISOM Sector 1 centred on Mogadishu and was covered by approximately 9,500 troops from Ugandan and Burundi. Sector 2 in southwest Somalia involved some 4,400 troops from the rehatted Kenyan force.[78] It

---

[75] Interview, US official, Djibouti, 22 November 2014.   [76] *Ibid.*

[77] At one stage the AU had contemplated a force of 35,500 troops to implement the new military strategy but this was rejected for a variety of political, financial and operational reasons. See *Report of the Chairperson of the Commission on the Joint AU-UN Benchmarking Exercise and the Review of AMISOM* (PSC/PR/2.(CCCXCIX), 10 October 2013), §5.

[78] The AU revealed that the Kenyan contribution was 4,460 personnel as well as providing Basic and Level-1 care for each battalion deployed and a Level-2 hospital to the mission. *Third Progress Report of the Chairperson of the Commission of the African Union on the Implementation of the Mandate of the AU Mission in Somalia (AMISOM), in Pursuance of Paragraph 21 of the United Nations Security Council Resolution 2036 (2012)* (S/2012/666, 24 August 2012), §16. Hereafter, *AU Third Progress Report* (2012).

covered such key towns as Afmadow, Jilib, Bualle, and Kismayo. In April 2013, a battalion from Sierra Leone deployed, replacing one of the Kenyan battalions (see Chapter 6). Sector 3 centred on the town of Baidoa and would comprise some 2,500 Ugandan and Burundian troops, supported by Ethiopian forces operating outside but in support of AMISOM. Sector 4 focused on the town of Beledweyne northeast of Mogadishu and would contain roughly 1,000 Djiboutian soldiers, again supported by non-AMISOM Ethiopian forces. AMISOM's maritime component was supposed to conduct limited maritime security operations and support land operations such as interdicting *al-Shabaab* logistic resupply into Kismayo, Haradhere, Marka, and Barawe, and protecting sea lines of communication.[79] In practice, AMISOM's handful of small boats was unable to meet such grand expectations.

The new CONOPS itself emerged when in the wake of the Kenyan and Ethiopian operations, Susana Malcorra, UN Under-Secretary-General for Field Support, asked the UNOAU to write a concept note about AMISOM as a precursor to thinking about a new CONOPS for the mission. During November 2011, UNOAU and AU staff laid the groundwork for a joint Technical Assessment Mission.[80] This was conducted between 5 and 17 December 2011 and involved representatives from the TFG, IGAD, Burundi, Uganda, Ethiopia, Kenya, and Djibouti. UNSOA, UNPOS, the United States and United Kingdom sat in on drafting sessions. The Assessment Mission concluded that 'for AMISOM to be able to conduct concurrent offensive operations throughout south-central Somalia, up to 35,000 troop and substantial resources would be required'.[81] In practice, this would be achieved by AMISOM fielding roughly half this number, and Somali forces the other half. This was rather problematic given that the AU had concluded that 'none' of the existing TFG security forces 'have the ability to support and sustain themselves logistically'.[82] Nevertheless, the UN Secretary-General recommended an increase of AMISOM's strength to 17,731 uniformed personnel, including 260 police officers and two formed police units (FPUs) of 140 personnel each.[83] Politically, the joint Assessment Mission was heralded as 'an exemplary model of collaboration between the two organizations under the leadership of the African Union'.[84]

The new CONOPS for an expanded AMISOM was then officially put to and endorsed by the AU's Peace and Security Council and the UN Security

---

[79] See PSC/PR/COMM.(CCCII), 2 December 2011. This communique also called for an air-exclusion zone to help cut off arms supplies to *al-Shabaab*.

[80] Interview, UNOAU official, Addis Ababa, 9 May 2012.

[81] *Special report of the Secretary-General on Somalia* (S/2012/74, 31 January 2012), §15.

[82] *Military Strategic Concept of Operations for AMISOM* (AU internal document, 14 February 2012), §15. Hereafter, *Military CONOPS* (2012).

[83] *Special report of the Secretary-General on Somalia* (31 January 2012), §18.

[84] *Ibid.*, §41.

Council on 5 January and 22 February 2012 respectively.[85] Specifically, UN Security Council resolution 2036 expanded AMISOM's mandate to

> include establishing a presence in the four sectors set out in the AMISOM strategic Concept of 5 January, and...to take all necessary measures as appropriate in those sectors in coordination with the Somali security forces to reduce the threat posed by Al Shabaab and other armed opposition groups in order to establish conditions for effective and legitimate governance across Somalia.[86]

AMISOM's military strategic objectives were finalized the following month as: (a) deplete military capabilities of armed opposition groups; (b) provide security to the Transitional Federal Institutions; (c) secure and protect AMISOM forces and other international actors; and (d) enhance the capacity and organization of Somali forces.[87] The desired end states were defined as follows:

> Strategic End State. The envisaged end state would be a significantly depleted military capacity of Al Shabaab and pirates and the threats they pose to Somalia and the sub-region, enhanced capacity and cohesion of the TFG military forces and police, expanded TFG authority, and a secure environment that allows the implementation of the End of Transition Roadmap as well as the gradual handover of responsibility to TFG Forces and take Somalia into the post-conflict peace building phase.
>
> Military End State. Somali National Forces take responsibility for security.[88]

With the new AMISOM CONOPS came two new decision-making mechanisms: the Military Operations Coordination Committee (MOCC) and Joint Coordination Mechanism (JCM). The MOCC comprised regional Chiefs of Defence under an AU chair and was tasked with providing strategic advice to the AU Commission to enable it to fully assume the management of AMISOM and to enhance coordination with the TFG and TCCs and other interested countries. The MOCC held its first meeting on 9 March 2012 and twenty-three more by September 2017. Over that time, it gradually came to usurp some of the strategic roles of the AMISOM Force Headquarters.

The JCM was designed as a consultative structure chaired by the AU Commissioner for Peace and Security and comprising regional ministers. It was mandated to undertake the following tasks: to advise the Commission on strategic and political issues regarding the deployment and operations of AMISOM; to review progress made on the implementation of the military effort in Somalia, with a view to making recommendations and providing advice on how best to enhance the effectiveness of the campaign and bring it to a successful end; to provide a forum for regular consultation and dialogue

---

[85] PSC/PR/COMM.(CCCVI), 5 January 2012 and S/RES/2036, 22 February 2012.
[86] S/RES/2036, 22 February 2012, §1.   [87] *Military CONOPS* (2012), §8.
[88] *Ibid.*, §10.

among the TCCs, other interested countries, and the Commission, among others. The JCM held its first meeting in Addis Ababa on 12 April 2012.

The two new bureaucratic mechanisms undoubtedly focused more high-level diplomatic attention on the details of AMISOM's activities. But they also generated some additional issues and it was not always clear that the extra bureaucratic layers produced more effective operations in the field. For one thing, they were established outside of the regular AU coordination structures for its peace operations. This was primarily because the mission's main TCCs wanted to secure more influence than the AU Commission over the strategic management of AMISOM. Arguably the main immediate issue arose from the fact that the MOCC's mandate was to provide advice, but it often went well beyond this to take decisions. In some respects this highlighted the weakness of the AU Commission and the Force Headquarters. It also prompted the Commission to try and establish a mission headquarters housing the SRCC and AMISOM's civilian staff in Mogadishu in order to be closer to the action.[89] On the other hand, the MOCC amplified the influence of some states. The key trio was Uganda, Ethiopia, and Kenya. Burundi was less influential and Djibouti and later Sierra Leone were initially not even invited.[90]

The other major innovation was the development and establishment of a new AMISOM force headquarters in Mogadishu, which was allocated eighty-five staff posts. When AMISOM involved just two TCCs operating in one city there was arguably no need for such a multinational force headquarters. But as the mission's scope expanded and the number of TCCs increased it made more sense. The process began in earnest in mid-August 2011 when the AU signed a memorandum of understanding with the Eastern Africa Standby Force's (EASF) command element based in Addis Ababa. Over the next few months, the EASF command finalized plans to deploy fourteen staff officers and fifty-seven trainers. At the time, this represented the first occasion when official elements of the African Standby Force deployed operationally. By early August 2012, fifty-two of the eighty-five force headquarters posts were deployed.[91] But it continued to suffer from staff shortages. Nor was there any official presence of the Somali security forces within the AMISOM force headquarters. One foreign military adviser stationed with the mission also noted a degree of suspicion of other nationalities and national cliques within the force headquarters that inhibited operational focus and synchronicity.[92]

---

[89] Communication, former AMISOM official, 22 October 2017.

[90] Interview, UNOAU official, Addis Ababa, 3 August 2012.

[91] *AU Third Progress Report* (2012), §23. Posts in the new force headquarters went to a range of African states beyond AMISOM's TCCs, in part to give as many countries as possible direct experience of being in that environment and to build AU capacity for subsequent missions.

[92] Interview, UK military adviser, Mogadishu, 4 January 2013 and communication 9 September 2014.

The new force headquarters also illuminated some other problems related to AMISOM's command and control structures.

Officially, AMISOM's operational authority flowed from the Chairperson of the AU Commission, to the Commissioner for Peace and Security, to the SRCC as Head of Mission. The AMISOM Force Commander was granted Operational Control of all AMISOM forces (as per AU command and control guidelines). He had the flexibility to tactically move forces between the mission's sectors to focus combat power as the operational environment changes. The Sector Commanders were granted tactical command of the forces assigned to them and retained operational command of their contingent forces. Sector Commands run by one country were granted operational command over the forces in their sector.

Naturally, coordination and synchronization challenges are present in all multinational forces, and as noted previously, AMISOM's were sometimes compounded by initial language and communications problems between the Ugandan and Burundian contingents. Between March 2007 and late 2011, AMISOM managed its activities through a Mission Headquarters in Nairobi and a small force headquarters in Mogadishu that was dominated by the UPDF. This had the negative effect of encouraging international interlocutors to bypass the SRCC, AMISOM's official head of mission, in Nairobi in favour of engaging the Force Commander in Mogadishu.[93] But as AMISOM extended across south-central Somalia this system became unsustainable.

In January 2012, regional defence ministers at the mission's TCC summit agreed on a new set of arrangements, raising the Force Commander to the rank of Lieutenant General and creating sector commands. This more extended configuration meant that secure and effective communications were vital if AMISOM was to be commanded centrally. Unfortunately, gaps in communication and information systems architecture sometimes prevented effective communication between Force and Sector headquarters and commanders on the ground (at battalion level and below). In subsequent years, there would even be examples of company level communication taking place using runners to pass information back and forth because they had no means of electronic communications![94] AMISOM's lack of a dedicated signal unit also undermined the mission's effectiveness in this regard. So too did TCC infantry units that did not always contain enough signalmen to staff existing communications nets. As late as 2015, numerous AMISOM units still lacked HF radios, which impeded command, control, and coordination at the tactical and operational levels.

---

[93] See, for example, Lamii Kromah, 'The Role of AMISOM's Civilian Component', *Conflict Trends*, Issue 2 (2010), p. 27.

[94] Interview, senior AMISOM official, Nairobi, 9 April 2015.

But the problems created by these circumstances were not purely technical. Political incentives frequently left some TCCs reluctant to follow orders from the Force Commander, making it impossible for AMISOM to establish a unified chain of command. As noted in this book's Introduction, one senior AMISOM commander summarized the situation by saying that his Force Headquarters had command but not control over AMISOM forces and therefore the best that could be achieved was coordination of the TCC operations.[95] By September 2015, the situation was so bad that the Chairperson of the AU Commission felt the need to emphasize that the MOCC should 'provide guidance to their respective sector commanders on the importance of complying with the AMISOM command and control'.[96] Although not the only guilty party, Kenyan troops in Sector 2 at times exemplified these problems. Not only was it Kenya that initially proposed carving AMISOM into distinct sectors—thereby 'creating areas of responsibility for each TCC'[97]—but Kenyan forces in Sector 2 were regularly and widely criticized for allegedly pursuing partisan agendas related to illicit commerce and support for particular politicians in Jubaland that caused tensions with both AMISOM Force Headquarters and the FGS.[98]

Finally, AMISOM's expansion across south-central Somalia created a new set of challenges related to coordinating activities across the mission's four sectors. Problems of coordination were exacerbated by the mission's inability to maintain a unified system of command and control but also by various technical challenges, notably problems of communications and language barriers. In retrospect, AMISOM's inability to ensure effective cooperation and conduct cross-sector operations provided *al-Shabaab* with sanctuaries along the mission's sector boundaries. *Al-Shabaab* was aware of AMISOM sector boundaries and sought to operate in the gaps between AU forces. There were several reasons for the lack of coordination. The first was the mission's inability to maintain a unified system of command and control, identified above. This put a premium on all sector headquarters having liaison officers from neighbouring sectors. But a second set of challenges were more technical, notably problems of communications and language barriers, which ultimately impeded operational effectiveness. Liaison officers would thus

---

[95] *Ibid.*   [96] AU doc. PSC/PR/2(DXLIV), 18 September 2015, §27.

[97] Indeed, the KDF had boasted about this in its official account of its Somalia campaign. KDF, *Operation Linda Nchi*, p. 265.

[98] See, for example, several reports of the UN's Somalia-Eritrea Monitoring Group and *Black and White: Kenya's Criminal Racket in Somalia* (Nairobi: Journalists for Justice, November 2012). In mid-2013, the FGS wrote a letter to the AU Commissioner for Peace and Security, via SRCC Annadif, protesting against Kenyan AMISOM troops, especially the Kenyan Sector 2 Commander Brigadier Kengere, for not obeying orders received from AMISOM Central Command in Mogadishu. The problem was resolved later in the year. *AMISOM Annual Report 2013* (AU internal document, 2013), §5.

often need to be bilingual, since there was no single common language across all AMISOM sectors. This, in turn, elevated the importance of AMISOM having a sufficient supply of reliable translators, both for work within AMISOM and for AMISOM's engagement with Somalis (see Chapter 12). However, by August 2012, AMISOM was still without a single civil affairs officer who could speak Somali.[99]

The challenges to AMISOM exercising a unified chain of command were real and significant. But they related principally to AMISOM's military component. The last key innovation in the 2012 CONOPS discussed here is the authorization of two Formed Police Units (FPUs).[100] It was only after *al-Shabaab* forces were pushed out of Mogadishu in August 2011, that AMISOM was able to deploy more police officers.[101] It took another year, but in early August 2012 an FPU from Uganda deployed to Mogadishu, and in mid-September it was joined by another FPU from Nigeria. These were the first ever FPUs deployed in an AU-led peace operation and hence required some revision from the standard UN model.[102] To help secure the presidential elections in late 2016 a platoon of thirty officers from each FPU was deployed to Kismayo and Baidoa.

AMISOM's FPUs served several purposes. First, they were intended to act as a bridge through which the Somali Police Force could gradually transition from a militarized policing strategy to civilianized policing focused on maintaining law, security, and good public order in Mogadishu. The FPUs could not arrest Somalis directly. Instead, they undertook guard duties, public order duties, and some patrolling in tandem with Somali police, who could arrest individuals.[103] Second, they served as a new and systematic point of cooperation and mentoring between AMISOM and the Somali police. Prior to this, for instance, individual AU police officers had to rely on military transport, which meant they were slow to move because they were never considered a top priority.[104] Third, the FPUs helped provide force protection to the mission's IPOs, which enabled the latter to more frequently interact with their local counterparts. This had previously been done by AMISOM's military

---

[99] Interview, UN official, Nairobi, 7 August 2012.

[100] It is not clear why the UN and AU authorized just two FPUs. It appears that no security assessment was undertaken in Mogadishu to determine how many FPUs were required to stabilize the city.

[101] Between January and August 2011, for instance, about 90 per cent of AMISOM's expenditure had been on its military component while just under 2 per cent was spent on its police. *AMISOM Financial Status: For Year 2011 and Cash Requirement for 2012* (AU internal document, 7 September 2011).

[102] For a more detailed discussion see Cedric de Coning, Meressa K. Dessu, and Ingvild Magnæs Gjelsvik, *The Role of Police in the African Union Mission in Somalia* (Oslo: Training for Peace, 2014).

[103] Interview, senior Ugandan police officer, Kampala, 15 August 2012.

[104] Interview, senior Somali police official, Mogadishu, 2 January 2013.

component, but this had raised problems, including related to the availability of military assets.[105] Finally, the FPUs were also intended to release and ease pressure off AMISOM's military to enable them to conduct military tasks and deploy beyond Mogadishu. AMISOM's FPUs were also intended to provide operational support to the mission's individual police officers.

As befits these tasks, the personnel for the Ugandan FPU were drawn from the Ugandan Field Force Unit, special police officers who had undergone both basic police and military training. Also included were a few members of Uganda's elite counterterrorism police. Although FPUs are usually designed to be self-sustaining, in reality AMISOM's FPUs required logistics and sustainment support. Ironically, this Ugandan FPU was originally assembled to deploy to UNAMID and received all the necessary equipment from the Canadian government. However, before it deployed to Darfur, the commander was given orders to go to Mogadishu instead.[106] After checking with the Canadian government, the FPU deployed to AMISOM.

EXPANSION OPERATIONS 2012

With its new concept of operations and suite of decision-making mechanisms, AMISOM spent the next nine months expanding its area of operations in addition to trying to stabilize Mogadishu. In Mogadishu, AMISOM spent much of 2012 carrying out 'consolidation operations'. These involved acquiring intelligence, usually gathered by local informants, about *al-Shabaab*'s remaining covert operatives and cells in the city and striking against them, usually at night.[107] The rest of the mission's effort went on capturing the remaining suburbs on the outskirts of the city. At this stage, some AMISOM officials even called for the mission to deploy troops to Puntland to prevent retreating *al-Shabaab* fighters establishing new bases in the Galgala Mountains.[108] This was not authorized and AMISOM's focus remained in its four existing land sectors.

Relatively little time was spent dealing with *al-Shabaab* defectors despite the fact that by February 2012 the Somali National Security Agency was receiving on average three to four defectors per day.[109] Defectors were supposed to be registered and placed on parole and then closely monitored. But there were no

---

[105] Communication, UN official, 31 July 2017.

[106] Interview, senior Ugandan police officer, Kampala, 15 August 2012.

[107] Interview, UPDF officer, Mogadishu, 5 January 2013.

[108] *Report of the 2nd AMISOM-TFG Information Sharing Meeting, 22nd to 24th November 2011, Bujumbura Burundi* (AU internal document, no date), p. 16.

[109] *Concept Note: Draft AMISOM Stabilization Plan for the Liberated Areas* (AU internal document February 2012).

resources to cater for needs of these and the roughly 3,000 disengaged former combatants.[110] The AU believed that *al-Shabaab*'s new 500-strong *Amniyat* (internal security) force was largely to stem an increasing number of defections.

In early April, roughly one hundred Ugandan and Burundian forces deployed to Baidoa as the advance team of 2,500 AMISOM troops that were envisaged to take over from the ENDF in Sector 3.[111] The plan was for UNSOA to deliver supplies to Baidoa by road from Kenya and Ethiopia as well as by commercial cargo aircraft. In early August, another 1,000 Burundi troops arrived there.[112]

Among the other operations one of the most notable was Operation *Free Shabelle*.[113] This was intended to capture the three main routes into Mogadishu used by *al-Shabaab*, namely, Jowhar Road, Afgoye-Baido Road, and Marka.[114] From 22–8 May, AMISOM succeeded in capturing the Afgoye corridor, a critical roadway linking the capital to the agricultural town of Afgoye on the Shabelle river. This was where an estimated 400,000 people displaced by fighting in Mogadishu since 2006 had congregated and where *al-Shabaab* was thought to have considerable influence and a significant concentration of fighters.[115] Table 5.1 shows AU and TFG estimates of *al-Shabaab* forces as of November 2011.

In order to avoid a large battle and hence high likelihood of civilian casualties in Afgoye, AMISOM forces employed deception. While pretending that the main AMISOM force was approaching by the main road, in reality they came from the flank and rear through bush terrain. This managed to lure a significant number of *al-Shabaab* forces into open terrain where they were quickly engaged by AMISOM's tanks, resulting in the destruction of over thirty enemy 'technicals'.[116] AMISOM's Afgoye operations were therefore a success, not least because they enabled the resumption of humanitarian services to the large number of IDPs. But they were undermined somewhat when some Abgal clan militias followed on behind AMISOM and proceeded

---

[110] *AU Third Progress Report* (2012), §12.

[111] *Report of the Chairperson of the African Union Commission on the implementation of the mandate of the African Union Mission in Somalia pursuant to paragraph 21 of the Security Council resolution 2036 (2012)* (UN S/2012/468, 1 June 2012), §15.

[112] *Fourth and final progress report of the Chairperson of the African Union Commission on the implementation of the mandate of the African Union Mission in Somalia pursuant to paragraph 21 of Security Council resolution 2036 (2012)*, (S/2012/764, 12 October 2012), §20. Hereafter, *AU Fourth Progress Report* (2012).

[113] To give a sense of the tempo of operations, during 2012, the UPDF conducted twenty-seven major operations: some alone, some with BNDF, and some with TFG. Interview, UPDF information officer, Mogadishu, 5 January 2013.

[114] Telephone interview, senior UPDF officer, 4 March 2015.

[115] At the time, Afgoye was thought to contain 'several hundred' *al-Shabaab* fighters. *AMISOM Force Protection Review* (Bancroft, September 2011), p. 13. ACOTA files.

[116] Telephone interview, senior UPDF officer, 4 March 2015.

Table 5.1. *Al-Shabaab*'s Dispersal of Forces, November 2011

Area of Deployment	Strength
Mogadishu	700–800
Lower Shabelle	1,000
Middle Shabelle	1,500
Lower Juba	1,500
Middle Juba	1,000
Hiiraan	600
Galgadud	1,000
Bakool	700
Bay	600
Gedo	800

Source: *Report of the 2nd AMISOM-TFG Information Sharing Meeting, 22nd to 24th November 2011, Bujumbura Burundi* (AU internal document, no date), p. 9.

to rape and loot. Obviously, such behaviour risked turning the locals against the AU and TFG.[117]

Shortly after this, on 30–1 May, Kenyan forces in Sector 2 captured the town of Afmadow, paving the way for an advance on Kismayo, which the KDF Chief of Defence Staff indicated he intended to capture by August.[118] To the northeast of Mogadishu in Sector 1, on 26 June, AMISOM forces took control of Balad without firing a shot. This removed *al-Shabaab* forces that had controlled the town for three years. It also paved the way for AMISOM to move on to capture Johwar, the regional capital of Middle Shabelle.

In late July, Afgoye again raised some controversy, but this time for the UK government, when two British soldiers were photographed with AMISOM forces in Elasha Biyaha and Afgoye, one of whom appeared to be talking to be child soldier.[119] They turned out to be part of Operation Backwell—a (preferably covert) UK training and assistance programme for the Somali security forces. The photos prompted the UK Ministry of Defence to acknowledge the 'small military support team' deployed to Mogadishu to help AMISOM fight *al-Shabaab*, although not its start date.[120]

To the southwest of Mogadishu, AMISOM identified the capture of the K50 airstrip as especially important because it would act as the logistics hub and staging area in the subsequent push further south towards the port town of Marka. This was achieved on 4 August, without meeting any significant *al-Shabaab* resistance.[121]

[117] Telephone interview, Somalia analyst, 2 June 2012.
[118] *SEMG Report*, 13 July 2012, p. 228.
[119] See Matthew Russell Lee, 'On Child Soldiers Next to UK Forces in Somalia', *Inner City Press*, 25 July 2012, http://www.innercitypress.com/uk1caacsom072512.html
[120] Jerome Starkey, 'British troops on mission to danger zone', *The Times*, 26 July 2012.
[121] *Operational Update—K50 Operation Dhanaane* (Bancroft, August 2012). ACOTA files.

In subsequent operations, AMISOM forces, with the help of Ethiopia, TFG, and aligned clan militias, gained considerable ground from *al-Shabaab* across Sectors 2, 3, and 4.

However, as AMISOM forces proceeded further from Mogadishu into the bush, two important problems emerged. First, communications proved increasingly problematic because AMISOM's Tetra radio system and cell phones became inoperable and the Burundian forces in particular lacked HF radios.[122] A second problem was that AMISOM's intelligence, surveillance, and reconnaissance (ISR) platforms were finding *al-Shabaab* forces but the mission lacked the combat aviation assets to interdict and destroy them.[123] As AMISOM advanced on Afgoye, for instance, its UAVs detected a convoy of about thirty 'technicals' leaving the area, but it had no combat helicopters with which to engage them in a decisive battle.[124] This was a major and persistent problem for AMISOM.

AMISOM's 2012 Strategic CONOPS had recommended fourteen rotary and fixed-wing aircraft to support the mission. However, in February 2012 UN Security Council resolution 2036 authorized an aviation component of up to twelve helicopters (nine utility and three attack). The AU then proposed reconfiguring this to six attack and six utility helicopters.[125] The AU emphasized that the helicopters were 'critical for operational as well as logistical support, specifically medical evacuation'.[126]

At this stage, the Kenyan forces were believed to have three attack and two utility helicopters operating in AMISOM Sector 2. However, they operated under KDF command not the AMISOM Force Commander and hence did not count as official AMISOM assets.[127] Ethiopia also operated various aviation assets, including attack and utility helicopters in AMISOM Sectors 3 and 4, but these too were national and not AU assets.[128] In mid-2012, AMISOM's helicopter problem appeared to be partially solved when Uganda signed a letter of assist with the AU and UNSOA to deploy six helicopters to AMISOM (three attack/tactical, two utility, and one for medical evacuation). They would

---

[122] *Ibid.*, p. 9.   [123] *Ibid.*, p. 9.
[124] Interview, UK military adviser, Nairobi, 6 August 2012. As noted in Chapter 4 (p. 118), in mid-2011, the US government had provided AMISOM with some UAVs. Ironically, UAVs became a somewhat controversial topic for AMISOM when in February 2012 the Force Commander complained to his main partners about unidentified UAV operations in Mogadishu, in part because a UAV nearly hit a passenger plane and one could crash into AMISOM's primary fuel depot. *SEMG Report*, 13 July 2012, pp. 224, 232. Nevertheless, evidence later emerged from some *al-Shabaab* defectors that they were afraid AMISOM or some other entity was tracking their movements and would strike them suddenly using drones. *Voices of Al-Shabaab* (UNSOM, 2016), p. 11.
[125] *Report of the AUC Chairperson* (1 June 2012), §19.
[126] *AU Third Progress Report* (2012), §18.
[127] Telephone interview, UNOAU official, 20 December 2012.
[128] Communication, former AMISOM official, 22 October 2017.

provide air assault, exploitation and pursuit operations, cover for troops, escort for convoys, rescue/evacuation missions, and airdrop forces. Unfortunately, in August 2012, AMISOM lost the scheduled provision of Ugandan military helicopters when three of them crashed on the slopes of Mount Kenya en route to be deployed in Somalia. As it turned out, AMISOM did not acquire any attack helicopters until December 2016, when three Kenyan helicopters were deployed.[129] Even then, the mission had no specific policies on the operational use and tasking of these air assets.[130]

At this point, most international attention focused on the port city of Kismayo, which was thought to be *al-Shabaab*'s new centre of gravity. In November 2011, Kismayo had been identified as 'Al-Shabaab's single largest revenue-generator and a strategic military fortress'.[131] In what was the last major operation of 2012, in late September, Kismayo was captured by AMISOM, Somali forces and Ras Kamboni militia in a Kenyan-led largely sea-borne assault.[132] It was notable that the KDF subsequently claimed AMISOM's other TCCs 'reneged on the joint operation arguing that Kismayo's capture was a Sector-2 affair as it fell within the KDF's Area of Responsibility'.[133] Once again, *al-Shabaab* fighters did not offer much resistance but chose instead to retreat. Before they left, however, *al-Shabaab* dismantled Radio Andalus, leaving the city without a local radio capability, and planted numerous IEDs and destroyed local infrastructure such as markets, water points, and schools.[134] In the following weeks, *al-Shabaab* used a variety of remote- and pressure-trigger IEDs to attack the occupying forces.

CONCLUSION

A few months after forcing *al-Shabaab*'s main forces out of Mogadishu, AMISOM achieved what it had wanted for years: additional TCCs. But it did so by integrating troops from two of Somalia's neighbouring states: Kenya and Djibouti. And neither of them joined for the most impartial of reasons.

[129] By mid-2015, AMISOM was operating nearly eighty landing zones, including some in Kenya. *AMISOM Force Headquarters Position Paper on Joint African Union/United Nations Benchmarking Exercise* (AU internal document, April 2015), Annex D, p. 2.

[130] Communication, UN official, 2 August 2017.

[131] *Report of the 2nd AMISOM-TFG Information Sharing Meeting*, p. 13.

[132] In mid-June, the Kenyan government had reportedly asked the EU and United States to use some of its naval assets deployed off the Somali coast as part of the international anti-piracy coalition to shell targets on land in the run up to the assault on Kismayo. 'Somalia: slow progress towards the end of the Transition', *A Week in the Horn of Africa* (Ethiopia MFA), 15 June 2012, https://www.yumpu.com/en/document/view/39834166/15-june-2012-embassy-of-the-federal-democratic-republic-of-

[133] KDF, *Operation Linda Nichi*, p. 38. [134] *AU Fourth Progress Report* (2012), §13.

Moreover, Somalia's third and arguably most important neighbour, Ethiopia, also re-engaged militarily but kept its troops outside of AMISOM. Henceforth, AMISOM's political centre of gravity would coincide more with these 'frontline states'. The second major development was that AMISOM massively expanded its area of operations. This increased from one city to cover the whole of south-central Somalia, an area roughly the size of Iraq. Nevertheless, with reinforcements sent by Uganda and Burundi and the additional troops from the 'frontline states', AMISOM enjoyed considerable military success: it forced *al-Shabaab* to give up control of numerous settlements and generally defeated the militants when they stood and fought. The battle at Dayniile remained the exception to that rule. But AMISOM soon became more frustrated. Not only did *al-Shabaab* usually retreat to fight another day on its own preferred, asymmetric terms, but when AMISOM could locate concentrations of *al-Shabaab* fighters it lacked the combat aviation assets to interdict and destroy them. Once again, therefore, diplomatic attention turned to the question of how AMISOM's advances on the military track could be translated into progress on the political track. This would prove difficult and AMISOM was about to enter into a period of consolidation.

6

Consolidation

September 2012 to December 2013

It took twenty-one years, but in August and September 2012 a small group of Somali elites selected the key players in a new Federal Government, thereby officially ending Somalia's political transition. This was an important mile-stone for AMISOM, which had been tasked to protect the TFG and facilitate this transition. The TFG was often a counterproductive partner in AMISOM's fight against *al-Shabaab*. As the UN Monitoring Group had observed, there had been 'pervasive corruption within the transitional federal institutions' wherein 'the systematic misappropriation, embezzlement and outright theft of public resources have essentially become a system of governance, embodied in the popular Somali phrase *"Maxaa igu jiraa*?" ("What's in it for me?")'.[1] During 2009 and 2010, for instance, it was estimated that $7 out of every $10 received by the TFG never made it into state coffers. And this was after the TFG had contracted PricewaterhouseCoopers Associates Africa (PWC) to provide financial management, tracking, and monitoring of development donor funds.[2] By late 2014, the Monitoring Group had accused the Federal Government of diverting 70–80 per cent of the funds it received to advance 'partisan agendas that constitute threats to peace and security'.[3]

The process that eventually produced the FGS was based on the Garowe Principles, named after the Somali National Consultative Constitutional Con-ference that took place in Garowe, Puntland, 21–3 December 2011. These dealt with the structure, size, and basis of representation and selection criteria for establishing the new federal Parliament and a federal constitution by a (temporary) constituent assembly. On 15–17 February 2012 a second confer-ence was convened which produced the Garowe II Principles on 18 February. In the debates that followed Somali elites concluded that their country would

---

[1] *SEMG Report*, 13 July 2012, p. 7. See also S/RES/2067, 18 September 2012, §7.
[2] Wikileak Cable, 09NAIROBI1460, 10 July 2009, §1.
[3] *Report of the Monitoring Group on Somalia and Eritrea pursuant to Security Council resolution 2111 (2013): Somalia* (S/2014/726, 13 October 2014), p. 9.

have a two-chamber Parliament: the lower house would have 275 seats (with at least 30 per cent going to women) while the upper house would have 54 seats (three members for each of Somalia's eighteen administrative regions, which were to be the same ones as in 1991 when Siad Barre was overthrown). The National Constituent Assembly, which would implement the process, was to have 1,000 members, at least 30 per cent of whom must be women. They would be selected by signatories of the 2011 Roadmap assisted by traditional leaders and civil society and based on the 4.5 formula.

After much behind-the-scenes haggling as well as allegations of corruption and intimidation, in late August 2012 Somalia's new federal MPs were sworn into office. Then, on 10 September 2012, these parliamentarians elected Hassan Sheikh Mohamud to be President. To his own evident surprise, Hassan Sheikh beat the incumbent TFG President Sharif Sheikh Ahmed. A former civic activist and university dean, Hassan Sheikh quickly asserted that it was his sovereign government's prerogative to determine the nature and timing of outside assistance since it was no longer a transitional mechanism. He also set out a six-pillar strategy that focused on making progress in the areas of stability, economic recovery, peace building (including reconciliation and building trust), service delivery in the areas of health, education, and the environment, international relations, and the unity and integrity of Somalia. Later, the six pillars were boiled down to three top priorities: security, reform of the judicial system, and public finance management reform.[4] To prove he was serious, Hassan Sheikh fired some of the country's top security officials, including the head of the Somali Armed Forces, his deputy, and the head of the Navy. They were replaced with commanders who had been in the diaspora, prompting critics to argue that these people were out of touch with the recent events in Somalia. In clan terms, Hassan Sheikh's presidency was mainly associated with the Abgaal Hawiye clan. But it also witnessed the rise of *Damul Jadid* ('New Blood'), a faction of *Al-Islaah*, a moderate Somali Islamist movement that emerged in the 1970s and was affiliated with Egypt's Muslim Brotherhood.[5] Under Hassan Sheikh's rule adherents of *Damul Jadid* assumed key positions in his administration.

It was in this new political context that AMISOM continued its war against *al-Shabaab*. Not surprisingly, AMISOM was forced to evolve once more as most international partners reviewed their Somalia policies. The mission's mandate was once again revised by both the AU and UN and in June 2013 AMISOM was joined in Somalia by a new UN Assistance Mission (UNSOM), which replaced UNPOS. At around the same time, AMISOM also welcomed

---

[4] President Hassan Sheikh Mohamoud, 'The Future of Governance in Somalia', speech to CSIS, Washington DC, 17 January 2013, http://bit.ly/Yz2ffi

[5] Matt Bryden, *Somalia Redux? Assessing the New Somali Federal Government* (Washington DC: CSIS, August 2013), p. 8.

Sierra Leone as its fifth TCC, which integrated a battalion of troops with the Kenyan forces in Sector 2. For most of the next year, however, AMISOM adopted a posture of consolidation that emphasized the defence of its positions and supply routes. It also had to respond to a number of criticisms made about the activities of its Kenyan contingent in Sector 2, especially those related to the illicit trade in charcoal and the fighting that broke out during the formation of the new Interim Jubaland Administration in southern Somalia. In the second half of 2013, however, *al-Shabaab* intensified its asymmetric attacks across Somalia but also in Kenya. This led to more calls for AMISOM to readopt an offensive posture. After *al-Shabaab* fighters attacked Nairobi's affluent Westgate Mall in September 2013 these calls intensified and AMISOM was granted a 'surge' capacity of over 4,000 additional troops to go back on the offensive.

In order to analyse these issues, the chapter begins with a summary of the different reviews and mandate revisions that took place during late 2012 and 2013. It then assesses Sierra Leone's decision to become AMISOM's fifth TCC. The third section explores some of the problems that were raised for AMISOM by the creation of the new Interim Jubaland Administration in mid-2013, while the final section discusses how the Westgate attack in particular stimulated a renewed push for AMISOM to end its period of consolidation.

REVIEWS, MANDATES, AND BENCHMARKS

The selection of the new Federal Government prompted most international actors to revisit their engagement with Somalia. The AU was no exception and it started yet another round of reflection about what role(s) AMISOM should play.

Ironically, shortly after the Federal Government was established, AMISOM adopted a more defensive posture, brought on in large part by fears of overstretch and the gap between its mandated tasks and the mission's actual capabilities. Of particular importance was the continued 'lack of force multipliers and overstretched communication lines'.[6] But there were other problems as well. The mission was still struggling to maintain its fleet of vehicles and its civilian and police components were badly short-staffed: it had only twenty-one civilian staff and ninety-one individual police officers deployed in Mogadishu. The mission was becoming increasingly concerned that most of its 'liberated areas' in south-central Somalia were 'now in the hands of clan militias that are tenuously linked to the National Security Forces'.[7] It was also

---

[6] *AU Fourth Progress Report* (2012), §12.   [7] *Ibid*, §18, §24, §20, §30.

struggling to get consistent water supply to its far-flung forces, especially around Baidoa, and lacked resources for dealing with the increasing number of disengaging combatants and defectors from *al-Shabaab*.

After reflecting on the formation of the new FGS and its 'Six Pillar Policy', on 7 November 2012, UN Security Council resolution 2073 revised AMISOM's mandate to carry out the following tasks:

a) maintain a presence in the four sectors set out in the AMISOM Strategic Concept of 5 January 2012, and in those sectors, in coordination with the SNSF, reduce the threat posed by Al Shabaab and other armed opposition groups in order to establish conditions for effective and legitimate governance across Somalia;

b) support dialogue and reconciliation in Somalia by assisting with the free movement, safe passage and protection of all those involved with the peace and reconciliation process in Somalia;

c) provide, as appropriate, protection to the Somali authorities to help them carry out their functions of government, and security for key infrastructure;

d) assist, within its capabilities, and in coordination with other parties, with implementation of the National Security and Stabilization Plan, in particular the effective re-establishment and training of all-inclusive SNSF;

e) contribute, as may be requested and within capabilities, to the creation of the necessary security conditions for the provision of humanitarian assistance;

f) protect its personnel, facilities, installations, equipment and mission, and to ensure the security and freedom of movement of its personnel, as well as of United Nations personnel carrying out functions mandated by the Security Council.[8]

And yet in spite of its mandate to reduce the threat posed by *al-Shabaab*, in practice from late 2012 AMISOM effectively assumed a defensive posture designed to consolidate its recent territorial gains. As discussed below, AMISOM would not resume offensive operations against *al-Shabaab* until 31 October 2013. *Al-Shabaab*, on the other hand, took this as an opportunity to intensify its asymmetric attacks on AMISOM and the new government.

The AU also engaged in another review of its engagement with Somalia and what role(s) AMISOM should play in it. To that end, in December 2012 the AU assembled a team to conduct a strategic review of AMISOM.[9] It was tasked

---

[8] S/RES/2073, 7 November 2012, §1.

[9] Although the initial plan was for the AU and UN to conduct a joint strategic assessment, this did not happen. Next, it was proposed that the AU and UN should conduct parallel assessments—perhaps facilitated by UNOAU—but that idea also failed to materialize.

with working out how best to engage with the new Federal Government and support its priorities, and finding a sustainable solution to AMISOM's chronic funding problems.

The review team noted that AMISOM had achieved a key objective of transferring power from the TFG to the new Federal Government but that 'significant sustained effort' was required to liberate remaining territory held by *al-Shabaab*. AMISOM therefore needed 'a robust peace enforcement capacity', but there was growing frustration that resources were not forthcoming, including 'the lack of predictable funding for AMISOM, which spills over into uncertainty and fragility for the consolidation of the peace process in Somalia'.[10] The AU team concluded that any future peace operation should pursue four strategic objectives: '(1) secure the sovereignty and territorial integrity of Somalia; (2) enhance the capacity of the defence and public safety institutions; (3) support the establishment of effective governance, and; (4) facilitate the conduct of general elections by 2016'.[11] Since the lack of resources available to AMISOM rendered the status quo untenable, the review team assessed three principal options for the AU:

1. handover AMISOM to a UN peacekeeping operation;
2. enhance AMISOM to work alongside a UN peacebuilding mission; and
3. establish a new joint AU-UN mission.[12]

They concluded that AMISOM should make the transition to a new joint arrangement, whereby two parallel AU and UN missions would come together at the strategic level under a Joint Special Representative. In their words:

"As the status quo is not an option, and option 1 (UN peacekeeping) is not feasible at this stage, the remaining options are option 2 (enhance AMISOM) and option 3 (a new joint AU-UN mission). As option 2 does not provide for sustainable and predictable funding for AMISOM, the Review Team therefore recommends option 3."[13]

However, because such a joint mechanism would take time to develop, the AU team recommended that an enhanced AMISOM should be developed as a prelude to its preferred joint AU–UN arrangement.[14] The AU also wanted the UN to authorize a new peacebuilding office to focus on supporting the Federal Government's priorities, including the empowerment and restructuring of the Somali security sector. At the heart of this new joint arrangement would be a more predictable and long-term source of financial support for the AU mission, which would come via the UN's assessed peacekeeping contributions.

---

[10] *Report of the African Union Commission on the Strategic Review of the African Union Mission in Somalia* (AU internal document, 16 January 2013), §6.

[11] *Ibid.*, §9.   [12] *Ibid.*, §11–12.

[13] *Ibid.*, §13. See also S/2013/134, 5 March 2013, §50.   [14] *Ibid.*, §14.

Meanwhile, in New York, on the back of its own review, in January 2013 UN Secretary-General Ban Ki-Moon recommended that the UN Security Council create a new UN Assistance Mission (UNSOM) to deliver political and peacebuilding support with a presence across Somalia alongside AMISOM, UNSOA, and a UN Country Team.[15] (UNPOS was closed and UNSOM duly established on 3 June 2013 under Security Council resolution 2102.)

On 27 February 2013, following its Strategic Review of AMISOM, the AU Peace and Security Council revised the mission's mandate once again. It also called on the UN to help AMISOM 'establish special training teams to enhance the capacity of Somalia's National Defence and Public Safety Institutions, and enhance its civilian capacity to support the FGS efforts to restore effective governance, promote reconciliation, human rights and rule of law, and ensure service delivery in the recovered areas'.[16]

Just over a week later, the UN Security Council extended AMISOM's operations for an additional year and set out a slightly different mandate than the one detailed by the AU Peace and Security Council (see Table 6.1). This added an additional task to AMISOM's previous mandate as set out in UN Security Council resolution 2073 (7 November 2012), namely, 'To assist, within its existing civilian capability, the Federal Government of Somalia, in collaboration with the United Nations, to extend state authority in areas recovered from Al-Shabaab'.[17] The Security Council also encouraged 'AMISOM to develop further an effective approach to the protection of civilians, as requested by the AU Peace and Security Council'.[18] Finally, the Council also requested AMISOM 'to strengthen child and women's protection in its activities and operations', 'to prevent sexual violence, and sexual exploitation and abuse, by applying policies consistent with the United Nations zero-tolerance policy on sexual exploitation and abuse in the context of peacekeeping' and 'the AU to establish a system to address systematically allegations of misconduct'.[19]

In early April, and despite the new mandates, AMISOM's Military Operations Coordination Committee recommended the mission should not undertake further expansion operations.[20] For the most part, this simply reflected the reality on the ground where AMISOM's offensive operations had stopped in late 2012. Probably the main exception occurred in mid-February 2013

---

[15] S/2013/69, 31 January 2013, §75c.

[16] PSC/PR/COMM(CCCLVI), 27 February 2013, §8.

[17] S/RES/2093, 6 March 2013, §1.

[18] S/RES/2093, 6 March 2013, §10. This was reiterated in S/RES/2124, 12 November 2013, §11 and S/RES/2182, 24 October 2014, §31.

[19] S/RES/2093, 6 March 2013, §13–15.

[20] *Report of the Joint African Union–United Nations Mission on the Benchmarks for a UN Peacekeeping Operation in Somalia and Assessment of AMISOM and Somali National Security Forces* (unpublished document, 2 October 2013), §2. Hereafter, *Joint Benchmarking Report (2013)*. The UN Secretary-General's technical assessment mission to Somalia shared this assessment (17–29 March 2013). See S/2013/239, 19 April 2013, §9.

Table 6.1. AU and UN mandates for AMISOM compared (2013)

AU Peace and Security Council 27 February 2013	UN Security Council Resolution 2093 6 March 2013
(a) take all necessary measures, as appropriate, and in coordination with the Somalia National Defence and Public Safety Institutions, to reduce the threat posed by Al-Shabaab and other armed opposition groups,	(a) To maintain a presence in the four sectors set out in the AMISOM Strategic Concept of 5 January 2012, and in those sectors, in coordination with the Security Forces of the Federal Government of Somalia, reduce the threat posed by Al-Shabaab and other armed opposition groups, including receiving, on a transitory basis, defectors, as appropriate, and in coordination with the United Nations, in order to establish conditions for effective and legitimate governance across Somalia;
(b) assist in consolidating and expanding the control of the FGS over its national territory,	
(c) assist the FGS in establishing conditions for effective and legitimate governance across Somalia, through support, as appropriate, in the areas of security, including the protection of Somali institutions and key infrastructure, governance, rule of law and delivery of basic services,	(b) To support dialogue and reconciliation in Somalia by assisting with the free movement, safe passage and protection of all those involved with the peace and reconciliation process in Somalia;
(d) provide, within its capabilities and as appropriate, technical and other support for the enhancement of the capacity of the Somalia State institutions, particularly the National Defence, Public Safety and Public Service Institutions,	(c) To provide, as appropriate, protection to the Federal Government of Somalia to help them carry out their functions of government, and security for key infrastructure;
(e) support the FGS in establishing the required institutions and conducive conditions for the conduct of free, fair and transparent elections by 2016, in accordance with the Provisional Constitution,	(d) To assist, within its capabilities, and in coordination with other parties, with implementation of the Somali national security plans, through training and mentoring of the Security Forces of the Federal Government of Somalia, including through joint operations;
(f) liaise with humanitarian actors and facilitate, as may be required and within its capabilities, humanitarian assistance in Somalia, as well as the resettlement of internally displaced persons and the return of refugees,	(e) To contribute, as may be requested and within capabilities, to the creation of the necessary security conditions for the provision of humanitarian assistance;
(g) facilitate coordinated support by relevant AU institutions and structures towards the stabilization and reconstruction of Somalia, and	(f) To assist, within its existing civilian capability, the Federal Government of Somalia, in collaboration with the United Nations, to extend state authority in areas recovered from Al-Shabaab;
(h) provide protection to AU and UN personnel, installations and equipment, including the right of self-defence;	(g) To protect its personnel, facilities, installations, equipment and mission, and to ensure the security and freedom of movement of its personnel, as well as of United Nations personnel carrying out functions mandated by the Security Council;

Source: PSC/PR/COMM(CCCLVI), 27 February 2013; S/RES/2093, 6 March 2013.

when about 1,700 AMISOM and SNA troops liberated three towns in Lower Shabelle (Janaale, Barire, and Aw Dheegle) situated on the main road linking Barawe to Burhakaba, the objective of a future AMISOM counter-*Shabaab* offensive.[21]

The decision was reiterated in June when the AU announced that AMISOM's lack of additional capabilities meant the mission had reached 'its operational limit' since it lacked 'all the required force enablers'. As a consequence, AMISOM would no longer engage in 'major advances to recover more territory from Al Shabaab'.[22] Instead, AMISOM's assets were used to protect supply routes and existing locations, including by conducting cordon and search operations for *al-Shabaab* militants hiding in settlements recently recovered by AMISOM/Somali forces. Neither task was insignificant. For example, route clearance (of dense vegetation) and road repair operations along AMISOM's main supply routes were critical in preventing further IED and ambush attacks. In addition, road construction also sped up travel, which benefited AMISOM and local people. It was therefore an important part of the AU's civil affairs engagement with the locals. Particularly along the roughly 240 km route from Mogadishu to Baidoa, AMISOM engineers would operate in tandem with a security platoon. On several occasions, local trucks carrying fruit would stop and give some to the security detail as a way of saying thanks.[23] Another related issue was the need to clear illegal checkpoints along the supply routes. Attempts by ill-disciplined Somali forces to extort money from passers-by at illegal checkpoints led to many fights, as did AMISOM and SNA attempts to dismantle them.[24]

On the other hand, reducing AMISOM's offensive operations handed the initiative back to *al-Shabaab*. Moreover, the subsequent deterioration in the security situation combined with the Federal Government's lack of political capacity made it difficult for the government to conduct the necessary outreach throughout the country, which also hindered AMISOM.

It was in this context that a few months later the AU and UN decided to undertake yet another assessment of their engagement in Somalia by establishing the Joint AU–UN Mission on the benchmarks for a United Nations Peacekeeping Operation in Somalia.[25]

Conducted between 26 August and 6 September 2013 the benchmarking mission offered a sober assessment of the security situation in south-central Somalia, warning that many of AMISOM's gains were at risk of reversal if its

---

[21] Bancroft Situational Report 10–14 February 2013. ACOTA files.

[22] PSC/PR/2.(CCCLXXIX), 13 June 2013. Quotes from §27, §72, and §16.

[23] Bancroft Situational Report 25–28 January 2013. ACOTA files.

[24] Bancroft Situational Report 29 January–1 February 2013. ACOTA files.

[25] The idea of a benchmarking mission was first welcomed in 'Statement by the President of the Security Council' (S/PRST/2013/7, 6 June 2013).

defensive posture continued.[26] It cautioned against 'rehatting' AMISOM into a UN peacekeeping operation and recommended instead enhancing the AU mission so it could once again go on the offensive against *al-Shabaab* and support the development of an effective set of Somali national security forces capable of eventually taking the lead in those operations. Crucially, however, the benchmarking mission also cautioned that any military offensive must be followed by stabilization activities conducted by AMISOM and the Federal Government in order to provide a viable alternative set of governance structures that would enable the delivery of basic services in settlements captured from *al-Shabaab*. The team summarized one of their main findings in the following manner:

Al Shabaab is increasingly fractured and politically weak with, paradoxically, a strengthened ability to perpetrate destructive asymmetrical attacks. Al Shabaab is considerably weaker than it was in 2011 or early 2012, but it requires far less resources to conduct insurgent and terrorist attacks than it does to wage conventional warfare, hold territory, govern people and provide services. This means that even though Al Shabaab has lost significant territory and resources, it would likely continue employing lesser resources to conduct a protracted insurgency campaign.

The joint mission deems it critical to resume expansion operations against Al Shabaab strongholds outside Mogadishu and its main lines of communication and supplies in order to minimise the threat of asymmetrical attacks. The idea behind the recommendations of the joint mission is to defeat Al Shabaab in their major rural hideouts and making it as costly as possible for them to exist and easier for the SNA to dislodge elements that melt into the population, forcing an eventual total defeat.[27]

With regard to when and whether AMISOM should transition to a UN peacekeeping operation, the review team suggested the decision should be made based on analysis of the following eight benchmarks:[28]

1. Political agreement, supported by federal and relevant regional/local authorities, on the process to finalize the federal vision and formation of administrations and states, including through the constitutional review and the electoral process.

2. Extension of state authority through local administrations in areas recovered from Al Shabaab in line with the provisional constitution, delivering basic security and assistance to the local population.

---

[26] *Joint Benchmarking Report* (2013). The report's recommendations were summarized in *Report of the Chairperson of the Commission on the Joint AU-UN Benchmarking Exercise and the Review of the African Union Mission in Somalia* (PSC/PR/2.(CCCXCIX), 10 October 2013) and *Letter Dated 14 October 2013 from the Secretary-General addressed to the President of the Security Council* (S/2013/606, 14 October 2013).

[27] *Joint Benchmarking Report (2013)*, §11–12.   [28] *Ibid.*, §17.

3. Degrading Al Shabaab to the level that it is no longer an effective force through a comprehensive strategy that includes political, economic and military components. Specifically, Al Shabaab should no longer be capable of undertaking major combat operations or control key military strategic objectives, including financial avenues, and is limited in its ability to conduct attacks.

4. A significant improvement in the physical security situation with 30 per cent to 50 per cent reduction in Al Shabaab attacks using improvised explosive devices (IEDs). Improved control of access of key urban areas, including Mogadishu, Marka, Kismayo, Baidoa and Belet-weyne, and improved security along main supply routes.

5. SNA is capable of holding the majority of major cities and key roads in south central Somalia achieved by a trained and equipped critical mass, assessed by the mission as at least 10,000 cohesive SNA force, with clear and effective command and control and capable of holding cleared areas.

6. Broad agreement on the major security arrangements, in line with the political process, set by the FGS within the context of the federal vision agreed by major political stakeholders; in particular on the role and functions of the police service.

7. In view of the envisioned elections in 2016, it is important that at least 4,000 trained SNP elements are provided with basic equipment and deployed with sustainment, are able to perform basic police functions in the major populations centers of south central, contributing to peaceful elections, and maintaining law and order within a more permissive security environment.

8. Consent of the Federal Government and regional authorities, as well as important segments of civil society, to the deployment of a UN peacekeeping operation.

Of course, these benchmarks were very far from being met, and hence there was no prospect of the UN deploying a peacekeeping operation in the foreseeable future.

ENTER SIERRA LEONE

In April 2013, Sierra Leone became AMISOM's fifth TCC when it deployed a battalion of soldiers alongside the Kenyan forces in Sector 2 in Tabda, Dhobley, and Kismayo.[29] Like Djibouti, the deployment took much longer than planned,

---

[29] Sierra Leone also deployed a few military officers to AMISOM's force headquarters and about forty individual police officers.

with Sierra Leone reportedly pledging a battalion to AMISOM as early as May 2009.[30] It was not until August 2011, however, that Sierra Leone sent a reconnaissance team to Addis Ababa, Nairobi, and Mogadishu as part of the preparations for that deployment and on 17 August Sierra Leone's Minister of Defence and National Security made that pledge public.[31]

The long delay arose from concerns about supplies of ammunition and other essential equipment items, including APCs and later the need to ensure stability during Sierra Leone's general elections (held in November 2012).[32] Sierra Leone had signed a memorandum of understanding with the AU to join AMISOM in February 2012. In April, the Republic of Sierra Leone Armed Forces (RSLAF) sent another reconnaissance team to Somalia, which included a British officer from the International Military Advisory and Training Team (IMATT).[33] After an initial proposal that the Sierra Leoneans should replace the Kenyan forces in Kismayo, it was later decided that the battalion would divide into companies and co-deploy with the KDF across Sector 2, ostensibly in order to reduce the risk of *al-Shabaab* attack. By August 2012, the Sierra Leone battalion was trained and operationally ready to go but still lacked key equipment.[34] The RSLAF's lack of capabilities meant it alone was unable to meet the mission's basic equipment standards. The battalion thus eventually deployed on a 'dry lease' basis whereby logistical and other support would come from partners, principally the United States and United Kingdom.

When they arrived, Sierra Leone's peacekeepers were widely seen as useful additions to AMISOM. Most of the RSLAF peacekeepers were Muslims, many spoke Arabic (one of Somalia's official languages, alongside Somali), and about sixty-five were women.[35] Moreover, the distinct lack of a national political agenda in Somalia meant Sierra Leone was considered by many Somalis to be a far more neutral player than neighbouring states that joined AMISOM.[36]

Several factors motivated Sierra Leone's decision to join AMISOM. However, the most important related to domestic politics in Sierra Leone after the civil war that ended in early 2002, namely, the international process to reconstruct and reform the country's security sector.[37] As Albrecht and Haenlein concluded in their detailed study of this question, 'the need to

[30] Wikleak Cable 09ADDISABABA1139, 14 May 2009.
[31] 'Sierra Leone to contribute one battalion of soldiers for Somalia', *Standard Times Press*, no date, http://standardtimespress.org/?p=589
[32] Peter Albrecht and Cathy Haenlein, 'Sierra Leone's Post-Conflict Peacekeepers', *RUSI Journal*, 160:1 (2015), p. 30.
[33] Interview, UK official, Nairobi, 6 August 2012.
[34] Interview, UN official, Addis Ababa, 3 August 2012.
[35] Debra Liang-Fenton, 'Sierra Leone Sends Women Peacekeepers to Somalia', US Institute of Peace, 23 April 2014, http://www.usip.org/olivebranch/sierra-leone-sends-women-peacekeepers-somalia
[36] Albrecht and Haenlein, 'Sierra Leone's', p. 31.   [37] *Ibid.*, pp. 26–36.

bring the armed forces under civilian control, and establish a focus that would be broadly accepted by the population, was paramount. Of the options available, contribution to peacekeeping emerged as the most significant, providing a clear purpose and direction (and the chance to generate an income)'.[38]

While official statements by Sierra Leonean officials stressed their desire to deploy peacekeepers abroad as payback for earlier international efforts to stabilize their country, with Sierra Leone's key security partners being the United Kingdom and United States, there was also a convergence of interests around maintaining global stability, and particularly in combating terrorism abroad.[39]

But such sentiments were meaningless without an army capable of expeditionary deployment. In turn, therefore, the key to understanding Sierra Leone's participation in AMISOM lies within the institutional dynamics of the RSLAF. The United Kingdom was the RSLAF's principal security partner from 2000 when the IMATT was established to provide a wide range of training, advisory and institution-building activities. Sierra Leone became a US ACOTA partner in May 2009. This was important because although the United Kingdom had trained five companies for peacekeeping duties, the RSLAF still lacked the equipment required for high-intensity peace operations, including protected mobility such as APCs. As the former head of the IMATT observed, 'The bottom line is that they can't afford to do anything else [beyond peace operations]. The only training they do is ... funded by the UK or the US, in support of peacekeeping ... other [external] support is minimal'.[40] It was the United States that provided the majority of the equipment for the AMISOM deployment, but this was not without its problems.

The first problem was that the United States would not order the relevant heavy military equipment for the battalion until Sierra Leone had signed the memorandum of understanding with the AU after previously having its fingers burnt by other countries.[41] Specifically, the Casspir APCs that the Sierra Leoneans would use required at least nine months to prepare and transport from South Africa to the Kenya–Somali border. The second problem was an argument about who would provide ammunition. While Sierra Leone thought the United States would provide ammunition in the same way it had done for Uganda, this was just a one-off US deal with Uganda, not a general commitment to AMISOM contributors.[42]

A related factor was the need to create some pride in the RSLAF among ordinary Sierra Leoneans. For a military that had developed a terrible

---

[38] *Ibid.*, p. 33.   [39] *Ibid.*, p. 28.   [40] Cited in *ibid.*, p. 29.
[41] Communication, US official, 1 September 2012.
[42] Interview, US official, Addis Ababa, 30 July 2012. UNSOA was not permitted to buy ammunition for AMISOM contributing countries.

reputation during the country's civil war—exemplified by the common use of the derogatory term 'SOBELS', soldiers-by-day-rebels-by-night—peacekeeping offered an opportunity to rehabilitate the army's public image. It also allowed Sierra Leone to export peace and security abroad rather than spill-over effects of civil war. The focus on peace operations also allowed the RSLAF to acquire some operational experience. As a former IMATT commander put it,

> If it were not for PSOs, [the RSLAF's] overall operational effectiveness would be degraded. Their contributions to PSOs allow them to keep some of their effect-iveness. That 75 per cent [of RSLAF resources are used] in support of PSOs is in itself not a bad thing, because if they were not doing that, they would do no military work at all.[43]

Finally, peace operations were also valued as a source of acquiring funds for the RSLAF through reimbursements.

The quid pro quo for the United Kingdom and United States was that they would support the RSLAF's ambition to become peacekeepers only if it significantly downsized. This it did, reducing its numbers from 14,000 in 2003 to 8,500 by 2010.[44] This meant that when Sierra Leone's battalion deployed to Somalia in 2013, one-fifth of the RSLAF was involved in or preparing for this deployment.

After a relatively positive tour of duty, Sierra Leone's initial battalion withdrew from Somalia in January 2015 as a consequence of the Ebola pandemic back home. This had prompted Somalia's President Hassan Sheikh Mohamud to announce in August 2014 that no new troops from Sierra Leone could be deployed to his country. After the Ebola pandemic was brought under control, in 2016, Sierra Leone pledged it would deploy AMISOM's third FPU, hopefully by late 2017.[45] It did not.

In sum, Sierra Leone joined AMISOM primarily for institutional reasons connected to the RSLAF's process of transformation. The secondary factors were the need to enhance relations with its principal security partners, the United Kingdom and the United States, and to acquire financial support for the army via peacekeeping reimbursements.

FIGHTING FOR JUBALAND

Shortly after the Sierra Leonean battalion deployed, in June 2013 major controversy arose when the FGS accused Kenyan forces in Kismayo of

---

[43] Cited in Albrecht and Haenlein, 'Sierra Leone's', p. 29.   [44] Cited in *ibid.*, p. 29.
[45] Communication, UN official, 31 July 2017.

working directly against its personnel in a blatant violation of AMISOM's mandate.[46] Specifically, the Somali government accused the Kenyans of supporting Ahmed Madobe, a former ally of al-Shabaab and leader of the Ras Kamboni militia, and to that end manipulating political processes in the controversial new 'Jubaland State'.[47] Following these allegations, the government called for Kenyan soldiers in AMISOM's Sector 2 to be replaced with different forces that would uphold AMISOM's mandate.

The clash between Kenya's narrow national agenda and the new Federal Government had two principal drivers. The first was disputes over the nature and implementation of federalism. Specifically, Somalis remained intensely divided over how much authority the new Federal Government in Mogadishu should have over the political arrangements of the clans, including the autonomous largely 'ethno-states' of Somaliland and Puntland, which had existed for decades. The situation was well summarized by Nicholas Kay, the new head of UNSOM, in the following manner:

> The heart of the political challenge is simple to describe, if rather difficult to solve. After 22 years of conflict, power and control of resources and revenue are fragmented. The strong centralist State has ceased to exist. Different regions and different people now hold different bits of power. That is why Somalis have decided that a federal model is the only system that will work in this new reality. The task now is to reconcile and agree among themselves exactly how federalism will work in practice. How will they share power, revenue, resources and responsibilities in a way that benefits all of Somalia? Those are difficult issues, but ones that need political solutions.[48]

When the Federal Government assumed office, international actors recognized it as the legitimate sovereign authority, but it had no real capacity to enforce its decisions and extend its authority beyond Mogadishu. The Federal Government thus felt compelled to respond to various de facto regional authorities across the country, including those in Somaliland, Puntland, Jubaland, Galmudug, and

---

[46] See 'Extremely Urgent: Kismayo Conflict', letter sent by Somalia's Deputy Prime Minister to the African Union, 30 June 2013. Copy in author's possession.

[47] Ahmed Mohammed Islaan aka Ahmed Madobe was formerly among the most radical members of *al-Shabaab*'s 'nationalist' faction. A member of the Darod Ogaden clan, he helped to organize an *al-Qa'ida* training camp in Ras Kamboni during the 1990s, and publicly boasted of sheltering the fleeing perpetrators of the 1998 bombing of the US Embassy in Nairobi. In 2007, he was wounded and received treatment in an Ethiopian hospital and was captured by the Ethiopians, where he stayed until 2009. His subsequent militia brigade was among *al-Shabaab*'s strongest military allies until a dispute over the distribution of the revenues from the port of Kismayo. When *al-Shabaab* refused to share those revenues, Madobe abandoned his allegiance to *al-Qa'ida*. He fought and lost a battle for Kismayo against *al-Shabaab* and subsequently defected from them in February 2010, at which point he became Kenya's preferred local ally in Jubaland. AMISOM's leadership also believed the KDF paid stipends to the Ras Kamboni militia, which did not help negative local perceptions. Interview, AMISOM senior official, Djibouti, 29 February 2016.

[48] UN document S/PV.7030, 12 September 2013, p. 2.

Hiraan. The Federal Government's immediate dilemma was whether to focus on securing Mogadishu and its environs and leave the regions to their own devices, and thus look weak; or try to extend its authority beyond Banadir region and potentially lose to these regional entities, thereby looking even weaker. President Hassan Sheikh's administration chose the second approach; first by initiating a process of dialogue, and then by becoming more forceful, especially in the south with the de facto authorities in Jubaland.

The second contentious issue was interference by Somalia's neighbours. Many Somalis believed that it was Kenyan and Ethiopian policy to keep Somalia weak and divided, and hence for economic and national security reasons they would seek to undermine the creation of a strong central government in Mogadishu. AMISOM became entangled in this issue because the Federal Government was worried that it might become an instrument of IGAD's agenda, which was dominated by Ethiopia and Kenya.

IGAD's agenda crystalized in June 2012 when Kenya initiated a process to establish a Jubaland state under the IGAD Grand Stabilization Plan, which had been agreed in January 2012.[49] The Somali Federal Government's position was that it should lead any such process. Its suspicions of ulterior motives were confirmed when Kenya and Ethiopia signed the *Memorandum of Understanding between the IGAD Joint committee for the Grand Stabilization of South Central Somalia* on 6 December 2012. This set out a framework whereby a Joint Committee comprising Ethiopia and Kenya would take the lead in implementing IGAD's Grand Stabilization Plan 'to support the development of an inclusive process, in determining the political and administrative arrangements for the liberated areas' (Preamble). The memorandum's objective was to facilitate stabilization, reconciliation, re-establish government institutions, including at regional and district levels, and share information (Article 5).

The next key development occurred in February 2013 when some 500 delegates gathered in Kismayo to discuss the status of Jubaland. The Federal Government promptly declared this conference unconstitutional and called for it to be disbanded. The delegates refused and in May 2013 they elected Ahmed Madobe as President of Jubaland.[50] This prompted the elders from several other clans to declare their own presidents of Jubaland, notably the Darod/Marehan clan's declaration that Colonel Barre Adan Hiraale was now President.

The activities of Kenyan forces in Kismayo also opened a major rift in the Somali Parliament, where on 25 May members tabled a motion to censure the KDF. Yet Nairobi repeatedly refused calls by the Somali Parliament and senior government officials to redeploy its troops to Mogadishu and surrender

---

[49] As discussed in Chapter 5, Kenya had pushed its 'Jubaland Initiative' since 2009.
[50] For IGAD's view of the process see Report of the IGAD Confidence Building Mission to Mogadishu and Kismayo 16–19 May 2013. At http://halgan.net/kutub/REPORT-ON-THE-IGAD-MISSION-TO-MOGADISHU-AND-KISMAYO-16.pdf

Kismayo to more clan-neutral Ugandan or Burundian forces. Kenyan support for creating a new Jubaland state was seen by the Federal Government as undermining its efforts to establish federal authority beyond Mogadishu. In an attempt to counter Kenya's military influence, the Somali President signed a military agreement with Turkey, which threatened an oppositional realigning of Mogadishu's interests with Turkey as well as Egypt and Djibouti.[51]

The crisis intensified in June 2013, when fighting erupted in Kismayo between Ras Kamboni and Darod/Marehan militia who were allied with the Federal Government. Ras Kamboni forces prevailed but not before the Kenyan commander in Kismayo had arrested a colonel in the Somali Army, who had been sent to Kismayo to oversee the integration of the various militia into the national army. Remarkably, in an effort to strengthen its position, the Federal Government even struck up an alliance with local leader, Barre Hiiraale, who declared that his forces were co-located with *al-Shabaab* and planning joint military operations against Madobe's forces.[52]

At the same time, Kenyan troops were accused of breaking the UN ban on the export of charcoal, and of confiscating 50 per cent of revenues generated at the lucrative deep-water port.[53] Kismayo had become particularly important as a site for the export of charcoal made from the region's acacia forests. According to the UN Monitoring Group, roughly 80 per cent of this charcoal was for export and 20 per cent for local consumption. In December 2011, the TFG had requested that the UN ban all imports of Somali charcoal, which were exported almost exclusively from *al-Shabaab* areas.[54] The UN Security Council subsequently decided that 'all Member States shall take the necessary measures to prevent the direct or indirect import of charcoal from Somalia, whether or not such charcoal originated in Somalia'.[55] Consequently, when Kenyan/TFG forces arrived in Kismayo in September they found thousands of bags of charcoal (worth many millions of dollars) throughout the city and outlying areas. However, what happened to them and who pocketed the profits remained murky. Certainly, the local business community was clear that they wanted the ban on charcoal exports lifted.[56] Critics alleged that the KDF in AMISOM were pocketing some of the proceeds from the illicit trade in charcoal, in large part because of their ability to control Kismayo port.[57] In response, on 4 August, AMISOM

---

[51] 'Somalia's Jubbaland conundrum', *Jane's Islamic Affairs Analyst*, May 2013, pp. 4–6.

[52] Bryden, *Somalia Redux?*, p. 22.

[53] See *SEMG Report*, 12 July 2013, pp. 38–9 and Annex 9. See also subsequent Monitoring Group reports, especially *SEMG Report*, 13 October 2014.

[54] *Special report of the Secretary-General on Somalia* (S/2012/74, 31 January 2012), §8.

[55] S/RES/2036, 22 February 2012, §22.

[56] 'Letter from the Jubba Business Committee to the Somali Federal Government, the African Union and the United Nations—subject: Release Charcoal stock in Jubba to Trade', 22 October 2012.

[57] Journalists for Justice, *Black and White: Kenya's Criminal Racket in Somalia*.

TCCs met with President Hassan Sheikh and agreed to recognize the authority of the Federal Government over Kismayo port and airport, and expressed their intention to deploy a multinational AMISOM presence there as requested by the Federal Government.[58] In late 2013 a company of Sierra Leonean and a company of Burundian troops were also deployed to Sector Kismayo, but it is unclear if the Federal Government was able to control the port.

After considerable diplomatic wrangling, an agreement was signed on 27 August 2013 in Addis Ababa. The deal was basically a loss for the Federal Government and a win for Madobe, whose position as leader of an Interim Juba Administration, consisting of Gedo, Lower Juba, and Middle Juba regions, was solidified for up to two years.[59] For Somalia's other potential interim regional administrations the deal signalled that the Federal Government could be overcome. In addition, in Baidoa, capital of the neighbouring Bay region, the deal was criticized because it implied the Federal Government had recognized Jubaland's claims to certain disputed border areas that were also claimed by the nascent Baidoa administration.[60]

But the episode also raised big questions for AMISOM, including about the limits of its central command and control structures and its ability to function as a coherent force rather than several disconnected, national parts.[61] This was crucial because if AMISOM was perceived by Somalis to be a vehicle for neighbouring states to pursue their narrow national agendas it would severely limit the mission's ability to achieve its objectives, hobble its strategic communications, and send hugely unhelpful signals about the wider ability of the AU to effectively steer its peace operations. It also raised interesting questions about the extent to which the Federal Government was willing to work with *al-Shabaab* forces to defeat a mutual enemy. Finally, the episode illustrated how there was sometimes a murky distinction between threats posed by *al-Shabaab* and those more deeply rooted in clan and subclan rivalries.

Similar sets of issues were raised in early 2014 about Ethiopia's lack of neutrality in the competition to run the new Interim South West Administration. In this case, Ethiopian and Burundian forces in AMISOM temporarily blockaded the conference halls in Baidoa of one of the two rival factions bidding to control the emerging Interim South West Administration.[62]

---

[58] S/2013/521, 3 September 2013, §8.

[59] For a good analysis of the agreement see 'Two Cheers for the Jubba Deal', *Africa Confidential*, 54:18, 6 September 2013, p. 6.

[60] Communication, AMISOM official, 26 November 2013.

[61] See also SRCC Annadif's criticism of the KDF Sector 2 commander General Kengere in Chapter 5, footnote 98.

[62] 'Somalia's response to the federalism crisis in Baidoa', *Somalia Newsroom*, 26 March 2014, https://somalianewsroom.com/2014/03/26/analysis-somalias-response-to-the-federalism-crisis-in-baidoa/

AFTER WESTGATE

On 21 September 2013, *al-Shabaab* fighters attacked the Westgate Mall in Nairobi, Kenya killing sixty-seven people and wounding over 200 others. According to Kenya's parliamentary inquiry into the attack, it was conducted by four gunmen (three Somali nationals and a Norwegian citizen of Somali origin), all of whom died in the subsequent four-day siege.[63] The inquiry listed Westgate as the twenty-eighth terrorist attack in the country since Kenyan forces intervened in Somalia in October 2011. It concluded that a confluence of factors had left Kenya particularly vulnerable to such attacks: its porous border with Somalia, endemic corruption, and poor levels of preparedness among its security officials, youth radicalization (with over 500 Kenyan youth recruited into *al-Shabaab*), the proliferation of small arms and light weapons, and the influx of more than 600,000 Somali refugees into Kenya. Overall, the inquiry lamented that despite relevant general information about an impending terror attack on such a target, there had been a 'nationwide systemic failure' on the part of numerous government departments, confusion among government agencies in responding to the attack, and disgraceful looting of premises within the mall by some Kenyan soldiers and police.

In the wake of several smaller scale attacks by *al-Shabaab* sympathizers in Nairobi and Mombasa, and egged-on by elements of the country's media, the Kenyan government conducted a massive sweep and relocation of some 4,000 suspected 'terrorists'—dubbed Operation Usalama Watch. This involved house-to-house searches by police, principally of ethnic Somalis living in or around the Eastleigh and South C districts of Nairobi, many of whom were subsequently detained in Safaricom Kasarani stadium, as well as Mombasa and various towns in central Kenya.[64]

This episode revealed two things pertinent to the wider international effort to defeat *al-Shabaab*. First, elements of the Kenyan media and political leadership played directly into *al-Shabaab*'s hands by scapegoating ethnic Somalis as a whole, refugees, and Kenyan citizens alike. This is precisely the type of behaviour *al-Shabaab* previously used to recruit fighters and it duly released another recruitment video in mid-May 2014 following Operation Usalama Watch. Second, the episode showcased corruption within Kenya's

---

[63] *Report of the Joint Committee on Administration and National Security; and Defence and Foreign Relations on the Inquiry into the Westgate Terrorist Attack, and other Terror Attacks in Mandera in North-Eastern and Kilifi in the Coastal Region* (Kenya National Assembly, Eleventh Parliament-First Session, December 2013). In spite of this inquiry, many of the details of the attack, including the number of attackers, remain a source of controversy.

[64] See *Joint Letter to UN High Commissioner for Human Rights Navanethem Pillay Regarding Violations in the Context of Kenyan Counterterrorism Operations*, 29 May 2014, http://www.hrw.org/news/2014/05/29/joint-letter-un-high-commissioner-human-rights-navanethem-pillay-regarding-violation

security forces operating at home, some of whom used the operation as a way to make money; accusing people of lacking genuine identification documents—including one member of the Kenya senate—and subsequently releasing those who could afford their bribes.[65] If this was how KDF forces behaved in their own capital city why should anyone assume they would behave differently in Somalia?

Beyond the domestic debates in Kenya that intensified after the Westgate attack, the assault also affected the wider war against *al-Shabaab*. First, although it wasn't *al-Shabaab*'s first terrorist 'spectacular', the siege received unprecedented international media attention that shone a spotlight on the state of *al-Shabaab* and efforts to defeat it.[66] Second, the attack gave renewed impetus to those calling for a new, more offensive phase in the war against *al-Shabaab*.

A combination of internal factors and external connections explain why *al-Shabaab* attacked Westgate Mall. It was partly an attempt to stir up ethnic and religious tensions within Kenya and punish one of AMISOM's TCCs in the same way that *al-Shabaab* had attacked the restaurant and rugby club in Kampala in 2010. And like the Kampala attack, AMISOM responded by intensifying its war against *al-Shabaab*. But the Westgate attack was also an attempt by *al-Shabaab*'s leader, Ahmed Godane, to settle the future direction of the movement and to demonstrate his potency to *al-Qa'ida*'s central command. As one security professional working with AMISOM put it, the Westgate attack was a way for Godane to remind *al-Qa'ida* leader Ayman al-Zawahiri that *al-Shabaab* was still a relevant player on the global jihadi scene.[67]

Godane had moved *al-Shabaab* even closer to *al-Qa'ida* when in late June 2013 he orchestrated an internal purge of his organization's leadership.[68] This involved executing several top commanders, including two of *al-Shabaab*'s co-founders: second-in-command Ibrahim al-Alfghani (Ibrahim Haji Jama Mead aka Sheikh Abu Bakr Zaylai) and Abul Hamid Hashi Olhayi (also known as Burhan). In addition, Godane had over a dozen other senior figures put under arrest in Barawe, one of *al-Shabaab*'s remaining strongholds 250 km south of Mogadishu, and by one estimate killed off 200 members of

---

[65] See 'Kenya: Halt crackdown on Somalis', *Human Rights Watch*, press release, 11 April 2014, http://www.hrw.org/news/2014/04/11/kenya-halt-crackdown-somalis

[66] For a useful summary of the international media debates and chronology of the attack see *The Guardian*'s special section 'Westgate mall attacks', http://www.theguardian.com/world/westgate-mall-attacks

[67] Communication, Bancroft official, 7 October 2013.

[68] For overviews of Godane's purge and its precipitating factors see Matt Bryden, *The Reinvention of Al-Shabaab: A Strategy of Choice or Necessity?* (Washington DC: CSIS, February 2014), pp. 3–6 and Stig Jarle Hansen, 'An In-Depth Look at Al-Shabab's Internal Divisions', *CTC Sentinel*, 7:2 (2014), pp. 10–11.

al-Shabaab's Amniyat.[69] Other top leaders fled for their lives, including Mukhtar Robow and Sheikh Hassan Dahir Aweys, the latter reportedly ending up in the Federal Government's custody.

The targeted senior figures had previously accused Godane of a brutal and un-Islamic style of leadership and of destroying *al-Shabaab's shura*, which had previously been the organization's top decision-making authority.[70] To take just one prominent example, in an open letter sent to *al-Qa'ida* leader Ayman al-Zawahiri in March 2013, al-Afghani blamed *al-Shabaab's* misfortunes not on the military prowess of its opponents but on the unbecoming personal conduct and dictatorial leadership of Emir Godane. He accused Godane of being tyrannical and demanding blind obedience, straying from the true path of jihad, failing to consult other leaders, and placing personal desires above the requisites of Sharia and neglecting Islamic teachings of fairness, kindness, and gentleness.[71] For his part, Sheikh Mukhtar Robow Ali, known as Abu Mansur, former deputy leader and spokesman for *al-Shabaab* had said in a recorded speech circulated on some Somali websites that Godane 'refused to listen to us and is interested nothing else, but in power'.[72]

This purge appeared to be Godane's way of crushing the various sources of internal dissent that had been brewing over several related issues. As noted in Chapters 3 and 4, these included blame for the failed 2010 Ramadan offensive in Mogadishu and the expulsion of international relief agencies in the 2011 famine. But it was also illustrative of the more general debate about *al-Shabaab's* priorities, strategies, and tactics as it ceded more and more territory to AMISOM and the SNA.

Leaving aside the Westgate assault, Godane had increased the tempo of *al-Shabaab* asymmetric attacks during 2013 and following his purge.[73] Among the most spectacular were those conducted against the Mogadishu courthouse (14 April 2013), the UN compound (19 June 2013), and the Turkish embassy (27 July 2013). But there were also major suicide and complex attacks elsewhere, including two deadly incidents in Beledweyne in October and November which killed over forty people.[74] These attacks strengthened the hand of those pushing for a more offensive approach against *al-Shabaab*, not least within the UN secretariat and the US government.

[69] Ken Menkhaus, 'Al-Shabab's Capabilities Post-Westgate', *CTC Sentinel*, 7:2 (2014), p. 5.
[70] The executive *shura* had approximately 8–10 members with a larger *shura* of 35–40 members convened as required.
[71] See Hansen, 'An In-Depth Look', pp. 10–11.
[72] Ahmednor Ugas, 'Al Shabaab leader speaks out', *SomaliaCurrent*, 20 September 2013, https://archive.is/9xZrh
[73] For some figures on the increased number of al-Shabaab attacks in Mogadishu during 2013 see S/2013/521, 3 September 2013, §14.
[74] 'Somali suicide bombing kills AU soldiers in Beledweyne', *BBC News*, 19 October 2013, http://www.bbc.co.uk/news/world-africa-24595012; Bancroft Situational Report, 16–22 November 2013, p. 1. ACOTA files.

In Washington, the Westgate attack confirmed the Obama administration's earlier decision to bolster its military engagement with the Horn of Africa. During 2013 the US military created three crisis response forces for Africa. In May, a 500-strong Special-Purpose Marine Air-Ground Task Force Crisis Response unit focused on northwest Africa was formed and temporarily based at Moron Air Base, Spain. In June, the US Army established an East African Response Force (EARF) to respond to contingencies such as the attack on the US Embassy in Benghazi, Libya in September 2012.[75] And in October, the AFRICOM commander's in-extremis force was established, based out of Fort Carson, Colorado. The creation of these forces occurred in tandem with an increased tempo of US kinetic operations and support for various African actors in the war against *al-Shabaab*, including, in October 2013, the deployment of approximately two-dozen military advisers to Somalia to support AMISOM and Somali security forces.[76] The United States also conducted sporadic air strikes and special forces operations, including a failed attempt to apprehend Ikrimah—a chief planner in *al-Shabaab*'s Kenyan wing of the organization—from the movement's stronghold of Barawe in October 2013.[77]

In New York, the Westgate and other attacks prompted the UN Secretary-General to reiterate the warning of the joint benchmarking review that 'the political progress made over the last year and the military gains against Al-Shabaab that have been achieved in recent years are at a serious risk of being reversed'.[78] In response, he suggested that *al-Shabaab*'s capacity to launch asymmetric attacks must be reduced. This, in turn, required a two-pronged strategy: an effective resumption of the military campaign against *al-Shabaab* to stifle its capacity to forcefully recruit, train, and finance its operations, and improving the capacity of the Somali forces to enable a gradual reduction of the combat role of AMISOM in Somalia.

These recommendations were subsequently debated at the UN Security Council during October 2013. Somalia's Foreign Minister represented the dominant view at these discussions when she said that AMISOM's defensive posture 'provided Al-Shabaab with the breathing room to regroup and take the offensive'.[79] The very next day, AMISOM announced that it had resumed military operations against *al-Shabaab*. Led by the KDF, these operations

---

[75] Based in Djibouti, the EARF's area of operations includes Burundi, Djibouti, Eritrea, Ethiopia, Kenya, Rwanda, Somalia, Tanzania, and Uganda. It deployed for the first time on 14 December 2013 to protect the US Embassy and personnel in Juba, South Sudan.

[76] Craig Whitlock, 'U.S. has deployed military advisers to Somalia, officials say', *Washington Post*, 10 January 2014.

[77] See Nicholas Kulish and Eric Schmitt, '"Imperfect Intelligence" Said to Hinder U.S. Raid on Militant in Somalia', *New York Times*, 8 October 2013; 'Terrorism Threat in the Country', reportedly produced by the Kenyan National Intelligence Service, September 2013, http://publicintelligence.net/kenya-shabaab-file/

[78] 'Letter Dated 14 October 2013', S/2013/606, p. 3.

[79] UN doc. S/PV.7054, 30 October 2013, p. 6.

apparently targeted training camps and senior commanders in the tri-border area between Middle Juba, Lower Shabelle, and Bay region.[80]

The subsequent discussions in Addis Ababa and New York eventually produced UN Security Council resolution 2124 on 12 November 2013. This authorized enhanced capabilities for AMISOM in three main areas so that it could conduct offensive operations against *al-Shabaab*. First, it increased AMISOM's strength from 17,731 to 22,126 uniformed personnel via a 'surge' capacity of three infantry battalions and a range of support units for a period of eighteen to twenty-four months.[81] It also reiterated its call for the mission to receive various force enablers and multipliers, including AMISOM's aviation component of up to twelve military helicopters.[82] This was particularly important because as the UN Secretary-General made clear, 'it is not realistic for AMISOM to achieve the desired effect of resuming the military campaign [against *al-Shabaab*] without air assets'.[83] Second, the resolution proposed changes to enhance AMISOM's planning and strategic management capabilities and new systems to address allegations of misconduct and ensure that any AMISOM detainees are treated in strict compliance with applicable obligations under international humanitarian law and human rights law. Third, resolution 2124 also expanded the UNSOA logistical support package for AMISOM to encompass the additional personnel and provide food and water, fuel, transport, tents and in-theatre medical evacuation for Somali National Army troops engaged in joint operations with AMISOM (see Chapter 8).

Security Council resolution 2124 affirmed Ethiopia's new commitment to change its long-standing position of supporting AMISOM from outside.[84] Negotiations then focused on the precise terms of integrating some of Ethiopia's forces into AMISOM. As discussed in Chapter 7, over 4,000 ENDF soldiers would join AMISOM in January 2014. This would require yet another new Concept of Operations for AMISOM. Officially, the process of revising AMISOM's 2012 Concept of Operations began after 4 August 2013 when AMISOM TCCs, Ethiopia, and Somalia issued a communiqué arguing that the mission needed a new strategic concept more in line with the prevailing circumstances in south-central Somalia.[85] The plan was to develop a new Concept of Operations that would reconfigure AMISOM's forces so they

---

[80] AMISOM Press Release, 31 October 2013, http://amisom-au.org/2013/10/amisom-resumes-military-operations-against-al-shabaab/

[81] The surge was extended by the UN Security Council in S/RES/2232, 28 July 2015, §3.

[82] As provided for in S/RES/2036, 22 February 2012, §6.

[83] 'Letter Dated 14 October 2013', S/2013/606, p. 6.

[84] Although it did not integrate any military units into AMISOM, Ethiopia had placed about ten staff officers in the mission's force headquarters since February 2012.

[85] The communiqué is at http://www.hiiraan.com/Pdf_Files/2013/FINAL_COMMUNIQUE_OF_THE_SUMMIT_OF_HEADS_OF_STATES.pdf

could conduct sustained offensive operations against *al-Shabaab*, strengthen the multidimensional nature of the mission, and bolster the SNSF as a necessary part of the mission's exit strategy. To that end, the 2014 Concept of Operations was designed to reconfigure AMISOM to achieve four strategic objectives: secure the sovereignty and territorial integrity of Somalia by helping to neutralize *al-Shabaab*; enhance the capacity of Somalia's national security forces to enable them to take full responsibility for the country's security; support the establishment of effective governance structures, especially in the areas recovered from *al-Shabaab*; and facilitate the holding of general elections in 2016.[86] To succeed, AMISOM would have to use its new 'surge' capacity to good effect.

CONCLUSION

Faced with a new political terrain after Somalia officially ended its period of 'transitional' governments, AMISOM underwent another series of reviews and mandate revisions. This time around, however, the emphasis was placed firmly on consolidating the mission's hard-won territorial gains. During this period AMISOM still suffered from some severe challenges, most notably related to political developments in Sector 2 and some of the KDF's activities. In the second half of 2013, however, *al-Shabaab* began to intensify its asymmetric attacks against AMISOM and the new Federal Government. Spurred on by Godane's internal purge, *al-Shabaab* also stepped up its operations in Kenya. Particularly after the Westgate attack, AMISOM and its key partners decided that it was in danger of losing its gains if it remained on the defensive. In late 2013, therefore, AMISOM restarted offensive operations and was authorized by the UN Security Council to use a new surge capacity to once again put *al-Shabaab* on the back foot. But as the new head of AMISOM, Mahamat Saleh Annadif, correctly pointed out in September 2013, one problem with surging forward was that 'the more territory we liberate, the more we become dispersed'.[87] As Chapter 7 discusses, this would have some deadly consequences for AMISOM.

---

[86] *Revised Concept of Operations for AMISOM* (AU internal document, January 2014), §13.
[87] S/PV.7030, 12 September 2013, p. 6.

7

Surge

January 2014 to May 2017

AMISOM's new Concept of Operations adopted in January 2014 included the temporary 'surge' in capacity authorized by the UN Security Council in November 2013. It also set out a new force posture for the mission based on six land sectors and the previous maritime sectors. The land sector boundaries were revised in mid-March. Although the overall AMISOM area of operations did not change, this involved creating a new Sector 5 to the northeast of Mogadishu, revising all the land sector boundaries, and creating a new Sector Kismayo (see Figure I.3).

According to the UN, the surge forces were supposed to total 4,395 troops comprising three infantry battalions (2,550), training team personnel (220), logistics units (1,000), an engineering enabling unit (190), a signals unit (117), a port security unit (312) and a civilian casualty tracking analysis and response cell (CCTARC) (6).[1] In practice, however, the surge did not materialize as planned—AMISOM acquired more combat troops but not the badly needed logistics and mobility enablers. As the subsequent 2015 joint AU–UN bench-marking review noted, the envisaged 'logistics unit, engineering enabling unit, signals unit, port security unit and CCTARC unit were either not deployed fully or could not be deployed as mission assets as envisaged under the CONOPS'.[2] Nor did AMISOM gain any military helicopters. Instead, Ethiopian troops accounted for almost the entire surge.

Nevertheless, the surge did stimulate a new phase of major operations for AMISOM from March 2014 to December 2016.[3] These succeeded in

---

[1] As set out in 'Letter dated 14 October 2013 from the Secretary-General addressed to the President of the Security Council' (S/2013/606, 14 October 2013). The CCTARC had been authorized in UN Security Council resolution 2036, 22 February 2012, §17.

[2] *Report of the Joint African Union–United Nations Mission on the Benchmarks for a United Nations Peacekeeping Operation in Somalia and recommendations on the next steps in the military campaign* (30 June 2015), §12. Hereafter, *Joint Benchmarking Review* (2015).

[3] It is notable that in November 2016, AMISOM's Military Operations Coordination Committee requested up to 4,000 additional troops beyond the existing surge capacity for a six-month

displacing *al-Shabaab* forces from more than two dozen strategic ports and towns. Usually, however, *al-Shabaab* forces withdrew without a fight. This chapter therefore begins with an analysis of why Ethiopia finally decided to integrate some of its troops into AMISOM in January 2014 followed by a summary of the four major expansion and consolidation operations that the AU mission undertook over the next two years, namely, operations Eagle, Indian Ocean, Ocean Build, and Juba Corridor. The third section then discusses the subsequent round of mandate revisions and review process that took place in light of these operations and produced yet another new Concept of Operations for the mission in August 2015. A major consequence of these operations was that AMISOM acquired more territory and settlements to help administer. This, in turn, generated a new force posture that relied on dozens of new Forward Operating Bases (FOBs). Often garrisoned by just a company of troops, the subsequent archipelago of FOBs required a major effort by both UNSOA and the mission TCCs to sustain, and some of them were left vulnerable to *al-Shabaab* attacks. The fourth section therefore discusses some of the main problems caused by this new force structure and the major attempts by *al-Shabaab* to overrun AMISOM bases. Finally, the chapter returns to the most fundamental and perennial problem facing AMISOM, namely, the lack of a political settlement and national reconciliation among Somalia's governing elites. However, at least on paper, some progress was made in this area in early 2017 with the (s)election of a new Federal Government and in May with the conclusion of a Security Pact signed at the London Somalia conference. This included for the first time a vision of a new national security architecture that had ostensibly been agreed by both the Federal Government and Somalia's regional entities. It remains to be seen whether the pact retains regional buy-in and whether it can be implemented in the field.

ETHIOPIA JOINS AMISOM

Ethiopia has been the most important external actor in Somali affairs in the twenty-first century, having a bigger strategic impact on local politics than any other actor. Broadly speaking, Ethiopia's multidimensional engagement in Somalia pursued three connected goals: minimizing irredentism, maintaining a fairly pliable government in Somalia which would not act as a major rival in the region, and promoting a federalist approach to Somali state-building

period to conduct offensive operations. This request was not authorized by the UN Security Council. See AMISOM Press Statement, 11 November 2016, http://www.peaceau.org/uploads/press-statement-mocc-11.11.2016v2.pdf

(drawing inspiration from Ethiopia's own federal constitution and the idea of a building-block approach, this gave a key place to Somaliland and other regional entities beyond the Federal Government).[4] This meant that despite Addis Ababa's regular willingness to intervene militarily in Somalia, defeating *al-Shabaab* had never been the ENDF's primary objective. Rather, it was to contain the threat away from Ethiopian territory.[5]

In relation to AMISOM, it was Ethiopia's 2006 intervention to oust the SCIC and install the TFG in Mogadishu that spurred the establishment of AMISOM.[6] Simply put, AMISOM was Ethiopia's way out of Mogadishu as the risk of becoming stuck in a political and military quagmire increased, casualties mounted, and the financial costs grew.

As discussed in Chapter 1, in June 2007, Ethiopia's Prime Minister Meles Zenawi had offered a variety of reasons for his 2006 intervention in Somalia. And as discussed in Chapter 5, the 2011 intervention was at IGAD's request and represented an attempt to open up a third front against *al-Shabaab* in the wake of Kenya's Operation *Linda Nchi*. This unknown number of ENDF troops subsequently remained in Somalia and supported AMISOM forces in Sectors 3 and 4. Then, as noted in Chapter 6, during the second half of 2013, Ethiopia began to shift its long-standing refusal to join AMISOM.

Since 2011, Ethiopia's main public justification for keeping its troops out of AMISOM was 'efficiency'. In sum, it was thought better for Ethiopian soldiers to operate solely under Ethiopian commanders.[7] Following discussions that took place as part of the Joint AU–UN benchmarking mission, by late 2013, this was apparently no longer a major concern and Ethiopia changed its approach from operating outside of the mission to integrating most of its existing troops already inside Somalia into AMISOM. In reality, of course, AMISOM's loose command and control system meant that all its TCCs retained considerable autonomy of action. The ENDF thus retained operational command of its troops since the AMISOM force headquarters had no practical way of controlling them. Roughly 4,000 ENDF troops were already deployed in AMISOM Sectors 3 (shared with Kenya) and 4 (shared with Djibouti), but one company would later deploy in Sector Kismayo in 2015 after Sierra Leone's withdrawal.

Given Ethiopia's long-standing preference to conduct unilateral military operations in Somalia and AMISOM's weak force headquarters, financial issues were probably the main reason why the ENDF integrated some of its troops into AMISOM.[8] This concern seemed to be borne out in the

---

[4] Interview, Ethiopian official, Addis Ababa, 31 July 2012.

[5] Interview, US military official, Addis Ababa, 27 April 2016.

[6] For details see Bruton and Williams, *Counterinsurgency*, pp. 9–11, 37–41.

[7] Interview, Ethiopian analyst, Addis Ababa, 16 October 2013; Heaton, 'Somalia: On Scene in Baidoa'.

[8] Communication, Ethiopian analyst, 14 November 2013.

subsequent negotiations over the official memorandum of understanding with the AU. During the discussions between Ethiopia and the AU it became apparent that the AU's preference was for the ENDF to contribute two infantry battalions but also crucial specialist capabilities with another country providing the third infantry battalion identified in the 'surge'.[9] Ultimately, however, three ENDF infantry battalions were deployed. The other details revolved around working out Ethiopia's reimbursement requests for their troops, logistics and contingent-owned equipment. There were also command and control issues to discuss because there would be additional ENDF forces inside Somalia that would not integrate into AMISOM, including some aviation assets.[10] Ethiopia also declined to provide military helicopters for AMISOM, saying that it was instead honouring a UN request to deploy its spare capacity in this area to the peacekeeping force in Abyei, where it was the sole major TCC. As noted in Chapter 5, however, Ethiopia operated attack and utility helicopters in Somalia but refused to place them under AMISOM command and control.

After joining AMISOM, and like all the other TCCs, Ethiopian forces received monthly allowances payments (provided by the European Union) and logistical support from UNSOA. As with its UN peacekeeping deployments, the Ethiopian government chose to retain just over half of the troop allowances for use by its defence sector and just under half to the soldiers.[11] Like Kenya, Ethiopia continued to conduct unilateral operations in Somalia in support of its AMISOM contingent, although some of these additional forces were withdrawn in late 2016 and early 2017.[12] The stated reason for the ENDF withdrawals was lack of international (financial) support, but they opened the door for *al-Shabaab* to return to some of these settlements, often exacting retribution on the local inhabitants for collaborating with the Ethiopian forces.[13] They also prompted, in November 2016, the AU to call for a temporary increase 'of up to 4,000 troops [for AMISOM] for a maximum period of six months to conduct offensive operations'.[14]

Institutional rationales were also part of the equation, but they do not explain the timing of Ethiopia's decision to join AMISOM and played only a minimal role in the conduct of the ENDF's operations in Somalia. The ENDF's most important external partner was the United States. Having become an

---

[9] Communication, senior US official, Addis Ababa, 13 November 2013. [10] *Ibid.*

[11] Communication, EU official, 15 January 2014.

[12] James Jeffrey, 'Ethiopian troop withdrawal from Somalia exposes peacekeeping problems', *France 24*, 16 December 2016, http://www.france24.com/en/20161215-ethiopian-troops-withdraw-highlighting-peacekeeping-internationally-funded-peacekeeping

[13] 'Ethiopia withdraws troops in Somalia over 'lack of support'', *BBC News*, 26 October 2016, http://www.bbc.co.uk/news/world-africa-37775555

[14] 'Outcome of the 21st MOCC meeting on AMISOM', AU Press Statement, 11 November 2016, http://www.peaceau.org/uploads/press-statement-mocc-11.11.2016v2.pdf

ACOTA partner in January 1998, the ENDF once again became eligible to receive US military aid under Section 505 of the US Foreign Assistance Act in January 2003. However, this support was focused principally on Ethiopia's roles in various UN peacekeeping operations including in Darfur and Liberia, not its operations in AMISOM.[15] In mid-2014, Ethiopia was chosen as one of six African states (also including Uganda) to receive additional support under the new US African Rapid Response Peacekeeping Partnership established by President Obama. This provided a range of support for Ethiopia's broader peacekeeping activities rather than its AMISOM operations specifically, but did include fungible items, notably a C-130 aircraft.[16]

In sum, like Kenya, Ethiopia's initial preference was to address security threats emanating from Somalia via unilateral action. Only much later did Ethiopia integrate some of its forces into AMISOM. This was done primarily for financial reasons and because the ENDF's concerns about retaining control of its operations was facilitated by AMISOM's weak force headquarters. Unlike all the other AMISOM TCCs, institutional concerns to derive security assistance packages were not a major concern of the ENDF for its operations in Somalia.

CLEAR. HOLD. PROTECT. BUILD. AMISOM'S MAJOR OPERATIONS, 2014–16

With over 4,000 Ethiopian troops now officially part of AMISOM, the mission started to deploy its 'surge' capacity. To that end, from March 2014 to December 2016, AMISOM embarked on four major operations, most in conjunction with the SNA and other allied militias:

- Operation Eagle (3–31 March 2014).
- Operation Indian Ocean (25 August–31 October 2014).
- Operation Ocean Build (1 November 2014–July 2015).
- Operation Juba Corridor (July–November 2015).

These were a mixture of expansion and stabilization missions to clear *al-Shabaab* from selected settlements, hold and then stabilize those settlements by protecting the local population, and building in them the prospect of a future better than that offered by *al-Shabaab*.

First up was Operation Eagle. It was intended to clear and then hold about a dozen selected *al-Shabaab* strongholds across south-central Somalia by

---

[15] ACOTA Partner Summary: Ethiopia, 1 August 2013. ACOTA files.
[16] Interview, US official, Addis Ababa, 27 April 2016.

separating the militants from the population and isolating them from their sources of support.

To give just one example of what was entailed, the planning and execution of the operations to recover the town of Qoryoley took two weeks, from 12–26 March, and involved numerous actors. Qoryoley was identified as a key target because *al-Shabaab* was suspected of orchestrating its attacks on various towns including Marka and Janaale from there and Buulo Mareer.[17] The operation required considerable coordination and planning to execute successfully. As was common, it involved a mix of forces, in this case two UPDF battalions, some special forces, elements of two SNA brigades, and Bancroft mentors. UNSOA provided helicopter support for casualty evacuation, which proved efficient and boosted morale, while a forward-based vehicle maintenance team fixed damaged Casspirs so as not to slow the advance. The AMISOM and SNA forces feigned attack from the south but enveloped the town from the north. It was effective and the town was successfully recovered. Indeed, one of the only problems identified was that gunners on some of the UPDF's fighting vehicles were too short to see over their weapons and thus could not deliver fire accurately.[18]

More generally, however, AMISOM was still facing a wide range of challenges as it embarked on Operation Eagle. For example, a lessons learned workshop in March 2014 identified thirty-eight lessons to improve upon related to pre-deployment training, mission support, equipment issues, logistics planning and delivery, weapons and ammunition management, media training, command and control infrastructure, joint operations, SNA training, international humanitarian law, and C-IED issues.[19]

Later, an internal review of Operation Eagle conducted in May 2014 identified further problems.[20] Most importantly, it concluded that while AMISOM had recovered its targeted settlements, this had generally displaced rather than destroyed *al-Shabaab*'s combat capabilities.[21] In other words, the 'clear' of clear/hold/build was only partially implemented since *al-Shabaab* forces often withdrew without a fight, lurked in the vicinity, or left some fighters to blend with the local population. This posed subsequent problems for the hold and especially build phases. The review also noted that there were

---

[17] *After Action Report: Qoryoley Offensive, 12–26 March 2014* (Bancroft, 2014). ACOTA files.

[18] This was also the case in the operation to recover Barawe in October 2014. *After Action Report: Operation Indian Ocean, Barawe, 28 September–11 October 2014* (Bancroft, 2014). ACOTA files.

[19] *Report on AMISOM Lessons Learned Workshop*, Addis Ababa, 17–21 March 2014 (AU internal document, 2014).

[20] *After Action Review: Lessons Identified, 12–13 May 2014* (AU internal document, May 2014), p. 1.

[21] The towns recovered in Operation Eagle were Rab Dhuure, Xuduur, Wajid, Burdubo, Bulo Burto, Warshik, Maxaas, Qurunlaw, Qoryoley, and Cell Buur.

often significant coordination problems between AMISOM, the SNA, and UNSOA as well as problems related to communications, logistical support, and lack of intelligence. Part of the problems occurred because of poor sequencing of operations; for instance, Operation Eagle was conducted while AMISOM's relief in place was still taking place.[22] The report also noted the SNA did not fully participate and the lack of attack helicopters reduced AMISOM's effectiveness.[23] There was also a lack of translators in Sectors 2–5, and the ones that were utilized sometimes suffered from poor skills and conflicting agendas, often related to their clan identity.[24]

Next up was Operation Indian Ocean, which ran from August to October 2014 and had similar objectives and intent to its predecessor. Indian Ocean succeeded in recovering twelve settlements, including *al-Shabaab*'s operations centre at Buulo Mareer and its new headquarters at Barawe in October.[25] Combined with Operation Eagle, this represented an estimated 68 per cent of the strategic locations *al-Shabaab* had controlled at the start of 2014. AMISOM and SNA forces also suffered few fatalities, with the AMISOM Force Commander noting that by September 2014 Operation Indian Ocean had resulted in three AMISOM and three SNA fatalities.[26] A boost to morale occurred on 1 September 2014, when a US strike killed *al-Shabaab*'s leader, Ahmed Godane, along with five suspected members of the militants' leadership.

While coordination with the SNA and logistics support with UNSOA improved significantly during Indian Ocean, there were still familiar problems. At times, large numbers of SNA soldiers did not have or did not wear issued uniforms, making them indistinguishable from *al-Shabaab* fighters.[27] Although Indian Ocean saw improved communication between AMISOM and UNSOA, there were still requests for logistical support that did not give UNSOA enough time to deliver the needed items.[28] The poor condition of many vehicles once again led to frequent breakdowns of AMISOM's Casspirs and Rinkhals, which risked slowing advancing troops and required repair in the field or recovery back to base. There were also approximately 7,300 local inhabitants displaced during the operation, not all of whom received adequate

---

[22] *After Action Review: Lessons Identified, 12–13 May 2014*, p. 1.   [23] *Ibid.*, p. 4.
[24] *Ibid.*, p. 3.
[25] The towns recovered in Operation Indian Ocean were Barawe, Golweyn and Jeero, Kurutunwarey, Bulogadud, Tiyeeglow, Jalalaqsi, Dhingaras, Raga Cell, Cadale, Xajicale, Fidow, and Haro Lugoole. *AMISOM Force Headquarters Position Paper on Joint African Union/United Nations Benchmarking Exercise* (AU internal document, April 2015).
[26] *Phase 1 and Phase 2 of Operation Indian Ocean Report* (AU internal document, September 2014), p. 3.
[27] *After Action Report: Operation Indian Ocean, Fidow and Jalalaqsi, 28 August–3 September 2014* (Bancroft, 2014). ACOTA files.
[28] *After Action Report: Operation Indian Ocean: Buulo Mareer and Kurtunwarey, 25 August–1 September 2014* (Bancroft, 2014). ACOTA files.

humanitarian assistance.[29] Once again, fewer Quick Impact Projects (QIPs) occurred than planned (only about a dozen), although the ones that did focused, quite reasonably, on water issues such as wells, bore holes, and sanitation, or infrastructure, such as improving medical facilities, schools, and bridges.[30]

It is worth noting here that AMISOM too struggled with water provision. Water in many areas of Somalia is already in scarcity so AMISOM had to employ a variety of techniques to secure sufficient water sources. In towns where there were private wells, AMISOM bought access (such as in Marka and Baidoa). But relying on local resources that were not secure posed a risk. Furthermore, over time, it could strain local resources for residents. As a result, water trucking occurred along the Mogadishu to Baidoa corridor between Baledogle and Burhakaba. Not surprisingly, in areas where AMISOM's FOBs relied upon water trucking, *al-Shabaab* often chose to target water bowsers in their ambushes.[31]

The conduct of operations Eagle and Indian Ocean also exposed the inability of some AMISOM forces to adequately perform anti-ambush procedures. This was important because although *al-Shabaab* forces usually retreated in the face of AMISOM/SNA assaults, there were occasions where they put up resistance from prepared defensive positions and obstacles, as in Buulo Mareer, or carried out ambushes on AMISOM and SNA convoys, which put a premium on the troops knowing anti-ambush drills and vehicle recovery procedures. In May 2014, for example, *al-Shabaab* killed between thirty and forty SNA soldiers in an ambush on a convoy near Jalalaqsi.[32] Similarly, during the operations to capture Barawe, *al-Shabaab* ambushed AMISOM and SNA convoys on 4, 7, and 11 October, injuring nine UPDF and killing two SNA troops.[33] *Al-Shabaab* subsequently continued to ambush AMISOM convoys, perhaps most notably in two major incidents near Jame'ada (June 2015) where an estimated thirty Ethiopian troops were killed and near Golweyn (July 2017) where over twenty Ugandan AMISOM troops were reportedly killed.[34] Finally, AMISOM and SNA were shown to possess

---

[29] *Operations Order (OPO) 08/2014—Operation Ocean Build* (AU internal document, November 2014), p. 2.

[30] *Operations Order 01/2015—Operation Juba Corridor* (AU internal document, November 2014), Annex D, p. 1.

[31] Communication, Bancroft official, 1 March 2015.

[32] *Operations Order 08/2014—Operation Ocean Build*, p.2.

[33] Barawe itself was recovered on 6 October with no resistance. *After Action Report: Operation Indian Ocean, Barawe, 28 September–11 October 2014* (Bancroft, 2014). ACOTA files.

[34] See, Caleb Weiss, 'Shabaab release images from the ambush of Ethiopian troops', *Long War Journal*, 19 June 2015, http://www.longwarjournal.org/archives/2015/06/shabaab-releases-images-from-the-ambush-of-ethiopian-troops.php and 'African Union troops killed in al-Shabab ambush', *AlJazeera*, 30 July 2017, http://www.aljazeera.com/news/2017/07/african-union-troops-killed-al-shabab-ambush-170730195320158.html

insufficient understanding of the '5Ss' of questioning procedures for detainees (search, silence, segregate, safeguard, speed to rear).

The third big operation during this period was Ocean Build, conducted from November 2014 to July 2015. With this operation AMISOM's approach shifted from 'clear-hold-build' to a 'hold-protect-build' approach. This placed more emphasis on consolidating and stabilizing the areas recently recovered from *al-Shabaab*.[35] The mission objectives were to stabilize the newly recovered settlements by protecting the local population, easing their suffering, and thereby win their support. This would then facilitate the extension of Federal Government authority.[36] The plan was to consolidate the gains made during operations Eagle and Indian Ocean by protecting the populations in the newly recovered settlements as well as the routes to them. In theory, this would enable Federal Government personnel to access these areas in order to establish interim District Administrations and District Peace and Stability Committees as part of the government's stabilization strategy.[37] In practice, this did not happen consistently. The desired end state was defined as liberated areas that were protected and stabilized, thus paving the way for further offensive operations against *al-Shabaab*. Along the way, discipline amongst AMISOM and SNA forces was vital to maintain local support.

The subsequent operations involved a whole host of challenges related to stabilization that are analysed in detail in Chapter 12. Suffice to say here that by April 2015, the AMISOM Force Commander had identified twenty-eight challenges that had arisen during the course of the recent operations (see Table 7.1). To a greater or lesser degree, all of them impacted on Operation Ocean Build and therefore any subsequent gains should be applauded.

The intent behind Ocean Build was to promote stabilization by holding the key population centres and protecting their inhabitants, as well as by enhancing security of movement along the main supply routes. This would enable the Federal Government, the UN, and NGOs to project security, governance, and humanitarian assistance and the subsequent peace dividends. AMISOM was also to devote more attention to improving the SNA's ability to support the Federal Government and contribute to joint operations with AMISOM. Importantly, AMISOM was also called on to monitor clan conflicts, which had sometimes erupted after *al-Shabaab* forces withdrew.[38] In the event of clan conflict, the Federal Government was to mediate and attempt to resolve tensions as quickly as possible.

Finally, in July 2015, AMISOM launched Operation Juba Corridor, conducted principally by Ethiopian and Kenyan forces with support from the

---

[35] *Operations Order 08/2014—Operation Ocean Build.*   [36] *Ibid.*, p.4.

[37] *Report of the Secretary-General on Somalia January 2015* (S/2015/51, 23 January 2015), §26–8.

[38] *SEMG Report*, 19 October 2015, p. 6.

Table 7.1. Operational challenges facing AMISOM, April 2015

1. Contingents spread across sector boundaries	2. Inadequate force protection equipment	3. Reliance on local interpreters inhibits operational security	4. Lack of command and control system between AMISOM and SNA
5. Inadequate communications	6. Inadequate medical care and training	7. No Hand over/Take over procedures for officers during rotation	8. Absence of DDR–SSR coordination
9. Inadequate force multipliers	10. Lack of night casualty evacuation capability	11. No plan for military drawdown and increase in Formed Police Units	12. Interclan and political conflicts
13. Inadequate maritime security capabilities	14. Strategy to open the main supply routes	15. Absence of stabilization plan	16. Lack of proper human resource management for the SNA
17. Insufficiently agile logistics support	18. Inadequate coordination between AMISOM and partners	19. Inadequate QIPs in liberated areas	20. Insufficient SNA support
21. Limited night fighting capabilities	22. Lack of rapidly deployable reserve unit	23. Lack of infrastructure development plan	24. Lack of militia integration plan
25. Inadequate spare parts for maintenance	26. Old, outdated maps	27. Insufficient force levels	28. Lack of strategic vision for 2016 elections

Source: AMISOM Force Headquarters Position Paper on Joint African Union/United Nations Benchmarking Exercise (AU internal document, April 2015), pp. 14–16.

SNA and local militia. It aimed to expel *al-Shabaab* from its last remaining strongholds in the Gedo, Bakool, and Bay regions of Somalia, particularly along the Juba river valley, isolate its fighters from the local population, and clear AMISOM's main supply routes.[39] The operation's official objectives were to 'destroy, secure, consolidate and enhance the stabilization process'.[40]

The plan was for the operation to unfold in five sequential phases stretching until December 2016.[41] Phase 1 involved shaping operations during June 2015. Phase 2 called for limited offensive operations across three Sectors during July and August. Phase 3 was envisaged as the decisive offensive operations that should take place from September to January 2016. Phase 4 would entail any subsequent offensive operations between February and April 2016. And Phase 5

---

[39] 'AMISOM Press Statement', 19 July 2015, http://somaliamediamonitoring.org/july-20-2015-morning-headlines/. Just prior to the operation, AMISOM estimated *al-Shabaab* had between 6,000 and 6,500 fighters with 3,000 in Sector 3 and 2,000 in Sector 2. *AMISOM Force Headquarters Position Paper (2015)*, Annex A, p. 3. See also *Operations Order 01/2015— Operation Juba Corridor*, Annex B, pp. 3–4.

[40] *Operations Order 01/2015—Operation Juba Corridor*, pp. 8–10.   [41] *Ibid.*, pp. 5–7.

would represent the consolidation and hand over to Somali forces from May to December.

Shortly after starting operations, AMISOM troops—supported by an unknown number of additional Ethiopian forces[42]—successfully seized Baardheere, in Gedo region, and Diinsoor, in Bay region in July. Diinsoor was thought to have become *al-Shabaab*'s headquarters after the militants lost Barawe. The operation also targeted suspected *al-Shabaab* positions in the Hiraan and Galguduud regions, including Halgan.[43]

Once again, however, the operation failed to destroy rather than displace most of *al-Shabaab*'s key combat capabilities. The operation also stalled and coordinated offensive operations petered out. In part, the failure to destroy the *al-Shabaab* forces in the Juba Valley was because AMISOM remained a generally slower force than its enemy and still lacked the aviation assets to strike them from depth. The use of Kenyan and Ethiopian aviation did not solve this problem. But there were also further coordination problems, this time between the Kenyan and Ethiopian troops and the Ugandans who were criticized for not providing the necessary blocking force at the required time and place.

The result was that the operation that petered out before it was scheduled to end and a long pause occurred. It was not until August 2016 that AMISOM and its key partners developed plans for Operation Juba Corridor 2. This time around the plan was for the new operation to unfold in three phases from September 2016 to March 2017.[44] Phase 1 would take place up to mid-September and involve the necessary reconfiguration and preparation of the relevant forces. Phase 2 would see the execution of the mission from mid-September until the end of December. The plan was to destroy *al-Shabaab* capabilities in the Juba Valley but also along the northeastern coast. Targeting about a dozen towns in these areas the operational mantra was to 'degrade, secure, consolidate and enhance the stabilization process'. Phase 3, from January to March 2017 would focus on the consolidation and stabilization of the newly recovered areas and key supply routes.

However, once again, the operation failed to unfold as planned.[45] This time the main problem was that both Ethiopia and Kenya identified additional non-AMISOM forces that would be necessary to achieve the operation's objectives and requested that they receive logistical support. Specifically, in

---

[42] In July 2015, it was reported that approximately 3,000 ENDF troops had entered Somalia's Gedo region. '3,000 Ethiopia troops cross into Somalia', *Daily Nation* (Kenya), 9 July 2015, http://www.nation.co.ke/news/africa/3-000-Ethiopia-troops-cross-into-Somalia/-/1066/2781280/-/fesx5tz/-/index.html

[43] *Report of the Secretary-General on Somalia* (S/2015/702, 11 September 2015), §12.

[44] *Force Commander Operations Order 01/2016: Operation Juba Corridor II* (AU internal document, 29 August 2016).

[45] This paragraph is based on communication, senior UNSOS official, 1 November 2016.

late September 2016, UNSOS was asked to provide additional logistical support for roughly 1,300 non-AMISOM Ethiopian troops, 1,600 non-AMISOM Kenyan troops, non-AMISOM air assets from both countries, and an additional 5,400 SNA and regional forces beyond those listed in the *Guulwade* (Victory) Plan (see Chapter 9). This proved impossible because UNSOS support to operations in Somalia could only be to forces mandated by the UN Security Council, and UNSOS had no such mandate to support these troops; even if authorized, UNSOS would require much more time to prepare logistics support for this large number of additional forces; and UNSOS did not have the capacity to provide such support, certainly not within the time frame proposed. With no other bilateral support available for these non-AMISOM forces, the operation petered out once again. Instead of a series of offensives, AMISOM's main focus turned to securing the Somali election process.

Overall, therefore, AMISOM ended these operations with *al-Shabaab* removed from a large number of settlements. The result was a considerably expanded footprint of AMISOM and SNA bases. But the operations had not destroyed as many of *al-Shabaab*'s combat capabilities as hoped and AMISOM and the SNA were left with many stabilization challenges, which are analysed in Chapter 12. Of course, as these operations unfolded, AMISOM's international partners were revising their policies accordingly.

MORE MANDATES AND BENCHMARKS

As AMISOM was embarking on Operation Juba Corridor, the UN and AU decided to conduct another benchmarking review of their engagement in Somalia. In its report, completed in June 2015, the review team concluded that AMISOM should not transition into a UN peacekeeping operation before the end of 2016 at the earliest because the conditions in south-central Somalia were not appropriate.[46] In the interim period, the benchmarking review called

---

[46] The 2015 benchmarks for the transition of AMISOM into a UN peacekeeping operation were:

1. Political agreement on the finalization of a federal vision and formation of administrations and states.
2. Extension of state authority through local administrations in recovered areas, in line with the provisional constitution.
3. Degrading *al-Shabaab* to the point that it is no longer an effective force through a comprehensive strategy that includes political, economic and security components.
4. A significant improvement in the physical security situation, with improved control in major cities and access to key urban centres.
5. Improved capability of the Somali security institutions to hold the majority of territory in the areas of operation of AMISOM with a critical mass of trained and equipped security personnel.

for a renewed push along three principal lines of effort: enabling the political process in Somalia at the national, regional, and local levels; restarting offensive operations against *al-Shabaab* targeting their remaining strongholds and separating them from the local population; and enabling consolidation and stabilization efforts.

The review also reiterated that in order for AMISOM to be 'more cohesive and effective', it desperately needed key enablers, especially helicopters, APCs, and intelligence capabilities. One dimension of this challenge was that such enabling units were in relatively short supply in Africa and unlikely to be deployable in Somalia for a mixture of political and practical reasons. The mission also needed better, centralized command and control, more coordination between national contingents to conduct cross-sector operations, and better information sharing about national operations. This time around, the review emphasized that 'offensive operations must aim at severely degrading Al Shabaab capacities rather than being terrain oriented, and that offensive operations not be determined or limited by AMISOM and/or SNA's respective sector boundaries'.[47] It also recommended that Puntland be included in AMISOM's Concept of Operations because some *al-Shabaab* fighters had moved into the region.[48] The benchmarking review formed the basis for AMISOM's latest Concept of Operations, which was adopted in August 2015 (see p. 191).

In line with the analysis conducted by the joint benchmarking review, on 28 July 2015, the UN Security Council passed resolution 2232 which endorsed a revised security strategy for Somalia. The new strategy was to be guided by three objectives:

1. continuing offensive operations against *al-Shabaab* strongholds;

2. enabling the political process at all levels, including through securing critical political processes throughout Somalia; and

3. enabling stabilization efforts through supporting the delivery of security for the Somali people to facilitate the wider process of peacebuilding and

---

6. Broad agreement on the major security arrangements, in line with the political process, set by the FGS within the context of the federal vision agreed by major political stakeholders.
7. Police services with essential training and equipment provide security and basic law and order functions in major population centers, creating an environment conducive for political processes, economic activities, and the delivery of basic social services.
8. The consent of the Federal Government and the support of important segments of the Somali population for the deployment of a United Nations peacekeeping operation.

Joint Benchmarking Review (2015), §42.

[47] *Ibid.*, §55.
[48] Puntland authorities rejected such an expansion, arguing instead for more resources to be given to their local security forces. Abdiqani Hassan, 'Puntland seeks resources as Somali militants enter its territory', *Reuters*, 6 August 2015, http://www.reuters.com/article/2015/08/06/us-somalia-security-puntland-idUSKCN0QB1W720150806

reconciliation, including through the gradual handing over of security responsibilities from AMISOM to the SNA and subsequently to the Somali police force.[49]

Among other things, it also called for AMISOM to undergo

a structured and targeted reconfiguration'. This was in order 'to enable a surge in its efficiency, in particular by strengthening command and control structures, enhancing cross-sector operations, examining sector boundaries, generating a dedicated special forces' capability under the authority of the Force Commander, which should operate alongside existing Somali special forces, generating all the requisite specialized units…, ensuring that all force enablers and multipliers operate under the authority of the Special Representative of the Chairperson of the AU Commission and Force Commander, and taking into account progress achieved in offensive operations against Al Shabaab and other terrorist organisations, by gradually, and in a limited manner, and where appropriate, reconfiguring AMISOM uniformed personnel in favour of police personnel within the authorized AMISOM personnel ceiling.[50]

It should be noted, however, that the Joint Benchmarking Review made much stronger recommendations about the need to develop more policing capabilities within AMISOM and in Somalia than was evident in the UN Security Council resolution.[51] The Security Council's insertion of language that suggested the shift to policing should be 'in a limited manner' and 'where appropriate' (Resolution 2232, op.§6) was used by some of AMISOM's TCCs to water down the recommendation and avoid implementing it.[52]

The same three strategic objectives proposed by the benchmarking team also became the basis for AMISOM's new Concept of Operations. Notably, however, the document also identified a series of risks facing AMISOM. One of which was summarized as follows: 'Should the FGS fail to deliver critical services and authority in line with its capacity development, the population may not enjoy the expected peace dividend, and this will undermine its perceived effectiveness and legitimacy, as well as support to AMISOM'.[53] As discussed below, this warning was sadly prescient.

In terms of its mandate, AMISOM subsequently enjoyed nearly a year without any further revisions. Then, in June 2016, the AU PSC officially endorsed AMISOM's new 'priority tasks' as set out in the revised CONOPS:

AMISOM support and contribution to securing the electoral process in Somalia in coordination with the Elections Security Taskforce within the Mission area;

---

[49] S/RES/2232, 28 July 2015, §5.   [50] *Ibid.*, §6.

[51] See *Joint Benchmarking Review* (2015), §66–8, 77–8, and Annex 1.

[52] Telephone interview, member of the benchmarking team, 7 September 2017.

[53] *Draft Harmonised AMISOM Strategic Concept of Operations* (AU internal document, August 2015), §24.

more targeted and effective offensive operations by AMISOM and SNSF against Al Shaabab; implementation of the established Joint Technical Intelligence Committees, in order to improve intelligence sharing and management; and enhanced Command and Control by urgently filling structures of AMISOM's Strategic, Operational and Tactical headquarters with dedicated and qualified personnel.[54]

And in what would become an intensely debated topic, the PSC also noted 'the indicative timelines of AMISOM's exit strategy'.[55] As the Somali election process ramped up, AMISOM was required to devote more of its resources to securing various venues and persons associated with them. Having been scheduled to occur in August 2016, the process did not actually finish until January 2017. During this period, it occupied the attention of almost the entire Somali political class, and international partners found it very difficult to make significant progress on AMISOM's operations. Naturally, all of this distracted from the effort to degrade *al-Shabaab*.

In New York in resolution 2297, most of the same conclusions were reached but AMISOM's mandate was repackaged somewhat. Specifically, the UN Security Council authorized AMISOM to pursue three strategic objectives, four priority tasks, and six essential tasks.[56]

The three strategic objectives were to: reduce the threat posed by *al-Shabaab* and other armed opposition groups; provide security in order to enable the political process at all levels as well as stabilization efforts, reconciliation, and peacebuilding in Somalia; and enable the gradual handing over of security responsibilities from AMISOM to the Somali security forces contingent on abilities of the Somali security forces.[57]

AMISOM's four 'priority tasks' were:

1. To continue to conduct offensive operations against al-Shabaab and other armed opposition groups;

2. To maintain a presence in the sectors set out in the AMISOM Concept of Operations in order to establish conditions for effective and legitimate governance across Somalia, in coordination with the Somali security forces;

3. To assist with the free movement, safe passage and protection of all those involved with the peace and reconciliation process in Somalia, and ensure the security of the electoral process in Somalia as a key requirement;

4. To secure key supply routes including to areas recovered from al-Shabaab, in particular those essential to improving the humanitarian situation, and those critical for logistical support to AMISOM, underscoring that the delivery of logistics remains a joint responsibility between the United Nations and AU.[58]

---

[54] PSC/PR/COMM(DCVIII), 29 June 2016, §7.   [55] *Ibid.*, §10.
[56] S/RES/2297, 7 July 2016, §5–7.   [57] *Ibid.*, §5.   [58] *Ibid.*, §6.

AMISOM's six 'essential tasks' were:

1. To conduct joint operations with the Somali security forces, within its capabilities, in coordination with other parties, as part of the implementation of the Somali national security plans and to contribute to the wider effort of training and mentoring of the security forces of the FGS;

2. To contribute, within its capabilities as may be requested, to the creation of the necessary security conditions for the provision of humanitarian assistance;

3. To engage with communities in recovered areas, and promote understanding between AMISOM and local populations, within its capabilities, which will allow for longer term stabilization by the United Nations Country Team and other actors;

4. To provide and assist, as appropriate, protection to the Somali authorities to help them carry out their functions of government, and security for key infrastructure;

5. To protect its personnel, facilities, installations, equipment and mission, and to ensure the security and freedom of movement of its personnel, as well as of United Nations personnel carrying out functions mandated by the Security Council;

6. To receive on a transitory basis, defectors, as appropriate, and in coordination with the United Nations.[59]

While this formulation provided a neat summary of AMISOM's ambitions, in the field, the mission was struggling to overcome a range of challenges. Arguably, none of them were more important than ensuring a force posture that facilitated these objectives and tasks. But as the next section discusses, this proved difficult and at times exposed AMISOM to deadly attacks by *al-Shabaab*.

FORCE POSTURE AND FORCE PROTECTION

As AMISOM and SNA forces recovered more settlements, so the AU mission adopted a more dispersed force posture with troops positioned to secure these towns. This put a premium on the rapid and effective construction of the FOBs. It also put significant pressure on the AMISOM troops deployed in them. Life on the mission's remote FOBs was tough. Most of the peacekeepers were deployed for roughly a year before rotation, often in only company-sized units, with meager defences, sparse accommodation, facilities, and supplies,

---

[59] *Ibid.*, §7.

and with patrols exposing them to significant risks against an enemy they often could not identify but who usually had them under surveillance.

As AMISOM's FOBs became more numerous and important, so the mission's engineer enabling unit increased in salience. Comprising UPDF and BNDF troops under UNSOA control and with the support of Bancroft mentors, the unit used bulldozers and front-end loaders to construct AMISOM's new FOBs. Construction usually involved clearing dense brush from 100m stand-off areas outside the base, constructing perimeter defences (usually with HESCO barriers), upgrading/repairing roads between and inside bases, by-passes where needed, and defensive weapons positions.[60] However, adopting this posture and building these new FOBs had some negative repercussions.

First, this configuration of forces reduced AMISOM's ability to engage in active patrolling, a key task during any peace operation. It was especially important as a means of engaging the local population and learning potentially crucial information about *al-Shabaab*'s activities. Active patrolling had proved a key part of dismantling *al-Shabaab* structures in each populated area and also correlated with reductions in the number of attacks against AMISOM units compared to assuming more defensive postures in FOBs. When AMISOM forces had gone on long-range patrols from larger bases and lived amongst local populations—sometimes for several weeks at a time—this increased their situational awareness. It is notable that AMISOM was very effective when its troops regularly engaged the local Somali population and first suffered the loss of an FOB in 2015. Over time, however, life in the FOBs encouraged a reluctance to patrol, or what the UN Monitoring Group referred to as 'barracks mode', consolidating forces 'thereby further inhibiting engagement with local communities'.[61] There was also increased demand for armoured vehicles, particularly Mine Resistant Ambush Protected (MRAP) vehicles, to enhance force protection while AMISOM personnel moved around.

Second, sustaining operations across more than eighty locations, some of which were in very remote locations, required AMISOM to engage a large number of its troops in escorting supplies for the FOBs instead of conducting operations against *al-Shabaab*. It was also a more expensive force configuration and approach, since it placed a premium on the mission acquiring more MRAPs or using limited aviation assets to deliver supplies. This also had knock-on effects for the vulnerability of the Main Supply Routes (MSRs).

---

[60] See, for example, *After Action Review: Engineer Enabling Unit BNDF FOB Qurunlow, 26 May-14 June 2014* (Bancroft, 2014). ACOTA files.

[61] *Report of the Monitoring Group on Somalia and Eritrea pursuant to Security Council resolution 2244 (2015): Somalia* (S/2016/919, 31 October 2016), §21. This was also the view of a significant proportion of local Somalis polled by the AU–UN IST. See *Citizens Perception of Peace and Stabilization Initiative in Somalia* (UNSOM and AU, Mid-line Report, August 2016), pp. 30–1.

Securing the MSRs over long distances with poor infrastructure proved especially challenging as *al-Shabaab* regularly engaged in ambushes and IED attacks against AMISOM convoys, including targeting particularly vulnerable vehicles such as water bowsers. This all left AMISOM and its partners with a range of unpleasant options to ensure convoy security and open up the MSRs: proactively target *al-Shabaab* concentrations near the routes; picket the route with AU and SNA forces providing checkpoints and Quick Reaction Forces (QRFs) at regular intervals; hold the routes with mobile vehicle patrols (expensive on fuel and vulnerable to IEDs); provide armed escorts for large convoys; or develop AMISOM projects along the MSRs with the aim of winning over the local population.[62]

In December 2016, AMISOM embarked on a new Operation Antelope to solve some of these problems in Sector 5. Specifically, the Burundian contingent, the mission's engineering enabling unit, and UNSOS jointly embarked on a three-month operation to rehabilitate over 150 km of roadways in order to open four key supply routes in HirShabelle region in AMISOM's Sector 5.[63] This was intended to enhance the security of the routes, save money (because it was too expensive to continue delivering supplies by air), and enable more rapid access by emergency and humanitarian services. The plan was also intended to boost local commerce by enabling civilians to buy and sell goods and services more quickly. By mid-2017, however, it was clear that the operation had failed to achieve its main objectives. In part this was down to a lack of support from the Burundian contingent (the plan had been drafted by Western advisers) and in part because a concentration of *al-Shabaab* forces northeast of Jowhar made clearing that section of the supply routes impossible without significant fighting.[64]

A third problem raised by this force configuration was the opportunity it afforded *al-Shabaab* to attack AMISOM at the time and place of its choosing. Consequently, between June 2015 and January 2017, *al-Shabaab* launched five major attacks against AMISOM FOBs at Leego (June 2015), Janaale (September 2015), El Adde (January 2016), Halgan (June 2016), and Kulbiyow (January 2017) (see Figure 7.1). These attacks were made possible by the dispersal of AMISOM's forces across a huge area, including positioning garrisons of company strength or fewer in remote FOB sites. This gave *al-Shabaab* an opportunity. Poor preparation by individual commanders combined with the lack of adequate base defences would also enable *al-Shabaab* to achieve these victories at relatively low cost and by deploying almost identical tactics in each

[62] *AMISOM Force Headquarters Position Paper (2015)*, p. 19.

[63] 'AMISOM launches Operation Antelope in HirShabelle state', AMISOM press release, 17 December 2016, http://amisom-au.org/2016/12/amisom-launches-operation-antelope-in-hirshabelle-state/

[64] Communication, AMISOM official, 17 June 2017.

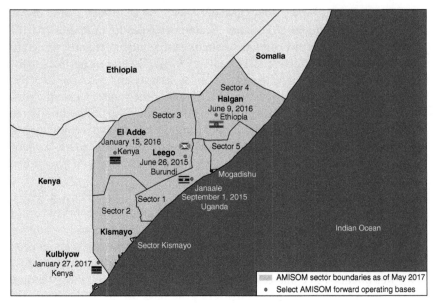

Fig. 7.1. Major *Al-Shabaab* Attacks on AMISOM's Forward Operating Bases, 2015–17

case. Interestingly, three of the subsequent FOB attacks occurred during the troop rotation phase, prompting AMISOM to change its procedures to rotate troops incrementally and not en masse.[65]

But before summarizing the FOB attacks during 2015, 2016, and 2017, it is instructive to revisit some earlier cases where *al-Shabaab* tried but failed to overrun AMISOM's bases. The best example is the case of Hoosingo in AMISOM's Sector 2.

Just before dawn on 4 April 2012, an estimated 500-strong force of *al-Shabaab* fighters supported by four 'technicals' and a media team attacked the Kenyan FOB at Hoosingo in south Somalia near to the Kenyan border.[66] They did so in waves, the first of which was destroyed after trip flares triggered their arrival. But *al-Shabaab* attacked in six subsequent waves in brave but poorly organized formations. Some of them were killed less than 30 m from the KDF's forward trenches. Fortunately for the defenders, air support was called in and arrived three hours later at 08.30 hours. The battle was over by 10.30 hours. While *al-Shabaab*'s fatalities were estimated at over one hundred, the KDF and TFG forces there suffered only five wounded and no fatalities. Key to the successful defence was an early warning of a potential attack from

---

[65] Notes from MOCC Debrief, 18 February 2016, p. 2.

[66] UK Armed Forces, *Report on RSLAF Recce to AMISOM Sector 2 from 7–9 May 2012* (unpublished document, 21 May 2012). For the official KDF account, see KDF, *Operation Linda Nchi*, pp. 175–87.

the nearby TFG base and KDF troops being put on high alert and waiting for any such attack. Good leadership was also important.

Similarly, on 4 February 2013, *al-Shabaab* conducted coordinated attacks on three AMISOM FOBs in Shalambooti, K50 and Tredisha/Elasha Biyaha using small arms, rockets, and mortars. None did any significant damage.[67] In all these cases it was notable that *al-Shabaab* did not manage to breach the AMISOM perimeter. During 2014, however, it appears that the militants started experimenting with the use of suicide vehicle-borne IEDs, initially by driving them into AMISOM convoys, that might provide the necessary impetus to breach AMISOM's defences.[68] In 2015, *al-Shabaab* employed them to even more deadly effect against AMISOM FOBs.

It appears that AMISOM did not predict its FOBs could be overrun until a few weeks before it happened. In an internal report written in April 2015, AMISOM's Force Commander described *al-Shabaab* as having 'evolved from a predominantly conventional force with a terror element, to a guerilla force with the occasional ability to mount larger scale operations'.[69] He went on to conclude that *al-Shabaab*'s main intent would most likely 'seek to degrade AMISOM capabilities through harassing attacks, laying IEDs and ambushes on resupply convoys along the MSRs. Amniyat will continue to conduct special ops'.[70] On 10 June, however, AMISOM's plan for Operation Juba Corridor warned that 'the AS [*al-Shabaab*] threat of targeted attacks on AMISOM/SNSF bases, FGS personnel and vital installations remain prevalent'.[71] Later in the same document, however, AMISOM concluded that *al-Shabaab* 'lacks the trained personnel and suitable vehicles to mass numbers and fight conventionally against AMISOM forces. Instead, it will rely on asymmetric attacks, using small numbers to conduct raids and avoid large scale confrontations'.[72] They may not have represented 'large-scale' confrontations, but just two weeks later *al-Shabaab* forces overran AMISOM's FOB at Leego and over the next thirty months would launch similar attacks on four other bases at Janaale, El Adde, Halgan, and Kulbiyow.

Leego

Just before dawn on 26 June an estimated 300 *al-Shabaab* fighters attacked AMISOM's FOB at Leego, which was garrisoned by about 120 Burundian

---

[67] Bancroft Situational Report 2–5 February 2013. ACOTA files.
[68] *Operations Order 08/2014—Operation Ocean Build*, p. 15.
[69] *AMISOM Force Headquarters Position Paper (2015)*, p. 4.
[70] *Ibid.*, p. 22. See also Annex A, p. 9.
[71] *Operations Order 01/2015—Operation Juba Corridor*, Annex B, p. 1.
[72] *Ibid.*, Annex B, p. 9.

troops.[73] Leego was the most remote outpost for the Burundian contingent in Sector 3 (at the time, the BNDF had troops spread across three AMISOM sectors). The attack began with a suicide vehicle-borne IED designed to take out the base's front gate and main defences. The vehicle-borne IED was immediately followed by waves of *al-Shabaab* infantry supported by 'technicals'. The base was overrun within a few hours and those BNDF who could do so retreated. Although *al-Shabaab* claimed they had killed 'more than 80 Burundian crusaders',[74] AMISOM registered fifty-four dead.[75] It took AMISOM forty-eight hours to get reinforcements to Leego by road (a journey that would have taken less than thirty minutes by helicopter) by which time *al-Shabaab* had ransacked the base and stolen all useful equipment including vehicles, generators, radios, weapons, and uniforms.[76] *Al-Shabaab* fighters videoed the battle and some of their war crimes perpetrated on Burundian soldiers. The video material was later edited and disseminated by *Al-Kataib*.

Janaale

The next major attack on an AMISOM FOB came at Janaale in Sector 1 on 1 September 2015, one year to the day that a US strike had killed *al-Shabaab*'s leader, Ahmed Godane.[77] Janaale FOB was garrisoned by nearly 200 Ugandan soldiers. *Al-Shabaab* used the same tactics as Leego, starting with a suicide vehicle-borne IED followed by a massed infantry assault supported by 'technicals'. On this occasion, they also cut off the base from any potential land reinforcements by destroying a bridge that served as the main route to the base.[78] The UPDF troops fought for several hours but subsequently retreated. The reported number of fatalities in the Ugandan press varied but eventually settled on nineteen. *Al-Shabaab*'s video claimed they had killed over '50 Ugandan crusaders'.[79] A CNN investigation cited 'Western sources' that as

---

[73] In April 2015, AMISOM had recorded two platoons of sixty-eight BNDF troops in Leego. *AMISOM Force Headquarters Position Paper (2015)*, Annex B, Appendix 2.

[74] 'Avenging the Honour of Our Prophet: Storming the Burundian Crusaders' Base Leego', video released by *Al-Kataib*, 23 September 2015.

[75] AMISOM SITREP as at 29 June 2015, p. 2.

[76] Telephone interview, senior AMISOM official, 7 November 2015.

[77] For journalistic accounts see, for example, Siraje Lubwama, 'Uganda: New Report Slams UPDF Commanders in Somalia', *The Observer* (Kampala), 5 August 2016; Daniel Kaliniki, 'Death in the morning: why AMISOM soldiers had little fighting chance in Janaale', *The East African*, 26 September 2016.

[78] *Report of the Monitoring Group on Somalia and Eritrea pursuant to Security Council resolution2182 (2014): Somalia* (S/2015/801, 19 October 2015), §91. Hereafter, *SEMG Report*, 19 October 2015.

[79] 'Storming a Ugandan Crusader Base', *Al-Kataib*, released 8 November 2015.

many as fifty AMISOM troops were killed.[80] The true number remains unclear to me. *Al-Shabaab* also took an unknown number of UPDF hostages, some of whom subsequently appeared in their propaganda videos. In Janaale it took AMISOM about eight hours to get reinforcements there when helicopters could have made the journey in about thirty minutes.[81] In this case, much blame fell on the performance of the UPDF base commander who it was alleged had not responded adequately to warnings about a potential attack and had not prepared his force sufficiently. As President Museveni put it, 'Our commanders were asleep. Asleep, not alert. And we have suspended those commanders'.[82]

El Adde

Just before dawn on 15 January 2016, an estimated several hundred *al-Shabaab* fighters attacked and overran AMISOM's FOB at El Adde in Gedo region.[83] It was garrisoned at the time by roughly 200 KDF troops. Once again, *al-Shabaab* employed the same tactics of attacking with two suicide vehicle-borne IEDs followed by massed infantry supported by 'technicals'. Once again, the battle lasted for several hours before the base was overrun. Following several failed rescue attempts, KDF ground troops finally reached the base on 18 January and retook full control of the camp the following day.[84] In the interim period, *al-Shabaab* made off with significant amounts of equipment, weapons and ammunition, and vehicles. The militants also took an unknown number of KDF soldiers hostage. As with the UPDF troops captured at Janaale, the Kenyan hostages were subsequently featured in *al-Shabaab* propaganda.[85] While the Kenyan government did not provide an official number of its fatalities, *al-Shabaab* claimed it had killed more than one hundred KDF soldiers. The real number of KDF dead was probably over 160 with perhaps as many as a dozen soldiers taken hostage.[86] This would make it,

---

[80] Robyn Kriel and Briana Duggan, 'Military sources: Al-Shabaab attack in Somalia kills dozens of AU troops', *CNN*, 3 September 2015, http://www.cnn.com/2015/09/03/africa/somalia-al-shabaab-attack/index.html

[81] Telephone interview, senior AMISOM official, 7 November 2015.

[82] Cited in 'Al-Shabaab Attack—UPDF Commanders to Face Court Martial', *The Observer* (Kampala), 12 September 2015.

[83] For a more detailed analysis see Paul D. Williams, *The Battle at El Adde* (International Peace Institute, July 2016).

[84] 'The Chief of Defence Force's Press Statement on Elade Update', Kenya Ministry of Defence, 21 January 2016, p. 3, www.mod.go.ke/wp-content/uploads/2016/01/CDF-press-conference-Elade-21-Jan.pdf

[85] For example, 'The Sheikh Abu-Yahya Al-Libi Raid', *Al-Kataib*, released 10 April 2016.

[86] An AMISOM assessment concluded 'over 150 KDF soldiers were killed and an unknown number of others captured'. *On Ceel Cadde: Lessons identified from the pre- and post-attack onto*

by far, AMISOM's deadliest day, surpassing the battle at Dayniile in October 2011 analysed in Chapter 4. It was also the worst defeat in the KDF's history. In the days following the battle, Kenya carried out an intense air campaign in Gedo that killed at least twelve civilians and destroyed homes, water points, and livestock.[87] *Al-Shabaab*, on the other hand, paid a bonus of between $200 and $400 to each of its fighters who survived the battle.[88]

The UN Monitoring Group concluded that the attacks at Leego, Janaale, and El Adde reinforced AMISOM's tendency to operate in 'barracks mode'.[89] This was true. But for some of AMISOM's leaders and their partners, El Adde proved to be the wake-up call that business as usual should not be allowed to continue. This combined with the fact that Operation Juba Corridor had ground to a virtual standstill prompted two notable developments.

First, it finally generated some serious introspection from the TCCs. Part of the reason why Juba Corridor proved so difficult to sustain was the lack of cross-sector coordination between AMISOM's national contingents. This, in turn, was a symptom of the mission's weak command and control structures (see Chapter 5). In order to fix this problem, on 28 February 2016 the heads of AMISOM's TCCs signed the Djibouti Declaration. This stressed

> the need for effective AMISOM Command and Control in order to achieve active synergy of the Mission's efforts against Al Shabab and therefore directs AMISOM contingents to fully support the Force Commander in his exercise of effective and accountable command of all military units assigned to the Mission.[90]

This was an astounding acknowledgement that for years, AMISOM's TCCs had often ignored the Force Commander. As the Head of AMISOM put it at the summit, the Djibouti Declaration formally recognizes and legitimizes the AMISOM Force Commander's authority over the TCC Contingent Commanders. Moreover, it gave the Force Commander 'the power, as a measure of last resort, to undertake the necessary procedures to remove and repatriate TCC contingent commanders or personnel within the Force Headquarters if they fail to deliver on their objectives or carry out their orders as directed by the Force Headquarters'.[91] This was sensible theory, but it would require real political will from the AMISOM TCCs to implement it in the field.

A debate then ensued over which country should assume the position of AMISOM Force Commander. Ironically, the position remained vacant for

---

the *AMISOM CP* (AMISOM Mission Analysis Cell, 23 January 2016), p. 1. Communications with AMISOM, UN, and EU officials, January 2016.

[87] *SEMG Report*, 31 October 2016, pp. 169–70.　　　[88] *Ibid.*, p. 70.　　　[89] *Ibid.*, §21.

[90] Djibouti Declaration, Djibouti, 28 February 2016, at https://www.un.int/djibouti/news/summit-troop-and-police-contributing-countries-african-union-mission-somalia-amisom. The same point was made in *Report on AMISOM Lessons Learned Conference, Nairobi, Kenya, 9–10 March 2017* (AU Commission, 2017), §12, http://www.peaceau.org/uploads/ll-eng-1.pdf

[91] Remarks by AMISOM SRCC Francisco Madeira, Djibouti, 27 February 2016. Copy in author's possession.

several months because of internal haggling over the details of the post. Ethiopia initially stepped forward to assume the role but would do so only if it could bring an additional 1,000 ENDF troops into the operation and deploy some of its soldiers to Mogadishu.[92] Both the AU and several key partners saw this as a distinctly bad idea and instead the Force Commander position went to Djibouti. This would really test the commitments made on paper in the Djibouti Declaration. And for the most part, the TCCs failed the test.

The second development was that the El Adde attack prompted the Force Commander to assess all AMISOM and SNA operational positions, troop dispositions, camp security, and effective joint operations, as well as the design, construction, and organization of all FOBs. All these elements should have been coordinated to address the threat posed by *al-Shabaab* and enable an effective AMISOM response. His assessment concluded that AMISOM's existing force configuration was badly flawed and that all the mission's FOBs should be garrisoned by at least two companies and that each sector should generate QRFs to ensure rapid response mobility.[93] If implemented, this would presumably have reduced the likelihood of *al-Shabaab* overrunning AMISOM bases. But it would also have significant implications for the number of settlements AMISOM could help protect and presumably reduce the resources free to undertake other operations.[94] Before all these issues were ironed out, AMISOM was once again put to the test, this time in Halgan.

Halgan

The importance of these defensive procedures and engaging with the local community were illustrated on 9 June 2016 when as many as 500 *al-Shabaab* fighters attacked the Ethiopian FOB at Halgan. The militants used the same tactics as before but also deployed an additional 100–150 fighters to block the road from Buulobarde to prevent the Ethiopians receiving any reinforcement from the Djiboutian contingent there.[95] This time, however, the ENDF troops successfully repelled the attack. Although the initial suicide vehicle-borne IED caused significant damage and breached the base perimeter, the ENDF were able to prevent *al-Shabaab* fighters overrunning their defences. This was in large part because the Ethiopian troops had previously been alerted to the possibility of an imminent attack by local sources and an element of the Ethiopian forces had been stationed outside the base and was able to create a killing zone that decimated the attacking forces. In addition, the base was

---

[92] Communication, US official, 16 February 2016.
[93] Interviews, AMISOM, AU and UN officials, Djibouti, February 2016.
[94] Communication, US official, 16 February 2016.
[95] *SEMG Report*, 31 October 2016, §23.

able to receive support from both ENDF and UNSOA helicopters, the former providing fire support, the latter casualty evacuation and delivery of supplies. Nevertheless, the fighting was bloody and the Ethiopians probably suffered about forty fatalities. In comparison, however, *al-Shabaab* lost anywhere between 140 and 245 of its fighters and much of their equipment.[96]

Kulbiyow

The final major *al-Shabaab* attack discussed here came at Kulbiyow on 27 January 2017. This base was garrisoned by about 120 KDF troops. Perhaps most notably, the base was in Kenya but located immediately adjacent to the Somali border. It had long operated as part of the AMISOM force and Sector 2 command and control structures.[97] Once again, *al-Shabaab* fighters initiated the attack before dawn with two suicide vehicle-borne IEDs and then followed up with infantry and 'technicals'. And once again, after some resistance, the defenders retreated from the base. It appears that *al-Shabaab* was able to spend some time in control of the base, but Kenyan reinforcements were able to recapture it later that day.[98] Estimates of KDF fatalities ranged from fifteen to around thirty.[99]

As with all modern battles, the major *al-Shabaab* attacks on AMISOM's FOBs since June 2015 demonstrated the importance of several operational and tactical factors. But they also highlighted the importance of engaging the local population in order to receive relevant information about any enemy preparations for such an attack. In the one case where AMISOM forces had established good relations with the local community, the attack was repulsed. In a slightly different form, this reflected AMISOM's perennial problem that the mission was essentially a rather blunt military tool that could not defeat *al-Shabaab* without sustained local support and leadership. In other words, it was the level of progress on the political track that would determine the fate of AMISOM and *al-Shabaab* alike. And here, the news for most of AMISOM's ten years was depressing.

[96] Interview, EU official, Nairobi, 14 December 2016; Anwar Muktar, 'AMISOM thwarts Al-Shabaab attack on Ethiopian forces at Halgan', Ethiopian Mission to UN, Geneva, 17 June 2016, http://www.ethiopianmission.ch/2016/06/17/amisom-thwarts-al-shabaab-attack-on-ethiopian-forces-at-halgan/

[97] See, for example, *AMISOM Force Headquarters Position Paper (2015)*, Annex B, Appendix 2.

[98] For a breakdown of events see Jacob Beeders, 'What happened at Kulbiyow, Somalia', *bellingcat*, 21 March 2017, https://www.bellingcat.com/news/africa/2017/03/21/happened-kulbiyow-somalia-open-source-investigation/ and Conway Waddington, 'The Kulbiyow Attack Uncovered', *African Defence Review*, 22 May 2017, https://www.africandefence.net/analysis-of-competing-claims-about-the-january-2017-al-shabaab-attack-on-the-kdf-base-at-kulbiyow/

[99] Communication, Somali analyst, 15 February 2017.

THE SOLUTION LIES WITH POLITICS NOT PEACEKEEPERS

Hassan Sheikh's presidency from 2012 to January 2017 had failed to live up to the initial expectations of locals and AMISOM's international partners. A major part of this was his inability to make real progress on either corruption or national reconciliation. As a result, there was no sustainable political settlement between Somalia's governing elites and too little progress on clarifying the nature of federalism and finalizing the country's constitution.

As noted above, AMISOM could not defeat *al-Shabaab*. At best, its peacekeepers could provide the space in which Somalis could defeat it themselves. And for this to happen, Somali's political, business, religious, and clan elites would have to reconcile, develop a shared vision of governance for their country, and commit to an agreement on the principles guiding the security sector, including the relevant command and control and revenue sharing arrangements. During Hassan Sheikh's presidency, progress was too little and too late on all counts. AMISOM was thus forced to operate in a context of regular political infighting between Somalia's leaders that took the focus away from winning the war against *al-Shabaab*. The subsequent lack of a political settlement between Somalia's bickering elites presented AMISOM with a wide range of problems and undermined its ability to effectively implement its mandated tasks.

Arguably the most fundamental problem was that the process of constructing a federal state in Somalia not only failed to make sufficient progress but sometimes actively generated conflict between the subsequent centres of power. AMISOM was mandated to support the Federal Government, but the mission had to operate in a context defined by the lack of an overarching political settlement setting out how Somalia should be governed and by whom. The underlying problem, as the UN Monitoring Group on Somalia put it, was the inability of 'Somalia's political elite to prioritize the long-term goals of State-building over the short-term capture of State resources'.[100] To this we might add the inability of external actors to use the right approach to produce genuine peacemaking and reconciliation.

There was also an economic dimension to this problem inasmuch as prominent elites in Mogadishu and elsewhere had become accustomed to benefiting from a situation where the rule of law was not enforced, where humanitarian and other crises proliferated, where they could gain access to considerable revenue streams with little accountability, and where there was no need to pay taxation to a federal government.[101] These were the 'Moneylords', noted in Chapter 3. In Mogadishu, for example, such individuals often ran

---

[100] *SEMG Report*, 19 October 2015, p. 6.
[101] On the concept of Somali 'crisis lords', see Bryden, *Somalia Redux?*

their own private security firms, which also brought in additional resources and reported to them directly. In comparison, having to rely on state military and police forces would require giving up some control over security provision and payment of taxes. In such circumstances, those elites that were making money out of the existing insecurity would likely see the rise of a functioning set of state institutions as a threat to their livelihoods.

The lack of elite agreement left Somalia without a consensus on some fundamental issues. First, until early 2016 there was no consensus over how to form the next political dispensation, and therefore no way to get genuine buy-in and support from Somali citizens and international donors alike. When a decision was finally made, Somalia's external partners ended up endorsing the Federal Government's version, despite the fact this was rejected by important regions such as Puntland as well as Somaliland. Second, in the security sphere, Somalia was left without a national security strategy setting out the vision for and roles of its armed forces. Without such a document there could be no clarity on how to build national security forces and what their respective roles and responsibilities would entail. As discussed in Chapter 9, the misleadingly named *Guulwade* (Victory) Plan, which emerged in 2015, was a poor substitute. Third, the numerous rounds of political infighting amongst Somalia's political elites distracted them from building a genuinely national army and police force and taking the fight to *al-Shabaab*.

Instead of national political consensus to take on *al-Shabaab*, AMISOM was stuck in the middle of bickering Somali politicians arguing over how to interpret the country's provincial constitution, which had been adopted in 2012. In Mogadishu, MPs lost confidence in the executive, twice attempted to impeach the President, and regularly changed Prime Ministers. In the regions, conflict occurred along two axes: against the Federal Government, and among different actors struggling to gain power within particular regions themselves. The problem for the Federal Government was that although it was recognized as the legitimate sovereign authority by most external actors, it lacked the power to impose its preferred political outcomes on other regional actors. This was demonstrated first in August 2013 when Ahmed Madobe won control of the Interim Jubaland Administration (see Chapter 6). Since then, the Interim South West Administration formed in June 2014, the Interim Galmudug Administration in July 2015, and the Interim Hiraan and Middle Shabelle Administration in late 2016 (see Figure 7.2).

The process of establishing these administrations created considerable (and sometimes violent) conflict among the participants. For AMISOM, this generated several headaches. First, it distracted national leaders from implementing President Hassan Sheikh's top priorities, which he had defined in September 2012 as 'security, security, and security'. Second, it gave AMISOM an additional set of tasks related to providing security and logistical support at the numerous regional conferences and meetings across

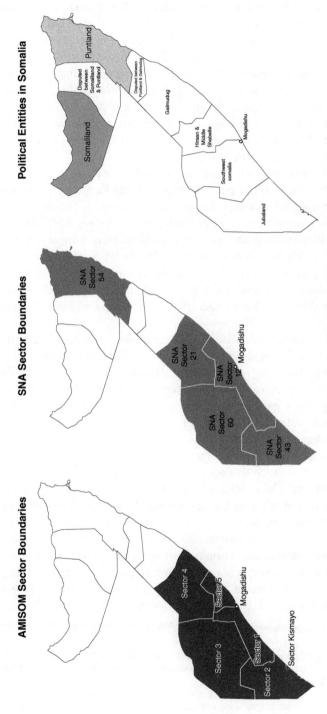

Fig. 7.2. Comparing AMISOM and SNA Sectors and Somalia's Interim Political Entities (2016)

south-central Somalia that took place in the process of establishing the Interim Regional Administration (IRAs). The mission did this successfully, but it diverted resources from the offensives against *al-Shabaab*. Third, it was notable that most of the influential players in the process of establishing the IRAs derived their power from clan affiliations rather than political parties or religious movements. This highlighted that *al-Shabaab* was not the only security threat facing the Federal Government and AMISOM. Indeed, clan conflicts over the newly recovered towns, intercommunal clashes, and fighting over land and water resources had often intensified after *al-Shabaab* withdrew from its strongholds.[102]

An additional problem was that AMISOM's mandate to support the Federal Government sometimes put it at odds with the local regional power brokers, who saw the SNA as a clan dominated institution.[103] The situation was made even more complicated and confusing when certain AMISOM contingents ignored that mandate and struck up unofficial relationships with those actors, some of which put them in conflict with the FGS (discussed in Chapter 6). AMISOM was therefore left without an effective local security partner and to fight *al-Shabaab* while walking through the political minefield of forces established by the IRAs, other clan militias, and additional armed groups such as *Ahlu Sunna Wal Jamaa*.

Finally, failure to finalize the constitution and political infighting among Somali elites also made it impossible to hold general elections in Somalia in 2016. This also negatively affected AMISOM's objective to pacify the country and implement its planned exit strategy. In July 2015, the Federal Government finally, publicly gave up on the original 'Vision 2016' idea of holding one-person one-vote elections. Instead, it opted to pursue a process of intra-elite consultations and selection aimed at enhancing the legitimacy of whatever government emerged from that process.[104] As it turned out, the process involved a more inclusive selection process than the 2012 version. This time, 135 traditional elders selected just over 14,000 Somalis who then played a practical role in selecting the new federal Parliament and hence President.

After these select Somali citizens elected roughly 320 MPs in late 2016, in January 2017 the parliamentarians eventually elected Mohamed Abdullahi Mohamed, nicknamed 'Farmajo', to serve as Somalia's President. A dual US-Somali citizen with a Master's degree in political science, he had previously been Prime Minister of Somalia for eight months from September 2010 before being sacked as part of the insider dealing that brokered the TFGs

---

[102] See *ibid.*, p. 6.

[103] See, for example, Tristan McConnell, 'Inside the fight for Somalia's future', *GlobalPost*, 29 May 2014, http://www.globalpost.com/dispatch/news/regions/africa/140528/inside-the-fight-somalias-future

[104] See The Somalia National Consultative Forum on the Electoral Process in 2016, *Facilitation Guide* (no date), https://www.scribd.com/doc/287843236/Facilitation-Guide

self-declared extension of its tenure in June 2011. Once again, the selection process was marred by allegations of systemic corruption. Nevertheless, 'Farmajo' emerged as an initially popular President with many ordinary Somalis and, importantly, many members of the SNA because of the importance he had placed on paying their salaries.

From AMISOM's perspective, one of the most important things the new Federal Government could deliver was a vision of Somalia's national security architecture agreed by both Mogadishu and the regions. In mid-April 2017, it appeared that 'Farmajo' might have delivered just such a vision.

Specifically, a political framework agreement was adopted which proposed a Somali national security architecture that dealt with the number of Somali national security forces, their distribution across the federal and state level, the command and control structures, and the fiscal responsibilities for the respective forces. Potentially, this agreement represented a major step forward for international attempts to stabilize Somalia because it held the promise that the Federal Government and Somalia's various regional administrations had finally agreed a shared political vision for the security sector.

The new architecture envisaged a 22,000-strong SNA, including 4,000 special forces, as well as 32,000 Somali police, including the coastguard and *Darwish*. It also involved the reconfiguration of the SNA's operational sectors to align with the boundaries of Somalia's Federal Member States. Each sector would also be home to a 500-strong battalion of *Danab* special forces, coordinated centrally from their brigade headquarters in Baledogle (see Chapter 9 for more details). Most importantly, the agreement envisaged a new system of command and control based on a reconfigured National Security Council (NSC) that included the presidents of Somalia's regions. This would be linked to a system of Regional Security Council's that would implement the strategic decisions made by the NSC.

The national security architecture was linked to the Federal Government's broader Vision 2027 that set out a ten-year timetable for Somalia to develop a fully integrated set of national security forces operating under the civilian oversight and strategic direction of the Ministry of Defence acting to defend the Constitution of Somalia, the country's territorial integrity, and defeating *al-Shabaab* with limited external support.

In May 2017, this framework agreement became part of the London Security Pact.[105] Attended by forty-two of Somalia's partners, the London conference endorsed the Somali government's new national security architecture plan, as well as the existing National Security Policy (June 2016), and National Strategy and Action Plan for Preventing and Countering Violent Extremism (September 2016). Taken together they comprised a new 'Security

---

[105] The full security pact is available at https://www.gov.uk/government/publications/london-somalia-conference-2017-security-pact

Pact' that set out the 'agreed vision of Somali-led security institutions and forces that are affordable, acceptable, accountable and have the ability to provide the security and protection that the people of Somalia deserve and need, in accordance with international humanitarian and human rights standards, as part of a comprehensive approach to security'. In substantive terms, the new Security Pact involved a political agreement between the Federal Government and the regional administrations on the country's national security architecture, a plan for reforming Somalia's security sector through the attainment of envisaged milestones over the next ten years, commitments from international partners to support these milestones, and an agreement that the transition from AMISOM to Somali security forces from 2018 should be conditions-based and have clear target dates linked to the security sector milestones.[106]

It had taken more than ten years, but AMISOM finally had a political pathway out of Somalia—it just had to be successfully implemented. Critics, however, warned that AMISOM's international partners had endorsed the pact before ensuring it had genuine buy-in from Somalia's regional member states and had probably underestimated the extent to which implementing the pact would generate resistance from spoilers who benefited politically and economically from the existing, largely informal security arrangements.

CONCLUSION

Stimulated in large part by the Westgate attack in September 2013, AMISOM's surge capacity finally saw some Ethiopian forces integrated into the mission. It also stimulated a new series of operations designed to clear *al-Shabaab* from strategic settlements across south-central Somalia, hold those areas and protect their populations, and then in tandem with the Somali authorities, deliver a real peace dividend to the local inhabitants to persuade them not to support *al-Shabaab*. These operations had a distinctly mixed record. In gaining considerable territory AMISOM did weaken *al-Shabaab* and its sources of finance and support. But it also dispersed AMISOM's forces and in some areas left them vulnerable. This vulnerability was ruthlessly exploited by *al-Shabaab* on several occasions and hundreds of AMISOM peacekeepers died as their FOBs were overrun. There were also negative effects when AMISOM subsequently withdrew its forces from some of these FOBs. In some cases, FOBs were abandoned in areas where AMISOM had provided little in the way of practical

---

[106] On 30 August 2017, UN Security Council resolution 2372 authorized AMISOM to withdraw 1,000 troops and add an additional 500 police by 31 December 2017. S/RES/2372, 30 August 2017.

protection for local civilians. But in those where AMISOM troops had played significant protection and deterrent roles, their withdrawal meant that local Somalis were exposed to *al-Shabaab*'s retribution. This had a predictable negative effect on AMISOM's efforts to win 'hearts and minds'.

Finally, in late 2016 and early 2017 a small portion of Somali citizens chose another new Federal Government. This one at least developed a new national security architecture that had the potential to unite the Federal Government and the regions behind one shared vision. It had taken AMISOM ten years to get to this point. It remains to be seen how long it will need to put itself out of business.

Part I of this book has told the story of AMISOM's first ten years. Part II now turns to offer an analysis of the mission's six main operational challenges. These are challenges that bedevil most contemporary peace operations, namely, sustaining effective logistics; reforming the host state's security sector; protecting civilians; developing effective strategic communications; delivering stabilization; and implementing an effective exit strategy. These are the subjects of Chapters 8–13.

Part II

Challenges

8

Logistics

Logistics support in peace operations is about ensuring the necessary movement and maintenance of a mission's personnel and equipment. It includes: the transportation of personnel to, within, and from the mission's area of operations; the transport, storage, maintenance, and eventual evacuation or disposal of mission equipment; the acquisition, distribution, and ultimate disposal of mission supplies; the acquisition or construction, maintenance, and operation of mission facilities, such as accommodation, offices, and warehouses; and the acquisition or provision of services required in the mission, such as catering or cleaning.[1] A peace operation's precise logistics support requirements depend on its mandate, size, composition, and operating environment. While even the best logistics support cannot in itself guarantee mission success, inadequate support can cripple a mission, making logistics 'the arbiter of strategic opportunity'.[2]

Unlike some national military operations, logistics support in multinational peace operations is based on a range of partnerships, including between states, international organizations, and commercial contractors. These circumstances inevitably raise questions related to the coordination and control of logistics support.

In AMISOM's case, officially, its Mission Support Component was responsible for the overall management of all support functions for the mission based on the integration of military, civilian, and contracted resources. But in practice, at the start of the mission it was Uganda that provided logistics to its troops with support from some external partners. The key initial partners were the United States and United Kingdom who in January 2007 hired DynCorp International to act as AMISOM's 'de facto quartermaster'.[3] In

---

[1] See Katharina P. Coleman and Paul D. Williams, *Logistics Partnerships in Peace Operations* (New York: International Peace Institute, June 2017).

[2] Colin S. Gray, *Fighting Talk: Forty Maxims on War, Peace, and Strategy* (London: Praeger, 2007), Chapter 28.

[3] See http://www.dyn-intl.com/what-we-do/contingency-operations/somalia-case-study.aspx [Accessed June 2012.] Among other services, DynCorp provided air transport for the deployment of personnel, outfitted field camps, food and medicines, and over 80 per cent of the

retrospect, the UPDF's General Katumba Wamala acknowledged that DynCorp's 'services... enabled us to achieve what many critics looked at as a mission impossible. DynCorp International stood with us even during the most challenging time of the deployment and did not waver even when one of the aircraft was shot at'. Moreover, unlike most peace operations, AMISOM had almost no support from the host government and had to construct most of its own buildings and repair the decrepit infrastructure in its initial areas of deployment. All that the UPDF were able to purchase locally were some rations, including some cows, fresh vegetables, and rice. These purchases were facilitated by Somali businessmen based in Uganda who connected AMISOM with local businesses in Mogadishu.[4] This situation was soon deemed inadequate and the AU requested UN assistance to plug the many gaps that had emerged.

As discussed in Chapter 3, the UN's assistance came in the form of the UN Support Office for AMISOM (UNSOA), which was requested in UN Security Council Resolution 1863 in January 2009. Shortly thereafter, UN Secretary-General Ban Ki-moon decided that the package should be delivered through a stand-alone support office overseen by the Department of Field Support (DFS).

UNSOA was an unprecedented response to the AU's request. First, it was the first time that the UN had established a new mission to use its assessed peacekeeping contributions to directly support a non-UN regional peace operation.[5] Second, it was the first field mission led by DFS.[6] And third, it pioneered the 'light footprint' concept and outsourcing model to deliver services in a non-permissive environment.

Initially, UNSOA was intended to raise AMISOM's operational standards in order to facilitate its transition into a UN peacekeeping operation, but that day never came. Instead, UNSOA underwent two reviews, in September 2012 and July–September 2015, in order to make it more effective. As a result of the 2015 strategic review, UNSOA transitioned into the UN Support Office for Somalia (UNSOS) on 9 November 2015.[7]

AMISOM vehicle fleet, by delivering and managing over one hundred new and remanufactured commercial, military, and armoured vehicles. On 9 March 2009, AMISOM suffered another significant blow when one of its transport planes crashed into Lake Victoria shortly after take-off from Entebbe. The plane, operated by DynCorp, was carrying eleven passengers, all of whom were killed. They included the Burundian deputy AMISOM contingent commander Brigadier General Saloum Nkikumana. Wikileak Cable 09KAMPALA254, 9 March 2009.

[4] Interview, officer in the initial UPDF battle-group, Washington DC, 23 October 2013.

[5] In 2007, the cost of the UN's light and heavy support packages to the AU Mission in Sudan (AMIS) was borne by the UNMIS budget, but no new mission was created.

[6] *UNSOA Scoping Exercise Opportunities for Policy and Best Practices Support, Nairobi 24–28 September 2012* (UN internal document, 2012), §3.

[7] UNSOS was mandated to support AMISOM, the UN Assistance Mission for Somalia (UNSOM), the Somali National Army, and the Somali Police Force on joint operations with

This chapter analyses five sets of challenges related to logistics support that constrained AMISOM's operational effectiveness. These revolved around the expanding scope of UNSOA's mandated tasks; the clash between the UN and the AU's organizational cultures; the highly insecure operating environment in Somalia; the problems posed by the size of UNSOA's theatre of operations from 2012; and some of the idiosyncrasies of its principal client, AMISOM. UNSOA had a mixed record but overall produced positive results for AMISOM and demonstrated a new, flexible mechanism for the UN to deliver field support. The chapter concludes by identifying six lessons UNSOA's experience offers for future peace operations, especially in Africa.

CHALLENGE 1: AN EXPANDING LIST OF TASKS

The first major challenge was keeping pace with AMISOM's growing list of logistical needs and the fact that UNSOA's mandate included activities unrelated to AMISOM and was repeatedly expanded without a commensurate increase in resources. As the 2015 strategic review of UNSOA noted, between 2009 and the end of 2015, the mission's mandate was expanded at least eight times.[8] In quantitative terms, the number of uniformed personnel UNSOA was supposed to support went from 8,000 in 2009 to nearly 33,500 by November 2013 (plus an additional 750 civilians).[9] Geographically, UNSOA's area of operations increased by 4,000 times during the same period (from a few blocks of central Mogadishu to the whole of south-central Somalia) to take account of AMISOM's expansion beyond the capital city. To make matters worse, it was tasked with supporting five different entities (not all of which were even in Somalia).[10] To do all this, UNSOA's personnel numbers were only increased from the initially authorized 249 to 450.[11] Similarly, its annual budget grew only 2.8 times, from $214 million to $513 million, and most of this was to cover the introduction of major equipment reimbursement and associated operational costs in 2012 (see Figure 8.1 and below).

AMISOM. See S/RES/2245, 9 November 2015. Apart from being a more accurately named mission, UNSOS was intended to enhance mechanisms for monitoring compliance with the UN's human rights due diligence policy (HRDDP) and protection of civilians as well as help AMISOM develop an environmental policy to lower its carbon footprint and energy usage.

[8] *Letter Dated 7 October 2015 from the Secretary-General Addressed to the President of the Security Council* (S/2015/762, 7 October 2015). Hereafter, UNSG, *Letter Dated 7 October 2015.*

[9] This figure represents AMISOM plus the 10,900 troops from the Somali National Army conducting coordinated operations with AMISOM. See S/RES/2124, 12 November 2013.

[10] The entities were: AMISOM, UNSOM, the Somali National Army, the UN Monitoring Group on Somalia and Eritrea, and the UN special envoy for the Great Lakes region.

[11] For the 2009/10 fiscal year, the total staff costs for UNSOA were $22.2 million. For 2015/16, they were $54.3 million.

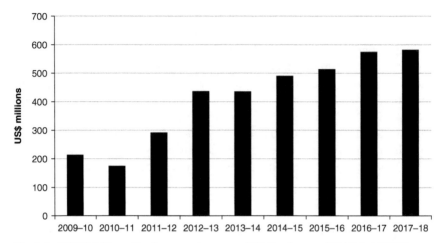

Fig. 8.1. UNSOA/S total budget requirements, UN fiscal years 2009/10–2017/18

Source: UN Peacekeeping, 'Financing Peacekeeping', www.un.org/en/peacekeeping/operations/financing.shtml#gadocs

The expansion of UNSOA's tasks occurred in several phases. Its initial task was to raise operational standards for 8,000 AMISOM troops to transition into a UN peacekeeping operation. At this point AMISOM's area of operations was roughly 100 square kilometres. Between 2009 and late 2011, the initial package expanded to include services normally included as self-sustainment in the UN peacekeeping model (such as catering, communications, and cleaning and sanitary services), the provision of explosive hazard management capacities, and strategic communications. It is notable that the latter involved UNSOA managing a public information strategy for AMISOM via the AU–UN Information Support Team.

During 2012, AMISOM's area of operations expanded to over 400,000 square kilometres, and the force increased to 17,731 personnel. In addition, UN Security Council Resolution 2036 expanded UNSOA's support package to include reimbursement of major contingent-owned equipment, a major additional set of costs, and support for up to seventy AMISOM civilian personnel.

The initial lack of UNSOA support for AMISOM's civilian and police components generated criticism from the AU. In September 2011, the AU PSC requested that the UN Security Council 'authorize the enhancement of the support package . . . to take into account the . . . fact that AMISOM is a multidimensional mission with military, police and civilian components'.[12] The AU's specific complaint was that UNSOA was 'essentially directed at the military component of AMISOM, thus excluding the police and civilian

---

[12] *Report of the Chairperson of the Commission on the Situation in Somalia* (PSC/PR/2 (CCXCIII), 13 September 2011), §14.

Table 8.1. Companies operating in AMISOM base camp, September 2012

• Bancroft Global Development	• DEEQA Construction & Water Well Drilling Ltd	• Supreme Fuel
• DynCorp International	• Saahib Enterprises	• ADNA Company
• PAE	• AIG International	• Agility Logistics Ltd
• UNMAS	• East African Brothers Co.	• Stars General Trading Ltd
• Alpha Logistics	• International Cleaners	
• RA International	• SAAB	• Global Vision
• SKA Logistics	• African Skies Limited	• Nationwide Enterprises
• TIKA	• Mogadishu General Service	
• Camel Trading & Construction Company		• Gossamer Crossing
		• APCO Group
		• AU/UN IST

Source: *Hand/Takeover Report for Sector One Commander* (AMISOM internal document, September 2012), pp. 13–14.

components. This approach negates the very essence of the multi-dimensional nature of AMISOM and affects the effectiveness of the Mission in delivering support to the Somali people'.[13]

Contingent-owned equipment turned out to be the other main source of controversy. Initially, the AU had promised to reimburse AMISOM TCCs for the use of equipment they owned, but this did not happen in practice because of the AU's lack of funds. The UK therefore volunteered to cover this cost at UN 'wet lease' rates through the UN Trust Fund for AMISOM and advocated intensely during 2011 for this to be covered by UN assessed contributions.[14] Moreover, the annex of Resolution 2036 stated that in order to avoid donors paying for equipment twice, AMISOM TCCs could not receive UN reimbursement for equipment that had been donated to them for use in AMISOM. UNSOA was also required to establish logistical hubs in each of AMISOM's four new sectors (see Figure I.3). Other areas that UNSOA took on included helping to train AMISOM troops in areas such as dispensing first aid, controlling movement, supply engineering, operating information technology (IT) systems, and using kitchens, as well as assisting AMISOM in dealing with ex-combatants.[15] Table 8.1 provides a snapshot of the range of contractors that were operating within AMISOM's main base camp, almost all of which were engaged in some aspect of logistics support.

Then in 2013, UNSOA was mandated to provide support services to the new UNSOM, which replaced the smaller UNPOS.[16] Unlike UNPOS, UNSOM would be permanently based in Mogadishu (and would subsequently deploy

---

[13] *Ibid.*, §49.   [14] Communication, senior UNSOA official, 1 August 2014.
[15] UNSOA, *Scoping Exercise*, §12–13; and Clarke, UNSOA study, p. 100.
[16] S/RES/2102, 2 May 2013.

staff across the south-central regions). UNSOA was tasked with supporting the mission, including logistically, and with building its accommodations. This was quite demanding given that UNSOM's personnel were split; some were in the new Bancroft-built camp in the airport compound, and others in the compound of the UN Mine Action Service (formerly the UN compound).[17]

UNSOA's engagement with UNSOM was costly in two senses. First, UNSOM required much greater expenditure of time, money, and other resources than UNPOS, and being effectively collocated with UNSOA meant that it was often given priority attention. Second, after UNSOM was established, UNSOA's director had a dual reporting line to both UNSOM's special representative and the head of DFS. The practical effect was that UNSOA was stretched in both directions, which generated discontent within AMISOM and the UN. Some personnel within UNSOM felt that they were initially just an afterthought, with UNSOA's principal focus on AMISOM.[18] In distinct contrast, some AMISOM commanders felt that UNSOA became primarily focused on supporting UNSOM and that AMISOM's needs became secondary.[19] One former UNSOA official echoed this view, claiming that setting up UNSOM broke UNSOA, which in turn affected AMISOM.[20]

In November 2013, UN Security Council Resolution 2124 authorized another major expansion of UNSOA's tasks. Not only were AMISOM's numbers increased to over 22,000, but UNSOA was also tasked with providing non-lethal support to 10,900 personnel of the Somali National Army engaged in joint operations with AMISOM (consisting of food, water, fuel, transport, tents, and in-theatre medical evacuation). This support was funded by the now renamed 'UN Trust Fund for AMISOM and the Somali National Army', not the UN's assessed peacekeeping contributions (like most of UNSOA's activities). Moreover, UNSOA personnel in Nairobi were mandated to provide support to the special envoy of the UN Secretary-General for the Great Lakes region and the Monitoring Group for Somalia and Eritrea. It is also worth noting that in July 2015, the UN Secretary-General recommended that UNSOA provide a non-lethal support package to 3,000 security forces in Puntland, but the Security Council decided not to authorize it.[21]

Overall, these various expansions of UNSOA's tasks led the 2015 strategic review to the conclusion that UNSOA's name had become a misnomer—it was not serving as a 'support office' to AMISOM. Moreover, the mission was massively under-resourced and suffered from 'a progressively widening gap

---

[17] Interview, senior UNSOA official, telephone, 22 July 2013.
[18] Communications with UN officials, 2 September 2016; 11 January 2017.
[19] Communication, former AMISOM official, 19 July 2016.
[20] Communication, former UNSOA official, 20 August 2015.
[21] For details, see UNSG, *Letter Dated 7 October 2015*, §15, 61–7.

between mandated tasks and its capacity to deliver'. In sum, UNSOA's 'overall capacity' was deemed 'simply inadequate'.[22]

CHALLENGE 2: CLASH OF ORGANIZATIONAL CULTURES

At the operational level, UNSOA represented the UN and AU's most intense attempt to develop a strategic partnership on peace operations. It also represented a foray into somewhat uncharted territory for both organizations, which put them on a steep learning curve. The second set of challenges for AMISOM and UNSOA consequently stemmed from the differences between the doctrinal and organizational cultures of the UN and the AU concerning peace operations. This challenge had several dimensions: doctrinal differences, bureaucratic challenges, and the resulting problems of building trust and ensuring coordination among the relevant players.

The basic contours of UN–AU doctrinal disagreements about peace operations can be summarized quickly. The UN's peacekeeping doctrine is based on three basic principles: (1) consent of the main conflict parties, particularly of the host-country government; (2) impartiality; and (3) non-use of force except in self-defence and defence of the mandate. On the basis of more than six decades and nearly seventy missions, the UN believes peacekeeping is unlikely to succeed where one or more of the following conditions are not in place: (1) a peace to keep, with the signing of a ceasefire or peace agreement as one (but not the only) important indicator of when parties are genuinely seeking peace; (2) positive regional engagement; (3) the full backing of a united Security Council; and (4) a clear and achievable mandate with resources to match.[23]

The AU does not have an official doctrine for its 'peace support operations', but its emerging practices suggest a significantly different approach from UN peacekeeping. This is in part because AU peace operations are intended to address the entire spectrum of conflict management challenges and in part because they are more willing to engage in combat against particular target groups.[24] As articulated in its major January 2012 report on UN–AU cooperation, the AU argued that the UN's peacekeeping doctrine renders it unable to 'deploy a peace mission ... in a situation like Somalia ... even though

---

[22] *Ibid.*, §54, 70, 79.

[23] UN DPKO/DFS, *United Nations Peacekeeping Operations: Principles and Guidelines* (New York: UN, 2008), pp. 49–51.

[24] For more details on the AU approach see Cedric de Coning, Linnéa Gelot, and John Karlsrud (eds.), *The Future of African Peace Operations* (London: Zed, 2016).

significant advances have been made on the ground'. Unlike the UN, the AU claims it developed 'a different peacekeeping doctrine; instead of waiting for a peace to keep, the AU views peacekeeping as an opportunity to establish peace before keeping it'.[25]

These different approaches could generate significantly divergent notions of the purpose, configuration, and force requirements for peace operations within the UN and AU. They did just that in Somalia. In sum, UNSOA was rooted in an organization that was prepared to do no more than robust forms of peacekeeping but had to support an AU mission that was fighting a war.

From these differences there flowed a number of bureaucratic challenges. First, the UN bureaucracy was slow and hence unable to cope with the high tempo of AMISOM's war-fighting operations. A senior UNSOA official noted that the mission's financial model meant that items of over $1 million needed for its core tasks required approval from New York (as was the case for all mission support components of UN peacekeeping operations). For non-core items, approval was required for anything over $500,000.[26] The mission could only purchase at its discretion items that cost less than these thresholds. (By 2012, the core requirements threshold had increased to $2 million.[27]) Hence, when UNSOA staff wrote contracts for items such as wells or prefabricated structures in August and September 2009, they were presented in New York in March 2010 and not processed until May, with work starting in Somalia in July and August 2010.

This was a problem not only for UNSOA but for UN peace operations more generally; in mid-2015 the High-Level Independent Panel on Peace Operations concluded that 'the current administrative framework for peace operations is often slow, cumbersome and averse to risk'.[28] Even by 2015, UNSOA's administrative framework took, on average, 180 days to recruit someone off a roster, 288 days to have purchases off a system contract delivered, and 114 days to amend an existing contract.[29]

This inefficiency led to political fights to give UNSOA some flexibility. After Malcorra departed DFS, efforts were made to ensure some continuity and retain the 'light footprint' approach (see p. 225). Nevertheless, UNSOA's leadership experienced persistent conflicts with New York, especially the

---

[25] Of course, numerous UN peacekeeping operations have also deployed into areas of ongoing armed conflict. *Report of the Chairperson of the Commission on the Partnership between the African Union and the United Nations on Peace and Security: Towards Greater Strategic Coherence* (PSC/PR/2.(CCCVII), 9 January 2012), §71.

[26] Interview, senior UNSOA official, Mogadishu, 3 January 2013.

[27] Telephone interview, DFS official, 21 October 2013.

[28] Report of the Secretary-General, *The Future of United Nations Peace Operations: Implementation of the Recommendations of the High-Level Independent Panel on Peace Operations*, (A/70/357–S/2015/682, 17 June 2015), §76.

[29] UNSG, *Letter Dated 7 October 2015*, §32.

Office of Legal Affairs, the Office of Central Support Services, and the controller. The routine pace at which these offices processed requests did not remotely match the needs of UNSOA and AMISOM in the field. As noted in Chapter 7, Operation Eagle (March 2014) was just one example where logistics planning and delivery proved too slow. The lack of a sense of urgency also generated considerable frustration among UNSOA staff, as memorandums of understanding were left unsigned for months. Initially, UNSOA had just one desk officer in New York, and his job became to act as a sort of messenger reminding people that UNSOA contracts needed a rapid turnaround.[30]

Even if New York had attended to UNSOA's needs more urgently, however, it is unlikely it could have overcome the fundamental problem: that a mission based on mechanisms designed for peacekeeping was being asked to support a war-fighting operation. One of the ways UNSOA personnel tried to bridge the gap was to procure goods and services on an exigency basis to meet the immediate operational requirements (i.e., procurement processes were fast-tracked on the grounds that if the service was not provided quickly people would die).[31] The UN had used a similar approach following major crisis situations, including the mission start-up in Darfur in 2008 and the 2010 earthquake in Haiti.[32] This did not solve the problem entirely but was a reasonable Band-Aid.

The disjuncture between UNSOA's structures designed for peacekeeping and the realities of war in Somalia manifested itself in several ways. First was the sheer volume of supplies required by UNSOA because the tempo of AMISOM operations was far higher than the UN norm. As one senior UNSOA official recalled, 'We were operating at roughly ten times the UN's standard rate for medical supplies but we had to have long fights with New York to get them to understand this'.[33] Not only was UNSOA using more supplies than a standard UN peacekeeping operation, but it was also comparatively under-resourced compared to other examples of such operations. In late 2011, for example, UNSOA's chief of technical services noted his mission's relative lack of resources (see Table 8.2).

A second manifestation of this disjuncture was the way the UNSOA package was stripped of anything that might be considered payment for

---

[30] Interview, senior UNSOA official, Nairobi, 13 December 2012.

[31] Clarke, UNSOA study, p. 92; and communication with DFS official, 2 September 2016. Rule 105.16 (vii) in the UN's financial rules and regulations allows for the formal methods of solicitation to be waived under exigent circumstances. Under General Assembly Decision 54/468 (7 April 2000), an exigency is defined for the purposes of procurement as 'an exceptional compelling and emergent need, not resulting from poor planning or management or from concerns over the availability of funds, that will lead to serious damage, loss or injury to property or persons if not addressed immediately'.

[32] UNSOA, *Scoping Exercise*, §11.

[33] Interview, senior UNSOA official, Mogadishu, 3 January 2013.

Table 8.2. Comparing UNSOA resources to select UN peacekeeping operations

	UNMIL	UNMIS	UNOCI	UNSOA (2011–12)
Military	8,069	9,450	7,250	12,000
Operational Costs (US$ million)	161.3	386.5	155	212.5
Total Support Staff	1,518	3,072	1,051	294
Troops to Staff	5.3	3.1	6.9	40.8
Operational Cost to Staff ($)	106,000	126,000	148,000	723,000

Source: Michael Hanrahan, Chief Technical Services UNSOA, briefing 20 September 2011, http://www.docstoc.com/docs/106459303/TAM-Backbrief-to-MilAd

military personnel, military hardware, or any kind of lease arrangement with the Ugandan or Burundian army to provide such equipment.[34] Consequently, UNSOA did not provide ammunition, which was still done through arrangements with bilateral partners or by the AMISOM TCCs themselves. Even a few years later, there was no funding from the UN assessed peacekeeping contributions to support the establishment of an AMISOM force headquarters or civilian staff in Mogadishu. Money for these mechanisms all had to come out of the Trust Fund for AMISOM and the Somali National Army, where donations usually came with caveats about what they could be spent on.[35] In 2009, for instance, Japan provided funds for outreach activities, but UNSOA could not spend the money because of the dire security situation. Similarly, the UK's initial contribution of $10 million could not be used to reimburse TCCs for use of lethal equipment they owned.[36] Finally, contributions to the trust fund were rarely transparent, and it was often unclear to AMISOM how the money was being disbursed and spent. Some AU officials joked that the UN was running an 'UNtrustworthy fund'.[37]

A third example of the organizational culture clash was the UN and AU's different views on how to fight Somalia's insurgents. A senior Ugandan officer recalled that initially the vehicles his troops received from bilateral partners were painted white, which is standard policy for UN peacekeeping operations. Even some of the Ugandan tanks were white. After he complained that this left AMISOM troops engaged in war-fighting badly exposed, UNSOA provided paint for them to be changed to the usual military colors. Another example was that UN standard peacekeeping procedures did not permit UNSOA to pay for medicines for AMISOM troops to distribute to local civilians. The Ugandan officer's response was that he needed information from the civilians and for them to realize that AMISOM was not the enemy. Medicines and water, he argued, should be used as a bridge to connect with the local population.[38]

---

[34] Clarke, UNSOA study, p. 60.   [35] *Ibid.*, pp. 61, 100–1.
[36] Communication, senior UNSOA official, 1 August 2014.
[37] Communication, former AMISOM official, 19 July 2016.
[38] Interview, senior UPDF officer, Mogadishu, 3 January 2013.

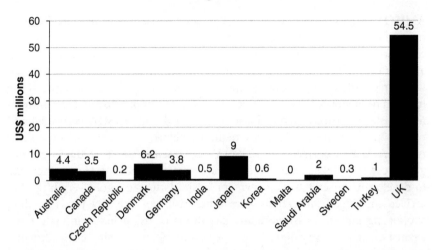

Fig. 8.2. Contributions to Trust Fund for AMISOM and the Somali National Army (up to 2015)

Source: Compiled by author.

Another commander said AMISOM was ultimately in Somalia to protect civilians so it should help them whenever it could, and win hearts and minds in the process.[39] As a result, AMISOM used its own limited supplies and sought bilateral donations from some personal friends of senior Ugandan officers. Similarly, UNSOA would not provide support to Somali security forces, who lacked basic supplies. AMISOM commanders, who had to develop working relations with the Somali troops on the frontlines, ended up sharing their own supplies.[40] Overall, these commanders concluded that Somalia was a learning experience for UNSOA and that it should have been more flexible.

A fourth case involved confusion over the type of equipment UNSOA was able to provide. Officially, UNSOA was limited to non-lethal support to AMISOM. But the lines quickly blurred over fighting vehicles. AMISOM thought UNSOA would provide it with frontline fighting vehicles in the form of APCs. UNSOA, however, said it would only provide vehicles for headquarters operations and that fighting vehicles would have to be sourced via the UN Trust Fund for AMISOM or bilateral support packages.[41]

Finally, there were accountability challenges. The problem here was that AMISOM did not share the UN's many rules and regulations for accountability and did not consistently punish its personnel who violated its rules. Even on basic issues such as accounting for supplies in a transparent manner,

---

[39] Interview, senior UPDF officer, telephone, 4 March 2015.   [40] *Ibid.*

[41] Secure military radios also became a source of contention. Ammunition was clearly outside UNSOA's mandate and hence was provided either by the TCCs themselves or by bilateral donors. Clarke, UNSOA study, pp. 79–80.

AMISOM forces were not organized to provide such information. Keeping track of fuel was a constant source of stress, as thousands of litres disappeared each month from vehicles that were supposed to remain on the main base. In another example, generators powering the force headquarters and the hospital would regularly stop working in the middle of the night because some of the fuel had been stolen.[42] The creation of the Joint Support Operations Centre in Mogadishu in 2010, which collocated AMISOM and UNSOA personnel and processed all AMISOM logistics requests, helped overcome some of these issues. A related obstacle for UNSOA's contractors was that they were not given access to UN software because they were not UN staff. Hence, they had to develop from scratch their own spreadsheets to catalogue everything that arrived in Mogadishu. There were other risks for the UN too, including supporting an AU mission facing allegations of using indiscriminate force against civilians, engaging in sexual exploitation, and causing environmental damage through poor wastewater management (AMISOM had no environmental baseline study or AU policy to guide its operations).[43]

It was therefore hardly surprising that UNSOA's mantra became 'One Mission–One Team' in an attempt to bridge some of these gaps.[44] But it was not always successful. AMISOM's assault to capture the town of Jowhar in late 2012 provides a good example of the operational problems that ensued. As a senior UNSOA official recalled, the Information Support Team had been sending film crews to document AMISOM operations in real time and hence needed to be kept informed about what was going on. For the Jowhar operation, however, AMISOM did not inform UNSOA until twelve hours after it captured the town. As a result, UNSOA was unable to get the required resources to the theatre in advance and no film crew showed up for twenty-four hours.[45]

Instances like this generated frustration on both sides and left UNSOA unable to meet AMISOM's needs. AMISOM was therefore less likely to always keep UNSOA in its information loop. Over time, these issues reduced the level of trust between the operations. The problem was only compounded by the fact that UNSOA did not have a reporting line to AU headquarters.[46] Multiple coordination problems emerged. For example, during the Afgoye operation in May 2012, the Ugandan contingent conducted the operation, and only then called for the logistics support to provide food and water. UNSOA meanwhile had no idea the operation was underway.[47] This prompted renewed efforts to co-locate UNSOA and AMISOM staff to avoid such problems. And yet, as

---

[42] *Ibid.*, pp. 81–2.   [43] UNSG, *Letter Dated 7 October 2015*, §36–7.
[44] Clarke, UNSOA study, p. 66.
[45] Interview, senior UNSOA official, Nairobi, 13 December 2012.
[46] UNSOA, *Scoping Exercise*, §24.
[47] Communication, UNPOS official, 20 December 2012.

noted in Chapter 7, coordination lapses were still evident between UNSOA, AMISOM, and the Somali National Army as late as March 2014 during the conduct of Operation Eagle.[48]

CHALLENGE 3: INSECURITY IN SOMALIA

A third set of challenges facing AMISOM and UNSOA stemmed from the highly dangerous operating environment in Somalia. In response, UNSOA developed a new model of operations in order to remotely manage most tasks from Nairobi. This approach was driven by three main factors: insecurity in Mogadishu, the desire to keep down financial costs, and a determination to maintain a 'light footprint' in terms of UN personnel.[49] Fundamentally, therefore, the security situation in Mogadishu drove the provision of AMISOM's logistics.[50] As the UN Secretary-General would later summarize, the situation presented UNSOA with the challenge of how to 'stay and deliver' its programmes in partnership with the AU.[51]

The security risks dictated that UNSOA's 'light footprint' relied upon contractors who were willing to assume considerable risks—if the money was right. Deploying UN personnel to Somalia was out of the question because the UN Department of Safety and Security initially assessed Mogadishu as a Phase V security risk, meaning international UN staff must evacuate immediately. UNSOA therefore deployed a few of its old UN hands to Mogadishu as contractors to set up support from the Somali side. Naturally, working in this environment required a different skill set and approach than more traditional UN peacekeeping operations.[52] To take just one example, UNSOA was tasked with maintaining and repairing AMISOM's fleet of over 700 combat and support vehicles. But the insecure environment meant that when vehicles broke down near the frontlines, UNSOA faced huge challenges in getting them back to its workshop in the rear.[53]

UNSOA's reliance on contractors and AMISOM personnel to undertake tasks that would usually be performed by UN staff was thus entirely understandable.[54] Its solution was to adopt remote management and a light footprint—namely, running the mission out of Nairobi and using contractors for most of the work in Mogadishu—to provide logistical support in the war-torn city. Later on, this led to conflicts between UNSOA and New York, and then within UNSOA itself,

---

[48] *Report of After Action Review for Operation Eagle* (AU internal document, 5 June 2014).
[49] UNSOA, *Scoping Exercise*, §8.
[50] Telephone interview, DFS official, 21 October 2013.
[51] UNSG, *Letter Dated 7 October 2015*, §7.
[52] Telephone interview, DFS official, 21 October 2013.   [53] *Ibid.*
[54] UNSOA, *Scoping Exercise*, §9.

as more new UN staff working on the mission preferred to operate according to the traditional UN framework for getting things done.[55]

A good example of UNSOA's reliance on contractors was its approach to air services. Whereas most UN peacekeeping operations have their own fleet of aircraft, UNSOA decided instead to lease seats on commercial aircraft.[56] Instead of paying for a plane and crew to be on standby throughout the year, UNSOA signed agreements with three companies to provide planes (and sometimes certain numbers of seats on planes) as and when they were needed. This allowed UNSOA to hire the most suitable plane for the required passengers or cargo.[57] It also saved money. As an internal analysis of UNSOA concluded, 'In the first three years of operations, UNSOA spent $4.2 million on flights, or 70 percent of the initial $6 million budget, which was meant to pay for one UN plane for one year'.[58] Similarly, the 2012 UNSOA review estimated that this approach produced savings of up to 60 per cent.[59] But outsourcing flights generated political pushback in New York, even though UNSOA had no other feasible option in its start-up phase. This pushback largely came down to international politics, because the majority of long-term charter agreements for UN missions are struck with companies from a handful of powerful UN member states.[60] UNSOA's use of local air charters was ended in early 2013 as security conditions improved.[61]

The extensive use of contractors meant that AMISOM's support was ultimately dependent upon a four-way partnership with UNSOA, the various private firms involved, and the bilateral donors that supplied the ammunition and lethal equipment.[62] As noted above, while outsourcing to firms resulted in considerable cost savings and efficiency for UNSOA, it also raised the problem of giving contractors access to UN information systems and generated some political pushback from powerful member states. For AMISOM, this outsourcing enabled the delivery of services the UN would have been unable to provide but raised additional concerns about operational security and safeguarding against leaked information while fighting its war.[63]

CHALLENGE 4: THE TYRANNY OF DISTANCE

A fourth challenge stemmed from the massive increase in AMISOM's area of operations once it pushed *al-Shabaab* forces out of Mogadishu in August 2011

[55] Interviews, senior UNSOA officials, Nairobi, 13 December 2012 and telephone, 17 July 2014.
[56] Telephone interview, DFS official, 21 October 2013.
[57] Clarke, UNSOA study, p. 72. A similar approach was adopted for sea transport. See pp. 76–7.
[58] *Ibid.*, p. 74.   [59] Telephone interview, DFS official, 21 October 2013.
[60] Clarke, UNSOA study, p. 74.   [61] *Ibid.*, p. 76.
[62] Interview, senior UNSOA official, Mogadishu, 3 January 2013.   [63] *Ibid.*

and started to spread out from the city in early 2012. The area it covered went from roughly 100 square kilometres to over 400,000 with personnel in more than eighty locations. While it was possible to stretch some of UNSOA's resources when AMISOM operated in just parts of Mogadishu, it was impossible for UNSOA to cope with the logistical challenges presented by AMISOM's new mandate and force posture from early 2012 when its operations expanded across south-central Somalia (see Table 8.3).

While logistical support to AMISOM forces in Mogadishu was difficult, there was a major seaport and airport to bring supplies in, and UNSOA personnel became familiar with the locales and could prepare accordingly. As AMISOM spread beyond Mogadishu, other problems emerged. First, as AMISOM deployed further inland from Mogadishu and the Somali border regions, it needed to arrange alternative lines of communication beyond the sea route from Mombasa. Interestingly, even after AMISOM gained control of the port of Marka in August 2012, southwest of Mogadishu, UNSOA continued to supply the town by road from Mogadishu. Yet, as one senior UPDF officer complained, it would have saved both AMISOM lives and equipment if its force in Marka was supplied by a small ship from Mogadishu rather than by road: a dangerous journey that took about eight hours on a poor road surface with the risk of ambush compared to about one hour by sea from Mogadishu.[64] It remains unclear to me why UNSOA did not use this option.

Second, insecurity along the main supply routes meant that even contractors would not take the risk. Consequently, AMISOM's TCCs were made 'responsible for the delivery of goods and services from UNSOA logistics hubs to the 'front line' or more insecure areas'.[65] This, in turn, required UNSOA to train those forces in how to conduct such operations. Moreover, the distances started to expose AMISOM's lack of enabling units, which might have been able to open up major ground supply routes for UNSOA to provide support. In particular, in addition to logistics personnel, AMISOM emphasized the need for 'heavy transport and logistics assets to move goods and services forward, along with combat engineers and aviation assets to secure, recce and support convoys along the Lines of Communication'.[66] Even when such assets did arrive, AMISOM did not have sufficient personnel to operate them. Hence, some heavy transport equipment and an engineering plant provided by UNSOA and donors to allow the movement of goods, food, and water sat idle. Nor did AMISOM have sufficient medical staff for the medical facilities needed in each sector.[67]

Third, UNSOA had to deal with long logistics supply chains, and the process of constructing AMISOM's supply routes was difficult, dangerous

---

[64] Communication, senior UPDF officer, 12 February 2015.
[65] *Military CONOPS* (2012), Annex D, §4.   [66] *Ibid.*, Annex D, §6.
[67] Communication, senior UNSOA official, 30 December 2012.

Table 8.3. Distances between Somali cities (kilometres)

	Beledweyne	Baidoa	Bardera	Bosaso	Adado	Dolo	Galkayo	Garowe	Kismayo	Mogadishu
Beledweyne										
Baidoa	585									
Bardera	782	197								
Bosaso	1,053	1,638	1,835							
Adado	245	830	1,027	570						
Dolo	807	222	258	1,860	1,052					
Galkayo	373	958	1,155	680	128	1,180				
Garowe	611	1,196	1,393	442	366	1,418	238			
Kismayo	803	527	330	1,856	1,048	588	1,176	1,414		
Mogadishu	343	242	439	1,396	588	464	716	954	460	

(because of regular *al-Shabaab* attacks), and slow.[68] It is notable just how significant the journeys involved were. For example, in 2012 AMISOM estimated that while the trip from Mogadishu to Kismayo (the Sector 2 headquarters) took one hour in a helicopter and forty-five minutes by fixed-wing plane, it would take up to four days to drive. Getting from Mogadishu to Beledweyne (in Sector 4) was a two-hour helicopter ride or a two-day drive, and getting to Baidoa (in Sector 3) took forty-five minutes by helicopter but also two days to drive (see Table 8.3).[69] For emergency medical evacuation, road transport was often out of the question, but UNSOA had only two contracted civilian helicopters, and air operations were very expensive. More-over, evacuated casualties had to be taken to Mogadishu to ensure effective medical support because of the lack of medical support elsewhere.[70] By 2015, there were some more utility helicopters available, but UNSOS still had to meet a very large demand for casualty and medical evacuations. During 2015, UNSOS aviation had to evacuate by air 1,233 patients, principally from AMISOM and the SNA, as well as human remains. During 2016, the figure was 1,436 patients.[71]

Finally, once again, the need to meet AMISOM's rapid reaction require-ments over such large distances fell afoul of cumbersome UN bureaucratic procedures.[72] With AMISOM forces capturing more and more towns, UNSOA fell further behind the pace of the operations.[73] In part, this was because UN standards are generally used to supply static forces, whereas AMISOM needed to be mobile. With the expanded geographic area, UNSOA's leadership thought it would be impossible to meet them. The basics might just be doable if corners were cut, but senior UNSOA officials recommended that the phrase 'to UN standard' be removed from the mandate.[74]

CHALLENGE 5: AMISOM AS A CLIENT

The final challenge analysed here stemmed from some of AMISOM's limita-tions as UNSOA's principal client. In sum, while UNSOA was not a perfect

---

[68] *Ibid.*   [69] *Military CONOPS* (2012), p. 2.

[70] Telephone interview, UNOAU official, 20 December 2012. For a self-assessment of one of the firms contracted to provide air medical evacuations, see Adam Low and Bettina Vadera, 'Air Medical Evacuations from a Developing World Conflict Zone', *Air Medical Journal*, 30:6 (2011), pp. 313–16.

[71] Confidential UNSOS documents, 2016 and 2017. Copy in author's possession.

[72] Interview, senior UNSOA official, Nairobi, 13 December 2012.

[73] Telephone interview, UNOAU official, 20 December 2012.

[74] Interview, senior UNSOA official, Mogadishu, 3 January 2013.

match for AMISOM's needs, the AU mission was also not in a position to work well and efficiently with its UN partner.

As noted above, some of the tensions stemmed from UNSOA's inability to keep pace with AMISOM's demands, others from misunderstandings and misaligned expectations on both sides. But as a client, AMISOM had some significant limitations. First, the many complex issues began to overwhelm the three AMISOM political officers who were present by mid-2012.[75] Second, many of AMISOM's specialists in these areas rotated every six to nine months, making it difficult to build institutional memory and relationships.[76] Third, it was not until 2012 that AMISOM established a multinational force headquarters. This left UNSOA to deal with a fragmented mission where the national contingents often adopted their own way of doing things.[77]

Things became more complicated once Djibouti joined the mission in December 2011, and Kenya in the first half of 2012. Both of these new TCCs caused UNSOA headaches. As analysed in Chapter 5, Djibouti took nearly a year to deploy its first battalion, soaked up significant UNSOA resources, and caused much aggravation in the process. UNSOA's relationship with the Kenyans was also fraught, not least because the government in Nairobi wanted reimbursement for its maritime assets. UNSOA refused, not only because they were not AMISOM assets but also because the Kenyans had engaged in indiscriminate shelling of local targets. AMISOM's Sector 2 functioned as a unilateral Kenyan operation, and UNSOA was regularly left completely without information as it worked to establish a presence in the port of Kismayo to deal with all the logistical requirements.[78]

As noted above, the fact that AMISOM failed to generate sufficient enabling units also made UNSOA's task more difficult. For example, UN Security Council Resolution 2124 (2013) authorized 1,845 uniformed personnel to serve as enabling units, but only a few of them materialized in the mission, and those that did were deployed as contingent rather than mission assets. Even by 2015, AMISOM had only one-third of the organic support assets of a normal UN peacekeeping operation.[79] Nor were AMISOM's troops very mobile, possessing only about 30 per cent of the mobility support capabilities of a similarly sized UN mission.[80] As a result, UNSOA had to provide many services by air because the main supply routes were in such a bad state of disrepair or were insecure. The 2015 strategic review later concluded this was 'operationally and financially unsustainable'.[81]

---

[75] Interview, AMISOM official, Nairobi, 7 August 2012.

[76] UNSOA, *Scoping Exercise*, §20.

[77] Telephone interview, DPKO official, 21 October 2013.

[78] Interview, senior UNSOA official, Nairobi, 13 December 2012.

[79] Communication, senior UNSOA official, 22 September 2015.

[80] UNSG, *Letter Dated 7 October 2015*, §40–1.   [81] *Ibid.*, §42. See also §85.

The compromise worked out during 2012 was that UNSOA would operate on a 'hub and spoke' approach: UNSOA would deliver supplies to the sector hubs and battalion headquarters, then AMISOM would be responsible for moving the supplies to its forward operating bases.[82] But AMISOM's expansion across more and more territory with more bases necessitated more logistical support as the force broke down into smaller, more dispersed units. For instance, while a battalion based in Mogadishu might need two fuel trucks because the fuel only has to go from the seaport to the base compound, a battalion deploying and breaking down to company level needs seven fuel trucks.[83] Overall, UNSOA struggled to effectively implement this model. The 2015 strategic review later concluded that it could not work unless AMISOM's individual contingents provided more of their own equipment.[84]

Nor was AMISOM always able to make requests in a timely and appropriate manner. Before the force headquarters was established in 2012, AMISOM had operated without any staff officers, so there was nobody dedicated to such tasks as ordering logistics, medical, and engineering items. Even when eighty-five headquarters staff posts were created, it took time to fill them. Moreover, when AMISOM communicated its needs, UNSOA personnel would usually be handed long lists of items. Lists were problematic because they lacked the narrative context that would enable UNSOA to prioritize between items that were crucial and those that could wait or be ignored.[85]

Finally, even when UNSOA instigated positive reforms within AMISOM, it was met with resistance. For example, when UNSOA first arrived, AMISOM was cooking without refrigeration and using charcoal. Not only did this lead to the wet beriberi outbreak (discussed in Chapter 3), but much of the charcoal came from areas of southern Somalia controlled by *al-Shabaab* (see Chapter 6). Although this did not break the UN ban on Somali charcoal exports, it was politically counterproductive. UNSOA therefore introduced hundred-person kitchens powered by diesel burners, but it took time to train AMISOM cooks to use them, and some soldiers initially resisted the change.[86] This change also raised AMISOM's expectations, but UNSOA then struggled to meet similar standards for the contingents out in the sectors.

ASSESSING UNSOA

How should we assess UNSOA's efforts to provide AMISOM's logistics in light of these challenges? Naturally, UNSOA's own publications provide glowing

---

[82] *Ibid.*, §43.   [83] Interview, senior UNSOA official, Mogadishu, 3 January 2013.

[84] UNSG, *Letter Dated 7 October 2015*, §87.

[85] Interview, senior UNSOA official, Mogadishu, 3 January 2013.

[86] Clarke, UNSOA study, pp. 84–5.

reviews. Its 2015 handbook, for instance, included ten brief testimonies praising UNSOA from senior AMISOM military commanders and the head of mission.[87] Other forms of assessment, including by the UN, were mixed. Between 2011 and 2015, for instance, the UN's Office of Internal Oversight Services conducted several audits of some aspects of UNSOA's operations. On the positive side, rations were provided in a timely manner and in the requested quantities, and UNSOA's risk management, control, and governance processes at the Mombasa support base were deemed satisfactory.[88] On the negative side, recruitment of staff suffered from initially high vacancy rates and subsequent delays; the management of UNSOA's procurement activities was only partially satisfactory; its use of vehicles in Kenya was only partially satisfactory; its management of fuel was rated as unsatisfactory overall, principally because of inaccurate financial reporting and noncompliance with mandates and regulations; and its management of air operations was also deemed unsatisfactory overall, mainly because of a lack of efficient and effective operations and noncompliance with mandates and regulations.[89]

So how should UNSOA's provision of logistics support to AMISOM be judged overall? UNSOA had some scathing critics. One US official, for instance, referred to it as 'a defunct organization' that was 'at the heart' of AMISOM's failures.[90] But this verdict is too harsh. First, it is important to recall that UNSOA was a political compromise forged because the UN's most powerful member states did not want to deploy a UN peacekeeping operation in Somalia. Its design and level of resources reflected that deal. Second, UNSOA was created as an attempt to help a struggling AU mission that operated in only a few parts of one city, and it had no clear exit strategy or plan in case those circumstances changed. Third, UNSOA was also constrained by the fact that it was an unprecedented (and contentious) experiment, in part because it was a logistics mechanism without a leading political arm. While it worked with two UN political missions in Somalia, neither was able to provide strong political leadership: UNPOS had enormous challenges even getting personnel into Somalia, let alone leading politically, while UNSOM managed a larger presence but also struggled to take the political reins. Hence, UNSOA often found itself providing logistics in something close to a political vacuum.[91]

---

[87] UNSOA, *UNSOA*, 2015, pp. 11–13, https://unsoa.unmissions.org/sites/default/files/unsoa-booklet.pdf

[88] UN Office of Internal Oversight Services (OIOS), Internal Audit Reports AP2010/638/03, 25 February 2011; and AP2011/638/02, 30 September 2011, https://oios.un.org/page?slug=report

[89] See, in order, OIOS, Internal Audit Reports AP2010/638/05, 25 February 2011; AP2011/638/04, 1 May 2012; AP2012/638/08, 8 November 2013; AP2013/638/05, 8 August 2014; and AP2013/638/01, 28 January 2015, https://oios.un.org/page?slug=report

[90] Communication, US official, Djibouti, 22 November 2014.

[91] Telephone interview, DFS official, 21 October 2013.

With regard to the five challenges discussed above, UNSOA's record was mixed. UNSOA coped reasonably well with its regularly expanding list of tasks. Its arrival in Somalia clearly constituted a major improvement on what existed before. As one AMISOM officer noted, 'Before UNSOA, the logistical challenges were huge'.[92] The 2012 review was also broadly positive. 'Overall', it concluded, 'the UNSOA model has been successful in providing an effective logistics backbone for AMISOM operations in Somalia'.[93] AMISOM and donor personnel also gave positive assessments. As one former AMISOM force commander recalled, with its roots in the UN's bureaucratic systems, UNSOA should be commended for doing a job that it was not formatted for.[94] Similarly, one EU military officer recalled that his days working with AMISOM before UNSOA were shocking because of the dire state of AMISOM's logistics support. Despite its limitations, he admired UNSOA as 'a unique instrument to help Africa in its hour of need'. Ultimately, he concluded, UNSOA had saved the lives of AMISOM personnel.[95] This is an accurate assessment.

The 'light footprint' approach was also an entirely reasonable and innovative approach to dealing with the security situation in Somalia. Especially in the early years, there was no other plausible choice but to innovate along these lines. UNSOA's reliance on contractors was sensible, even though it caused some political frictions in New York. In financial terms, and despite working in a much more insecure environment than most UN missions, UNSOA managed to generate a significant impact at a much cheaper rate than other UN peacekeeping operations. This was in large part because of its extensive use of contractors, which in this case provided good value for money compared to the costs involved if the UN had deployed a full peacekeeping operation.[96] In that sense, as the 2015 strategic review concluded, 'The light footprint approach has been broadly successful', particularly in its highly efficient use of resources.[97] Indeed, the AU recognized UNSOA's relative success when it called for the UN to establish similar mechanisms for the African missions in Mali (2013) and the Central African Republic (2014).[98]

Indeed, what else could reasonably be expected of UNSOA given the available resources? Even by the 2014/15 fiscal year, for instance, UNSOA had about 700 civilian staff to support over 34,000 personnel working in a variety of different entities in several different countries. This translated into a terrible staff-to-supported-personnel ratio of 1:48. By way of comparison, other UN missions in the region had equivalent ratios of 1:5 (MONUSCO

---

[92] Telephone interview, AMISOM official, 29 July 2012.
[93] UNSOA, *Scoping Exercise*, Summary.
[94] Communication, former senior AMISOM commander, 12 February 2015.
[95] Interview, EU official, Nairobi, 15 December 2012.
[96] Interview, UK official, Kampala, 13 August 2012.
[97] UNSG, *Letter Dated 7 October 2015*, §79.   [98] *Ibid.*

and UNAMID) and 1:4 (UNMISS).[99] This suggests UNSOA was basically designed to fail, and the 'light footprint' was the only way it could achieve even partial success.

In contrast, UNSOA struggled to overcome the clash of organizational cultures between the UN and AMISOM. The central problem was that UNSOA was based in frameworks designed for peacekeeping but tasked with supporting a war-fighting mission. The predictable result was that AMISOM's more intense tempo of operations simply overwhelmed UNSOA, especially once the mission expanded beyond Mogadishu. As the 2012 review exercise noted, this led 'some AMISOM personnel [to conclude] the logistics operation is still playing catch up with the security operations on the ground'.[100] Even as late as 2015, the strategic review identified several important capability gaps that UNSOA was unable to fill, including provision of water in remote locations, field defence supplies, maintenance services, tentage for tactical deployments, recruitment and administrative support, and mobility. There were also significant delays in constructing the UNSOM regional offices and AMISOM sector hubs outside Mogadishu.[101] Nevertheless, it is unreasonable to expect UNSOA to overcome such huge organizational differences. And by working together in the field, UNSOA and AMISOM personnel were able to better understand one another and develop tactical innovations to mitigate some very difficult problems.

Finally, UNSOA was never going to be able to meet all of AMISOM's war-fighting needs. This was obvious from the start, and expectations should have been managed accordingly. In addition, the UNSOA–AMISOM partnership broke one of the cardinal rules of war: commanders should always be in control of their logistics. While generally sympathetic to UNSOA, several senior AMISOM commanders saw their separation from their logistical support as fundamentally problematic and ill-advised, as would most military commanders. UNSOA's principal weakness was thus its structural design and the political terms on which it was established. As a top Ugandan commander put it, 'I did not like having to rely on outside parties for our logistics because it put our force at risk'.[102] Similarly, a former AMISOM force commander suggested that 'a fighting force relying on the UN supply chain is a big challenge because they are not compatible'.[103] Another described UNSOA's logistics package as a suboptimal 'push' rather than a 'pull' system: UN officials determined what to give AMISOM commanders and when (push), rather than AMISOM commanders being given the freedom to determine

---

[99] UNSOA official, presentation at the Africa Logistics Council, Addis Ababa, June 2015.
[100] UNSOA, *Scoping Exercise*, §30.   [101] UNSG, *Letter Dated 7 October 2015*, §22.
[102] Interview, senior UPDF officer, Kampala, 14 August 2012.
[103] Cited in Clarke, UNSOA study, p. 93.

what they needed and when (pull).[104] All of this was true, but UNSOA personnel were not in a position to change the nature of their relationship. Rather, the problem originated from the inability of the AU and the AMISOM TCCs to provide adequate logistics for their troops in Somalia.

LESSONS

In mid-2012, a UN lessons learned workshop on the delivery of logistical support to AMISOM had drawn six major lessons.[105] First, AMISOM had limited capacity to absorb international logistical support and needed to accelerate recruitment, manage rotations more effectively, and ensure retention of personnel in key areas. Second, the AU, AMISOM, UNSOA, and the TCCs needed to share information more effectively and in a timely manner to enable joint planning. Third, once information was shared, it needed to be channelled to the right people at the right time and in the right way so that information is interpreted in the way it was meant. This would require streamlined communication channels and standardizing some elements of documentation and reporting formats. Fourth, UNSOA struggled to strike a healthy balance between being flexible, nimble, and responsive on the one hand and being compliant with relevant rules and regulations and accountable on the other. Fifth, UNSOA and AMISOM did not always optimize the management, prioritization, access utilization, control, and accountability of their assets and resources. Finally, the workshop highlighted the weakness of AMISOM's strategic communications not only to counteract *al-Shabaab* propaganda but also to ensure complete understanding and buy-in to the AU mission by all its personnel.

For the most part, these lessons still resonate in mid-2017. Despite massively improving the level of logistical support available to AMISOM, UNSOA struggled to meet the needs of a loose multinational force engaged in sustained maneuver warfare. This was partly because UNSOA was based on UN procedures, mechanisms, and frameworks that were designed for more traditional UN peacekeeping operations in relatively benign environments rather than a war-fighting mission. UNSOA was able to paper over the cracks while AMISOM operated in just one city (Mogadishu). But as the AU forces spread across south-central Somalia, the logistical challenges increased exponentially. This put UNSOA staff in an impossible position and frustrated AMISOM

---

[104] Communication, senior AMISOM official, 20 June 2013.
[105] *Report of the Lessons Learned Workshop on the Delivery of Logistical Support to the AMISOM by the UNSOA*, Nairobi, 30 April–1 May 2012 (internal AU–UN document, no date).

commanders because the UN was unable to deliver the logistical support they required.

It is highly unlikely that the factors that coalesced to produce the multiple partnerships on which AMISOM rested will reoccur. Hence, a relationship exactly like that between UNSOA and AMISOM is unlikely to be replicated. Nevertheless, important debates continue about what support the UN should provide to African regional peace operations, either as part of a transition into UN peacekeeping operations or when that prospect is not on the horizon.[106]

With this in mind, six lessons can be drawn from UNSOA's experience. First, it is always unwise to separate control over logistical functions from the operational commander concerned. This should be avoided in all peace operations that are primarily military, and especially in those involving combat operations.

Second, despite some pioneering efforts by innovative individuals, the UN's bureaucratic rules and procedures were unable to quickly and flexibly provide the level of logistical support to conduct sustained maneuver warfare with forces dispersed over large distances. If the UN Security Council were to repeat such an arrangement in the future, new mechanisms for supporting enforcement operations—whether by regional or UN forces—will be needed.

Third, when using the UN's assessed peacekeeping contributions, regional organizations must put in place mechanisms to ensure accountability and a reasonable degree of transparency to guard against problems related to civilian harm.[107] Since 2013, this led to many conversations between the UN and AMISOM over whether the AU could prove that the mission met the requirements set out in the human rights due diligence policy (HRDDP) on UN support to non-UN security forces.

Fourth, the UNSOA story illustrates the need for better information sharing between all stakeholders, in this case, the UN (at both headquarters and in the field), the AU, the EU, and other AMISOM partners. An appropriate balance will need to be found to address concerns about operational security in warfighting missions. While it should be acknowledged that different organizations have their own processes and procedures that cannot easily be changed to suit others, the UN's HRDDP should set the standard for such inter-organizational assistance.

Fifth, in AMISOM's case, UNSOA struggled in part because it was not well prepared to support the development of Somalia's national security forces. In

---

[106] See, for example, *Letter Dated 2 January 2015 from the Secretary-General Addressed to the President of the Security Council* (S/2015/3, 5 January 2015); and *Report of the Joint African Union-United Nations Review of Available Mechanisms to Finance and Support African Union Peace Support Operations Authorized by the United Nations Security Council* (A/71/410–S/2016/809, 28 September 2016). Hereafter, *AU-UN Joint Review* (2016).

[107] A point made by the High-Level Independent Panel on Peace Operations in *The Future of United Nations Peace Operations*, §61c; and in *AU-UN Joint Review* (2016).

this case, building legitimate, inclusive, and professional Somali security forces was a crucial part of AMISOM's exit strategy, but UNSOA struggled for many of the same reasons as AMISOM (which are analysed in Chapter 9).

Finally, UNSOA's experience suggests that a better link is needed between the field operations and the planning processes in New York and Addis Ababa, with more emphasis on risk and crisis management. To that end, the UN and regional organizations should reflect on whether future peace enforcement operations should operate under a different set of rules than peacekeeping missions. This could include using support mechanisms designed to use a range of 'special measures' that go well beyond the existing six-month UN crisis response and mission start-up measures and provide much greater operational flexibility than is currently available through the 'exigency' mechanism.[108]

[108] See UNSOA, *Scoping Exercise*, Summary.

9

Security Sector Reform

In July 2017, the AU PSC announced that in partnership with the UN and the Somali Federal Government and as part of its attempts to move forward with AMISOM's exit strategy, it needed to conduct a comprehensive verification of the SNA and Police Force across all sectors of operations.[1] For its part, during the May 2017 Joint Review of AMISOM, the Federal Government acknowledged the value of 'a Joint Verification exercise'.[2] Among other things, the verification exercise was intended to catalogue basic information such as the identities of Somali security personnel, their locations and unit affiliations, as well as their weapons and equipment.[3] The fact that there were so many fundamental 'known unknowns' about the Somali security forces in July 2017 spoke volumes about what a difficult partner Somalia had been for AMISOM.

Especially from 2009, AMISOM had to grapple with two big issues related to its host's security forces. First, how best to cooperate and coordinate with the existing Somali security forces in order to fight an effective war against *al-Shabaab*? And second, how to help build a new set of ostensibly 'national' security forces that could make the AU mission redundant, while simultaneously fighting that war? While the official aspiration was to build a legitimate, inclusive, professional, effective, and sustainable SNA, for AMISOM's purposes, all that was required was an SNA good enough to reduce and contain the threat posed by *al-Shabaab* to a tolerable level. But even this less ambitious goal was a far more daunting undertaking than just 'reforming' the Somali security sector. In part, this was because most of it, especially the army, had to be built almost entirely from scratch. As one 2017 study put it, 'The list of needs is so fundamental that it is no exaggeration to suggest that Somalia is building its army from the very foundation'.[4] But it was also because of the

---

[1] PSC/PR/COM.(DCC), 12 July 2017, §15.

[2] SNA presentation to AMISOM Joint Review team, Mogadishu, 23 May 2017.

[3] The name was subsequently changed to the Operational Readiness Assessment, which got underway in September 2017.

[4] Paul R. Camacho and Ibrahim Mohamed Abukar, *Somalia's Security: The Reconstruction of the Somali National Army* (Mogadishu: Center for Policy Analysis and Research, February 2017), p. 11.

lack of political consensus among Somali elites about the vision guiding the country's security sector and how to win the war against *al-Shabaab.*

In short, AMISOM's most fundamental problem was that the politics of Somali security sector reform (SSR) were not conducive to building a national army. Security sector issues were inherently political and hence genuine progress needed the country's political elites to reconcile and agree on a shared vision and roadmap for their national security architecture and forces. But this did not happen. Without it, Somali ownership was impossible and external partners had no stable national security architecture into which to plug their assistance.[5] Moreover, building a 'national' army in the absence of a national consensus about what the Somali state is and how it should be governed was a risky endeavour, particularly in a context where AMISOM had to fight a war simultaneously and the relationship between the multiple armed groups could change quickly.[6] But this was AMISOM's daunting task.

None of these things should have come as a surprise to anyone versed in the basic principles of counterinsurgency and SSR. In counterinsurgency, it is widely accepted that success hinges on the ability of foreign forces to handover operations to an effective and legitimate local authority, and, in turn, for indigenous military forces to be gradually replaced by civilian authorities.[7] As discussed at length in Chapters 12 and 13, AMISOM struggled along both these dimensions. Similarly, guidelines for successful SSR emphasize that trying to achieve it during political instability and without national consensus on the vision and structures guiding the sector is a recipe for failure. Attempts to reform the security sector must also strike an appropriate balance between operational support and institutional reform, the latter always being inherently political. As US government guidance on SSR put it, 'Success and sustainability depend on developing the institutions and processes that support security forces as well as the human capacity to lead and manage them'.[8] Once again, the SNA had huge gaps related to its supporting institutions and human capacity. The AU's own policy framework on SSR, developed from 2008 but not officially adopted until January 2013, identified nine 'fundamental core elements' on which attempts to achieve SSR would hinge. They included an accurate needs assessment, a national security strategy, institutional, legal, and security policy frameworks, democratic control and oversight mechanisms, adequate resource mobilization, funding and accountability, and monitoring and evaluation

---

[5] *Security Sector Assessment* (June 2011), p. 33.

[6] Although debate continues over whether Somaliland will reunify with the rest of Somalia, this chapter focuses only on AMISOM's area of operations in the south-central region.

[7] See, for example, *US Government Counterinsurgency Guide* (US Government, January 2009), https://www.state.gov/documents/organization/119629.pdf

[8] *Security Sector Reform* (US AID, Department of Defense, Department of State, February 2009), p. 5. https://www.state.gov/documents/organization/115810.pdf

mechanisms.[9] The Somali security sector lacked all of these elements during AMISOM's first decade of operations.

To analyse how AMISOM grappled with these huge challenges, this chapter proceeds in three parts. It starts with a brief overview of how Somalia's armed forces evolved since independence, focusing on the period since 2008 when the basis of today's SNA was formed. Throughout the twenty-first century, the armed forces remained fragmented and their institutions and structures largely dysfunctional. The second section then examines seven major challenges that made AMISOM's mandate to enhance the SNA particularly difficult. The final section reflects on some of the principal lessons that can be identified from AMISOM's experience.

During the period under review, AMISOM and its international partners usually defined the Somali security sector broadly to encompass not solely the SNA but also the Somali Police Force, the national intelligence services, coastguard, air force, corrections/custodian officers, as well as judicial institutions. This recognized that countering *al-Shabaab* would ultimately require more than a heavily militarized approach to include community-based policing and intelligence as well as broader initiatives such as education, encouraging defections, and amnesty programmes. Nevertheless, the principal focus of this chapter is on the SNA, which initially was AMISOM's main partner in this endeavour. The Somali Police Force became a much more important part of AMISOM's work from 2012 but is discussed in Chapter 12 as part of the debate about undertaking stabilization operations.

EVOLUTION OF THE SOMALI ARMED FORCES

Although Somalia had established a police force in 1943, it was not until April 1960 that its Armed Forces was formed by the merger of the Italian and British mandates' mobile security forces. Initially, these numbered between 2,000 and 5,000.[10] For most of the next two decades, the Armed Forces focused heavily on pursuing an irredentist agenda designed to unite the Somali populations spread across the wider Horn of Africa. Ultimately, this led to the decision to invade Ethiopia in 1977, which resulted in the Somalis suffering a crushing defeat within less than a year. During the 1980s, the Armed Forces became increasingly politicized and its officer corps distorted by President Siad Barre's promotion of officers from his preferred clans, mainly Marehan and related Darod. By the time Somalia's civil war got underway in 1987, the Armed

[9] *Policy Framework on Security Sector Reform* (Addis Ababa: AU, 2013), Section D.

[10] Colin Robinson, 'Revisiting the rise and fall of the Somali Armed Forces, 1960–2012', *Defense & Security Analysis*, 32:3 (2016), p. 239.

Forces had effectively started disintegrating as Barre lost control of large parts of the country.[11]

The SNA subsequently ceased to exist until the new transitional Somali authorities tried to resurrect it between 2000 and 2005. The first effort to rebuild a national army was made by the TNG in 2000, which recruited freelance gunmen and members of Siad Barre's military.[12] These did not all carry over to 2004 when the new TFG formed its military in Jowhar. They comprised some troops from Barre's military but also Puntland militias and other clan militias from the Jowhar area. When the TFG moved to Baidoa in 2005 it also recruited some clan militias from the Bay region.[13]

On paper at least, the SNA were part of the Somali National Security and Stabilization Plan (NSSP), which the TFG adopted in June 2006.[14] The NSSP was intended 'to serve as the main conduit for supporting collaboration between the TFG and its international partners for sustained, coherent, harmonized and complimentary security sector stabilization in Somalia'.[15] It was subsequently revised several times because it was originally intended to serve as guidance during the transitional governance period. Revisions were developed in light of recommendations made by two security sector assessments conducted during 2009 and 2011.[16] Rather ominously, the 2009 assessment concluded that: 'Security Sector Reform efforts will probably falter—and quite possibly even fail—without a broader political foundation that promotes good governance, transparency and accountability within the Transitional timeframe'.[17]

The basis of today's SNA, however, lay in the merger of the TFG's security forces with those of the ARS–Djibouti faction as stipulated in the August 2008 Djibouti Agreement. These forces, which probably numbered just over 5,000 troops (about 3,000 from the TFG and about 2,000 from the ARS-Djibouti, who were mostly militia from the Islamic Courts), were to be given UN support to build their capacity to restore the security sector and the rule of law.[18] The

---

[11] *Ibid.*, p. 241.

[12] Mohamed Mubarak, 'Somali military has more problems than lack of guns', *African Arguments*, 28 February 2014, http://africanarguments.org/2014/02/26/somali-military-has-more-problems-than-lack-of-guns-by-mohamed-mubarak/

[13] *Ibid.*

[14] *Report of the Chairperson of the Commission on the Situation in Somalia* (PSC/PR/2(LXIX), 19 January 2007), §33.

[15] Cited in the President's Foreword to the 2011 Somali NSSP.

[16] The 2009 assessment was compiled outside of Somalia, largely donor-led and based on interviews with key actors. It was limited to south-central Somalia for political reasons and was stimulated by donor concerns about the TFG forces. The 2011 assessment was carried out in Somalia and was more Somali-driven and linked to the idea of developing a revised NSSP. Communication, contractor engaged in the process, 31 July 2012.

[17] *Somalia Security Sector Assessment* (AU, US, EU, TFG, World Bank and UN: 1 January 2010), §1i.

[18] 'Letter from the Secretary-General to the President of the Security Council' (S/2008/804, 19 December 2008), Annex.

Table 9.1. Estimated size of the Somali Armed Forces, 1963–2017

Date	Estimated Size	Source
1963	4,000	
1965	4,600	
1970	12,000	
1977	35,000–37,000	
May 2009	5,000–6,700	TFG and ARS–Djibouti
November 2009	6,400 (+ 6,270 aligned forces)	UN Monitoring Group
November 2010	8,000	AMISOM (CONOPS)
May 2011	10,106	TFG Security Officials
November 2011	10,299	AMISOM
February 2012	11,200	AMISOM (CONOPS)
September 2013	20,000 (inc. aligned militia)	UN Secretary-General
October 2013	12,000	Roger Carstens
January 2014	22,714	FGS and UN
January 2017	19,440	UN and World Bank
March 2017	24,684	FGS and UK
March 2017	Around 20,000 (inc. aligned militia)	AU–UN IST
May 2017	24,820 (+4,569 benefit recipients)	FGS

Sources: In order, Colin Robinson, 'Revisiting the rise and fall of the Somali Armed Forces, 1960–2012', *Defense & Security Analysis*, 32:3 (2016), pp. 240–1, 244 [first five rows]; *Report of the Monitoring Group on Somalia pursuant to Security Council resolution 1853 (2008)* (S/2010/91, 10 March 2010), §17; *AMISOM CONOPS* (AU internal document, November 2010), §21; *Report of a Security Sector Assessment Scoping Mission in Somalia* (Unpublished document prepared by former Somalia Senior Security and Military Officials, Mogadishu, June 2011), p. 5; *Report on TFG Military Forces (November 2011)* (AU internal document, November 2011); *AMISOM Military Strategic CONOPS* (AU internal document, 14 February 2012), §15; UN document S/2013/521, 3 September 2013, §29; Roger Carstens, 'Analog War: How to rid Somalia of al-Shabab once and for all—in six (not-so) easy steps', *Foreign Policy.com*, 7 October 2013; Minutes of the Defence Working Group meeting, Mogadishu (FGS/UN internal document, 29 January 2014), p. 9; *Somalia Security and Justice Public Expenditure Review* (UNSOM and World Bank, January 2017), p. 35; *Securing Payroll: Somali National Army* (FGS and DFID, March 2017); *Somali National Army Capability Assessment Report* (AU–UN IST, March 2017); SNA presentation to AMISOM Joint Review team, Mogadishu, 22 May 2017.

AU also wanted donor logistical and financial assistance to support AMISOM as well as the new Joint (TFG–ARS) Security Force, which it hoped would act as a buffer between AMISOM and hardline opposition forces.[19]

The high level of uncertainty involved when trying to count the number of personnel in the SNA is illustrated in Table 9.1. As noted above, this problem persisted through to mid-2017, but the issue of identifying members of the SNA was apparent from day one. In January 2009, for instance, AMISOM's Force Commander General Okello noted that both the TFG and ARS had submitted lists of names of soldiers to AMISOM to be placed into the Joint Security Force,

[19] Wikileak Cable 09ADDISABABA49, 12 January 2009.

but his troops had to scrutinize the lists of names 'one by one' to verify each individual's information and then issue them an ID card. Okello said AMISOM had issued approximately 800 ID cards thus far.[20] There was also a problem of distinguishing genuine 'fighters' from other 'freelancers' who were, as the UN Monitoring Group put it, '"on call" to varying degrees if required though always ready to collect salary and stipend payments when available'.[21]

By that stage, the Joint Security Force held about half of Mogadishu's sixteen districts. Arguably the most functional unit was the TFG's 867-strong presidential guard, based at the presidential compounds in Mogadishu and Baidoa.[22] The President also controlled the *Darwish*: traditionally a composite force carrying out military and police functions that generally operated independent from the SNA and answered directly to the President.[23]

In June 2009, the TFG signed a cooperation agreement with the Ethiopian-backed *Ahlu Sunna Wal Jamaa* (ASWJ) whereby the TFG would provide it with military and logistical support and consult the group on administrative issues in areas under its control. The ASWJ reportedly had about 10,000–12,000 soldiers, including 3,000 in Mogadishu.[24]

In November 2009, the UN Monitoring Group estimated there were 2,900 effective TFG armed forces, with roughly 3,500 additional troops unvetted, untrained, and unregistered.[25] The latter should therefore not be considered for international support.[26] On top of this, some 6,270 government-aligned troops were estimated to exist, mostly clan militia and, old, 'grey' soldiers from Barre's era.[27]

By May 2011, a second security sector assessment estimated there were 10,106 personnel in the SNA, excluding friendly militias such as ASWJ.[28] As discussed below, it also noted high levels of nepotism, corruption, and poor record-keeping and emphasized the urgent need for a biometric identification system across the entire Somali security sector. Rather optimistically, in August 2011, the UN Secretary-General concluded 'the biometric identification system initiated in January should cover the entire National Security Force in Mogadishu by October'.[29] It was still lacking as of late 2017. By this stage, the Federal Government, the United States, United Kingdom, and the United Arab Emirates all held SNA identification registries but none was fully comprehensive nor were they aligned.[30]

---

[20] Wikileak Cable, 09ADDISABABA717, 25 March 2009, §8.
[21] *SEMG Report*, 31 October 2016, Annex 2.1 §3.   [22] Robinson, 'Revisiting', p. 243.
[23] *Somalia Security Sector Assessment* (January 2010), §16a9b12b.   [24] *Ibid.*, §16a15.
[25] *SEMG Report*, 10 March 2010, §17.
[26] *Somalia Security Sector Assessment* (January 2010), §4ar.   [27] *Ibid.*, §16a9a.
[28] *Security Sector Assessment* (June 2011), p. 5.
[29] *Report of the Secretary-General on Somalia* (S/2011/549, 30 August 2011), §69.
[30] FGS/DFID, *Securing Payroll*, p. 41. Also *SEMG Report*, 31 October 2016, Annex 2.3.

By the end of 2011, AMISOM was also operating on the assumption that there were about 10,300 SNA troops organized into five brigades, with an additional 10,000 fighters in various aligned militia forces. But the AU concluded they were 'a fragmented disparate group' whose 'strong prevalence of clan identity...is the stumbling block to all efforts in organizing a national military force'.[31] Moreover, it observed that some of 'those who defect from Al Shabab are absorbed into the TFG without undergoing serious scrutiny and rehabilitation'.[32] A few months later, AMISOM's new CONOPS stated 11,200 SNA were operating in Mogadishu and another 11,000 (including ASWJ) were engaged in operations against *al-Shabaab* elsewhere. 'None of these forces', AMISOM concluded, 'have the ability to support and sustain themselves logistically'.[33] This was correct: the SNA had no dedicated logistical support system of its own.

As noted in Chapter 8, in November 2013, UNSOA was tasked with providing non-lethal support to 10,900 SNA personnel engaged in joint operations with AMISOM. Consisting of food, water, fuel, transport, tents, and in-theatre medical evacuation, this support was funded by the UN 'Trust Fund for AMISOM and the Somali National Army', not the UN's assessed peacekeeping contributions (like most of UNSOA's activities). UNSOA also had to conform to the UN's Human Rights Due Diligence Policy for supporting non-UN security forces, which is discussed in Chapter 10.

By mid-2014, a sixth SNA brigade had been established.[34] As more attention focused on supporting the SNA to coordinate operations with AMISOM, international partners and the Federal Government developed the *Guulwade* (Victory) plan.[35] Launched in March 2015, this was intended to revamp the SNA with international support but also to provide some structure for the roughly 10,000 SNA members that were not part of the UNSOA support package. The plan recognized that the SNA was little more than a collection of clan militias without a functioning, centralized command and control structure. It argued that in order to fight effectively the SNA needed better equipment, infrastructure, organization, and morale. In the short-term, it badly needed increased mobility and firepower to conduct effective operations. In essence therefore, the 'plan' was not so much a plan of action but a list of capability gaps that the SNA wanted to fill, with rough calculations of how much it would take to do it. The estimated costs were just under $85 million for equipment, vehicles, small arms and light weapons, training centres, medical

---

[31] *Report on TFG Military Forces (November 2011)* (AU internal document, November 2011), p. 1.

[32] *Ibid.*, p. 7.   [33] *Military Strategic CONOPS* (February 2012), §15.

[34] See UNSOM, *The Somali National Army* (UNSOM briefing Version 1.06, 31 January 2015).

[35] In June, the Federal Government launched its *Heegan* ('readiness') plan for the police force.

Table 9.2. Distribution of 10,900 SNA conducting joint operations with AMISOM (2015)

Region	AMISOM Sector	HR Trained (as at 9 Apr)	Guulwade Plan	HR Training Required
Banadir, Lower/Middle Shabelle	1 & 5	3,139	3,000	0
Bay, Bakool, Gedo	3	3,495	2,570	0
Hiraan, Galgaduud	4	2,137	2,000	0
Middle/Lower Jubba, Gedo	2/Kismayo	0	2,880	2,880
DANAB Battalion	Baladogle	300	450	150
	Totals	8,771	10,900	3,030

Source: Guulwade (Victory) Plan (SNA internal document, 9 April 2015), p. 1.

facilities and barracks but excluding operations and maintenance costs.[36] Some critics of the plan pointed to the clan composition of the 10,900, which was dominated by one of the Hawiye subclans. They suspected Hawiye leaders pushed the plan for precisely this reason.[37] There were also complaints from within the Somali government that some international partners pushed for the plan to focus too narrowly on the SNA troops that would be supported by UNSOA rather than the entire force.[38]

The distribution of the designated 10,900 SNA that would receive UNSOA support is shown in Table 9.2. It was particularly notable that any SNA in AMISOM's Sector 2 would be subject to consultation with the Interim Jubaland Administration on militia integration.

By the time of the 2017 London conference, the SNA was thought to comprise approximately 2,100 officers, 18,700 soldiers and non-commissioned officers, as well as nearly 3,900 orphans, disabled and retirees.[39] It was organized into twelve brigades, over thirty battalions, and had various special units including the presidential guard and headquarters units, military police, the *Danab* ('lightning') advanced infantry, and the health unit.

Resurrecting the name of a commando battalion used by the SNA before the civil war of the late 1980s, the *Danab* units deserve a special mention. After AMISOM expanded beyond Mogadishu it needed a credible Somali partner force that was disciplined and could assuage the international concerns about accountability and discipline.[40] During late 2011 and 2012, the United States supported Bancroft's efforts to pilot a special SNA advanced infantry platoon

---

[36] *Guulwade (Victory) Plan* (SNA internal document, 9 April 2015), p. 9.
[37] Communication, UN official, 1 September 2017.
[38] Interview, Somali government official, Djibouti, 27 February 2016.
[39] *Securing Payroll: Somali National Army* (FGS and DFID, internal document, March 2017), p. 6.
[40] This analysis is based on *Danab Battalion Update* (Bancroft Global Development briefing, November 2014). ACOTA files.

as proof of concept for what would become the *Danab* battalion. Once this was viewed as an operational success, during 2013 the Somali government and the United States supported its expansion to a company and then battalion with Bancroft providing training and mentoring, logistics coming via US contractors, and salary payments made through the PricewaterhouseCoopers mechanism. By July 2014, the first *Danab* company was fully operational and moved to its base in Baledogle. The following month it deployed during Operation Indian Ocean (analysed in Chapter 7). By early 2015, the second *Danab* company graduated and the command and support elements of the battalion took shape. At the time of writing, the third company was not fully operational.[41] Nevertheless, by recruiting personnel on the basis of merit from across all south-central Somalia's regions and paying, equipping and mentoring them consistently, the *Danab* units represented an important symbol of what military professionalism in Somalia could look like. The rest of the SNA, however, remained well short of such standards.

KEY CHALLENGES TO BUILDING AN EFFECTIVE SNA

AMISOM and its partners faced a daunting task to build legitimate and effective national security forces in Somalia. This section analyses the seven principal challenges, namely, the legacies of two decades of state collapse; the problem of building an army while simultaneously fighting a war; the negative effects of clan dynamics; the debilitating effects of corruption; the problems involved with carrying out military integration of numerous armed factions; the long list of capability gaps afflicting the armed forces; and the difficulties of coordinating the activities of multiple partners.

Legacies of State Collapse

Between 1991 and 2000 Somalia had no official central government, and from 2000 to 2012 it had only transitional authorities. This extended period of state collapse led most of the local population to find alternative security providers instead of a central government. As noted in Chapter 1, Menkhaus had described this trend as 'governance without government', whereby a variety of non-state actors and informal systems of adaptation delivered services 'in the prolonged absence of a central government'.[42] Once international efforts started to resurrect a Somali central government through the TNG and TFG in

---

[41] Communication, Bancroft official, 5 August 2017.
[42] Menkhaus, 'Governance without Government', p. 74.

the 2000s, this produced a hybrid political order in which the official governing authorities had to compete or negotiate for authority with other non-state entities to play the role of key security provider. More often than not, it was clan militias that protected local populations across most of the country.[43] Nevertheless, most international efforts to stabilize Somalia proceeded largely top-down to resurrect a strong central government centred on Mogadishu and without ensuring that reconciliation took place between the centre and the various regional authorities.[44]

These developments generated a variety of symptoms that made it difficult for AMISOM to help build an effective SNA. First, there was a widespread and deep distrust that the central government would be an impartial actor or could really deliver genuine security. This bred a strong inclination towards continued reliance on non-state actors, which made it difficult to attract recruits to the SNA. Indeed, for those actors that saw a strong central government as a potential threat, the idea of giving it an effective army was a recipe for disaster and marginalizing other groups.

Second, this situation generated strong loyalties to actors beyond the central government, which complicated any attempt to build an SNA with a unified and coherent command and control system.

More broadly, prolonged state collapse meant that when the central government did establish new institutions they were dysfunctional and hence sometimes simply reaffirmed people's faith in government incompetence and the need for alternatives. To take just one example, without sustainable revenue it would be impossible to build an effective SNA. Yet Somalia had a completely dysfunctional Central Bank. Consequently, international agencies had to rely on Xawala or PricewaterhouseCoopers (which was contracted to support the TFG) to handle some important financial matters and could not stop many corrupt financial transactions involving unregistered private and even foreign governments.[45] In such circumstances there was little prospect of generating sustainable revenues, let alone establishing a workable procurement system for a military.

A fourth dimension was the legacy of such a long period without a functioning military system. Combined with Somalia's youthful population, this left many young potential SNA recruits confused about the meaning of a federal state and how it was supposed to function.[46] It also left behind a missing generation of officers available to the armed forces. As one senior TFG commander put it in 2011, 'the most critical gap in the existing forces was the lack of young officers and junior officers. Most officers are old: "less than 50" are younger.

---

[43] *SEMG Report*, 18 July 2011, p. 11.

[44] See, for example, Tobias Hagmann, *Stabilization, Extraversion and Political Settlements in Somalia* (Nairobi: Rift Valley Institute, 2016).

[45] *Security Sector Assessment* (June 2011), pp.30–1.   [46] *Brief Report* (October 2011).

The older officers find it difficult to lead the young soldiers, physically and mentally'.[47] The poor levels of literacy and education in many areas further increased the difficulty of creating an effective military.

Finally, it should be noted that before the IRAs came to life in 2016, there was no political entity at the subfederal level that had any official legitimacy to discuss the politics of security. It was only after the creation of these entities that legitimate answers to the questions of security governance could be provided. Before that, it had been a Mogadishu-focused process.

Reforming While Fighting

Most recent international SSR programmes were designed to take place during peacetime or immediately after the war in question had ended in some form of political settlement. In Somalia, however, AMISOM had to help build the SNA while simultaneously fighting a war against *al-Shabaab*. As a result, there was a real tension between the guidelines and principles that had been developed for successful SSR and the practical realities facing AMISOM and the SNA on the ground.

Ideally, without a carefully crafted peace process, a government committed to (and putting resources behind) the endeavour, and an agreed national security framework, international assistance to the Somali security sector is very vulnerable to high waste, and potentially counterproductive.[48] In practice, however, reform had to begin while the SNA was at war, in the absence of a peace process, and without an agreed national security strategy and force structure. Speaking in May 2013, the UN's senior military advisor in Somalia acknowledged this problem when he pointed to 'a real tension trying to train these [SNA] forces when they are at war' because 'no one has the luxury of pulling them out; they are essential in the fight against Al-Shabab'.[49]

The practical debate thus revolved around how best to fight the war and build the SNA. While the US–FGS plan was to focus on building the *Danab* battalion, some senior AMISOM officials offered another view.[50] This assumed that trying to create an elite force in the middle of a war would not solve the fundamental problems and hence it would have been better to provide some minimum logistical support/allowance to SNA and allied militias in the regions, with the emphasis on taking the fight to *al-Shabaab* and winning the war.

[47] Cited in Robinson, 'Revisiting', p. 246.
[48] UNSOM, *The Somali National Army*, p. 21 and communication, Colin Robinson, 6 August 2017.
[49] 'Somali Security Sector Reform', *IRIN*, 13 May 2013, http://www.irinnews.org/analysis/2013/05/13/somali-security-sector-reform
[50] Communication, former senior AMISOM official, 13 September 2017.

Thereafter, international partners could focus on reconstructing a professional set of Somali security forces.

Other operational challenges were created as well. During 2009, when AMISOM and the TFG were fighting to maintain control of parts of Mogadishu, the lack of even basic equipment such as uniforms left AMISOM commanders concerned about potential problems in distinguishing non-uniformed TFG troops and allied militias during combat (see also Chapter 3). Other deficiencies led TFG commanders to worry that even when they captured new territory there was little commitment by some of their 'front line' troops to hold it.[51] In mid-2011, at the height of the battle for Mogadishu, the lack of basic communications equipment and skills on the Somali side meant that there was only 'limited coordination' between AMISOM and Somali forces, which made 'it difficult to conduct joint planning and operations to contain insurgent groups fighting against the TFG'.[52]

To make matters more difficult, Somalia was what one contractor working with the SNA called a 'distributed battlefield', that is, a large territory with few troops.[53] In such terrain, emphasis should be placed on small battalions as the focal point of the army rather than brigades and success rested on the ability to operate with 'small unit tactics, mobile strike teams, civil affairs, and simplified logistics'. But these were tools that would take time, resources, and training to master, none of which were available to the SNA at the time.

Clan Politics

Clan politics also significantly undermined the process of building a professional SNA. In his careful study of the Somali Armed Forces, Colin Robinson concluded 'Clan loyalties exceeding loyalties to the center is the principal obstacle to rebuilding an effective national army for Somalia'.[54] He went on to note how 'clan ties trump virtually everything, business interests sometimes excluded'.[55]

The roots of major clan divisions and agendas rupturing the SNA can be traced back to Siad Barre's efforts to consolidate his rule during the 1980s.[56] This came after an aborted coup in 1978, when Barre responded by loading the armed forces with his Marehan and related Darod officers. Clan dynamics was a major obstacle to building an effective SNA ever since. With the implosion of the central government in 1991, clan dynamics became even more important

---

[51] Wikileak Cable 09NAIROBI1962, 18 September 2009, §2.
[52] *Security Sector Assessment* (June 2011), p. 6.   [53] Carstens, 'Analog War'.
[54] Robinson, 'Revisiting', p. 245.
[55] *Ibid.*, p. 246. On the importance of business interests, see Ahmad, 'The Security Bazaar'.
[56] Before 1976, the armed forces sought a balance between the major clans, even specifying the proportional number of recruits from each district. See Robinson, 'Revisiting'.

as most individuals turned to their clans, subclans or sub-subclans to provide for their security instead of the state.

By the time of the first TFG administration, the struggle over Mogadishu was interpreted by many Somalis as primarily a conflict involving a Darod-led TFG trying to reassert Darod dominance over a primarily Hawiye city. Following the selection of the second TFG administration in January 2009, the Hawiye/Habir Gir and Hawiye/Ayr increased their power over the military sphere around Mogadishu.[57]

Clan politics also caused problems as AMISOM and the TFG forces moved beyond Mogadishu from late 2011. With *al-Shabaab* still in control of most of south-central Somalia, this left relatively few areas from which the SNA could recruit new soldiers. Specifically, the Banadir region around Mogadishu that AMISOM recovered was dominated by particular clans and subclans, which were then directly reflected in the composition of new recruits entering the army. One internal AMISOM analysis concluded that the 'monster of clan' infected the whole enterprise. 'Clan identity within the forces', the AU noted, 'is the stumbling block to all efforts in organizing a national military force'.[58] The practical consequence of the preponderance of certain clans was that the ostensibly 'national' army was perceived by most citizens outside Mogadishu as a partisan force dominated by particular subclans. When those forces operated outside their areas of influence they were perceived as illegitimate by the locals.

Clan politics also had debilitating effects on achieving a unified command and control structure within the SNA because rank-and-file troops often displayed loyalty to clan (and other actors, including previous warlords) rather than the Federal Government. With battalions and some brigades largely organized around clan lines, this reduced formal interaction and collaboration between them. Indeed, in some cases clan conflicts stopped collaboration between battalions within the same brigade.[59] As an UNSOM report observed, the subsequent dynamic within the units saw most of them revolve around one strong leader with senior personnel from the same clan; if company and platoon commanders were not of the same clan, however, command authority quickly broke down.[60] Most of these commanders had little formal training but considerable militia experience. This is why some experts concluded that the importance of subclan dynamics dictated that painstaking local-level negotiations were required to find command solutions.[61]

Finally, clan politics undermined the potential for the new SNA to act as a unifying symbol for Somalia. Multiclan SNA units were potentially important

---

[57] 'Leaked SEMG letter, S/AC.29/2014/COMM.13 (OC.8), 6 February 2014', p. 5 cited in UNSOM, *The Somali National Army*, p. 15.

[58] AU, *Report on TFG* (November 2011), pp. 9 and 1.   [59] *Ibid.*, p. 6.

[60] UNSOM, *The Somali National Army*, p. 6.

[61] Matt Bryden and Jeremy Brickhill, 'Disarming Somalia: lessons in stabilisation from a collapsed state', *Conflict, Security & Development*, 10:2 (2010), pp. 239–62.

symbols of national unity.[62] But almost the only place they existed was in the *Danab* advanced infantry battalion where recruits were selected on merit across clan. An SNA that remained largely segregated along clan lines could not act as much of a unifying force.

Corruption

In 2016, Transparency International noted that according to its annual Corruption Perceptions Index, Somalia was ranked as the world's most corrupt country for ten years in a row.[63] Not surprisingly, therefore, corruption amongst senior commanders and Somali political elites was another major challenge to building an effective SNA. Given the lack of de facto loyalty of most rank-and-file troops to the Federal Government, allegiance had to be bought. As one US official put it in June 2009, the TFG had 'constantly to purchase loyalty to motivate militias to fight in its defense'.[64] But the chronic corruption among Somali politicians meant that much of the money ostensibly earmarked for the SNA was stolen.

A distinction should be drawn, however, between elite corruption and the practices of rank-and-file soldiers. Elite corruption involved relatively wealthy and powerful individuals stealing large sums of money and working to oppose strong, government-led rule of law in order to further their narrow economic interests. In July 2012, for instance, the UN Monitoring Group identified 'pervasive corruption within the transitional federal institutions'. The group concluded that 'the systematic misappropriation, embezzlement and outright theft of public resources have essentially become a system of governance, embodied in the popular Somali phrase "Maxaa igu jiraa?" ("What's in it for me?")'.[65] It estimated that $7 out of every $10 received by the TFG in 2009 and 2010 never made it into government coffers and remained unaccounted for.

At the other end of the political pyramid, SNA soldiers were asked to risk their lives often without being given meagre salaries, equipment and rations, or medical care. Their survival sometimes depended on extorting money or food from alternative sources, taking multiple jobs, or selling their equipment. This was still corruption but of a qualitatively different kind. Nevertheless, not only did it turn elements of the local population against them, it also left the troops vulnerable to exploitation. In 2009, for instance, the AMISOM Force Commander told the UN technical assessment mission that *al-Shabaab* was

---

[62] On the important symbolic roles of national armies in the unifying war-torn territories see Roy Licklider, 'Introduction' in Roy Licklider (ed.), *New Armies from Old* (Washington DC: Georgetown University Press, 2014).

[63] Details of the Index are at www.transparency.org

[64] Wikileak Cable 09ADDISABABA1409, 26 June 2009, §4 and 6.

[65] *SEMG Report*, 13 July 2012, p. 7.

offering TFG fighters $50 a month to swap sides, and this was a serious proposal given how many of them lacked food and equipment.[66] Later that year, the Mayor of Mogadishu had quipped that he had 6,000–7,000 TFG soldiers on payday but only 2,000–3,000 when it was time to fight.[67]

AMISOM was so concerned about the potential for the TFG troops to sell their equipment and the weak or non-existent accountability mechanisms that they concluded the TFG should not be permitted to stockpile internationally provided military supplies, such as fuel and ammunition.[68] AMISOM also decided to oversee 'the storage and dispensation' of the TFG's arms and ammunition and rations 'in order to stem the Government corruption that had surfaced in previous years'.[69] This led TFG commanders to complain that they were being undermined by AMISOM's unwillingness to provide them with sufficient ammunition.[70] Nevertheless, AMISOM was unable to prevent ammunition leaking 'from the custody of Government and militia commanders to the illicit market'.[71] By 2011, the UN Monitoring Group thought TFG and aligned forces sold between one-third and one-half of their ammunition.[72]

Military Integration

As noted above, in the hybrid political order that emerged after Somalia's period of state collapse it was not surprising that a multitude of armed groups emerged. As Alice Hills noted, this meant that south-central Somalia displayed the characteristics of a 'security arena' in which numerous actors competed for dominance rather than an institutionalized 'security sector'.[73] For AMISOM, this meant that building a genuinely national Somali army would require some degree of military integration between at least some of these armed groups and persuading or coercing those that were left out to accept the outcome.

Military integration is the process whereby 'individuals are brought into the new military in positions similar to the ones they occupied in prior organizations'.[74] Over the last two decades, pursuing it after civil wars became what Licklider called 'the new normal' because it was thought to help solve three problems: 1) how to reduce the likelihood that the civil war will reignite;

---

[66] Wikileak Cable 09ADDISABABA110, 16 January 2009, §9.
[67] Wikileak Cable 09NAIROBI1798, 25 August 2009, §5.
[68] *Somalia Security Sector Assessment* (January 2010), §16a9b10.
[69] *SEMG Report*, 18 July 2011, §133. See also Wikileak Cable 09NAIROBI1520, 15 July 2009, §7.
[70] Wikileak Cable 09NAIROBI1370, 2 July 2009, §6.
[71] *SEMG Report*, 18 July 2011, §135.   [72] *Ibid.*, Annex 5.1, p. 231.
[73] Alice Hills, 'Security Sector or Security Arena? The Evidence from Somalia', *International Peacekeeping*, 21:2 (2014), pp. 165–80.
[74] Licklider, 'Introduction', p. 3.

2) how to reduce the overall number of soldiers in the country; and 3) how to forge a national identity between communities previously torn apart by war.[75] In contrast, building a strong army could increase the risk of coups and political leaders should avoid using the army to employ misfits and more former fighters than is financially sustainable in hope of bolstering stability.

In Somalia, of course, the war was not over and there was no peace process defining the terms of any integration process. Instead, as noted above, the SNA had developed organically as a composite of TFG forces, former Islamic Court fighters, and various clan/subclan-based militias. As the process of defining the IRAs took shape from 2013, regional forces became a more important part of this equation. Nor was there clarity over the extent or form of any potential DDR programme. Indeed, with fighting the principal source of livelihood for most militia, being disarmed and demobilized was hardly an attractive option. Nevertheless, as one analysis pointed out,

> Whatever the final formula devised for the composition of the SNA, the most important parameter is the requirement of integration; if the vast majority of soldiers do not develop a national identity and national allegiance above that of clan, region, and warlord—then it is a failed effort and prospects for a unified Somalia are endangered.[76]

For AMISOM, it raised the challenge of which entities to engage as part of the SNA or potentially a future part of it. The usual list was those groups 'aligned' with the government, but this could change. It also generated the problem mentioned above that either for clan-related or political reasons, many of the armed groups beyond Mogadishu were distrustful of any attempts to centralize control of the Somali armed forces. In other words, military integration was arguably necessary to form a national army, but it was also a deeply political process. As Ronald Krebs rightly concluded, it 'is, first and foremost, a local *political* problem, not a matter of *technical* expertise that local actors lack and whose secrets international actors must therefore impart'.[77] AMISOM therefore had to be careful to ensure that its technical efforts did not become a substitute for the more important effort to generate political reconciliation and national unity.

Capability Gaps

Even when launching its *Guulwade* (Victory) plan in 2015, the Federal Government acknowledged a long list of technical and infrastructural shortages

---

[75] *Ibid.*   [76] Camacho and Abukar, *Somalia's Security*, p. 7.
[77] Ronald Krebs, 'So What?' in Licklider (ed.), *New Armies from Old*, p. 255.

afflicting the SNA.[78] The principal gaps were mobility, especially armoured vehicles but also 'technicals', pickups, troop-carrying trucks, and specialist vehicles such as ambulances, water trucks, fuel bowsers, and recovery vehicles; all types of ammunition;[79] heavy weapons and the ability to maintain and repair them;[80] communications equipment, including military radios;[81] and field defences, especially force protection for defended positions and forward operating bases. The SNA also still had major shortages and problems related to training, logistics capacity, vehicle maintenance facilities, arms and ammunition storage facilities, medical support (especially facilities and resources to treat and stabilize patients forward in the sectors),[82] and adequate barracks to accommodate and maintain good control over its troops. The combined effect of these gaps was not only to reduce military effectiveness but also to undermine morale.

If this was the situation in April 2015, AMISOM had to work with much worse in previous years. It will suffice to briefly discuss three examples of deficient capabilities: the problems of desertion and identifying SNA personnel, poor levels of education, and a lack of regular salary payments.

For many years, SNA soldiers deserting and absconding occurred far too frequently. Some left because their real loyalty lay elsewhere. For others, it was the lack of regular pay, food, or other poor conditions of service. This problem was compounded by the lack of a comprehensive identification system. Even by 2017, the Federal Government had no comprehensive biometric identification system for its troops. Unsurprisingly, there was a long history of 'ghost soldiers' on the roll and stipends going to people who were dead, permanently injured, old persons, women partners, orphans, and disabled.[83] While some SNA troops used this state of confusion to engage in corruption and fraud,

---

[78] *Guulwade Plan*, pp. 2–8. Similarly long lists of equipment and infrastructural shortages can be found in *Security Sector Assessment* (June 2011) and *Brief Report* (October 2011).

[79] Although note that the UN Monitoring Group on Somalia concluded the SNA should have received about 9 million rounds of ammunition. *SEMG Report*, 19 October 2015, §136.

[80] In 2011, AMISOM estimated that 80 per cent of SNA weapons belonged to warlords, clans, and individuals rather than the Federal Government. AU, *Report on TFG* (November 2011), pp. 7–8. Small arms were also in short supply. For example, in May 2013, the colonel in the Gashandiga barracks in Mogadishu complained that he had just one hundred AK-47s for 600 soldiers. IRIN, 'Somali Security'. Since the UN arms embargo was partially lifted in 2013, however, the Somali government received over 17,500 weapons. *SEMG Report*, 19 October 2015, §136.

[81] For years, the TFG troops had to rely on commercial mobile phone networks for communications or walkie-talkie handsets. *Somalia Security Sector Assessment* (January 2010), §4ag and *Brief Report* (October 2011).

[82] By late 2011, the Martini Hospital in Mogadishu was the SNA's only medical facility. It had a twenty-bed capacity, one volunteer doctor, and about twelve nurses. AU, *Report on TFG* (November 2011), p. 5.

[83] AU, *Report on TFG* (November 2011), p. 8.

al-Shabaab exploited it in order to infiltrate the SNA to prosecute attacks on government installations and personnel.

Another problem was the generally low level of education and literacy of many recruits, which made some military speciality categories difficult to populate.[84] Some of this was down to successive Somali governments giving military ranks to clan and warlord militia commanders simply to appease these groups, resulting in 'an army of semi-literate officers at every level'.[85]

Third, the inability of successive governments to pay soldiers their salaries regularly and in full caused major problems, including desertion, corruption, and poor morale.[86] As Matt Bryden argued, paying salaries was ultimately 'much more important in building a professional force than obtaining new weapons and equipment'.[87] In response, some soldiers obtained two or more identification cards to draw multiple salaries when the money came while others worked second jobs in the private sector. And with AMISOM rationing bullets, it was not uncommon for TFG soldiers to sell some to buy food and *khat* and then abscond when they had used the rest.[88]

In 2009 and 2010, the United States and Italy started paying stipends to some SNA troops. By early 2014, the United States was paying just over 9,000 SNA soldiers $100 per month while Italy was paying about 3,300.[89] Turkey also provided direct budget support to the Federal Government, some of which was reportedly used to pay salaries.[90] Since the Federal Government was selected in September 2012, each soldier was supposed to receive a monthly wage of $260 ($100 from the government, $60 for rations, and $100 from a donor).

Opportunities for corruption—by senior officers and the rank-and-file troops—were increased because for years, salary payments were made in cash. This eventually prompted the government to use a PricewaterhouseCoopers mechanism to disburse funds using the mobile phone network, once the soldier's identity and bank details were verified. This system was still not extended across the entire SNA at the time of writing.[91]

---

[84] Camacho and Abukar, *Somalia's Security*, p. 8.   [85] Mubarak, 'Somali military'.

[86] For a list of SNA withdrawals and salary-related incidents between September 2015 and August 2016, see *SEMG Report*, 31 October 2016, Annex 2.6.

[87] IRIN, 'Somali Security'.   [88] *Security Sector Assessment* (June 2011), p. 26.

[89] Minutes of the Defence Working Group meeting, Mogadishu (FGS/UN internal document, 29 January 2014), pp. 3, 9. US payments started in 2009 after it sought authorization from the UN to supply the TFG with arms and ammunition despite the arms embargo imposed on Somalia in 1992. See Robinson, 'Revisiting', pp. 247–8. Italy stopped its payments after 2013. See *SEMG Report*, 10 March 2010, §191 and Robinson, 'Revisiting', p. 249.

[90] Robinson, 'Revisiting', p. 247.

[91] SNA troops outside of AMISOM Sectors 1 and 5—incorporating the capital, Mogadishu, and Middle and Lower Shabelle regions—were receiving little if any salary support. *SEMG Report*, 31 October 2016, Annex 2.2, §8.

Uncoordinated Partners

The final challenge discussed here was the uncoordinated nature of the assistance provided to the SNA by various external partners. Ideally, external assistance would be based on similar (or at least compatible) political objectives and vision as well as military doctrine, provide interoperable equipment and training on maintaining donated equipment, use standardized training programmes, and be based on an assessment of the SNA's needs. Indeed, in 2012, the new Somali government had asked external partners to ensure that they had a single 'door to knock on' to coordinate activities in this sector.[92] The reality was quite different, however. Most partners provided support to Somalia's security sector in ways that aligned with their own vision and strategic interests. Some Somalis saw this as a deliberate attempt to fragment their fledgling security sector and pointed out how various clandestine military operations run by Ethiopia, Kenya and the United States—sometimes involving various Somali actors—all complicated the issue.[93]

Even when partner agendas converged they were rarely well coordinated. It was not until early 2017, for example, that the Joint Training Symposium of partners adopted a Somali-owned training programme based on NATO standards.[94] Hence, for more than a decade the Somali armed forces received uncoordinated support from its partners.[95] In addition, the very limited human resources capacity in the Somali Ministry of Defence made it difficult to absorb and coordinate the assistance it received.[96] To take training programmes as just one example of poor coordination, since 2009, the TFG and SNA forces received training from Burundi, Djibouti, Ethiopia, Uganda, Kenya, EU, United States, United Kingdom, Turkey, the United Arab Emirates and even Sudan.[97] This was provided in several different languages, including English, French, Swahili, Amharic, Arabic, and meant that trainees returned with diverse military skills and doctrines only to find another form of military training skills and doctrine back home.[98] Unfortunately, partners did not keep track of the people they trained, which led to wide-ranging numbers of 90,000–100,000 soldiers having receiving training, probably some of them many times over.[99]

---

[92] 'Letter dated 19 April 2013 from the Secretary-General addressed to the President of the Security Council' (S/2013/239, 19 April 2013), Annex §43.

[93] Interview, FGS official, Djibouti, 27 February 2016.

[94] SNA presentation to AMISOM Joint Review team, Mogadishu, 23 May 2017.

[95] See, for example, the similar conclusions reached in *Somalia Security Sector Assessment* (January 2010); AU, *Report on TFG* (November 2011); *Security Sector Assessment* (June 2011); and *Brief Report* (October 2011).

[96] By mid-2017, the Somali Ministry of Defence only had about sixty civilian personnel, including support staff.

[97] See *Report on TFG Military Forces*, p. 9.   [98] *Brief Report* (October 2011).

[99] Telephone interview, UN official, 7 September 2017.

During the late 2000s, one expert concluded that 'most of the units that were trained defected'.[100] And as already noted in Chapter 2 (p. 71), in 2008 the Ethiopian government estimated that of the roughly 17,000 Somali security forces it had trained about 14,000 had defected or deserted. Some of these defections were due to the problem of infiltration whereby *al-Shabaab* fighters successfully posed as SNA recruits, benefited from training, and then returned to *al-Shabaab*. There was also the problem of poor facilities. Even by 2013, for instance, the principal training facility in Mogadishu—Jazeera camp—lacked adequate billets, sanitation, and manoeuvre space for exercises.[101] This was apparently why some recruits left. More fundamentally, training alone was not sufficient to build an effective army. As the 2009 Somali security sector assessment suggested, it 'may even be counterproductive if it is not followed up by a sustainable equipment/supply program and payment of salaries. If these requirements are not met, the risk of desertion/defection of trainees upon return to Somalia is high'.[102]

In its 2015 *Guulwade* Plan, the Federal Government sought to coordinate the assistance packages that its forces received from different partners around its new training plan. This involved establishing sector and combined training centres, mentors, and a schedule for training priorities for the SNA.[103] By that stage, AMISOM had established training teams in all Sectors to deliver training to the SNA, including on human rights, and developed an *SNA Training and Mentoring Concept* as set out in the mission's January 2014 CONOPS.

LESSONS

What lessons stand out from AMISOM's experiences with trying to build an effective SNA? First of all, the evidence from the last decade in Somalia suggests that the most fundamental issue is whether national politics is conducive to SSR. That is, was an elite consensus forged around a shared vision of the national security architecture, how to finance it, and how decisions will be taken within it? In Somalia between 2007 and 2017 the

---

[100] Hansen, *Al-Shabaab in Somalia*, p. 96.

[101] Carstens, 'Analog War'. The Jazeera Training Centre, located southwest of the Mogadishu International Airport, had trained Somali troops since at least 2010. It was part of AMISOM's capacity-building efforts for the TFG and to enhance joint operations. AMISOM's military training team provided tactics, drill and duties, signals (communications) and physical training wing. By 2012, there were forty-five instructors from Burundi, Kenya, and Uganda; twenty-five Somali instructors; and supplementary staff from the force headquarters who could provide more specialized training in areas such as communication, leadership, Civil–Military Coordination (CIMIC), and logistics.

[102] *Somalia Security Sector Assessment* (January 2010), §16a9b8j.

[103] *Guulwade Plan*, p. 5.

answer was a resounding no. The London Security Pact agreed in May 2017 and its envisaged National Security Council structure for Somalia stands as the best chance thus far to achieve such a consensus. But before that, AMISOM was left for ten years trying to encourage Somali elites to forge that consensus and take the difficult political decisions about the key issues of power-sharing between the centre and the regions, clan integration, and financing. The lesson to learn is that external actors must incentivize local political elites to take those difficult decisions as soon as possible because without such a foundation SSR can make little headway.

The second, and related lesson that follows is that international and local audiences should adopt realistic expectations for making progress on SSR when the usual conditions for success are absent but where political realities necessitate continued engagement. This will have significant repercussions for whether the political coalition supporting AMISOM holds, whether the mission can secure sustainable financing, and hence its prospects for implementing a successful exit strategy, as analysed in Chapter 13.

Third, at the operational level, a key lesson is that fighting together requires not only a shared strategic objective but also effective communication, coordination, and, crucially, mutual trust. Ultimately, trust must be earned, but it is more likely to develop where the different armed forces can regularly liaise within one another and, importantly, co-locate as often as possible. In AMISOM's case, there were not always sufficient liaison channels and certainly not enough co-location to develop truly joint operations. Even ten years on, AMISOM and the SNA were still trying to work out how to co-locate their forces and conduct joint operations. And as one Somali government official put it, 'What signal does it send to the locals when they see the SNA and AMISOM still not working very closely together and using two separate bases? It signals that AMISOM are really like an occupying force not working with the SNA'.[104]

In sum, from the vantage point of late 2017, AMISOM was still grappling with the two questions it started with: how to fight together with the SNA to wage an effective war against a common enemy and how to develop 'good enough' indigenous armed forces to allow the AU mission to withdraw?

[104] Interview, Somali government official, Djibouti, 27 February 2016.

10

Protecting Civilians

The unfolding of genocidal violence in the presence of UN peacekeepers in Rwanda (1994) and Srebrenica (1995) prompted a period of introspection among the world's governments that eventually produced a new commitment that peacekeepers would protect civilians. To that end, since 1999 the UN has almost always given its missions protection of civilians (POC) mandates.[1] The AU has done the same in most of its peace operations.[2] And yet, particularly during its first four years, AMISOM had a distinctly ambiguous relationship with civilian protection issues.

On the one hand, AMISOM was mandated to protect certain VIPs associated with the political reconciliation process as well as degrade *al-Shabaab* and other anti-government armed actors. The mission also regularly provided medical care, water, and humanitarian assistance to significant numbers of Somalia's stricken civilians. On the other hand, at times, AMISOM personnel were depicted as supporting a brutal occupying force in Mogadishu (the ENDF) and turning a blind eye to predatory behaviour by the TFG's security forces as well as other militias. The AU force was also accused of harming civilians both directly, through its indiscriminate fire policies, targeting of civilians that were mistaken for enemy fighters, and instances of sexual exploitation and abuse (SEA), and indirectly, by failing to protect others from *al-Shabaab* snipers and attacks.

Regardless of whether it had an explicit POC mandate, AMISOM had always been required to protect civilians as part of its obligations under International Humanitarian Law (IHL).[3] But, especially from 2010, AU and

---

[1] See Victoria Holt and Glyn Taylor with Max Kelly, *Protecting Civilians in the Context of UN Peacekeeping* (New York: UN DPKO and OCHA, 2009).

[2] See Jide M. Okeke and Paul D. Williams (eds.), *Protecting Civilians in African Union Peace Support Operations* (Durban, South Africa: ACCORD, March 2017).

[3] See Siobhan Wills, *Protecting Civilians: The Obligations of Peacekeepers* (Oxford: Oxford University Press, 2009). IHL requires parties to a conflict to take all feasible precautions to protect civilians under their control against the effects of attacks, including avoiding locating military objectives within or near densely populated areas and removing civilians from the vicinity of military objectives. The obligation to respect IHL does not depend on reciprocity by

AMISOM officials debated whether the mission should take on a more explicit and proactive approach to protecting civilians. This raised some big questions for the mission: What would such a proactive protection mandate mean in practice? Would it raise local expectations to unrealistic levels, or had local civilians always expected protection from AMISOM troops regardless of whether this was written into the mission's formal mandate?[4] Would a POC mandate require AMISOM to deploy many more police and other civilian experts? Assuming so, how would the mission acquire such additional resources? Finally, how could AMISOM ensure that its troops received effective training for conducting the military and policing tasks associated with the proactive POC?

Despite these debates, it was not until late May 2013 that AMISOM adopted a more explicit and proactive approach to POC involving the deliberate application of its resources to reduce civilian harm.[5] This included adopting a mission-wide POC strategy which defined the mission's main objectives in this area as 'protecting civilians from harm resulting from the conduct of AMISOM military operations' and 'strengthening civilian protection from harm resulting from the conduct of other actors in AMISOM's area of operations'.[6] AMISOM's POC strategy borrowed directly from the AU's four-tiered approach wherein the protection of civilians was conceptualized as 1) protection as part of the political process; 2) protection from physical violence; 3) rights-based protection; and 4) the establishment of a protective environment.[7]

The long delay in adopting a mission-wide POC strategy stemmed from several factors. First, the AU and AMISOM disseminated mixed messages about the status of POC issues. Second, during AMISOM's early years the AU was unprepared to support a POC mandate and only began developing guidelines on this topic during 2009. Third, there were prudential concerns about adopting a POC mandate because AMISOM struggled to protect its own personnel, let alone civilians, and was unlikely to receive the additional resources and capabilities that such a mandate would require. Adopting a POC mandate was thus thought likely to raise local expectations without

---

other belligerent forces. See ICRC, *Customary International Humanitarian Law* (Cambridge: Cambridge University Press, 2005), rules 22–4, citing Protocol I, articles 58(a–c), and 140).

[4] The AU has explicitly recognized that AMISOM has 'been widely expected to protect civilians in [its] areas of operations, without being explicitly mandated or resourced to do so'. *Report of the Strategic Retreat of the African Union Inter-Departmental Working Group on the Protection of Civilians*, Debre Zeyit, Ethiopia, 28–9 September 2011, p. 10.

[5] *Report of the Chairperson of the Commission on the Situation in Somalia* (PSC/PR/2. (CCCLXXIX), 13 June 2013), §49.

[6] *AMISOM Mission-Wide Protect of Civilians Strategy* (AU internal document, May 2013), p. 3.

[7] *Draft Guidelines for the Protection of Civilians in African Union Peace Support Operations* (AU Commission, March 2010).

necessarily providing the tools needed to meet them. Over time, however, AMISOM recognized the importance of POC in achieving its strategic objectives and adopted various policies to reduce civilian harm while carrying out its operations. AMISOM did not, however, reconfigure its operations to focus on delivering more proactive forms of POC but instead continued to pursue military operations designed to degrade *al-Shabaab* while trying to uphold its obligations under IHL. It did so without ever being given a mandate to proactively protect civilians.

This chapter discusses these issues in four parts. It begins by illustrating how the AU and AMISOM disseminated mixed messages on POC issues. Second, it highlights the AU's lack of experience in this area. The third section then analyses how AMISOM sometimes became a source of civilian harm in Mogadishu, and later beyond the city, while the fourth section summarizes the remedial policies AMISOM adopted to try and alleviate this problem. The conclusion reflects on the main lessons that emerge from AMISOM's experiences with civilian protection issues.

MIXED MESSAGES ON PROTECTING CIVILIANS

Prior to the mission-wide POC strategy that AMISOM adopted in May 2013, the AU and AMISOM's senior leadership had sent out a variety of mixed signals on civilian protection issues. These appear to be caused by a lack of coordination and coherence within the AU as well as different views about the mission's priorities.

One source of confusion came at the operational level in AMISOM's rules of engagement (ROE). AMISOM's initial ROE stipulated that any use of force should try to avoid collateral damage and that AMISOM troops *could* use force in some situations beyond self-defence including: 'To afford protection to civilians under imminent threat of physical violence'.[8] No other guidelines were specified, leaving a blurred line between AMISOM's obligation to uphold IHL (i.e., mitigate the level of harm caused to civilians due to the conduct of any military operations) and proactively protect civilians from threats. The February 2010 iteration of AMISOM's ROE also stated: 'Use of force, up to and including deadly force, to protect civilians, including humanitarian workers, under imminent threat of physical violence is authorized' (Rule No. 1.7). So did the Pocket Card version of the ROE issued to AMISOM troops, which stated: 'You are authorized to use force, up to and *including deadly force* ... To protect civilians, including humanitarian workers, under imminent threat of physical

---

[8] *Rules of Engagement for the Military Component of the AMISOM* (AU internal document, March 2007), §7h and §7k(1b).

violence'.[9] Thus while AMISOM troops did not have an explicit POC mandate their ROE told them they could use deadly force to protect civilians.

Mixed messages were also present at the strategic level where AU pronouncements emphasized the importance of POC for AMISOM but did not give the mission an explicit mandate to that effect. During 2009, the AU began to define its approach to civilian protection and in March 2010 it released, *Draft Guidelines for the Protection of Civilians in African Union Peace Support Operations*. In October that year, the AU PSC reaffirmed 'the AU's commitment to fully adhere to, and respect, International Humanitarian Law (IHL) in AMISOM's operations' and encouraged the Commission to 'mainstream' the AU's *Draft Guidelines* 'into the activities of AMISOM as the Mission does its utmost to avoid collateral civilian casualties'.[10] A Working Group on the Protection of Civilians was established within the AU Commission in February 2011, which was charged with developing and implementing AMISOM's 'mission-wide strategy on the protection of civilians' for the civilian population in its area of operations by the end of 2011.[11] In May 2011 the AU PSC held its first open session on POC during which it called on the Commission to develop 'an AMISOM approach for the protection of civilians' as a matter of priority.[12]

Even more confusingly, the 2011 AMISOM *Mission Implementation Plan* identified POC as one of AMISOM's five key diplomatic and political tasks for the period from March to September 2011. In its words: 'AMISOM is committed to the adherence and implementation of International Humanitarian Laws and Rules of Engagements approved for the mission. In this regard AUC is developing the wholesome policy and guidelines for protection of civilians'.[13] This was followed, in July 2011, by an AMISOM conference that called on the AU Commission to 'assist AMISOM to mainstream relevant parts of the four-tiered approach to protection into the work of the mission *under the current mandate*'.[14] Once again, this blurred the distinction between AMISOM protecting civilians in the limited sense of upholding IHL and the more proactive

---

[9] *AMISOM ROE Annex E: Soldiers' Pocket Card—Specific Rules for Use of Force*, §2.

[10] AU PSC communiqué (PSC/MIN/1/(CCXLIII), 15 October 2010).

[11] *Concept Paper: On the development of a mission-wide protection of civilians strategy for the AMISOM* (AU Commission internal document, 2011), p. 3. See also *Progress Report of the Chairperson of the Commission on the Development of Guidelines for the Protection of Civilians in African Union Peace Support Operations* (PSC/PR/2(CCLXXIX), 18 May 2011), §15.

[12] Press statement of the 279th meeting of the Peace and Security Council. (PSC/PR/BR. (CCLXXIX), 18 May 2011).

[13] *AMISOM MIP 2011*, §32e.

[14] *Outcome Document*, AU–AMISOM roundtable on enhancing respect for international humanitarian law in the implementation of AMISOM mandate, Kigali, Rwanda, 6–8 July 2011, p. 2 emphasis added. As noted above, the four-tier approach referred to the AU's understanding of: (i) protection through political process, (ii) protection from physical violence, (iii) rights-based protection, and (iv) the establishment of a protective environment.

approach that would require AMISOM to stop other threats to Somali civilians, most notably with regard to protection from physical violence. In contrast, the AU Commission's Working Group on POC made the mainstreaming of civilian protection in AMISOM largely synonymous with respect for IHL, stating: 'Where the protection of civilians is not considered a primary objective and is considered more as a means to an end, such as in the case of AMISOM, protection of civilians rests more on the respect of the mission for IHL and human rights law, as opposed to engaging in proactive protection activities'.[15]

Despite all these efforts to mainstream POC, when AMISOM's new Military Strategic Concept of Operations was adopted in January 2012 it made no mention of civilian protection. In March 2012, however, the brochure version of the AU's *Draft Guidelines for the Protection of Civilians*, included a foreword by Commissioner for Peace and Security Ramtane Lamamra who wrote that 'the AU operations in Darfur and in Somalia were, and remain, specifically mandated to ensure the protection of displaced persons and the delivery of humanitarian assistance, and to prevent serious human rights abuses from being committed against the civilian population'.[16] This seems to imply much more than simply upholding IHL. Finally, in June 2012 the AU PSC issued a statement that stressed the importance of 'mainstreaming' POC issues 'in standard operating procedures of AU peace support operations', and that 'PoC *must* form part of the mandate of future AU missions'.[17]

Unsurprisingly, these mixed messages caused confusion within AMISOM about the status of POC in the mission's activities. From my research, it appears that at least four views were evident:

1. AMISOM was actively engaged in POC, but only for the small subset of political leaders who were designated as VIPs in the Transitional Federal Institutions.

2. AMISOM was carrying out POC through its civil-military assistance, including facilitating humanitarian relief and giving medical care to civilians in Mogadishu.

3. AMISOM provided protection to some civilians as an unmandated byproduct of its defense of the TFG and its operations against *al-Shabaab*.

4. POC tasks were not currently conducted but should become an explicit part of AMISOM's mandate, even if it would likely raise local expectations to unrealistic levels.

---

[15] *Report of the Strategic Retreat*, p. 15.

[16] H.E. Ramtane Lamamra, 'Foreword' in *Draft Guidelines for the Protection of Civilians in African Union Peace Support Operations* (Addis Ababa: AU and Australian Government, 2012), p. 2.

[17] AU press statement (PSC/PR/BR/1.(CCCXXVI), 26 June 2012), p. 1. Emphasis added.

Not only were such divergent views indicative of incoherence within the mission, they also suggested radically different force postures and resourcing implications for AMISOM.[18]

LIMITED PREVIOUS EXPERIENCE

The AU was also reluctant to take on a proactive POC mandate in Somalia because of its lack of previous experience and related institutional unpreparedness. Before AMISOM's deployment in March 2007, only two AU peace operations had been given an explicit POC mandate, namely, AMIS in Darfur (2004–7) and the AU's monitoring mission in the Comoros (AMISEC, 2006). Neither operation stimulated an official lessons learned study on the AU's efforts to protect civilians. This absence of lessons learning occurred despite the AU Commission's acknowledgement that it would have been highly significant for 'the development of a body of knowledge and institutional memory' and 'as a valuable policy-making and training tool for future operations'.[19]

A second problem was that the AU's *Draft Guidelines* on POC were only produced in March 2010 and they borrowed heavily from the UN's parallel process of developing POC guidelines for its peacekeeping operations.[20] This was problematic because AMISOM was not a peacekeeping mission in the UN sense of the term. Rather it involved various war-fighting, VIP protection, and counterinsurgency elements which went well beyond the levels of force and tempo of operations generally expected in UN-led peacekeeping missions. AMISOM's mandate to protect the TFG and target *al-Shabaab* also made it a party to the armed conflict. This left AMISOM under constant threat of attack from anti-TFG forces and raised the risks of conducting the type of small-unit patrols which had been an essential part of POC strategies in some UN peace operations. AMISOM's predicament was further complicated by the lack of an effective national government, which would usually shoulder the

---

[18] See Lotze and Kasumba, 'AMISOM'.   [19] PSC/PR/2(CCLXXIX), 18 May 2011, §17.
[20] The UN DPKO and DFS utilized a three-tier approach to civilian protection. Tier 1 entailed protection by promoting a political process of conflict resolution to end the armed conflict that was a major source of threats to civilians. Tier 2 entailed providing protection from physical violence, which takes place in four broad phases (assurance and prevention, pre-emption, response, and consolidation). Tier 3 entailed establishing a protective environment that enhances the safety and supports the rights of civilians, i.e., promoting legal protection (especially international humanitarian law but also relevant human rights and refugee law), the facilitation of humanitarian assistance and advocacy, and support for national institutions. The three tiers were seen as 'mutually accommodating and should be taken forward simultaneously, in accordance with mission mandates and in light of the circumstances on the ground'. *Draft DPKO/DFS Operational Concept on the Protection of Civilians in United Nations Peacekeeping Operations* (New York: UN DPKO/DFS 2010), §15.

primary responsibility for ensuring civilian protection within its territory. In Mogadishu, however, the TFG lacked even rudimentary capabilities and its armed forces routinely harmed civilians.[21] AMISOM's status, posture, and operating environment thus raised major questions about the applicability of the UN's approach to POC.

Not surprisingly, therefore, the AU lacked even basic training modules in POC-related activities for AMISOM personnel; a point the AU recognized.[22] There was a similar dearth of operational concepts suitable for articulating what military and civilian tasks might actually be involved in carrying out a POC mandate. Even on the more limited issue of compliance with IHL, AMISOM had severe limitations, including having no legal advisers in IHL until 2010. This gave rise to confusion. It made the mission's senior leadership reluctant to comment publicly on controversial incidents and left lower ranks worried about potentially admitting responsibility for alleged IHL violations. There was also concern that AMISOM would become financially liable for any claims but had neither a mechanism to verify such claims nor any funds to pay reparations in legitimate cases.[23]

Compounding these problems, in its first few years AMISOM did not have enough troops for the job. As one former officer suggested: 'A force that cannot protect itself is unlikely to do well at protecting civilians'.[24] Recall, that AMISOM did not reach its initial authorized strength of 8,000 for nearly three and a half years (see Figure I.1).

Nor did AMISOM have enough police officers or civilian personnel, who would have been crucial for implementing many aspects of a POC mandate. In 2008, the AU authorized AMISOM to deploy 270 police officers to train, mentor, and monitor the SPF. However, insecurity in Mogadishu rendered it impossible for AU police to deploy. In 2010, the policing tasks were expanded to provide institutional and individual capacity development as well as security and operational support to the Somali Police Force. In October 2010, the UN Security Council authorized 260 IPOs and two FPUs for AMISOM. In practice, however, the security situation in Somalia restricted police operations outside of AMISOM's base camp and severely restricted deployment. By 31 December 2011, only thirty-four of the authorized 260 IPOs had deployed in the Mission area with another sixteen undergoing training in Kenya. It would take AMISOM until January 2014 to get over 90 per cent of its authorized 540 police. As discussed in Chapter 5, it was not until August

---

[21] Human Rights Watch, *Harsh War, Harsh Peace: Abuses by al-Shabaab, the Transitional Federal Government, and AMISOM in Somalia* (Human Rights Watch, 2010).

[22] See *Report of the Strategic Retreat* (2011), p. 16.

[23] Interviews, AU official, Nairobi, 7 August 2012 and AU adviser, Washington DC, 18 September 2012.

[24] Communication, senior AMISOM official, 20 April 2011.

2012 that AMISOM's first (Ugandan) FPU was deployed to Mogadishu, followed by a second FPU from Nigeria the following month.

There were even fewer civilian staff. By the end of December 2010, AMISOM had just fifty-three civilian staff. By January 2014, out of an AU authorized strength of 285 there were ninety-seven, including thirty-eight international staff, only twenty of whom were in Somalia (the rest were mainly Somali language assistants). Indeed, it is important to recall that AMISOM's civilian component only relocated to Mogadishu in May 2014.

Finally, AMISOM had no means to collect and analyse the type of information that is crucial for both ensuring compliance with IHL and more proactive POC initiatives. Although Mogadishu was clearly a very difficult place in which to verify reports of civilian casualties and identify the perpetrators, AMISOM's information-gathering mechanisms were severely limited and constrained. The AMISOM Mission Analysis Cell, for instance, struggled to complete its other tasks let alone collect the additional information that would have been necessary to support POC activities. Nor did AMISOM report on incidents appropriately. Indeed, it lacked adequate mechanisms for investigating episodes of collateral damage and potential violations of IHL.[25]

In sum, the AU was badly unprepared to carry out a POC mandate in Mogadishu even if it had wanted to do so.

CAUSING HARM

AMISOM's most controversial issue was the harm its own personnel caused civilians in Somalia. This failure to protect civilians also eroded the mission's legitimacy with local actors and hence undermined its effectiveness.

While exact figures are impossible to generate, large numbers of civilians were killed or injured as a direct result of fighting in Mogadishu during AMISOM's deployment. For example, Amnesty International reported that some 6,000 civilians were killed in attacks in 2007 alone.[26] The Somali NGO, Elman Peace and Human Rights Centre, estimated that in Mogadishu 1,739 civilians were killed in 2009, 2,200 in 2010, and around 1,400 in the first half of 2011.[27] Of course, these are only estimates, and most of these civilians were

---

[25] Communication, AMISOM official, 1 August 2010.

[26] Amnesty International, *Routinely Targeted: Attacks on Civilians in Somalia* (London: Amnesty International, AI Index AFR 52/006/2008, 2008), p. 1.

[27] Cited in CIVIC, *Civilian Harm in Somalia: Creating an Appropriate Response* (UNHCR and CIVIC, 2011), p. 18. Much later, UNSOM estimated that 2,078 civilians were killed between 1 January 2016 and 14 October 2017, most in Banadir region. UNSOM and OHCHR, *Protection of Civilians: Building the Foundation for Peace, Security and Human Rights in Somalia* (UNSOM and OHCHR, December 2017), p. 5.

probably killed due to the activities of the ENDF, the TFG's forces, and *al-Shabaab*. But local perceptions of reality count more than any objective indicators. An additional challenge was *al-Shabaab*'s tactics of using civilians as 'human shields', killing their own wounded and leaving them unarmed in an attempt to make them look like a civilian casualty.[28]

From its initial deployment until January 2009, AMISOM worked alongside the ENDF (see Chapter 2). The ENDF was not part of AMISOM, but the AU forces worked with them and suffered from a considerable degree of 'guilt by association' in the eyes of the local populace because of the ENDF's brutal approach towards local civilians.[29] Albeit to a lesser degree, AMISOM also suffered from guilt by association with the TFG forces who regularly committed crimes against local civilians because the mission was involved in training and supporting them in the fight against *al-Shabaab*.[30]

But guilt by association was not AMISOM's only problem; on numerous occasions several different parties accused the mission of actually causing civilian harm. In September 2008, for example, Sheikh Sharif Sheikh Ahmed accused AMISOM of 'brutality', 'war crimes', and indiscriminately killing 'over 100 people, including children, women, and elderly'.[31] Even in 2010, after the ENDF's departure, one Somali peace activist in Mogadishu summarized the perspective of many local civilians by saying: 'What is the difference between AMISOM and al-Shabab... AMISOM are killing me. And they [*al-Shabaab*] are also killing me'.[32] Some former *al-Shabaab* fighters have testified that their decision to fight against AMISOM was partly the result of feelings of hatred or a desire to seek revenge because of AMISOM's bombardment tactics.[33] AMISOM would also return fire after being attacked with heavy weapons without being able to observe where the shot fell and without being able to rapidly locate *al-Shabaab*'s heavy weapons.

At times, AMISOM also fired on civilians who were mistaken for enemy fighters. In September 2012, for example, a Kenyan AMISOM soldier shot dead six civilians in the run up to the assault on Kismayo: he apparently believed they were *al-Shabaab* fighters who had attacked his unit earlier that day.[34] A similar incident occurred in April 2016 when AMISOM troops

[28] CIVIC, *Civilian Harm in Somalia*, p. 2 and interviews, senior AMISOM officer, Kampala, 15 August 2012; EU official, Addis Ababa, 2 May 2012.

[29] See Amnesty International, *Routinely Targeted; Report of the Monitoring Group on Somalia Pursuant to Security Council resolution 1724 (2006)* (S/2007/436, 18 July 2007), pp. 12–13.

[30] Human Rights Watch, *Harsh War, Harsh Peace*.

[31] Alliance for the Re-Liberation of Somalia, 'AMISOM Brutality in Somalia', letter, 29 September 2008. Copy in author's possession.

[32] Quoted in CIVIC, *Civilian Harm in Somalia*, p. 42.

[33] See Muhsin Hassan, 'Understanding Drivers of Violent Extremism: The Case of al-Shabab and Somali Youth', *CTC Sentinel*, 5:8 (2012), p. 18.

[34] 'Kenyan AMISOM soldier kills six Somali civilians', *BBC News*, 24 September 2012, http://www.bbc.co.uk/news/world-africa-19698348

killed four civilians in a vehicle that was travelling towards their roadblock.[35] Other forms of collateral damage included civilians caught in crossfire and AMISOM vehicles injuring civilians through road accidents.[36]

A particularly difficult problem was raised if AMISOM caused casualties amongst relatives of members of the TFG's security forces, with whom AMISOM personnel had to work.

The other significant source of AMISOM personnel causing civilian harm was related to SEA. Instances of SEA in peace operations are notoriously difficult to verify. In AMISOM's case, most allegations of SEA that attracted the attention of international media and other organizations emerged after the mission had been on the ground for several years. It was only in March 2013 that the UN Security Council called on AMISOM to take measures to prevent SEA and address allegations of abuse.[37]

One of the earliest high-profile cases came in 2013 when a Somali woman claimed she was kidnapped (by a Somali man) and then subsequently held hostage, drugged, and gang raped by AU peacekeepers.[38] One NGO worker speculated that more cases weren't reported because local 'people were nervous to talk about AMISOM abuses because they thought it could destabilize the fragile peace'.[39]

The following month, the head of AMISOM, Mahamat Saleh Annadif, told the UN Security Council

> that the latest allegations of rape, made by a Somali woman against the Somali national forces and AMISOM, proved unfounded following several internal and external investigations. We in AMISOM have adopted a zero-tolerance policy on such issues. We now have at our disposal early-warning mechanisms and permanent investigation structures. We are also carrying out awareness-raising campaigns, both for AMISOM military staff and Somali populations. In that context, we have helped the Somali Government put in place a gender policy that will soon be presented to Parliament for a law to be adopted.[40]

In response, however, Human Rights Watch claimed that the subsequent investigation into this case conducted by the Somali TFG was 'marred by

---

[35] 'AMISOM regrets the loss of civilians lives in Bula Marer', AMISOM press release, PR/017/ 2016, 16 April 2016, http://amisom-au.org/2016/04/amisom-regrets-the-loss-of-civilian-lives-in-bula-marer/

[36] This was something that AMISOM also started to address. By mid-2011, for instance, if such an incident occurred involving an AU vehicle, a member of the Information Support Team (see Chapter 11) would be immediately required to draft a press release to apologize, even during the middle of the night. Interview, senior IST official, Washington DC, 3 October 2012.

[37] S/RES/2093, 6 March 2013, §14. See also *SEMG Report*, 12 July 2013. §141.

[38] Nicholas Kulish, 'African Union and Somalia to Investigate Rape Accusation', *New York Times*, 15 August 2013.

[39] Cited in *ibid.*   [40] S/PV.7030, 12 September 2013, p. 7.

mismanagement, opacity, and the harassment of the female rape survivor and support service providers'.[41]

The most detailed set of investigations into this issue occurred during 2014 and 2015. Based on research conducted in 2013 and 2014, in September 2014, Human Rights Watch released a report detailing twenty-four allegations that AMISOM personnel had sexually abused and exploited local women and girls.[42] The report alleged that AMISOM personnel used a range of tactics including using humanitarian assistance to coerce women and girls into sexual activity; approaching women and girls while they received medical assistance or water on AMISOM bases; enticed IDPs to work on the AMISOM base using Somali intermediaries; and giving women official badges to facilitate their entrance into AU bases. This chimed with that year's report by the UN Monitoring Group, which identified SEA occurring against female interpreters waiting for employment in AMISOM, soldiers exchanging humanitarian supplies for sex, or demanding sex in return for access to medical assistance, and using shopkeepers on AMISOM's main base to bring women onto the base for use as prostitutes.[43]

The AU's initial response was to deny the conclusions reached by Human Rights Watch.[44] However, behind the scenes, the AU and AMISOM launched an investigation into the allegations that was conducted between November 2014 and February 2015. The investigation team engaged with a total of 316 AMISOM personnel—via briefings, interviews, questionnaires, and focus group discussions—but faced many challenges and limitations in conducting their inquiry, including reluctance on the part of several TCCs to facilitate the investigation. They also noted that over 200 Somalis (male and female) resided inside the perimeter of AMISOM's main base at the Mogadishu International Airport, mostly selling goods or providing translation services.[45] (AMISOM's

---

[41] AMISOM and civil society representatives were initially included on the investigating committee but were later excluded due to alleged conflicts of interest. Human Rights Watch, 'Somalia: Deeply flawed rape inquiry', 10 November 2013, http://www.hrw.org/news/2013/11/10/somalia-deeply-flawed-rape-inquiry

[42] Human Rights Watch, *The Power these men have over us: Sexual exploitation and abuse by African Union Forces in Somalia* (Human Rights Watch, 2014).

[43] *SEMG Report*, 13 October 2014, §119 and Annexes 8.3 and 8.4. Additional evidence that appears to show Burundian troops soliciting local schoolgirls for prostitution during 2010 and 2011 is contained in 'Mogadishu Soldier', a documentary film produced by Torstein Grude (Piraya Film, 2017).

[44] 'The African Union strongly rejects the Conclusions contained in the Report of the Human Rights Watch on allegations on sexual exploitation and abuse by AMISOM', press release, 8 September 2014, http://www.peaceau.org/en/article/the-african-union-strongly-rejects-the-conclusions-contained-in-the-report-of-the-human-rights-watch-on-allegations-on-sexual-exploitation-and-abuse-by-amisom

[45] Kokunre Agbontaen-Eghafona, Aissatou Fall, Elizabeth Chipfakacha, *Assessment of Sexual Exploitation and Abuse in AMISOM*, report submitted to the AU Commission, March 2015, p. 62.

leadership subsequently decided to relocate these families and workers outside the main base camp.) The investigation found evidence that some AMISOM personnel had engaged in SEA of local civilians. Unfortunately, despite running to 106 pages, the subsequent report was of such a poor standard that it was never publicly released and instead the AU issued a detailed press release summarizing the principal findings and recommendations. This acknowledged two cases of SEA perpetrated by AMISOM personnel, the considerable lack of transparency about this issue within the mission, the reluctance of some TCCs to grant the inquiry an audience, and the inability of the team to establish the truth behind allegations that brothels were being run inside the AMISOM base camp.[46] The recommendations included that AMISOM's Conduct and Discipline Office must monitor all reported cases of SEA and that the AU Commission should establish an Office of Internal Oversight Services to investigate such issues.

REMEDIAL ACTION AND ITS LIMITS

By 2010 there was widespread agreement throughout the AU, AMISOM, and various international partners that levels of civilian harm in Mogadishu must be reduced. This was thought to be important for moral and legal reasons as well as pleasing the TFG. As Somalia's Deputy Minister for Interior and National Security had put it, 'Protecting the civilians is a key priority for the government. We are consulting with our military experts and the leaders of the AMISOM forces for ways of fighting against extremists while protecting the civilian population'. He went on to acknowledge, however, that while 'Somali forces and AMISOM will take precautions as we do not want to harm the people...This is easier said than done'.[47] Finally, it also made sense to make changes because causing civilian harm undermined AMISOM's strategic effectiveness as some of the victims or their families provided information or other support to *al-Shabaab*, or even joined the insurgents.

In order to change its policies AMISOM called on external contractors who helped design and implement new information and communication policies and advisers who helped design a new indirect-fire policy for the mission.

---

[46] 'The AU releases the key findings and recommendations of the report of investigations on sexual exploitation and abuse in Somalia', press release, 21 April 2015, http://www.peaceau.org/en/article/the-african-union-releases-the-key-findings-and-recommendations-of-the-report-of-investigations-on-sexual-exploitation-and-abuse-in-somalia

[47] Speech by H. E. Abdihakim Egeh Guled, Deputy Minister of Interior and National Security, 13 August 2011, http://www.somaliweyn.info/pages/news/Aug_11/13Aug8.html, accessed 1 August 2013.

AMISOM's 'strategic communication' challenge was to protect the mission's image by shifting the dominant narrative in its favour to explain that *al-Shabaab* was the key source of civilian casualties. As discussed in more detail in Chapter 11, in February 2010, AMISOM and the UN contracted a consortium of three companies to support AMISOM's strategic communications campaign: Albany Associates, Bell Pottinger, and Okapi Consulting. These firms developed a public information campaign to reinforce AMISOM's profile, credibility, and legitimacy and simultaneously undercut efforts to obstruct that narrative by the mission's opponents. This was pursued through a variety of means including launching Radio Bar-Kulan (Somali for 'meeting point'), publications such as the online *AMISOM Bulletin* and *AMISOM Quarterly Magazine*, facilitating media visits to Mogadishu for international journalists, organizing AMISOM media training workshops, producing video documentaries, drafting op-eds for senior officials, and maintaining AMISOM's website. Such initiatives were not a remedy for previous harm done by AMISOM, but within a year of the new campaign, reports accusing AMISOM of causing civilian casualties significantly decreased.

AMISOM's second major change was to endorse a new indirect-fire policy in spring 2011 (although it was only formally introduced into the revised AMISOM ROE in mid-2012).[48] This was designed with the help of outside advisers, notably from the Information Support Team and the Center for Civilians in Conflict (CIVIC). Bancroft Global Development later played a role in implementing the new policies. Drawing inspiration from the Somali tenets of *biri-ma-geydo* (which seeks to spare women and children and other innocents from the spear/armed conflict), the new indirect-fire policy involved a three-step process summarized as the '3A strategy'—for Avoid, Attribute, and Amend. Where possible AMISOM should avoid the use of indirect fire; where casualties occur, AMISOM should attribute responsibility to the perpetrator(s) by assessing and investigating incidents; and AMISOM should assist those who have been injured through emotional redress, medical care, and/or material assistance and make amends for civilian harm caused unintentionally by AMISOM, thus helping to build local support for the mission over the longer term. CIVIC recommended this course of action because they 'found that Somalis place importance on both recognition of their losses and tangible assistance. Offers of compensation are appreciated as an expression of regret and acknowledgment of the harm caused'.[49] In the initial steps, AMISOM's military component would lead, whereas in the final stages the leading role would be played by AMISOM's civilian component as well as perhaps UN agencies and international donors.

---

[48] Indirect fire is when a projectile is fired without relying on a direct line of sight between the weapon and its target.

[49] CIVIC, *Civilian Harm in Somalia*, p. 3.

The new policy required changes in policy and tactics as well as better equipment. In particular, AMISOM called for more sophisticated targeting equipment and locating equipment for mortars as well as the associated training and support. However, one analysis suggested the major problem with the new policy was the fact that AMISOM was told to implement it without any 'additional resources for training, mentoring and equipment such as weapons-tracking mechanisms or aerial drones which would greatly assist in tracking fire and determining response options'.[50]

In terms of tactical changes, AMISOM commanders instigated a number of mitigation/control measures designed to reduce the potential for causing civilian harm. These included troops being given relevant pre-deployment training, including in IHL, which instructed commanders on matters such as: (i) not to fire without authorization; (ii) designating 'no fire zones' in areas where civilians were known to be present (e.g., schools and hospitals); (iii) restricting counter-battery fire and unobserved fire; (iv) utilizing early warning mechanisms, including verbal warnings to people to vacate an area; (v) choosing not to use particular weapons; and (vi) exercising a high degree of restraint.[51]

As part of the 'attribute' step, AMISOM required some form of investigative capacity. Ideally, this should have operated in a context where the mission's personnel kept accurate records of incidents and war diaries at Contingent Command level as well as the Force Commander level, including detailed logs of use of heavy weapons and skirmishes/contacts. Calling on such records/ diaries would make it easier to refute false allegations. The external advisers called on AMISOM to establish a dedicated unit to collect and analyse such information: a Civilian Casualty Tracking, Analysis and Response Cell (CCTARC).[52] Accordingly, in February 2012, UN Security Council Resolution 2036 authorized AMISOM to establish a CCTARC.

Taken together, in December 2011 CIVIC concluded that 'AMISOM has recently shown clear improvement in its tactics. These include limiting the collateral impact of artillery, and committing to better civilian protection awareness and policies'.[53] This was true. But as two officials working with the AU concluded in 2012, it was also true that 'The protection of the Somali civilian population has been neglected by the international community for several years'.[54]

AMISOM also instituted boards of inquiry (BOIs) as an important aspect of boosting the mission's investigative and oversight capacity. BOIs were convened as required at contingent or headquarters level to investigate allegations

---

[50] Lotze and Kasumba, 'AMISOM', p. 23.
[51] Interview, senior AMISOM official, Kampala, 15 August 2012.
[52] CIVIC, *Civilian Harm in Somalia*, p. 4.   [53] *Ibid.*, p. 2.
[54] Lotze and Kasumba, 'AMISOM', p. 18.

of IHL and human rights violations and ensure accountability for the perpetrators. Headquarter-level BOIs were established for more serious incidents, including the death or serious injury of an AMISOM peacekeeper or major damage or loss resulting from suspected negligence, unsatisfactory control or accounting procedures, or in any other circumstances where responsibility for the loss or damage is unclear.[55] Some BOIs led to courts-martial, including in-mission courts-martial, repatriations, and criminal prosecutions of offenders.[56]

BOIs were also used to verify and address issues relating to civilian casualties in incidents involving AMISOM personnel and misconduct by AMISOM troops. The establishment of BOIs provided a mechanism to give a balanced account of civilian-related incidents in AMISOM's area of operations. They usually covered incidents related to traffic accidents, mistaken shootings, and even compensation to the families of some civilians killed in a bomb blast in July 2010.[57]

Even by this stage, however, it was clear that the new indirect-fire policy was already out of date in important respects and needed revision. As the advisers rightly noted, the 2011 policy had been designed before the arrival of the Kenyan forces, and thus before AMISOM had any airpower, which had a potentially major part to play in preventing or causing civilian harm; and there were now new relevant technologies that had not existed previously in the mission.[58] This situation called out for AMISOM to create a Force Fire Direction Centre and a related collateral damage estimate decision support tool to work in conjunction with the CCTARC, an action plan for which had been given funding by the British government.[59] However, despite the fact that the idea to establish a six-person CCTARC was endorsed by the UN Secretary-General in December 2011[60] and in UN Security Council Resolutions 2036 (22 February 2012) and 2124 (12 November 2013), and the UK government made available the necessary funding, the CCTARC did not become operational until late 2015 when its first officer began working out of the AMISOM Force Headquarters in Mogadishu. This delay was largely because of the controversy the CCTARC generated within AMISOM. As one IST official noted, both the head of mission, Ambassador Diarra, and some senior AMISOM commanders had been reluctant to move forward with the CCTARC, viewing it as a form of Western surveillance, especially given the way that the US-led coalitions in Afghanistan and Iraq had for a long time avoided counting

---

[55] *Brief note by AMISOM IHL/Human Rights Advisor to SRCC/AMISOM, 22 May 2017* (AU internal document, 2017).

[56] To my knowledge, the first court-martial convened in Somalia was by Uganda during 2013. Human Rights Watch, *The Power these men have over us*, p. 4.

[57] See *AMISOM Standard Operating Procedures for Processing Death and Disability Claims* (AU internal document, 2016) Annex A.

[58] Interview, AU adviser, Washington DC, 18 September 2012.   [59] *Ibid.*

[60] *Report of the Secretary-General on Somalia* (S/2011/759, 9 December 2011), §69.

civilian casualties.[61] Hence, even by mid-2017, the CCTARC had just two active technical staff and some military support staff that were insufficient to follow up on all allegations and verify civilian casualties in a timely manner.[62]

Another relevant but controversial issue was whether AMISOM should offer compensation for civilian harm caused by its personnel and actions. AMISOM had no such compensation scheme. Consequently, CIVIC called for the development of such a scheme on moral, strategic, and cultural grounds to acknowledge an error and responsibility, and help build better relations with the local population.[63] Until early 2011, there had only been one example of AMISOM making a compensation payment (of nearly $8,000), but this was for some camels that were killed by AMISOM troops.[64] Not surprisingly, this generated considerable anger among the local population. It also intensified the worries of some AU officials for the potential for 'floodgate' issues if AMISOM instigated any such compensation scheme. Specifically, they were concerned that 'every injured person in Mogadishu will claim he was hurt by AMISOM'.[65]

In subsequent years, the AU and AMISOM went on to develop a series of mechanisms to mitigate various sources of civilian harm and ensure greater accountability for the mission. Some of the most relevant are listed in Box 10.1.

To mention just a few examples, since November 2011, AMISOM contingent commanders and key appointment holders began receiving pre-deployment training in IHL, human rights, child protection, and protection of civilians. This was in addition to training on the key principles of the law of war. Nevertheless, not all troops deployed to Somalia received such training, nor was the effectiveness of such training formally assessed.[66] In November 2011, the AMISOM Force Commander and Somali women's and civil society organizations established a mechanism for information sharing and subsequently met on a monthly basis to discuss issues relating to protection of civilians and human rights. In line with the AU's new Gender Policy of 2009, AMISOM also established a Gender Unit. By March 2017, however, there were only two dedicated gender officers.[67] AMISOM also hired a senior IHL and human rights law expert to advise the mission's civilian leadership and

[61] Interview, senior IST official, Washington DC, 3 October 2012.
[62] Communication, UN official, 2 August 2017.
[63] CIVIC, *Civilian Harm in Somalia*, pp. 41–4.
[64] Interview, AU adviser, Washington DC, 18 September 2012.
[65] Cited in CIVIC, *Civilian Harm in Somalia*, p. 37.
[66] *Summary of Mapping Exercise for UNSCR2124 on the HRDDP by Senior IHL/Human Rights Advisor to AMISOM, May 2015* (AU internal document, 2015), p. 5.
[67] Compare this, for example, to the UN peacekeeping operations in DRC, which had sixteen; Darfur, which had fifteen; and South Sudan, which had ten. De Coning et al., 'The Role of the Civilian Component'.

Box 10.1. Examples of AU and AMISOM measures to mitigate civilian harm

---

- Development of a draft AU Conduct and Discipline Policy Framework
- Development of an AU Code of Ethics
- AMISOM Policy Guidance on Sexual Exploitation and Abuse (2013)
- AMISOM Force Commander's Legal Directive on Operations (February 2014)
- AMISOM Force Commander's Directive on the Protection of Children Rights (September 2014)
- The relocation of civilian shopkeepers outside AMISOM base camp
- Adoption of a Concept of Operations for AMISOM's civilian component
- Establishment of the Human Rights and Protection, and Gender units
- Establishing Boards of Inquiry
- Development of Standard Operating Procedures for the treatment of detainees (July 2014)
- Establishment of AMISOM's Civilian Casualty Tracking, Analysis and Response Cell (2015)
- Awareness-raising campaigns about the mission's zero tolerance of SEA
- Establishment of a toll-free hotline to confidentially report complaints

---

military commanders on the application of applicable IHL rules in the context of the armed conflict in Somalia.

In 2014, in collaboration with UNSOM, AMISOM also started conducting training of trainers in IHL and human rights for SNA commanders in charge of instructions in military schools and officers whose duties included military planning and execution.[68] Unfortunately, this came too late for the SNA troops that participated in Operation Eagle (March 2014), who did not receive training in human rights and IHL.[69]

After July 2011, an additional factor encouraged the AU and UN to push for further remedial initiatives, namely, the UN's adoption of its Human Rights Due Diligence Policy (HRDDP).[70] This applied in situations where the UN was providing support[71] to non-UN security forces, i.e., UNSOA to AMISOM and later to the SNA.[72] The policy sought to ensure that such support is consistent with the UN Charter's purposes and principles and relevant

---

[68] *Summary of Mapping Exercise for UNSCR2124*, p. 8.   [69] *Ibid.*, p. 12.

[70] The policy was made public in 2013. See *Human rights due diligence policy on United Nations support to non-United Nations security forces* (A/67/775–S/2013/110, 5 March 2013).

[71] 'Support' is understood to mean any of the following activities: training, mentoring, advisory services, capacity- and institution-building and other forms of technical; programmatic support to non-UN security forces; financial support; logistical support; and joint operations conducted by the UN forces and non-UN security forces.

[72] Non-UN security forces include both national security forces and peacekeeping forces of other international organizations.

international law, including IHL, human rights and refugee law. It stipulates that where a UN entity (in this case UNSOA) is contemplating providing support to non-UN security forces, it must exercise due diligence and first conduct an assessment of the risks involved in providing or not providing such support. Where there are substantial grounds for believing there is a significant risk of such violations taking place the UN entity must refrain from supporting the non-UN forces, unless it can establish measures to eliminate that risk or reduce it to acceptable levels.

For AMISOM, the HRDDP did not change the mission's existing international legal obligations but it did represent an obstacle to further political support from the UN, including UNSOA.[73] In April 2014, the Standard Operating Procedure for the implementation of HRDDP in Somalia was adopted. It provided guidance and created structures for the implementation of the policy in Somalia, including the UN–AMISOM Joint Working Group on HRDDP and the UN–HRDDP Task Force.

Even with these remedial initiatives, AMISOM was unable to eradicate all sources of civilian harm from among its own ranks and operations. Arguably, the two most serious examples were instances of lethal force used against local civilians and accusations that AMISOM personnel sexually abused some local women and girls (discussed above). The most prominent example of AMISOM personnel killing civilians came on 31 July 2015 when the AU acknowledged that Ugandan members of AMISOM killed seven civilians in Marka town. Three AMISOM personnel were subsequently indicted for this incident.[74] Allegations of sexual violence also continued, the most egregious case being an alleged rape incident involving fourteen Ethiopian troops against two children during 2016.[75]

LESSONS

What lessons can be drawn from AMISOM's ambiguous experiences with POC? First, it is clear that a small, under-resourced force that is unable to protect itself is hardly in a position to engage in proactive POC activities.

---

[73] *Note for the file on the HRDDP for the SRCC/HOM, Senior IHL/Human Rights Advisor to AMISOM, 16 June 2012* (AU internal document, 2012).

[74] 'Statement by AU Special Representative for Somalia and Head of AMISOM addressing the 31st July 2015 incident in Marka, Lower Shabelle Region of Somalia', 21 August 2015, http://amisom-au.org/2015/08/statement-by-the-african-union-special-representative-for-somalia-and-head-of-amisom-addressing-the-31st-july-2015-incident-in-marka-lower-shabelle-region-of-somalia/

[75] Report of the Secretary-General, *Special measures for protection from sexual exploitation and abuse* (A/71/818, 28 February 2017), Annex IV, C, p. 63.

AMISOM found itself in this position until at least late 2011. The best that could be hoped for in such circumstances is that the force conducted its operations in line with IHL. However, this was not always the case.

Second, it is also clear, regardless of whether AMISOM adopted an explicit POC mandate, that most local civilians expected AMISOM to protect them, not just to avoid harming them. It is therefore important to realize that even a mission like AMISOM that lacked an explicit POC mandate should work hard to minimize civilian harm in its area of operations because this inevitably erodes the mission's legitimacy, pushes victims and their families to aid opponents, and ultimately undermines the mission's effectiveness.

A third lesson is that it is important to be clear about what peacekeepers are being asked to do in relation to POC. Specifically, do their obligations end once they ensure respect for IHL, or are they expected also to conduct other proactive activities to reduce threats to civilian populations? AMISOM personnel were given a variety of unhelpful mixed messages on this issue.

A fourth lesson is that POC mandates require the investment of considerable resources and many specialized capabilities, especially if such tasks are to be compatible with the mission's war-fighting efforts. To be given even a chance of success, these capabilities must be built into the mission's Force Requirements and Concepts of Operations documents. Specifically, POC mandates require a multidimensional mission structure with sufficient military, police, and civilian components, mission-specific pre-deployment training regimes, appropriate means of mobility and coercive capacity, as well as analytical capabilities to gather, process, and act upon relevant intelligence and information. It is particularly important not to neglect the mission's analytical capabilities because it will only be possible to mitigate the main threats to civilian populations if the mission has an accurate understanding of what those threats are and where the risk of them occurring is most intense. In AMISOM's case, however, the mission lacked an appropriate force structure and enablers, it had insufficient analytical capabilities, and its personnel were not well versed in what military and other civilian tasks would be required to execute a proactive POC mandate.

Fifth, AMISOM's experience shows the value of remedial action, although this is certainly not the same thing as addressing the whole spectrum of POC challenges. From 2009, the AU leadership, AMISOM, and its partners took important steps to address some of the civilian protection challenges facing the mission. New approaches to strategic communications and indirect fire in particular enhanced AMISOM's ability to undercut *al-Shabaab*'s propaganda and guarded against an important cause of civilian harm. In contrast, issues of compensation were not adequately addressed, nor did the mission sufficiently bolster its analytical capabilities in this area. Remedial action thus had its limits and nor did it prevent all further incidents of AMISOM personnel killing local civilians and engaging in SEA.

A sixth lesson is that while POC is important during war-fighting operations for moral, legal, political, and strategic reasons, it becomes even more salient as operations shift towards broader stabilization tasks. These are analysed in detail in Chapter 12. In AMISOM's case, this occurred after the mission forced *al-Shabaab* to withdraw most of its fighters from Mogadishu in August 2011 and the mission's area of operations expanded across much of south-central Somalia. POC was crucial for that agenda because the Somali populations were the centres of gravity that needed defending from rebels who were willing to use violence to enforce civilian compliance with their agendas.[76] In such environments, ensuring compliance with IHL is not enough to succeed. More proactive measures need to be taken to keep civilians from harm.

[76] See A.W. Beadle, *Protecting Civilians While Fighting a War in Somalia—Drawing Lessons from Afghanistan* (NUPI Policy Brief, 10–2012, 2012).

11

Strategic Communications

Strategic communication is 'the purposeful use of communication by an organization to fulfill its mission.'[1] Or, more precisely, the 'coordinated actions, messages, images, and other forms of signaling or engagement intent to inform, influence, or persuade selected audiences to support national objectives'.[2] It is an important but often neglected dimension of modern peace operations. Its principal methods include audience analysis, goal setting, and message strategy. In UN peace operations, this task is normally the remit of the Public Information Unit (PIU). When AMISOM was deployed, however, the AU had almost zero capabilities in this area and so AMISOM deployed without the ability to wage an effective strategic communications campaign. This was a significant oversight. Even after ten years in the field, AMISOM's PIU had just one officer and one assistant.[3]

As AMISOM was deploying to Mogadishu in 2007, the US-led coalitions in Afghanistan and Iraq had concluded after several years of fighting that two elements of strategic communication were vital for success in counterinsurgency campaigns: in General David Petraeus's words, 'fight the information war relentlessly' and be 'first with the truth'.[4] Too often, AMISOM failed on both counts. In elaborating on these two mottos in his command guidance to coalition forces, General Petraeus argued they were crucial to success. 'Beat the insurgents, extremists, and criminals to the headlines', he wrote,

> and pre-empt rumors. Integrity is critical to this fight. Don't put lipstick on pigs. Acknowledge setbacks and failures, and then state what we've learned and how we'll respond.... Every action taken by the enemy and our forces has implications in the public arena. Develop and sustain a narrative that works, and continually drive the themes home through all forms of media.[5]

---

[1] Kirk Hallahan et al., 'Defining strategic communication', *International Journal of Strategic Communication* 1(1), pp. 3–35.
[2] Christopher Paul, *Strategic Communication: Origins, Concepts and Current Debates* (Santa Barbara, CA: Praeger, 2011), p. 3.
[3] de Coning et al., 'The Role of the Civilian Component'.
[4] General David H. Petraeus, 'Multi-National Force Iraq Commander's Counterinsurgency Guidance', *Military Review*, September–October 2008, p. 4.
[5] *Ibid.*

AMISOM in contrast started its operations with virtually no media presence or proactive communication strategy and operated with a 'bunker mentality' whereby media briefings were sporadic, poorly organized, the messaging confused and the tone defensive.[6] For its first thirty months, the resulting information vacuum played into the hands of opposition forces and undermined AMISOM's operational effectiveness. In particular, AMISOM suffered from three risks to its reputation with local Somalis and key international partners: incoherence of its narrative; opaqueness and lack of transparency; and problems related to civilian and AMISOM casualties and human rights violations perpetrated by the mission's personnel.[7]

In an attempt to remedy this situation and counter *al-Shabaab*'s narrative of events, in November 2009 UNSOA contracted a consortium of private firms that established the AU–UN Information Support Team (IST). Utilizing techniques employed in a variety of war zones, the IST's goal was to drive, as well as communicate AMISOM's success, improve the mission's media presence, and develop a communications strategy. Working with AMISOM's tiny PIU, the IST devised key strategic information objectives related to maintaining the cooperation and support of the local population, informing international opinion of AMISOM's progress in order to sustain support from TCCs and donors, and promoting a culture of peace and non-violence in Somalia to create an environment for national reconciliation.

Especially between 2010 and late 2012, the IST actively countered *al-Shabaab*'s strategic narrative in several respects, including building greater confidence in the mission and its effects. Later, however, several factors coalesced to see AMISOM struggle to deliver effective strategic communications. First, was the changing environment in which the IST was asked to operate, most notably AMISOM's expansion beyond Mogadishu and the inclusion of new TCCs (Kenya, Djibouti, Sierra Leone, and Ethiopia), which eroded the mission's coherence. Second, during late 2012 and early 2013, the UN and AU competed over which organization should lead politically in Somalia, which made the IST's tasks more challenging. When UNSOM deployed from mid-2013, there was a significant increase in international civilian staff in Mogadishu, which meant the IST was pulled in multiple, sometimes contradictory, directions. Finally, by the time a new set of firms took over the IST contract in late 2014, the IST had in some respects developed a different relationship with AMISOM, particularly over the scope for the IST's strategic communications experts to give autonomous advice to AMISOM's leadership. Unfortunately, this coincided with polling evidence that showed AMISOM's reputation with local Somali civilians reduced significantly during 2015 and 2016.

---

[6] *Final Report: Information Support Services to UNSOA/AMISOM: November 2009–November 2012* (Albany-CHIME internal document, 2012), p.78. Hereafter, IST, *Final Report*.
[7] Communication, former UNSOA official, 28 September 2017.

To address these issues, this chapter proceeds in four parts. In light of the need to know one's enemy, it begins with an analysis of *al-Shabaab*'s strategic communications and a brief assessment of its effectiveness. The second section then provides an overview of the AU–UN IST and its efforts to promote a particular strategic narrative about AMISOM and Somalia. The third section discusses the major challenges faced by the IST, paying particular attention to the roles of AMISOM's contributing countries. Among other things, the challenges faced by the IST demonstrate that successful strategic communications require more than just institutional capacity in the mission; they also require sustained, high-level political support from the key stakeholders beyond the mission to ensure that the agreed policies are implemented. The conclusion briefly identifies four main lessons that should be drawn from AMISOM's experiences with strategic communications.

AL-SHABAAB'S STRATEGIC COMMUNICATIONS

AMISOM's principal objective in the strategic communications realm was to prevent *al-Shabaab* dominating the narrative about Somalia. It therefore spent considerable time and effort to understand how *al-Shabaab* conducted its media operations. Since late 2006 and early 2007, *al-Shabaab*'s media strategy 'became an integral part of its insurgency'.[8] Over the next decade the organization ran a 'capable and adept... multi-faceted media and information operations campaign'.[9] Starting with postings on jihadi websites, mostly written in Arabic, and a film criticizing the Ethiopian intervention in December 2006, *al-Shabaab* soon created its own websites. When those sites were shut down by the hosting companies, *al-Shabaab*'s operatives utilized a wider range of social media and increased their video production. By 2010, its Media Department was rebranded as *Al-Kataib* ('brigades') Media Foundation and News Channel. This produced material in English and Somali, and then branched out into Swahili, Norwegian, Swedish, and even Urdu.[10]

The core elements of *al-Shabaab*'s strategic narrative over this period can be summarized reasonably succinctly:[11]

- There is only one truth, one Islam, and the world is divided between two irreconcilable poles—*Dar ul Harb* (Abode of War) and *Dar ul Islam* (Abode of Islam).

---

[8] Christopher Anzalone, *Continuity and Change: The evolution and resilience of Al-Shabab's media insurgency, 2006–2016* (Hate Speech International, November 2016), p. 4.

[9] *Ibid.*, p. 38.   [10] *Ibid.*, pp. 4, 30.

[11] See ICG, *Somalia's Divided Islamists* (Crisis Group Africa Briefing, No. 74, May 2010) and Anzalone, *Continuity and Change*, p. 10.

- Non-Muslims, especially Christians and Jews, are existential enemies and hence negotiation with them is not possible because of their inherent hostility toward Islam.
- True Islam is impossible under a secular state.
- Jihad and martyrdom are supreme acts of faith and *al-Shabaab*'s fighters are true, pious warriors of Islam because violence is the only path to victory.
- Its fighters are defending Islam (lands and Muslims) from unjust persecution and exacting legitimate retribution for oppression.

While money and clan loyalties certainly account for some of *al-Shabaab*'s fighters, others believed the basic ideas *al-Shabaab* propagated about the global oppression of Islam (e.g. in Iraq, Afghanistan, and Palestine) and that it was the Islamic Courts and other pious jihadis that had brought an end to the corrupt terror of the Mogadishu warlords in 2006.[12] Some *al-Shabaab* fighters were required to attend special courses that encouraged them to see Somalia within the wider context of global jihad, thereby counteracting their clan loyalties.[13]

Al-Shabaab's stated intention was to spread its version of Islamic order and justice by establishing a caliphate. Initially, the focus was within Somalia, but subsequently it extended across the wider region, especially after Kenya's October 2011 intervention. Here, *al-Shabaab* tried to frame its actions as defensive: reclaiming traditionally Muslim lands from disbelievers or as exacting legitimate retribution for anti-Muslim oppression perpetrated by Christians and other *kafirs*. Sometimes it went further, expressing global aspirations to ensure 'that the rule of the Quran governs the whole world', but more commonly the focus was regional, specifically 'to redraw the East African map'.[14]

To do so, *al-Shabaab* consistently sought to disseminate its messages to multiple audiences, including its own fighters and supporters, other local Somalis, the diaspora, Muslims across the wider region (including affiliates such as *Al-Hijra* and the Muslim Youth Center in Kenya), and the global jihadi movement, especially *al-Qa'ida*. Central throughout *al-Shabaab*'s media operations was the desire to discredit AMISOM and its contributing countries, position itself favourably within the broader transnational jihadi movement, and maintain exposure in the mass media to attract financial support and inspire new recruits.[15]

Al-Shabaab consistently depicted as weak, corrupt and illegitimate successive Somali 'governments' and AMISOM's contributing countries. In 2010, two

---

[12] Hansen, *Al-Shabaab in Somalia*, p. 45.　　　[13] *Ibid.*, p. 79.

[14] 'Mpeketoni: reclaiming back Muslims lands under Kenyan occupation', *Al-Kataib* video released March 2015.

[15] Anzalone, *Continuity and Change*, p. 13.

videos—titled, *The African Crusaders* and *Mogadishu: Crusaders' Graveyard*—
tried to pressure Burundi and Uganda to withdraw their troops from
AMISOM or their 'sons would continue to die in the streets of Mogadishu'.
They also argued AMISOM was covering up its real casualty figures and
did not care about the lives of its rank-and-file soldiers.[16] One particularly
successful method was *al-Shabaab*'s use of video to highlight its infiltration
of Somali authorities and AMISOM and showcase their incompetence
or their corruption, since their personnel were susceptible to bribes.[17]
Al-Shabaab also often claimed AMISOM TCCs were in Somalia principally
to relieve domestic economic pressures.[18]

Another persistent theme was to promote *al-Shabaab*'s prowess and potency
in Somalia but also across East Africa and the wider (jihadi) world.
Al-Shabaab warriors were portrayed as pious and justified in taking up arms
in defence of Islam. After its forces withdrew from Mogadishu in August 2011,
al-Shabaab made a virtue out of surviving and focused its media on harassing
Somali government and AMISOM forces and spreading its movement across
East Africa, most notably in Kenya.[19] Its films therefore started to reflect its
military tactics of hit-and-run-style attacks. Several were made about ambushes and massacres in Kenya, and later the militants moved on to exploit
the 'lone wolf' theme, including urging attacks on the United Kingdom and
United States.[20]

Operationally, *al-Shabaab*'s principal targets shifted according to circumstances. In 2005, the initial target was the TFG, which was portrayed as an
illegitimate, corrupt, and puppet government. From late 2006 until early 2009,
al-Shabaab's focus shifted to expelling the Ethiopian forces that had brought
the TFG to Mogadishu. When AMISOM arrived, *al-Shabaab* saw it as another
pro-Ethiopian external attempt by disbelievers to protect the TFG. When
Abdullahi Yusuf's TFG was replaced in January 2009 by a new administration
led by Sheik Sharif Sheik Ahmed, a former leading figure in the Supreme
Council of Islamic Courts, *al-Shabaab* denounced Sheikh Sharif's government
as traitors and continued to target its supporters.

From 2009 until late 2011, *al-Shabaab*'s principal targets were thus the
TFG and AMISOM's TCCs (Uganda and Burundi). During this period, its
single most potent message deployed against AMISOM was the mission's role
in inflicting civilian casualties in Mogadishu because of its indiscriminate
shellfire (see Chapter 10 and p. 291). This perception became widespread
amongst the Mogadishu populace and helped *al-Shabaab* recruit fighters and

---

[16] *Ibid.*, p. 31.
[17] See, for example, a video titled 'AMISOM and the Inevitable End', released in 2011.
[18] Anzalone, *Continuity and Change*, p. 27.
[19] See Matt Bryden, *The Reinvention of Al-Shabaab: A Strategy of Choice or Necessity?*
(Washington DC: CSIS Report, February 2014).
[20] Anzalone, *Continuity and Change*, pp. 21, 33.

encouraged local civilians to provide it with information about AMISOM's movements and procedures. Following the arrival of troops from Kenya, Ethiopia, and Djibouti in Somalia from late 2011, *al-Shabaab* expanded the scope of its messaging to include these countries. From September 2012, its main target for criticism was the new Federal Government of Somalia. Ironically, from May 2015, *al-Shabaab* was itself targeted by media operatives of the Islamic State with a series of films calling for *al-Shabaab* leaders to pledge allegiance to the Islamic State.[21]

Like any organization, *al-Shabaab*'s capabilities in this sphere derived from its people, finances, and the technologies it was able to employ. As discussed previously, *al-Shabaab* gathered funds from a variety of sources including diaspora donations, local taxation of commodities and transportation routes, illicit commerce, and donations from external supporters, including *al-Qa'ida* and its affiliates. Its information operations utilized various technologies, including leaflets, speeches, videos, radio programmes, press releases, a newspaper (*Milat Ibrahim*), and online newsletter (*Nashrada al-Jihad*).[22] *Al-Shabaab* leaders also presented their views through other media outlets, including *al-Qa'ida*-affiliated publications.

Arguably its two most important tools were radio and the internet. Radio was a particularly important medium in Somalia given the high levels of illiteracy and difficulty of distributing print media. *Al-Shabaab* ran a Ministry of Information that used a network of FM radio stations (and some TV stations) known as *al-Andalus*. They were given distinct numbers to refer to broadcast towns/areas but their broadcasts were coordinated and at least one hour per day was the same across all *Andalus* stations.[23] *Al-Shabaab* messages were also communicated via Radio Koran and Al-Furqan radio.

But beyond Somalia it was *al-Shabaab*'s use of the internet that made most impact. Indeed, the group's early use of micro-blogging and other forms of social media led one respected analyst to conclude its operatives were 'jihadi pioneers' in this area.[24] *Al-Shabaab*'s internet campaign began in earnest in late 2007, ironically to distance itself from the *Sharia* courts that had facilitated its rise to prominence during 2006. At that stage, *al-Shabaab*'s communications were circulated by the *al-Qa'ida*-affiliated Global Islamic Media Front. It also used YouTube as well as Hegan (its own website during 2007) and *Kataaib* (set up in southwest Somalia in early 2007 but hosted in Vancouver) websites. Stig Hansen has persuasively argued that *al-Shabaab* developed its internet capabilities because it lacked control over other traditional media outlets. The web also allowed it to communicate directly with international

---

[21] See *Ibid.*, p. 35.

[22] The Kenyan affiliate of *al-Shabaab* also produced a magazine, *Gaidi Mtaani*, reportedly since 2012. Hansen, *Al-Shabaab in Somalia*, p. 130.

[23] *Ibid.*, p.90.   [24] Anzalone, *Continuity and Change*, p. 22.

followers and potential recruits for which it used pan-Islamic symbols and depicted the war in Somalia as part of a wider global 'Clash of Civilizations'. To the Somali diaspora it painted a picture of Christian/apostate occupation (initially by Ethiopia but later also including Kenya and other AMISOM contributing countries).[25]

Al-Shabaab's websites, in turn, generated others established by sympathizers around the world. They contained battle reports depicting *al-Shabaab* successes (and later some suicide operations), biographies of 'martyrs', as well as the mutilation of Ethiopian troops and various attacks against AMISOM and Somali government soldiers. Some of *al-Shabaab*'s martyrs also tried to directly recruit successors in their final video testimonies. Eventually, *al-Shabaab* chose *Al-Kataib* as its public face.[26] Between 2007 and 2010, its productions commanded significant attention from the global jihadi network, including *al-Qa'ida* and its affiliates. However, this also caused problems within *al-Shabaab* since the more it appealed to this global jihadi audience, the less nationalistic it could be about its priorities and the struggle in Somalia. The tensions in the so-called 'nationalist' and 'global' wings of *al-Shabaab* featured prominently in arguments over its failed 2010 Ramadan offensive against AMISOM and the TFG, and during the famine which afflicted much of south-central Somalia in early 2011 (see Chapter 4). Indeed, from late 2011 to late 2012 there was a significant decrease in the popularity of key *al-Shabaab* websites AmiirNuur and Somalimemo.[27] It is also notable that during the 2011 battle for Mogadishu, AMISOM destroyed much of *al-Shabaab*'s communications infrastructure, with the exception of one mobile radio station that still broadcasts its communications.[28]

Since then, *al-Shabaab* utilized several forms of social media, including numerous Twitter accounts. On Twitter, *al-Shabaab* initially enjoyed considerable success. Its official @HSMPress handle, for instance, gained over 15,000 followers. Perhaps *al-Shabaab*'s most infamous episode was its live-tweeting of the attack on Westgate Mall in Nairobi in September 2013. But the militants turned away from officially using Twitter after the site administrators got quicker at closing down their accounts.[29] This prompted debate about the role of numerous so-called 'pro-*Shabaab*' (suspected unofficial *al-Shabaab*) accounts. One recent example was the @Daudoo account, which claimed to be run by an anonymous Somali journalist and attracted over 90,000 followers.[30] Twitter suspended the account in mid-2017. In the more restrictive context,

---

[25] Hansen, *Al-Shabaab in Somalia*, p. 64. [26] *Ibid.*, pp. 59–61.
[27] IST, *Final Report*, p. 96.
[28] Professor Stig Jarle Hansen cited in Robyn Kriel, *TV, Twitter and Telegram: How Do Jihadi Insurgents Attempt to Influence the Mass Media?* (Kings College London, Unpublished MA dissertation, 2017), p. 50.
[29] Anzalone, *Continuity and Change*, p. 22.
[30] See Kriel, *TV, Twitter and Telegram*, pp. 82–5.

al-Shabaab also stopped communicating with journalists by phone, and, with a few notable exceptions, face-to-face as well.[31] Instead, when it wanted to contact journalists, *al-Shabaab* turned to encrypted messaging applications—such as Telegram—'to ostensibly alert journalists of upcoming soon-to-be published material, but also to sharpen their relationship with members of the mass media or to explain their cause(s)'.[32]

In 2013, arguably the most authoritative external analyst on *al-Shabaab* concluded that the organization's propaganda effort should not be underestimated—'it is professional and conveys extremist views that can motivate youths to become terrorists on their own'.[33] This conclusion could be extended through to mid-2017.

Al-Shabaab's activities in this sphere were certainly not news to the IST, which conducted extensive analysis of them. The practical issue was translating a sophisticated understanding of *al-Shabaab*'s operations into an effective plan to combat them, with the correct priorities and appropriate resources. AMISOM's strategic communications initiatives also had to operate within a rather different set of rules than *al-Shabaab*, which often relied on gory and gratuitous 'shock and awe' tactics in its media.[34] As the next section suggests, sometimes the mission did this well, sometimes less so.

AMISOM'S STRATEGIC COMMUNICATIONS

Shortly after deploying to Mogadishu in mid-2009, UNSOA's leadership decided that AMISOM could not adequately communicate with the local population under the existing conditions. So it pushed to contract a service provider to mount an information campaign in support of AMISOM. In November 2009, AMISOM signed a Support Implementation Agreement on Public Information whereby a consortium of three firms was hired to drive its strategic communications to a variety of target audiences.[35] The three firms would subsequently form the AU–UN Information Support Team.

The UN concluded that in Somalia private firms would provide more effective operations than their standard PIU approach. As a senior UNSOA official recalled, the primary reason for establishing a commercially contracted capability was that it provided 'a means for the UN to transfer risk to a deployable commercial entity'.[36] This was largely because the intense insecurity in Mogadishu precluded the deployment of UN staff there. As was the case

---

[31] *Ibid.*, p. 50.   [32] See *Ibid.*, p. 13 and Chapter 7.
[33] Hansen, *Al-Shabaab in Somalia*, p. 141.
[34] Communication, IST official, 6 September 2017.   [35] IST, *Final Report*, pp. 3 and 5.
[36] Communication, former UNSOA official, 3 August 2017.

with UNSOA, a contracted capability permitted the deployment of personnel, as well as considerable flexibility in approach. This was not entirely unprecedented, since the UN had previously utilized contractors in some of its peacekeeping operations, including in South Sudan and DR Congo where they played a role in the establishment of local radio stations.[37]

Initially, the IST consortium comprised Bell Pottinger (part of Chime Communications plc), which provided the strategic oversight and production research and project management; Albany Associates Ltd, which led on project strategy and direction, press news, and media development; and Okapi Consulting, which set up Radio Bar-Kulan ('meeting place' in Somali) in Somalia, having previously established similar radio stations in the DR Congo, Central African Republic, and Croatia.[38] In terms of personnel, the IST built a team of consultants and staff recruited from the region and AMISOM TCCs as well as from Somalia itself who worked out of London, Nairobi and Mogadishu.[39] There were about twenty employees in the general IST and approximately another fifty running Radio Bar-Kulan. By early 2011, the forward team in Mogadishu was about ten strong.

At the time the IST contract began, AMISOM's strategic information objectives were: to maintain cooperation of the parties and the support of the local population; to inform international opinion in order to sustain support from the mission's TCCs and partners; and to foster a culture of peace and non-violence.[40] This was all very well, but AMISOM had no means to implement these objectives. Its own PIU had only one member of staff until 2011, when two new personnel were recruited.[41] AMISOM could also call on the lone Public Information Officer the UN had seconded to Addis Ababa to help boost the AU Commission's capability in this area.[42] But that was it. In retrospect, the IST team concluded: 'The resulting information vacuum and hostile misrepresentations of AMISOM's role played into the hands of opposition forces and undermined AMISOM's ability to accomplish its mandate'.[43] One senior IST official at the time therefore saw the consortium as 'a desperate and ultimately very successful attempt to reverse the appalling headlines emanating from Mogadishu about AMISOM'.[44]

Hence it was the IST that embarked on implementing a new information strategy for AMISOM. It did so through six core lines of effort.[45] First, it

[37] Communication, former senior IST official, 20 July 2017.
[38] Once established, project management of Radio Bar-Kulan was handed to Albany and Okapi Consulting dropped out of the consortium. IST, *Final Report*, pp. 9–10.
[39] *Ibid.*, pp. 29, 31.   [40] *Ibid.*, p. 7.
[41] *AMISOM Annual Report 2011* (AU internal document, no date), §82.
[42] Wikileak Cable 10ADDISABABA388, 24 February 2010, §2.
[43] IST, *Final Report*, p.78.
[44] Richard Bailey cited in Kriel, *TV, Twitter and Telegram*, p. 53.
[45] IST, *Final Report*, p. 8.

provided strategic communications and information support to execute a strategic communications plan.[46] Second, it provided research, monitoring, and analysis to map the information ecology and media landscape of Somalia, track public opinion, and test products to measure campaign effect. Third, it established a credible Somali-language radio station, Radio Bar-Kulan, which went on air on 1 March 2010 and began twenty-four-hour broadcasting exactly one year later.[47] The content was intended to emphasize the growing level of normalcy in Mogadishu, that the population could openly criticize *al-Shabaab*, and that it was legitimate of the TFG to relax *al-Shabaab*'s restrictions, such as watching football and texting freely.[48] The IST's fourth task was to establish a fast, professional, and consistent media capability for AMISOM. As part of this, it would produce and disseminate audio-visual material to support AMISOM's work and messages. Finally, it would conduct outreach to ordinary Somalis, key leaders, and the diaspora.

In addition to organizing press conferences, briefings and releases, and weekly information meetings to coordinate with partners at the UN compound in Nairobi, the IST also developed a variety of products to strengthen AMISOM's media presence, including a website for the mission launched in March 2010.[49] A media observatory site was implemented in June 2010 and shortly thereafter a summary of media reporting, including monitoring of *al-Shabaab*-affiliated radio.[50] Daily situation reports were also compiled and transmitted to the AU headquarters in Addis Ababa. Several publications were developed including the AMISOM fortnightly and quarterly bulletins. These were intended to keep stakeholders informed, maintain morale within the mission, and promote local ownership of the Somali peace process.[51] Numerous op-eds were also drafted on behalf of AMISOM's senior leadership and published in such outlets as *Foreign Policy* magazine and the *East African*, *New Vision*, *Monitor* and *New Times* newspapers. Thousands of printed desktop and wall calendars were also produced. The IST also facilitated media visits to Mogadishu for international journalists and from the TCCs and potential TCCs. In 2010, it began holding media training workshops in Nairobi for key AMISOM staff to equip them with skills in handling the media.[52]

---

[46] It also provided some support for the UN in Somalia and also the Federal Government, for instance, by providing vital equipment to the Ministry of Information to support Radio Mogadishu.

[47] See www.bar-kulan.com

[48] Communication, former senior IST official, 20 July 2017.

[49] See http://amisom-au.org. *AMISOM Annual Report 2010* (AU internal document, no date), §81.

[50] Via www.Somali-media.org (now defunct) and www.somaliamediamonitoring.org respectively.

[51] IST, *Final Report*, p. 52. The IST distributed some 4,000 copies of the quarterly magazine to international stakeholders.

[52] *AMISOM Annual Report 2010*, §82.

The IST also started to produce radio shows and video documentaries to support AMISOM's activities.[53] In 2010, for example, the production team produced 'The Misleaders', a radio drama of ten thirty-minute episodes exploring *al-Shabaab*'s recruitment methods that aired on Radio Shabelle. A follow-up ten episode series 'Happy People Can't Be Controlled', aired on Radio Frontier during 2011.[54] Video documentaries were also produced, usually based on material filmed by embedded reporters, for example, from the frontlines of the battle for Mogadishu in 2010 and 2011, with the KDF before the final assault on Kismayo in 2012, and clearing the road from Mogadishu to Baidoa.[55]

The IST was also keen to promote a more secure environment in which journalists could work within Somalia as part of its media sector development. With sixty-two journalists killed in Somalia between 1992 and 2017, it was one of the most dangerous places in the world to be a journalist.[56] This goal sometimes extended to the IST helping to provide physical security to journalists. For example, the IST established the Mogadishu Media House complete with computers and internet access as a safe house for journalists to meet, stay, and work.[57] In another episode in 2011, the IST provided equipment and technical support to the staff of Radio Shabelle who were trying to relocate out of an *al-Shabaab*-controlled part of Mogadishu.[58] This part of the IST project was called 'Lifeline'.

The overall goal of AMISOM's new communications strategy was: 'To obtain broad popular support and understanding of the role of AMISOM in protecting the sovereignty, rebuilding the national institutions and safeguarding natural resources as well as to promote the implementation of the peace agreement through supporting an all inclusive Somali dialogue'.[59] The IST proceeded to work on two main strands of this to reinforce the profile, credibility, and legitimacy of AMISOM, and to undermine the narratives produced by 'obstructionists' (insurgents, criminals, warlords, pirates, etc.).[60] It also tried to ensure there was a coherent AMISOM message and that the mission's personnel adhered to a single narrative (that challenged misconceptions) and explained their mandate and intentions to the Somali people. The IST summarized its work as an attempt to promote three principles of consistent and credible messaging, and confidence that the peace process could be reinforced through public participation and dialogue.[61]

---

[53] Examples include 'Gate of Hope', 'Somalia back from the brink', 'AMISOM Hospital', and the 'Mayor of Mogadishu'. In 2014, the UPDF also produced a twenty-three-minute film about AMISOM's successes titled 'Heroes in the Horn'.

[54] IST, *Final Report*, pp. 59–60.

[55] Interview, senior IST official, Mogadishu, 3 January 2013; communication, former senior IST official, 20 July 2017.

[56] 'Somalia', Committee to Protect Journalists, 2017, https://cpj.org/africa/somalia/

[57] IST, *Final Report*, p. 55.   [58] Communication, former senior IST official, 20 July 2017.

[59] IST, *Final Report*, p. 15.   [60] *Ibid.*, p. 20.   [61] *Ibid.*, p. 17.

The IST organized its activities to engage four clusters of target audiences.[62] These were defined as Somali audiences (especially political leaders, clan leaders, displaced people, local civilians, and rebels); regional audiences (Somalia's neighbouring countries, other regional players, refugees, and the region's civilian population); international audiences (notably the government and military of AMISOM's TCCs, international organizations, the Somali diaspora, NGOs with a presence in Somalia and the region, and other organizations with a credible global reach); and, finally, internal audiences (namely, AMISOM's leadership and spokespeople, AU civilian staff across the region, AMISOM troops, and UN partners). As well as outreach to media houses, particular attention was paid to 'potential change leaders' in each of these audiences, i.e., actors with status and respect to act as opinion leaders.[63]

The IST's core narrative about AMISOM and Somalia had several dimensions.[64] First, it emphasized that the TFG was a transitional mechanism 'to prepare the way for the establishment of legitimate and accountable public institutions, which respond to the desires and aspirations of the Somali people'. Second, AMISOM was portrayed as representing the whole of Africa and a friend of Somalia not an invading force. In particular, the IST promoted a narrative that AMISOM and the TFG were working in a constructive alliance to stabilize the country. In contrast, the IST depicted *al-Shabaab* as being controlled by foreigners linked to *al-Qa'ida*.[65] A third strand was to emphasize that AMISOM's progress depended on continued support of its TCCs but 'chiefly on the participation of Somalis themselves'.

For Somalis, the message was that AMISOM is here to help; for the region, AMISOM was portrayed as the natural African reaction to a fire in a neighbour's house; and for international audiences AMISOM was depicted as having a positive effect by providing an opportunity for political dialogue but it needed additional troops and donor support.[66]

By early 2012, the IST was focused on disseminating four basic stories to support the transition from war to peace. These focused on explaining how the TFG was established and what it was trying to achieve, a story of how the security environment was improving, a story about trying to achieve a settlement and reconciliation between Somalis, and a story focused on the negative traits and activities of what the IST called the 'obstructionists'.[67] As one senior IST official put it, 'We needed to change the messaging around AMISOM and Somalia: From conflict to post-conflict. From destruction to reconstruction. From failed state to emerging statehood'.[68]

Evidence from the IST's own polling suggests that their efforts were not in vain. The IST initially conducted three waves of opinion polling in November

---

[62] *Ibid.*, p. 21.   [63] *Ibid.*, p. 22.   [64] *Ibid.*, pp. 24, 25, 79 and 25 respectively.
[65] *Ibid.*, p. 5.   [66] *Ibid.*, pp. 26–7.   [67] *Ibid.*, p. 33.
[68] Interview, senior IST official, Mogadishu, 3 January 2013.

2009, October-November 2010, and December 2011 to January 2012.[69] Using a sample of 1,150 people in Mogadishu and its environs, the three polls indicated a significant positive shift in AMISOM's reputation.[70] In January 2010, almost one-third of Somalis polled said AMISOM was in Somalia to cause harm. By December 2011, however, this figure had dropped to 9 per cent. This was important because until 2011, 'The perception that AMISOM was the prime cause of civilian casualties in Mogadishu as a consequence of indiscriminate shell fire was the single most potent message deployed by Al-Shabaab, undermining much of AMISOM's broader success both with Somalis themselves and the international community'.[71] Yet as discussed in Chapter 10, by late 2011, the IST was able to claim that charges of civilian casualties caused by AMISOM had 'practically disappeared'.[72]

By the end of 2012, the IST concluded that AMISOM was seen as a 'trusted local partner' rather than 'a foreign occupier' and *al-Shabaab* as foreign-led and *al-Qa'ida*-affiliated.[73] More generally, as discussed in this book's Introduction, Somalia and AMISOM was being hailed as a potential model for responding to other international crises.[74] And yet, at the same time, the strategic terrain started to shift. With expansion beyond Mogadishu and the inclusion of two new TCCs (Kenya and Djibouti), AMISOM became a more disjointed mission. And in 2013, political competition between the AU and UN began to surface and affect the IST's work as its staff were pulled in multiple, sometimes contradictory directions.

In addition, a fourth round of similar IST polling of 1,031 adults conducted during March and April 2013 in Mogadishu and its environs suggested that 59 per cent felt AMISOM had been 'very' or 'fairly' effective at providing security for the local community.[75] Local respondents also urged AMISOM to provide more training for the SNA (mentioned by 70 per cent of respondents) and disarm militias (43 per cent). On the other hand, the same survey revealed only 50 per cent of respondents viewed AMISOM as a 'friendly force' compared to 30 per cent who felt it was not. Furthermore, more than half of all respondents believed Kenya (61 per cent) and Uganda (54 per cent)—at the time, AMISOM's most prominent TCCs—were involved in Somali affairs for their own interests rather than for the interests of Somalis (the answer in Burundi's case was 48 per cent, Djibouti 45 per cent, and Sierra Leone 39 per cent). On the positive side, similar polling conducted in October–November 2013 saw a rise in the proportion of respondents who viewed AMISOM as a

---

[69] IST, *Final Report*, pp. 37–8.   [70] *Ibid.*, pp. 81ff.   [71] *Ibid.*, p. 49.
[72] *Ibid.*, p. 86.   [73] *Ibid.*, p. 92.
[74] See, for example, an article coauthored by a former IST employee: Freear and de Coning, 'Lessons from AMISOM for Peace Operations in Mali'.
[75] *Mogadishu Polling Survey 2013 (Wave 2)* (IST internal document, 2013). Apparently, only 844 of the 1,031 people polled had heard of AMISOM.

friendly force—an average of 65 per cent of respondents across Mogadishu, Beledweyne, Kismayo, Baidoa, and Marka.[76]

Spurred in part by the changing external environment noted above, in late 2013 a basic system of Task Order (approvals) was put in place to de-conflict the use of IST resources by the UN and AU, and to try and refocus the IST's activities, which UNSOA thought had lost momentum in the changing environment.[77] This perturbed some IST staff because it was seen as altering the previous arrangement where the contractors—who were the strategic communications professionals—generated the concepts of work and then implemented them, to a more stifling situation where tasks were generated top-down.[78] There was also a growing sentiment that the new arrangement was intended to get the IST to do more 'crass public relations' work for the AU.[79]

AMISOM's media operations thus came to resemble the more standard UN PIU format rather than the IST's earlier more autonomous, research-led approach. It also brought more internally focused products and mission paraphernalia and merchandise such as AMISOM calendars, T-shirts, bags, etc. This reflected an increasing focus on production (i.e., the number of outputs became key) rather than the need to generate influence and specific political effects that reduced the risks to AMISOM's reputation with local Somalis. There was also a noticeable decrease in the number of media visits, although this usually fluctuated due to several factors, including the tempo of AMISOM operations and the new Federal Government developing its own embryonic capacity and hence the IST—which had provided accommodation, life support, and security for visiting journalists—became less vital. One outside journalist suggested that this might also have been due to the fact that AMISOM was increasingly only sharing media that independent journalists 'weren't interested in—such as your typical public relations products, ribbon-cutting, ceremonies etc.—and suppressed the things we were, often because it made them look bad, incompetent or beaten'.[80]

In late 2014, the IST transitioned from the original private firms, which lost the new UN contract.[81] It was won by Aethos, a specialist communications division of Aegis Defence Services Ltd, which was then subsequently bought out in 2015 by another private security company, Garda. Despite the change in contractors, some of the personnel remained the same. For example, some senior Aethos personnel had previously worked for Bell-Pottinger/CHIME and numerous lower ranking staff simply changed contracts. The Tasking

[76] Communication, IST official, February 2014.
[77] Communication, former UNSOA official, 3 August 2017.
[78] Communication, former IST senior official, 20 July 2017.
[79] Communication, former senior UNSOM official, 10 March 2017.
[80] Tristan McConnell cited in Kriel, *TV, Twitter and Telegram*, p. 78. [81] *Ibid.*, p. 53.

Order arrangement previously put in place continued under the new IST management.

Under these new arrangements, there were notable elements of both continuity and change at the IST. For example, the new team remained approximately fifty-strong, maintained a predominance of Somali speaking local staff in the field, and continued to organize media and communication pre-deployment trainings for AMISOM personnel.[82] The challenge was to keep these trainings regular enough to meet the demands posed by high turnover of AMISOM personnel. The IST also continued to produce official video programming, such as the 'AMISOM in Action' series examining key aspects of the mission's operations.

The approach to research products displayed elements of both continuity and change. The IST continued to compile research products as directed by AMISOM. These included assessments of the SNA, SPF, and countering *al-Shabaab* propaganda, as well as studies on the voices of ex-combatants and women's roles in Somali politics. It was noticeable, however, that the new arrangements saw a shift to a more centralized approach. Whereas previously, AMISOM leadership received some research products sent to them by the strategic communication advisers at IST, the new arrangement saw IST only able to respond to AMISOM's requests for communications support.[83] The former arrangement granted more autonomy to the strategic communications professionals to advise AMISOM.

In terms of novelty, at the strategic level, during 2015 and 2016, AMISOM (together with UNSOM) reconfigured their communication strategy based around a three-pronged campaign to push a security narrative (themed as 'Safe and Secure Somalia'), a political narrative (themed as 'Our Somalia'), and a future-state narrative (themed as 'Self-Reliant Somalia').[84] Operationally, there were some novel advances in the social media realm, with new AMISOM Facebook and Instagram accounts established. An outreach unit was also set up. This consisted of two staff operating out of the fortified Jazeera Hotel, very close to the Mogadishu International Airport. In mid-2017, the IST expanded these efforts when one Somali member of the outreach IST personnel was deployed to each of Baidoa, Beledweyne, and Kismayo.[85] In early 2016, the United States donated to AMISOM 'Radio-In-A-Box' communication capabilities in order to broadcast pro-Federal Government, pro-AMISOM and anti-*al-Shabaab* content to local target communities across south-central

---

[82] Thirty-seven such trainings were conducted between December 2014 and September 2017. Communication, IST official, 7 September 2017.

[83] Communications, IST official, 6 September 2017; senior UN official, 28 September 2017.

[84] *Citizens Perception of Peace and Stabilization Initiative in Somalia* (UNSOM and AU, Mid-line Report, August 2016), p. 10.

[85] Communications, IST official, 6 September 2017; senior UN official, 28 September 2017.

Somalia.[86] This gave AMISOM an additional form of outreach, which broadcast news messaging as well as dramas, Somali music, and talk shows featuring community call-in. AMISOM deployed the 'Radio-In-A-Box' in each sector except Kismayo, which did not implement the programme.[87]

Despite these various initiatives, AMISOM faced a significant strategic communications problem between 2014 and 2016 as the IST's opinion polling showed that Somali public opinion of the mission had become considerably less favourable.

In polls of 2,000 Somalis from Mogadishu, Baidoa, Beledweyne, and Kismayo conducted between December 2014 and February 2015, the IST found significant positive local perceptions of AMISOM.[88] For example, 76 per cent of respondents had some or a lot of 'confidence' and 80 per cent had some or a lot of 'trust' in AMISOM military, although the statistics for AMISOM police and civilian components were considerably lower. 52 per cent strongly or somewhat agreed that AMISOM presence would assist the Somali people to achieve peace, and over 60 per cent felt positive that AMISOM would enable the stabilization of Somalia. In particular, AMISOM's operations were credited with facilitating significant improvements in education (68 per cent), the competence of the SNA (52 per cent), freedom to use/own land (50 per cent), and the ease of doing business (49 per cent).[89] Interestingly, residents in Beledweyne felt significantly safer than those in Mogadishu, Kismayo, and Baidoa. This correlated with strongly positive views of AMISOM's Djiboutian contingent, which was playing a significantly larger role in managing local disputes there than the TCCs deployed in other parts of the country. Kismayo, in contrast, with mostly Kenyan troops, had the highest proportion of dissatisfaction with AMISOM.

However, the next major survey conducted during June and July 2016 saw AMISOM's popularity significantly diminish among local civilians. This survey polled 2,306 adults in Mogadishu, Baidoa, Beledweyne, Kismayo, and Garowe.[90] The context in which it was undertaken was mixed. On the one hand, almost all the socio-economic indicators measured by the IST improved across Somalia during 2015–16, except cost of living.[91] On the other, there was

---

[86] See 'AMISOM introduces 'Radio-In-A-box' to enhance communication with local populations', AMISOM Press release, February 2016, http://amisom-au.org/2016/02/amisom-introduces-radio-in-a-box-to-enhance-communication-with-local-populations/

[87] Farsight Africa Group, *Final Report: Radio in a Box Program* (Forcier, June 2017), pp. 6, 18.

[88] *Citizens Perception of Peace and Stabilization Initiatives in Somalia* (AUUN IST Final Presentation Report, July 2015).

[89] *Citizens' Perception of Peace and Stabilization Initiatives in Somalia* (Ipsos, Draft Summary Report, 2015), p. 7.

[90] *Citizens Perception of Peace and Stabilization Initiative in Somalia* (Ipsos Survey Report, unpublished document, July 2016). See also *Citizens Perception* (UNSOM and AU, August 2016), pp. 26–30.

[91] *Citizens Perception* (UNSOM and AU, August 2016), pp. 3, 24.

a significant overall decline in perceptions of security and AMISOM engaging in less constructive ways with the local population. Overall, support for AMISOM reduced by over half from 64 per cent to 28 per cent, and as discussed in more detail in Chapter 13, nearly half of Somali citizens polled (48 per cent) wanted AMISOM to leave immediately.

In more detail, 62 per cent of respondents said they received no services from AMISOM in 2016 compared to only 32 per cent in 2014. Overall, local support for AMISOM fell significantly from 2014, when 64 per cent of respondents had a lot or some support for AMISOM, to just 28 per cent in the 2016 survey. There was also a drop in assessments of AMISOM's performance. Whereas in 2014, 64 per cent were very or somewhat satisfied with AMISOM (with the worst figures coming from respondents in Baidoa and the best from Beledweyne), in 2016 the figure had dropped to 37 per cent (with the worst figures coming from respondents in Mogadishu and the best from Kismayo). Incredibly, by 2016, only 15 per cent of respondents viewed AMISOM as friendly and 55 per cent saw it as an unfriendly force. The worst figures (and a huge reversal from the previous year) came from Beledweyne, where 64 per cent now saw AMISOM as unfriendly and only 13 per cent as friendly. The most positive figures this time around came from Kismayo, where 22 per cent saw AMISOM as friendly and 42 per cent saw it as an unfriendly. In 2014, 56 per cent had seen AMISOM as a friendly force and only 14 per cent saw it as unfriendly. This was reflected in the overall assessment that by June 2016, 47 per cent had no confidence at all in AMISOM, 30 per cent some little confidence, and only 14 per cent had a lot of confidence in the mission.

Similar research conducted for UNSOM confirmed these negative trends (see also Chapter 13). By 2016, AMISOM was generating more negative than positive reactions from local Somalis, including the perception that despite receiving much higher remuneration, AMISOM personnel were working in 'safer' zones compared to the SNA troops who were more exposed. Criticisms over human rights abuses by AMISOM personnel also remained prominent and intensified calls for AMISOM to handover to Somali security forces.[92]

CHALLENGES

Although the IST provided AMISOM with an enormous boost to its strategic communications capacity, it also suffered from some major challenges and limitations. Indeed, one of the IST's own retrospective conclusions was that

---

[92] *Citizens' Perceptions of the United Nations in Somalia: A Qualitative Analysis* (UNSOM, 2016), pp. 5 and 16.

AMISOM never achieved the desired media and press 'rhythm' and remained essentially reactive and ad hoc in its approach to strategic communications.[93] Similarly, AMISOM itself identified a range of ongoing public information challenges. In late 2012, these were summarized as understaffing; lack of proper coordination and information-sharing; laborious statement clearance procedures that delayed information dissemination and inadequate harmonization of the statements that were produced; the security situation, which made information gathering very difficult; a lack of Crisis Communications guidelines; irregular media briefings; and the lack of high-level information coordination meetings since March 2011.[94] In addition, AMISOM's tiny PIU bemoaned the fact that it was overshadowed by the IST. In reality, there was no viable route for the PIU to meet AMISOM's strategic communications needs without the IST.

Of course, probably the most fundamental challenge was the operating environment in Somalia, which was exceptionally hostile, with few secure locations available for IST staff to live and operate. They ended up staying on Bancroft facilities until a separate compound was built for them within AMISOM's main base at the Mogadishu International Airport in 2012. Security concerns also restricted the amount of activity IST personnel could undertake in the sectors beyond Mogadishu.

A second, and perhaps surprising problem early on was selling some of the concepts to sceptical AMISOM commanders. This proved particularly difficult with regards to Radio Bar-Kulan when it became apparent that some of the AU's senior leadership thought they would be getting 'Radio AMISOM'. This reflected the Ugandan primacy in AMISOM at the time and the UPDF's experience in the Ugandan bush wars, which saw strategic communications as essentially pro-AMISOM propaganda.[95] In Somalia, however, what was required was an impartial and credible news outlet that was balanced, which meant at times being critical of AMISOM. Indeed, Albany Associates advertised Radio Bar-Kulan as 'a trusted independent, impartial observer of affairs in the country run by Somalis'.[96] This was unexpected and caused friction with some of AMISOM's senior leadership. Arguably, the turning point came after *al-Shabaab's* failed Ramadan Offensive in August and September 2010 when IST staff embedded with AMISOM on the front lines produced useful footage and escorted international media personalities, which eventually changed the perception of AMISOM from invaders to liberators. Overall, the IST concluded that it took about a year to dispel the UPDF's initial assumptions.[97]

[93] IST, *Final Report*, p. 106.
[94] *AMISOM Mission Implementation Plan 2012*, Annex D, p. 10.
[95] Communication, former IST senior official, 20 July 2017.
[96] Albany Associates, http://www.albanyassociates.com/projects/somalia [accessed 25 July 2017].
[97] IST, *Final Report*, p. 46.

Perhaps surprisingly, the IST found that AMISOM's civilian component was also reluctant to engage in its strategic communications plan. In one sense, the IST's relations with AMISOM force headquarters had been good in terms of access because the project lead was a senior Ugandan who had been the press secretary to Yoweri Museveni during the civil war. But while AMISOM's military came around, the IST concluded that the civilian component 'remained reluctant to shoulder its responsibilities with regard to the political communications process'.[98] This meant the IST had to do it for them. Having the head of mission based outside of Somalia with only short trips to Mogadishu also made it harder for AMISOM to maintain consistently positive relationships with local leaders.[99]

A third set of challenges revolved around the IST's relationship with the governments of AMISOM's contributing countries. In sum, AU and UN personnel would repeatedly contend with AMISOM TCCs pursuing their own, national communications goals, which often ignored the IST's advice. This was particularly apparent on information related to casualties (both locals and peacekeepers). Several dimensions of this challenge arose. First, as noted above, the military forces initially displayed a limited understanding of strategic communications. As a result, when they did deploy national media teams to their sectors, they tended to only produce news that was focused on their own country. This was to be expected, but it should not have come at the expense of strategic engagement with other audiences. It also reflected the wider tendency of the TCC contingent commanders to report back to their home capitals rather than through the AMISOM force headquarters. Especially in the first few years, there was also a problem of considerable mistrust of the local Somali population, which meant local IST staff were often excluded from entering AMISOM camps.[100]

Another dimension of this challenge was noted by prominent Somali intellectual Faisal Roble, who argued there was a tension between AMISOM's stated agenda of improving Somali governance and the fact that most of its TCCs (with the exception of Kenya and Sierra Leone) were run by autocratic regimes. There was an apparent contradiction, he argued, between AMISOM acting to 'steward Somalia to democracy' while its 'Godfather'—Ugandan President Museveni—'believes only in one party democracy!'[101] In some emergency cases, the IST had to try to build AMISOM's reputation as a source

---

[98] *Ibid.*, p. 35.

[99] Interviews, senior IST official, Washington DC, 3 October 2012; senior UPDF officer, Kampala, 14 August 2012; senior AMISOM official, Kampala, 15 August 2012.

[100] Communication, former IST senior official, 20 July 2017. Since the IST first established a presence in AMISOM's sectors, these personnel had been Somali staff. Communication, senior UN official, 28 September 2017.

[101] Faisal A. Roble remarks to the Institute for Horn of Africa Studies and Affairs conference, Minneapolis, October 2013, http://www.youtube.com/watch?v=iq3PfPwlzBk&feature=youtu.be

of credible information while some of its TCCs were caught lying. This was particularly apparent in relation to casualties and illicit trading of commodities. As veteran British journalist Tristan McConnell, who covered *al-Shabaab* for more than a decade, put it: 'the tendency of Kenya in particular to lie in its press statements means that we've reached the thoroughly disheartening situation in which the terrorists seem more honest than the government'.[102] As noted above, *al-Shabaab's* media products frequently highlighted the Kenyan government's lies. But the IST had only very limited contact, coordination, and influence over the KDF since they were often reluctant to accept any of the IST's advice.[103] This situation persisted, as was evident in the Kenyan government's incoherent media response to the battles at its bases at El Adde in January 2016 and Kulbiyow in January 2017 (see Chapter 7).

It was also noted that the example set by the United States on some of these issues did not help. As journalist Robyn Kriel noted, there tended to be intense secrecy about US strikes against *al-Shabaab*, which had taken place for over a decade and were often left unexplained. There was also little willingness to reveal any video footage from drones as was done for other parts of the world.[104] This reinforced the view of AMISOM TCCs that operational security should override strategic communications and they remained secretive about various aspects of their operations. As the IST acknowledged, probably more than any other issue, it was debates about acknowledging military casualties that 'led to serious issues of credibility'.[105]

The unhelpful attitude of some of the TCCs was also reflected in the limited media training available to most AMISOM personnel. Although the IST continued to provide pre-deployment and some other media and communications trainings, it also regularly identified the need for more and better training as a weakness. As noted in AMISOM's 2013 Strategic Directive, 'Ensuring that accurate information about the mandate, objectives and operations of AMISOM is disseminated as widely as possible, both within Somalia and beyond, is important with regards to ensuring the success of AMISOM operations and the attainment of the mandate of the Mission'.[106] And yet numerous mission personnel continued to make mistakes and there was little evidence of AMISOM's military component seriously buying into such declarations. In early 2013, for example, one of AMISOM's key spokespeople had no prior training in this area.[107] Probably the most infamous case occurred in March 2014 when a Burundian officer was quoted in local Somali media as

---

[102] Cited in Kriel, *TV, Twitter and Telegram*, p. 70.
[103] Communication, former UNSOA official, 3 August 2017.
[104] Kriel, *TV, Twitter and Telegram*, pp. 74–5.   [105] IST, *Final Report*, p. 56.
[106] *AMISOM Strategic Directive 2013*, section 19g.
[107] Communication, UK military adviser to AMISOM, 28 February 2014.

saying 'I don't want to defeat Al-Shabaab. I would rather scatter them to prolong my mission'.[108] Widely broadcast across Somali radio and other media sources, this gave the impression that AMISOM peacekeepers did not want their mission to succeed until they had made enough money to build their houses or buy cars back home (see also Chapter 13). IST officials also noted that the quality of media training varied across contributing countries. It was implemented first for Uganda, then Burundi, and then expanded to the other TCCs. While the UPDF pre-deployment package was generally praised, the performance of KDF officers came in for considerable criticism.[109]

The IST also faced several organizational challenges. Like most international actors operating in Somalia, it suffered at times from a lack of resources, a high turnover of personnel, and the inappropriate hiring of professionals who 'lacked cultural understanding, linguistics but also those with insight into the Somali culture'.[110] The IST's research component, for instance, struggled to produce consistently reliable and accurate products intended to help senior leaders better understand the operating environment. But while this was partly a problem of limited resources, it was also due to insecurity, and perhaps most fundamentally to the complexity of Somalia's clan dynamics and the shifting alliances between different armed actors. As discussed in Chapters 9 and 13, for example, even after ten years, the AU, UN, and even the Federal Government did not have an accurate list of who was in the SNA! There was also some controversy about the lack of Africans in senior management roles, with British ex-media, ex-armed forces, and ex-political communications personnel predominant.[111]

All of these challenges and limitations led to some missed opportunities to significantly damage *al-Shabaab*'s brand. To take just two examples, in 2011, one visiting journalist reported on how AMISOM had missed a good chance to exploit evidence of *al-Shabaab*'s regular references to sexual imagery and its abuse of women.[112] In one captured *al-Shabaab* position, AMISOM troops found 'the walls covered with doodles of the most obscene type', including scenes of rape, bestiality, and half-man, half-beast depictions not usually associated with pious Islamists. The discovery prompted one UN official to joke that 'to neutralize al-Shabaab as a fighting force, all AMISOM needed to

---

[108] Abdiwahab Sheikh Abdisamad, 'AMISOM must leave Somalia before 'Mission Creep' sets in', *The Star* (Kenya), 11 March 2014, http://www.the-star.co.ke/news/2014/03/11/amisom-must-leave-somalia-before-mission-creep-sets-in_c906058

[109] Interviews, Ugandan journalist, Kampala, 15 August 2012; senior IST official, Washington DC, 3 October 2012.

[110] Stephen Harley cited in Kriel, *TV, Twitter and Telegram*, pp. 72–3.

[111] Communication, senior UNSOM official, 10 March 2017.

[112] *Al-Shabaab* fighters regularly committed acts of sexual violence and abuse, including against children. See, for example, UN documents A/70/836-S/2016/360, 20 April 2016, §116, 118; S/2017/249, 15 April 2017, §55–6.

do was to fly in two planeloads of prostitutes from Bangkok and ferry them up to the front'.[113]

Another more recent example came in 2016 when the UN Secretary-General documented that *al-Shabaab* had been recruiting and using children to fight in some of their bloodiest battles.[114] Despite being given ample time to respond to the story, it took two weeks for AMISOM to formulate a counter-message.[115] As Robyn Kriel argued, this was a perfect occasion for AMISOM to paint *al-Shabaab* as cowards who pushed young children out front to fight their battles, but the opportunity was missed. One former IST official concluded that such lost opportunities reflected a broader and 'consistent failure to message in any way against al-Shabaab's high-profile attacks. There is no preparatory work in terms of reporting suspicions, no rapid response messaging once the incident starts (and) no follow-up messaging to clarify what happened'.[116]

LESSONS

The preceding analysis suggests that there was no viable route for AMISOM's tiny PIU to meet the mission's strategic communications needs. Without the IST, AMISOM would have had almost zero capabilities in this area. Like UNSOA, therefore, the IST was a necessary addition for AMISOM. As part of the IST's broader strategic communications strategy, polling evidence and broader debates about AMISOM in Addis Ababa, New York, Brussels, and Washington DC suggest that its work helped shift the tide against *al-Shabaab*'s initially dominant narrative.

As circumstances changed, however, so AMISOM's strategic communications needed to evolve as the nature of the threat from *al-Shabaab* altered, as the mission brought on more TCCs, as the new Federal Government of Somalia started to establish its own, albeit embryonic, strategic communications, and as the UN established a more significant field presence in Somalia. Despite the challenges and shortcomings discussed above, the IST played an innovative and important function for AMISOM. With an expanded UN mission authorized in 2013 and the shift into more of a stabilization mode from 2014, the terrain had shifted. This put a premium on supporting the

---

[113] Fergusson, *The World's Most Dangerous Place*, p. 117.

[114] Kriel, *TV, Twitter and Telegram*, pp. 62–3.

[115] 'Al-Shabaab violating human rights by recruiting child soldiers', AMISOM Video Release, 18 April 2016, https://www.youtube.com/watch?v=a1QZnU3N6VA

[116] Stephen Harley cited in Kriel, *TV, Twitter and Telegram*, pp. 86–7.

Somali authorities, which, like other components of AMISOM, had not been the IST's priority.

Arguably the most basic lesson is that deploying a mission without the capabilities to wage an effective strategic communications campaign is a major error. To ensure this is not repeated, the AU needs a standing strategic communications capability equipped to develop policy and plans, build coherence, as well as support robust communications operations in all its peace operations. Naturally, the precise nature of the strategic communications capabilities should be constituted in accordance with the needs on the ground.

A second lesson is to ensure coherence between a clear vision and sound policy to guide strategic communications. The mission leadership should clearly articulate the desired effects and clarify how particular audiences can be influenced to support the mission's goals. Moreover, as seen in AMISOM's case, it is not enough to devise a coherent policy; it must also be implemented by the countries contributing to the mission. To be effective also means building trust and remaining credible. Here, the issue of casualties (both civilians harmed by AMISOM and the mission's own casualties) most clearly demonstrated how the absence of a coherent policy between the AU and the mission's TCCs could have a disastrous impact on strategic communications. It was therefore unsurprising that the IST sometimes struggled to build trust both with some of the mission's contingents and with local Somali audiences.

A third lesson is that effective strategic communications in AMISOM required an expeditionary mindset and a willingness to take risks, including to generate and support media access in difficult circumstances. Like UNSOA's operations with regard to logistics, this could only plausibly be delivered in the early years by a contractor capability rather than a standard UN format PIU. And like UNSOA, the IST's experience demonstrates that in such an insecure and fluid environment as Somalia, contractual arrangements need to build in flexibility and a willingness to take some risks. In this case, the IST was initially designed to ensure a strategically focused and decentralized approach to project design, which was subsequently curtailed from 2013. But given the need to learn and evolve quickly on the job, the ability to take risks was crucial.

Finally, a related lesson is that the need for expertise about local conflict dynamics means that IST-like operations probably need a predominantly local team in order to ensure sustainable success. The challenge facing AMISOM early on was the absence of a Somali commercial capability able to manage an effort of the scope, scale, and complexity of the IST.[117] The situation improved over time and the IST maintained over 50 per cent local staff. But it remained difficult to hire and retain the best people, and the issue was sometimes

---

[117] Communication, former UNSOA official, 3 August 2017.

complicated by AMISOM's initial mistrust of Somalis, which often raised practical obstacles to running an effective campaign such as the inability to co-locate.

In sum, the IST may not have lifted AMISOM to a level where it lived up to General Petraeus's dictums about waging a relentless information war and being first with the truth, but it stands as a useful example of how strategic communications can effectively support a struggling peace operation.

12

Stabilization

In the twenty-first century, a growing number of peacekeepers from a variety of international organizations were mandated to carry out 'stabilization' tasks in theatres as diverse as Afghanistan, Iraq, Kosovo, Haiti, Mali, Central African Republic (CAR), and Democratic Republic of the Congo (DRC).[1] According to perhaps the most thorough analysis of what stabilization operations entail,

> Stabilisation is the process that supports states which are entering, enduring or emerging from conflict in order to: prevent or reduce violence; protect the population and key infrastructure; promote political processes and governance structures which lead to a political settlement that institutionalises non-violent contests for power; and prepares for sustainable social and economic development.[2]

Yet the theories and definitions of stabilization used by states and international organizations vary and remain contested. For example, although the UN's missions in Haiti since 2004, DRC since 2010, Mali since 2013, and CAR since 2014 all have the word 'stabilization' in their name, the UN still has no explicit definition of or framework for this concept, let alone a set of guiding principles for its field operations.[3] The same was true for the AU. Nevertheless, most actors engaged in stabilization concluded that military power can provide only part of the equation, and ultimately it is the ability to establish legitimate governance structures and deliver essential services to the local population that holds the key to successful stabilization.

As discussed below, AMISOM struggled on precisely this issue. In part, this was because Somalia's asymmetric threat environment made any stabilization efforts extremely difficult, especially considering AMISOM was never designed

---

[1] This chapter draws from Walter Lotze and Paul D. Williams, *The Surge to Stabilize: Lessons for the UN from the AU Experience in Somalia* (New York: International Peace Institute, May 2016).

[2] *Security and Stabilisation: The Military Contribution* (UK Ministry of Defence, Joint Doctrine Publication 3–40, November 2009), p. 239.

[3] David Curran and Paul Holtom, 'Resonating, Rejecting, Reinterpreting: Mapping the Stabilization Discourse in the United Nations Security Council, 2000–14', *Stability*, 4:1 (2015).

or equipped to be a force that operates in this type of situation. Hence, while AMISOM achieved some notable military successes by recovering dozens of settlements from *al-Shabaab*, the mission was unable to consistently deliver on the governance dimension of its stabilization agenda, in part because of its own military-heavy composition and in part because its local partners were unable (and sometimes unwilling) to do so. Officially, AMISOM had always been tasked with stabilizing Somalia.[4] In practice, however, it was only after the expulsion of *al-Shabaab*'s main forces from Mogadishu in August 2011 that the mission really began to design and try to implement concrete stabilization programmes.

Moreover, AMISOM was in a particularly difficult situation with regard to implementing a stabilization agenda for several additional reasons. First, AMISOM was mandated to support a host government that was weak and perceived as illegitimate by large segments of the local population. Second, AMISOM had to share its theatre of operations with a bewildering mix of armed actors, including external militaries as well as local forces. Third, AMISOM had to develop its stabilization agenda on an ad hoc basis and learn on the job. Not only did the AU have no official doctrine on stabilization, its doctrine on 'peace support operations' also said nothing about the concept. Nor was the need for stabilization operations foreseen in any of the roadmaps developed to guide the African Standby Force, which focused on more traditional conceptions of multidimensional peacekeeping and humanitarian military intervention.[5] The AU has now recognized at a strategic level that it needs to address this deficit, but the deficit remains.

To address these issues, the chapter proceeds in three parts. The first section summarizes the evolution of AMISOM's stabilization agenda. The second section identifies ten challenges that bedeviled its efforts in this area. The concluding section identifies nine lessons from AMISOM's experience in Somalia that might help in designing more effective stabilization operations elsewhere.

THE EVOLUTION OF AMISOM'S STABILIZATION AGENDA

As military successes against *al-Shabaab* continued during 2011, preparations were made to strengthen AMISOM's police and civilian components and to relocate them to Mogadishu. This shift aimed to transform AMISOM from an

---

[4] See PSC/PR/Comm(LXIX), 19 January 2007, §8 and S/RES1744, 20 February 2007, §4.
[5] See de Coning, Gelot, and Gelot (eds.), *The Future of African Peace Operations*.

almost purely military mission into a more multidimensional operation that could also support the stabilization of Mogadishu, and potentially of south-central Somalia once the security situation permitted.

In 2007, a small civilian team had been established in Nairobi, mostly to engage with the TFG and coordinate with UNPOS and the UN Country Team. AMISOM's civilian personnel were intended to complement its military and police components by helping to support political processes including dialogue and reconciliation, extend state authority, protect civilians and facilitate immediate humanitarian assistance, and provide support to the FGS in the implementation of its national stabilization and security plans.[6] Like the AU police, deployment was hampered by insecurity in Somalia and by the end of December 2010, AMISOM had only fifty-three civilian staff based in Nairobi. In 2011, steps were taken to strengthen this team and construct facilities in Mogadishu in anticipation of their redeployment.

The idea that AMISOM could play a stabilization role also gained traction with the UN. In September 2011, the UN Security Council welcomed the improvement of security in Mogadishu and requested that AMISOM work with Somalia's Transitional Federal Institutions to develop a stabilization plan for the capital city.[7] The Council also noted the important role an effective police presence could play in stabilizing Mogadishu and stressed the need to continue developing an effective Somali Police Force (SPF). Although AMISOM was authorized to deploy 260 individual police officers (IPOs) and two FPUs, in practice, the security situation in Somalia restricted police operations outside of AMISOM's base camp and severely restricted deployment. By 31 December 2011, only thirty-four of the authorized 260 IPOs had deployed to Somalia with another sixteen undergoing training in Kenya.

By this stage, AMISOM's police component was mandated to assist and support the SPF to build its operational, training, administrative, and management capacity; re-equip and rehabilitate its infrastructure; mobilize and manage its resources; and enforce the law to serve and protect Somali citizens under the law. This mandate envisaged AU police assisting in key areas of police reform; the development and delivery of short-term skills enhancement training; providing ongoing mentoring and advisory support to the SPF; the

---

[6] AMISOM civilian personnel were divided into substantive and support components. The substantive component, headed by the Deputy SRCC, comprised the Political Affairs, Civil Affairs, Humanitarian Liaison, Protection, Human Rights and Gender, Security Sector, and Public Information sections. The support component was responsible for providing administrative and logistical support on a mission-wide basis. It was led by the Head of Mission Support and divided into Integrated Support Services, Administrative Services and Finance, Accounting, and Budget.

[7] S/RES/2010, 30 September 2011. See also Yvonne Akpasom and Walter Lotze, 'The Shift to Stabilisation Operations: Considerations for African Peace Support Operations', *Conflict Trends* 2 (2014).

mobilization and management of resources; in law enforcement operations; and helping the SPF to reduce the fear of armed violent crime within communities, including kidnapping for ransom, as well as rid communities of the weapons of war.

In February 2012, the Security Council adopted Resolution 2036, which, among other things, specified three dimensions of stabilization where AMISOM should take on more of a role.[8] First, it called for AMISOM to support delivery of stabilization plans developed by the IGAD and the Somali TFG in areas already secured. Second, it called for AMISOM to establish an operational police component to help stabilize Mogadishu. Third, the Council indicated that, in making future decisions, it would take into account how far Somali security forces and AMISOM had consolidated security and stability throughout south-central Somalia on the basis of clear military objectives integrated into a political strategy.

Meanwhile, AMISOM had started drafting its own stabilization plan based on six pillars:[9]

1. TFG leadership, especially support for the National Reconciliation Steering Committee.

2. Establishment of multi-clan administrations, not based simply on a victor's peace model or the '4.5 formula' as these were viewed as being insufficiently representative of local preferences. Moreover, AMISOM interpreted evidence of the past twenty years as proof that 'clan coalitions are inherently unstable and exceptionally prone to manipulation and defections'.

3. Immediate service delivery, especially of food, water, shelter, demining, and law and order.

4. Pre-Disarmament, Demobilization, and Reintegration (DDR) for members of armed groups, including *al-Shabaab* fighters who wanted to demobilize.

5. Integration of some allied armed militias into the Somali security services.[10]

6. Coordination of international efforts on the ground.

The draft plan also emphasized that it was 'critical that all of AMISOM's efforts should be **Population Centric** in order to deprive the insurgency of a

---

[8] S/RES/2036, 22 February 2012.

[9] *Concept Note: Draft AMISOM Stabilization Plan for the Liberated Areas* (AU internal document, February 2012).

[10] Interestingly, AMISOM characterized these militias as 'anti-Al Shabaab but... not necessarily pro-TFG'. They included the Ras Kamboni Brigade fighting in the Lower Juba region, the Shabelle Valley Administration fighting in the Hiiraan region, and some factions of ASWJ, most of whom recognized the TFG but still operated independently. *Ibid.*

population base'.[11] The draft document called for the immediate development of an AU Stabilization Plan for the Liberated Areas.

To that end, AMISOM slowly began relocating its civilian personnel from Nairobi to a small mission headquarters in Mogadishu, providing limited political affairs, civil affairs, humanitarian liaison, and public information capabilities. The AU intended to slowly transform AMISOM from a military fighting machine into a multidimensional peace support operation focused on supporting the stabilization efforts of the Somali authorities and providing much-needed support to the Somali security forces.

Shortly thereafter, the UN Security Council also called for expanding the stabilization component of AMISOM's mandate. Specifically, it requested that AMISOM, within its capabilities, assist in the implementation of Somalia's newly developed National Security and Stabilization Plan. At the AU's request, the Security Council also extended logistical support for AMISOM's civilian component, underlining the importance of these civilians deploying swiftly to areas liberated from *al-Shabaab* to assist with stabilization efforts.[12] In light of the AU's Strategic Review of AMISOM (discussed in Chapter 6), in February 2013, the PSC revised AMISOM's mandate to include facilitating and coordinating support from relevant AU institutions and structures for the stabilization and reconstruction of Somalia.[13]

The following month, the UN Security Council gave the new Somali Federal Government more responsibility for the security and stabilization of areas recovered from *al-Shabaab* and moved AMISOM into more of a supporting role.[14] As noted in Chapter 6, the UN also replaced UNPOS, which had primarily operated from Nairobi, with the larger UNSOM, based in Mogadishu. UNSOM's mandate was to provide good offices and support to the Somali government's peace and reconciliation efforts and to coordinate international support to the development of the Somali security sector.[15]

Then, in April 2013, AMISOM issued its first mission-wide guidance on stabilization in the form of the *AMISOM Provisional Guidelines on Stabilisation Activities*. These guidelines provided the mission's first official definition of stabilization efforts as 'any post-conflict/-combat activities undertaken in order to facilitate and promote early recovery of the population and institutions in a locality that has been recovered from Al Shabaab'.[16] Based on this definition, all mission components would be engaged in stabilization activities, with the military focused on securing areas under the control of *al-Shabaab*, the police working to enhance the rule of law and public order,

---

[11] *Ibid.*   [12] S/RES/2073, 7 November 2012.

[13] PSC/PR/COMM(CCCLVI), 27 February 2013.   [14] S/RES/2093, 6 March 2013.

[15] S/RES/2102, 2 May 2013.

[16] *AMISOM Provisional Guidelines on Stabilisation Activities* (AMISOM internal document, 2013), p. 1.

and the civilian component undertaking activities 'in support of the military gains in Somalia'.[17] The overall aim of the stabilization efforts was to support the Federal Government in promoting safety, security, reconciliation, and development of local governance to foster 'normalcy' in the areas secured from *al-Shabaab*. While the guidelines provided a useful definition and overall strategic direction for the mission, they did not provide guidance on how to implement these tasks. By default, this was left to a working group within AMISOM, which was tasked with initiating QIPs with a ceiling of $10,000 each.

As discussed in Chapter 7, during its Operations Eagle and Indian Ocean conducted in 2014, AMISOM adopted a phased approach to stabilization.[18] The first stage was to separate *al-Shabaab* forces from the population and isolate the group from its sources of support. At which point, AMISOM would seize, secure, and stabilize key settlements. Having seized a settlement, AMISOM's theory of stabilization went as follows: Once the AMISOM commander declared an end of military 'combat security' operations, the second stage was reached when the security situation was deemed safe enough for external officials, including FGS, to visit and engage the local authorities and police forces could start taking over security tasks from the military. This would involve securing the MSRs, shaping operations, and conducting humanitarian needs assessments. The third stage occurred when the local community shared a sense of security, and enjoyed a level of access, space for dialogue, and engagement with partners in the new political process and for recovery activities to develop.[19]

To help in these endeavours, by January 2014, out of an authorized strength of 285 AMISOM civilian personnel there were ninety-seven, including thirty-eight international staff, but only twenty of whom were in Somalia (the rest were mainly Somali language assistants). AMISOM's civilian component relocated to Mogadishu in May 2014. On the policing side, by January 2014, AMISOM had deployed 514 police: the two FPUs (discussed in Chapter 5) plus 234 IPOs. By mid-2015, IPOs were deployed across all AMISOM sectors (in Mogadishu and Benadir region, Johwar, Kismayo, Baidoa, Dhobley, and Beledweyne).

At this point, the UN Security Council further refined the language of AMISOM's mandate to include 'Enabling stabilization efforts through supporting the delivery of security for the Somali people to facilitate the wider

---

[17] *Ibid.*, p. 1.

[18] The January 2014, AMISOM CONOPS had also conceived of stabilization as part of a phased approach following the mission's expansion operations and preceding and facilitating the handover of security responsibilities to Somali actors. *AMISOM CONOPS*, January 2014, pp. 14–15.

[19] *Report of the Joint African Union–United Nations Mission on the Benchmarks for a United Nations Peacekeeping Operation in Somalia and recommendations on the next steps in the military campaign* (30 June 2015), §64.

process of peacebuilding and reconciliation, including through the gradual handing over of security responsibilities from AMISOM to the SNA and subsequently to the Somali police force'.[20]

To give a sense of how these theories played out in practice, having recovered a town from *al-Shabaab*, AMISOM civil–military cooperation (CIMIC) personnel would conduct a rapid assessment of the humanitarian needs and identify any relevant QIPs.[21] Ideally, these would be coordinated with the other relevant actors providing similar services such as OCHA and local and international NGOs. AMISOM assessments used a stability matrix based on a traffic-light scale (red for unfavourable, green for favourable, yellow for moderate conditions) in order to quickly display broad comparative areas of need across the region. These rapid assessments covered humanitarian needs for water, food, healthcare, and the extent to which Somali authorities could provide such services, as well as indicators of concern for measuring stabilization, including the presence of a district commissioner, Somali police, disengaged combatants, and community-driven projects.

AMISOM's main attempt to provide for some of these needs in the period between the mission recovering an area and the arrival of other actors came in the form of QIPs. As the mission's 2013 Strategic Directive put it, the effective planning, delivery, and monitoring of QIPs is essential to ensuring that the civilian population in Somalia receives tangible peace dividends, and supports the operations of AMISOM.[22] They were mainly focused on water provision, e.g., renovation of wells and boreholes (not used to build new ones to avoid accusations of favouritism); sanitation and hygiene issues e.g. non-food items such as mosquito nets, Jerry cans and basins; and some infrastructure projects, including renewal of medical centres and hospitals, schools, and bridges. However, only sixteen relatively minor QIPs were realized as of March 2015 in four of AMISOM's Sectors.[23] (Between 2013 and November 2014, only three QIPs had been realized.[24])

To provide just one illustrative case of the military and governance challenges facing AMISOM's stabilization agenda, consider Bardheere, a relatively small market town that was recovered in July 2015, well after the AU mission first started pursing such policies. Located in the Gedo region of Jubaland State, it was recovered from *al-Shabaab* by AMISOM (Kenyan and Ethiopian) forces with support from the SNA, ASWJ, and Jubaland fighters.[25] As was

---

[20] S/RES/2232, 28 July 2015, §5.

[21] Communication, AMISOM official, 2 December 2014.

[22] *AMISOM 2013 Strategic Directive*, section 19b.

[23] *AMISOM Force Headquarters Position Paper on Joint African Union/United Nations Benchmarking Exercise* (AU internal document, April 2015), Annex C, p. 2.

[24] *Ibid.*, Annex C, p. 1.

[25] This paragraph draws from *Baardheere District* (Fragility Index and Maturity Model, internal UNSOM document, April 2017).

common, *al-Shabaab* mounted little initial resistance but dispersed its forces into the countryside and then returned to the outskirts to attack nearby SNA and AMISOM troops and travellers on the road routes out of the town. In order to provide governance, a 'caretaker' district administration was appointed by the Jubaland authorities to govern the town. This mainly comprised ASWJ military commanders, who participated in its recovery. The plan was to transition to more civilian administration, but this had not happened by April 2017. This stimulated some local resentment because of the predominance of Marehan and under-representation of Digil-Mirifle representatives on the district administration. The lack of any official police in the town led some SNA and ASWJ troops to assume de facto policing functions. The administration also had to make do without any official budget from either the Federal or Jubaland State governments. Perhaps as a result, some unpaid Jubaland forces were subsequently accused of engaging in extortion and robbery of the local community. A separate council of elders was established to adjudicate in clan/subclan disputes and in 2016 a District Peace and Stability Committee. That same year, Saudi Arabian funds paid for a new hospital but no mechanisms were established to ensure qualified health professionals and supplies were available at the new hospital. Given the risky nature of road travel, the UN and some commercial flights utilized the nearby airstrip, which was rehabilitated with assistance programmes from several international partners. To complicate matters further, Bardheere also received an influx of IDPs from the drought-affected areas of Bay region.

In sum, therefore, despite recovering the town, AMISOM struggled to destroy significant elements of *al-Shabaab*, establish legitimate and effective security and governance structures, escape unhelpful clan dynamics, and meet the humanitarian needs of the population and the subsequent additional IDPs that their presence attracted. It also highlighted the limited non-military actors available to assist with any stabilization initiatives.

CHALLENGES

Bardheere was illustrative of numerous other settlements where AMISOM tried to implement an effective stabilization strategy across south-central Somalia. In more general terms, the mission's stabilization agenda suffered from a number of political and operational challenges.

Lack of a Shared Stabilization Strategy

First, the Federal Government and the AU did not have a shared stabilization strategy when AMISOM and the SNA launched their expansion operations.[26] Moreover, military priorities generally dictated other actions. In anticipation of the expansion operations, the Federal Government had developed a stabilization plan by February 2014, one month before the start of Operation Eagle.[27] This plan was to be coordinated by Somalia's Ministry of the Interior and Federal Affairs. However, it was not effectively factored into the planning of military operations.[28] Military planning was thus undertaken largely in isolation from the stabilization planning undertaken by the Federal Government, the SPF, AMISOM's civilian and police components, UNSOM, the UN Country Team, as well as donors and NGOs. In addition, external critics saw it as designed in Mogadishu—principally by the UN Development Programme and a few members of the diaspora—and based on the dubious idea of parachuting police, judges, and other administrators from Mogadishu into liberated areas. This was thought highly unlikely to succeed because of local clan dynamics.[29]

Complicating matters further, many actors crucial to the stabilization efforts, in particular the UN Country Team, NGOs, and donors, were reluctant to be too closely associated with AMISOM. AMISOM was also reluctant to share its military planning with other actors, given the need to maintain operational security. As such, joint planning both within AMISOM and between AMISOM and other actors proved difficult. Communication and coordination were often weak, and establishing priorities and delivering support to areas recovered from *al-Shabaab* was challenging. This combination of factors left all other actors scrambling to coordinate their stabilization plans and responses after the military campaign was already underway.

Lagging Non-military Responses

Second, the speed of military operations far outpaced the speed of other stabilization responses. The Federal Government's stabilization plan, for instance, provided for the immediate deployment of caretaker administrations in recovered districts, followed by an inclusive local process to agree on interim administrations, which in turn would prepare and facilitate agreement on permanent administrations. The plan also called for support to local-level social and political reconciliation processes and peace dividend projects. In

---

[26] It is important to note that throughout the subsequent expansion operations, the SNA had no troops in AMISOM's Sector 2 because of disputes with the leadership over what in 2013 became the Interim Jubaland Administration.

[27] Federal Government of Somalia, *Stabilization Project Strategy*, version 30 August 2014.

[28] *Operation Eagle after Action Review Workshop: Stabilisation of Recovered Areas, Gender and Human Rights. Report of Working Group 4* (AMISOM internal document, 30 May 2015).

[29] Telephone interview, UN official, 7 September 2017.

terms of local-level security, the plan called for the recruitment of community volunteers to work with a limited number of trained police.

However, when the first towns were secured, the caretaker administrations had not even been selected or trained, and they were generally deployed several weeks or months after locations had been secured. In some cases, this raised serious tensions between local communities that had appointed their own interim administrations and the government-appointed administrations. In addition, as noted in Chapter 7, when government security forces did deploy, their arrival sometimes raised tensions with local populations and militias and, in several instances, resulted in the outbreak of new conflicts. Thus, as the expansion operations ended, they left a very unequal degree of governance and security in the locations recovered from *al-Shabaab*.

Misalignment of Security and Political Dimensions of the 'Surge'

A third challenge was that the security and political dimensions of the surge and the resultant stabilization operations were separated from one another. Since AMISOM's initial deployment, the division of labour between the AU and the UN had been clear. The AU, through AMISOM, was to take the lead on security operations—protecting the TFG and then the Federal Government, enhancing the capabilities of the Somali security forces, and undertaking joint operations with them against *al-Shabaab*. The UN, working first through UNPOS and then UNSOM, was to lead on the political side—providing good offices and engaging with the TFG to support the transition to the Federal Government, supporting the development of regional and local authorities, supporting the consolidation of the state and state authority, and coordinating international assistance to the Somali security sector. This division of labour—at times explicit, sometimes less so—was based on an understanding of comparative advantage: it was thought that the AU was best placed to conduct enforcement operations in a highly volatile and dangerous context, while the UN was best placed to act as guarantor of the political process (i.e., supporting implementation of federalism as set out in Somalia's provisional constitution and encouraging reconciliation).

While this approach proved quite successful in the initial years of engagement in Somalia, it was highly problematic during the expansion and stabilization phase since 2014. AMISOM and the SNA were rapidly expanding their military operations across south-central Somalia, while the UN focused its political engagement primarily on the Federal Government in Mogadishu and the regional administrations emerging around Baidoa, Beledweyne, and Kismayo. Thus, while the UN remained engaged at the federal and regional levels,

AMISOM military operations were increasingly engaging at the local level without the necessary linkages to the regional and federal political processes.

In addition, while the UN also worked in Puntland and Somaliland, AMISOM's engagement was limited to south-central Somalia, which caused significant challenges when *al-Shabaab* started moving forces into Puntland and developing a strong presence in Kenya. Thus, while the UN was able to operate politically in Puntland, there was no equivalent security cooperation to address the expanding threat posed by *al-Shabaab*. As both the security and the political operations in Somalia evolved along different trajectories, significant gaps arose and became increasingly difficult to bridge.

Fragmented Command and Control

A fragmented system of command and control, combined with weak multidimensionality, was AMISOM's fourth major challenge inhibiting its stabilization agenda. As a war-fighting operation, it was not surprising that AMISOM's multinational Force Headquarters did not exercise real operational control over all the mission's TCCs; this is to be expected in war-fighting coalitions where force headquarters focus on providing overall strategic command and direction and facilitating effective coordination between the national contingents.

In AMISOM's case, however, even these functions were limited, with the Force Headquarters in Mogadishu having limited influence on the actions of the TCCs in their respective sectors. During AMISOM's early years, this limited influence was exacerbated by the weak political leadership demonstrated by successive heads of the mission. This left a succession of AMISOM force commanders as the primary political points of contact with the TFG and then the Federal Government in Mogadishu. Nevertheless, AMISOM's military leadership in Mogadishu only ever held a coordinating, as opposed to a commanding, role over the operation after it expanded beyond the city.

Accordingly, the pace of operations, and the actions of the individual TCCs within their respective sectors, proved challenging to coordinate, let alone control. This had a particularly direct and counterproductive military effect by offering *al-Shabaab* relative sanctuary in the frontier areas between AMISOM's sector boundaries. *Al-Shabaab* quickly exploited the inability of AMISOM's different TCCs to coordinate cross-sector operations.

With regard to AMISOM's stabilization agenda, the fragmented command-and-control system was compounded by the military-heavy nature of the mission (see Table 12.1). Setting up a multidimensional mission headquarters following five years of an almost exclusively military presence in Mogadishu proved challenging. Integrating civilian and police personnel into AMISOM operations proved equally daunting. As such, the civilian and police components

Table 12.1. AMISOM budget summary, 2011 and 2013–16 (US$)

Budget line	2011	2013	2014	2015	2016
Military Component	150,531,684	226,809,726	270,261,584	278,879,302	281,506,596
Police Component	39,757,200	18,905,880	29,492,320	12,648,120	18,962,080
Civilian Component	10,948,882	14,107,535	12,298,257	16,891,673	14,744,429
Operational Cost	12,207,934	12,230,647	12,919,064	12,796,702	14,629,113
Other Support	7,629,859	2,255,000	8,248,578	4,943,575	4,958,444
Programme/Projects	22,541,970	6,213,976	8,393,661	6,595,041	19,664,012
Grand Total	**243,617,529**	**280,522,763**	**341,613,464**	**332,754,413**	**354,464,673**

Source: Data supplied by the AU Commission, 26 November 2016.

of AMISOM, more often than not, either worked in isolation from their military counterparts or scrambled to respond to the outcomes of the military operations. Effectively cooperating and coordinating with the Federal Government, UNSOM, and the UN Country Team on stabilization programmes thus became even more challenging as well. Competition regularly emerged between the UN and AMISOM and it also became apparent that the Federal Government did not want AMISOM to deploy a large civilian component, especially one directly engaged with crucial stabilization tasks in the recovered areas. Instead, the Somali authorities wanted any peace dividend to be delivered by its people not the AU.

Resilience of al-Shabaab

Fifth, the expansion operations were not able to significantly degrade *al-Shabaab*'s key fighting capabilities. With only a few exceptions, when faced with an AMISOM/SNA assault, *al-Shabaab* chose to withdraw its forces without a fight. Instead, its fighters usually pillaged local infrastructure, poisoned water supplies, and left boobytraps. *Al-Shabaab* had learned in the battles for Mogadishu and later on its outskirts at Afgoye that AMISOM had far superior conventional military power. From then on, the militants chose to fight conventional battles generally only on their terms. Hence, while AMISOM and SNA forces quickly displaced *al-Shabaab* forces, they did not dramatically degrade its combat capabilities. Some *al-Shabaab* fighters melted into the population, others redeployed elsewhere in Somalia, heading as far north as the Galgala mountains in Puntland, where they established new bases and training camps.[30] The number of *al-Shabaab* fighters captured or killed remained low, and *al-Shabaab* military equipment was rarely seized or destroyed.

---

[30] See Matt Bryden, *The Decline and Fall of Al-Shabaab? Think Again* (Sahan Report, April 2015), www.sahan.eu/wp-content/uploads/Bryden-Decline-and-Fall-of-Al-Shabaab.pdf

Having retreated, *al-Shabaab* fighters often set up camp several kilometres outside the recovered towns, then returned to harass them with raids and established roadblocks and taxation points along the entry routes to continue controlling the local population. *Al-Shabaab* was also able to harass AMISOM's supply routes, using a combination of IEDs and ambush attacks. In some cases, for AU and UN personnel, this left the recovered settlements feeling a lot like 'islands, beyond which movement was nearly impossible'.[31]

When Operations Eagle and Indian Ocean concluded in late 2014, *al-Shabaab*'s fighting capabilities had barely been degraded. Moreover, *al-Shabaab* continued to recruit and train new fighters, increasingly from Kenya. The militants also often left behind sleeper cells (usually formed of personnel from its clandestine intelligence wing, *Amniyat*) in some of the larger urban settlements and their fighters could still move freely across large swathes of south-central Somalia. This meant they could still exercise significant influence over local populations living in these areas and extract sufficient resources from them through taxation and other revenue streams—notably, illicit forms of commerce—to maintain highly effective operations against the Federal Government and AMISOM.[32]

The Lack of Force Enablers

Sixth, most of the force enablers and multipliers that had been authorized and which AMISOM desperately needed never arrived. As noted in Chapter 7, the recommended enabling units that made up the 'surge' for the most part either were not deployed or were deployed as TCC assets rather than mission assets. Regarding the police, the number of individual police officers was reduced in preparation for the deployment of a third Formed Police Unit to further support the transition to policing operations in either Mogadishu or Kismayo. But this unit did not arrive as planned, temporarily reducing AMISOM's overall policing capacity. Regarding civilian capacity, the AU struggled to recruit the additional civilian personnel authorized in 2013. They were intended to reinforce the mission headquarters in Mogadishu and slated for deployment to the sector headquarters and areas recently recovered from *al-Shabaab*. In effect, between 2014 and 2015, there was no tangible increase of civilian personnel in AMISOM. By June 2016, AMISOM civilian strength stood at 116 substantive and support personnel comprising fifty-eight international staff (with fifty-four deployed in Mogadishu and four in Nairobi),

---

[31] 'Letter dated 19 April 2013 from the Secretary-General addressed to the President of the Security Council' (S/2013/239, 19 April 2013), Annex §7.

[32] Bryden, *The Decline and Fall*.

nine Kenyan national staff, and forty-nine Somali national staff.[33] By March 2017, AMISOM had filled only 140 of its 240 allocated civilian posts.[34] As such, even after the surge, AMISOM was configured neither for conducting expansion operations nor for undertaking or supporting the planned stabilization tasks. And as discussed in Chapter 5, AMISOM had to conduct these offensive operations without a single military attack helicopter, which would have offered a means to rapidly strike *al-Shabaab* (and hence degrade some of its key combat capabilities), provide air cover for troops, escort convoys, enable rapid response to attacks, flying rescue/evacuation missions, and airdrop forces.

Continued Insecurity of the Somali Population

These challenges also led to a seventh major problem: some of the expansion operations did not tangibly increase security, or perceptions of security, for the Somali civilian population. Indeed, the joint SNA and AMISOM offensives indirectly increased the level of violence in several locations by pushing out *al-Shabaab* and leaving a power vacuum in its wake. Such situations were worsened by central and regional authorities failing to match the military effort with rapid deployment of interim administrations that could deliver basic services to the local populations.

A related problem was that AMISOM probably under-estimated the problems that other non-*al-Shabaab* armed groups could cause, especially clan militias. Clan violence, largely over leadership and resources, often reemerged as a significant threat, particularly in the newly recovered areas. The beginning of 2015 saw consistently high rates of clan violence, which increased humanitarian challenges, political marginalization of less powerful clans, and clan-related conflict over power and resources.[35] And in 2016, the UN reported 2,062 civilian casualties of conflict but estimated *al-Shabaab* was responsible for only just over half of them.[36]

Throughout these areas, Somali civilians continued to bear the brunt of the violence. In 2014, for example, an estimated two-thirds of all casualties from IED incidents were civilians.[37] Civilians also suffered from predatory behaviour by *al-Shabaab*, the SNA, and clan militias, ranging from illegal taxation and checkpoints to criminality to increased human rights abuses.[38] In

---

[33] *AMISOM Strategic CONOPS*, draft 17 June 2016, §38.

[34] de Coning et al., 'The Role of the Civilian Component'.

[35] *Somalia Security and Justice Public Expenditure Review* (UNSOM and World Bank, January 2017), p. 17.

[36] *Somalia Strategic Assessment Report* (unpublished UN document, 7 April 2017), p. 10.

[37] Communication, AMISOM official, 20 April 2015.

[38] In August 2017, an assessment of the main transit routes in south-central Somalia revealed eighty-two fee-paying checkpoints, twenty controlled by *al-Shabaab*, fifty-seven by the SNA, and

perhaps the worst-case scenario, AMISOM and the SNA sometimes vacated towns they had recovered from *al-Shabaab*, leaving civil administrators and ordinary citizens who had cooperated with them particularly vulnerable to reprisals. During 2015, examples included Tooratorow, Yaq Bari Weyne, Buufow, Ababay, Qoryooley, Awdheegle, and Golweyn.[39]

Difficulty Delivering Peace Dividends

This continued insecurity was compounded by an eighth challenge: the Federal Government and AMISOM's struggle to bring peace dividends to the growing civilian population coming under their control. *Al-Shabaab* increasingly resorted to destroying critical infrastructure when abandoning towns, taking generators and water pumps with them, blowing up wells, destroying bridges, ransacking medical facilities and schools, and even removing doors from prison cells. In *al-Shabaab*'s former headquarters of Barawe, militants completely gutted the hospital of its equipment, leaving a single SNA mobile clinic as the only medical facility available to the local population.[40]

Once AMISOM and government forces had entered a town, *al-Shabaab* worked to blockade it, preventing all access by road and ensuring that goods could not enter and people could not exit. AMISOM did not have the necessary forces to picket the roads or conduct regular convoys, and thus in many instances the only option was to deliver supplies for the mission and humanitarian assistance by air. This made humanitarian operations very costly and slow, given the small number of helicopters operated by the UN. In many locations, *al-Shabaab* also cut off farmers' access to their fields. As shortages of food and medical supplies rose, so too did the frustration of the civilian population.

The conduct of hearts-and-minds activities was also constrained by three factors. First, AMISOM had very limited CIMIC capacity, with only a small office at the Force Headquarters in Mogadishu and a handful of CIMIC officers in each sector. Second, the mission had a tiny budget for CIMIC and hearts-and-minds activities. Third, the AU did not have adequate systems and procedures in place for AMISOM to assess local needs, identify relevant QIPs, and deliver those projects on the ground. Projects were slow to be

---

five jointly by the SNA and Interim South-West Administration forces. Cited in *Report of the Monitoring Group on Somalia and Eritrea Pursuant to Resolutions 751 (1992) and 1907 (2009)* (S/2017/924, 2 November 2017), §167.

[39] 'AMISOM vacates 10 towns in Somalia amid Al-Shabaab's Ramadan attacks', *Somalia Newsroom*, 3 July 2015, https://somalianewsroom.com/2015/07/03/%E2%80%8Banalysis-amisom-vacates-10-towns-in-somalia-amid-al-shabaabs-ramadan-attacks/

[40] *After Action Report: Operation Indian Ocean, Phase 2, Part 2, Barawe* (Bancroft, October 2014). ACOTA files.

implemented, in some cases taking well over two years to complete, leading to frustration on all sides. Numerous attempts to streamline projects, work directly with bilateral donors, and work through the UN procurement system led to marginal improvements. However, AMISOM's ability to conduct hearts-and-minds operations was not commensurate with the pace and scale of its military operations, especially in a context where it was recovering areas that had been under *al-Shabaab* control for a relatively long period, in some cases almost ten years.

Faulty Key Assumptions

A ninth challenge was that a key assumption underpinning the security strategy developed for AMISOM's surge proved faulty. The temporary AMISOM surge endorsed by the AU PSC and the UN Security Council assumed that the SNA would be able to play a supporting and then leading role in the fight against *al-Shabaab*. As Somali forces assumed greater responsibility in the recovered areas, so the thinking went, AMISOM could move into a supporting role that would free up AU forces for other tasks. In reality, training, arming, and supporting the SNA forces proved challenging, which limited their operational capabilities. Often, AMISOM operations had to be slowed down or scrapped altogether when the SNA could not match their pace. As analysed in Chapter 9, the SNA's weaknesses stemmed from technical and infrastructural gaps and problems related to command and control, clan dynamics, and political leadership, which further eroded AMISOM's effectiveness. The same could also be said about the inability of the Federal Government to deploy legitimate and effective administrators and other civilians to help AMISOM forces 'hold' and 'build' these settlements.

Difficulty Providing Logistical Support

Finally, as discussed in Chapter 8, providing logistical support to the expansion operations was difficult. According to the UN's logistical support package for AMISOM and, later, for SNA forces working directly with AMISOM, it was UNSOA's responsibility to deliver logistics support. The mutually agreed concept of joint AU–UN logistical support had been based on an integrated civilian and military supply chain; UNSOA would be responsible for delivering to AMISOM sector headquarters, and AMISOM would be responsible for first-line support from the sector headquarters to its forward operating bases. To facilitate this support, UN Security Council Resolution 2124 had authorized the deployment of critical enabling units as part of AMISOM's temporary surge, including aviation assets and a transportation company.

However, critical shortfalls quickly arose when these enablers never arrived, *al-Shabaab* consistently attacked the main supply routes, and UNSOA's own budget constraints led to gaps in the logistics chain. As a result, logistical support could not keep pace with the expansion operations. This was entirely predictable, given that UNSOA had always struggled to apply UN rules, regulations, and ratios designed for standard UN peacekeeping operations to a rapidly expanding offensive campaign in an extremely hostile environment. In its war-fighting and stabilization mode, AMISOM's consumption rate of everything from tires for armoured vehicles to blood supplies and coffins far surpassed that of any mission the UN had ever before supported. Critically, when the AMISOM surge and a support package for the SNA were authorized, the UNSOA support package, which was designed to provide the logistical support to these operations, was left unchanged.[41]

LESSONS

What lessons should be identified from AMISOM's ongoing attempts to stabilize south-central Somalia? The first point to make is that missions must be appropriately configured to fulfil their mandate. Peace operations will struggle to fully succeed if they are not given appropriate means to achieve their mandated tasks. In this case, a military-heavy mission like AMISOM cannot be expected to deliver stabilization, which requires significant police and civilian capabilities. Moreover, a mission configured to undertake offensive operations and counterterrorism tasks will not be well suited to implementing stabilization programmes. AMISOM was forced to operate for years without some critical enablers and multipliers that rendered it almost impossible to significantly destroy *al-Shabaab*'s main combat forces.

A second lesson that emerges is the need to ensure that the political and military elements of a stabilization strategy are in sync. Successful stabilization requires military actions that support a viable political strategy. This will be very difficult to achieve if the military and the political dimensions of stabilization are separated from one another and carried out by different, uncoordinated actors, as often occurred in AMISOM's case. Developing the security sector is not an apolitical task, and ensuring nonviolent political processes requires a degree of security engagement.

A third lesson is that extending state authority is not synonymous with peacebuilding, at least in the short-term. A peace operation mandated to extend state authority in a context where the state is not widely accepted

---

[41] For additional details, see UNSG, *Letter Dated 7 October 2015*.

as legitimate will not always be viewed as an impartial force. In such circumstances, extending state authority is likely to generate conflict. Success will therefore depend on the ability to conduct effective reconciliation and peacebuilding processes with aggrieved actors at the same time as extending state authority.

AMISOM's experiences also suggest that territorial expansion is less important than degrading the capabilities of spoilers. Specifically, stabilization efforts focused on expanding territory and denying the opposition territorial control are unlikely to work where the opponent adopts asymmetric tactics. Extending a mission's responsibilities over new territory without degrading the opponent's combat capabilities risks overextending mission forces and leaving supply routes increasingly vulnerable. The opponent may simply adapt to losing territory by becoming more mobile and flexible, as was the case with *al-Shabaab*. Mission planning and resource allocation should therefore focus on separating opponents from the local population and degrading their combat capabilities rather than traditional objectives of territorial control.

Since no single actor can accomplish the stabilization agenda alone, it is crucial that strategic coordination occurs among the relevant partners, and that they recognize that this is principally a political rather than technical task. Importantly, implementing complex stabilization agendas involving numerous partners in the face of concerted hostility from some local actors requires *shared* planning assumptions, threat analysis, and operational responses. Moreover, where missions engage in essentially war-fighting activities, the headquarters of multinational forces are unlikely to exercise real control over TCCs. Instead, their principal function will probably be limited to ensuring unified political leadership and strategic coordination among the TCCs.

A sixth lesson is that failure to achieve such coordination can have negative political and military effects. This was certainly the case when AMISOM's TCCs failed to coordinate effectively. Politically, the inability of the Force Headquarters to ensure that all of AMISOM's TCCs followed the mission's mandate led many Somalis to view the mission in a negative light as providing cover for rogue TCCs. In military terms, when a mission loses local support, its personnel, particularly those in exposed forward operating bases, become especially vulnerable to attack. Moreover, lack of coordination between some of AMISOM's TCCs prevented the execution of cross-sector operations, which enabled *al-Shabaab* fighters to find sanctuary in the boundaries between AMISOM's sectors.

It also became apparent during AMISOM's operations that effective stabilization requires positive relationships between the peacekeepers and the local population. Simply put, implementing complex stabilization agendas is impossible without the support of local populations. Locals are best placed to identify insurgents and inform a peace operation of militants' movements and routines. Peacekeepers who do not develop positive relationships with local populations risk, at best, are operating without optimal information and, at worst, driving locals to collaborate with the insurgents. To date, AMISOM's experience with running small forward operating bases without regular active patrolling and substantive engagement with the local communities has not always provided a good model for forging positive ties with the local populations. Nor did its decision to withdraw from some settlements recently recovered from *al-Shabaab*. And as discussed in Chapter 11, effective and trusted public communications also plays a significant role here.

The penultimate lesson is that successful stabilization requires capable and legitimate local security forces. AMISOM struggled inasmuch as in large parts of the country, local security had been provided by a range of informal actors, usually clan-based and self-defence militias, and only relatively rarely by regional or certainly federal security forces.[42] This was a problem in both the military and policing sectors. It is fair to say that for too long AMISOM's international partners put too little emphasis on building effective Somali national security forces and the mission's ability to achieve stabilization goals suffered as a result. Sometimes donors were reluctant to invest much money in this area given the high levels of corruption and the lack of short-term positive results (see Chapter 9). Sometimes the UN Security Council was unwilling to authorize UN support where it was needed most.

The final point is to reiterate a conclusion that has appeared frequently in AMISOM's history, the mismatch between the UN's organizational frameworks for delivering logistics support and its bureaucratic culture and the needs of a mission essentially engaged in sustained manoeuvre warfare. As discussed in Chapter 8, it is never ideal to separate military commanders from their logistical support. And while the establishment of UNSOA had a major positive impact on AMISOM's logistical capabilities, it was always apparent that the UN's organizational culture, technical frameworks, and procurement rules would be insufficient to meet all of AMISOM's needs. This put UNSOA personnel in an impossible situation. When AMISOM operated in just part of one city (until early 2012), UNSOA could just about cover over most of the cracks. But when AMISOM's area of operations was extended across the whole of south-central Somalia, UNSOA was exposed as a chronically under-resourced mission that was not suited to operating in such an insecure environment. If peace operations are given war-fighting mandates, their personnel should rightly expect appropriate logistical support.

---

[42] For an overview of these in south-central Somalia, see Ken Menkhaus, *Non-State Security Providers and Political Formation in Somalia* (Gerda Henkel Stiftung, CSG Paper No. 5, April 2016).

13

Exit

All peace operations must end. But how should this be done responsibly while ensuring they achieve their mandated tasks? The short answer is by developing and implementing an effective exit strategy. This involves understanding how to marshal the resources necessary to achieve the mission's principal object-ives but also managing what might be called the 'politics of exit' because once the process of withdrawal begins in earnest it can generate its own unintended effects. In AMISOM's case, the mission's planners and leaders had thought about how the mission might end since day one. But, at times, the politics of AMISOM's withdrawal became another source of incoherence and tension between the mission's contributing countries and their key partners. Particu-larly, from late 2015, AMISOM's exit was used to justify various positions: for the TCCs it became a way of pushing for more sustainable sources of funding for the mission; for the EU and UN it would become part of the justification for gradually reapportioning and eventually reducing their funding to AMI-SOM; and for Somali politicians, it became a significant issue in the 2016/17 electoral process and a way for the Federal Government to demand more funds and support from its international partners.

Some of the challenges raised by the politics of AMISOM's exit were evident during 2015 and 2016 when the EU decided to place a cap on the amount of money it allocated to pay allowances for AMISOM's troops and FPUs. The EU also adopted measures to reduce its financial risks in case the AU failed to comply with its financial standards. These decisions contributed to three types of controversies that became tied up with the question of AMISOM's exit strategy and whether some TCCs might leave early.

First, the EU and AMISOM contributing countries argued over the appro-priate level of AMISOM allowances (see Figure 13.1). In 2007, the EU agreed to pay AMISOM's troop allowances, which were then set at a rate of US$500 per soldier per month. With only some 1,600 Ugandan troops deployed, this cost the EU approximately €0.7 million per month. In January 2009, the rate was increased to US$750 per soldier per month. This changed after the AU argued that its peacekeepers should get the same as their counterparts in UN peacekeeping operations. The EU therefore agreed to align its payments with

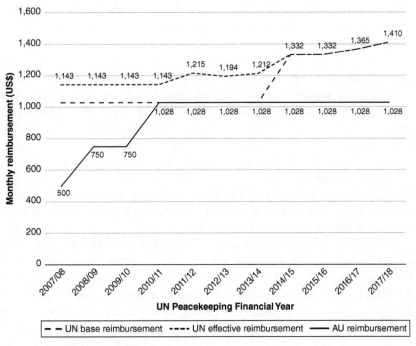

Fig. 13.1. Monthly Allowances for Uniformed Personnel in AMISOM and UN Peacekeeping Operations, 2007–2017 (US$)

the standard UN reimbursement rate, which was then US$1,028 per soldier per month, which it did from January 2011. By 2016, AMISOM had over 22,000 uniformed personnel, costing the EU about €22 million per month. In addition to allowances, the EU also paid for other costs, including training, death, and disability compensation for AMISOM peacekeepers killed or wounded and indirect costs such as supporting some AU personnel working in Addis Ababa and AMISOM offices in Nairobi and Mogadishu. In January 2016, the EU reduced its payment for AMISOM allowances by 20 per cent, from US$1,028 to US$822 per soldier per month.[1] This generated another round of arguments.

---

[1] To understand the EU's decision, it is necessary to recall that effective 1 July 2014, the UN raised its monthly base reimbursement rates for its peacekeepers from US$1,028 to US$1,322 per soldier. That rate was also set to increase gradually to US$1,410 per peacekeeper by 1 July 2017. This raised the question of whether the AU would also align its rate of AMISOM allowances with the new UN rate given that had been the rationale behind adopting the US$1,028 figure. In mid-2015, the Ugandan government argued that the EU should align its payments with the new UN peacekeeping rates. Unsurprisingly, the prospect of increasing the AMISOM allowances payments by approximately 30–40 per cent (up to approximately €32 million per month) triggered another round of debate within the EU. Its Member States decided instead to set a cap of €738/US$822 per peacekeeper per month starting on 1 January 2016. Notably, the EU did not reduce

Second, several AMISOM TCCs complained about delayed payment of allowances to peacekeepers in the field. Some claims suggested troops went without allowances for over a year.[2] As Burundi's Defence Minister, Emmanuel Ntahomvukiye, put it, '11 months of delay in paying troop allowances have demoralized our troops in Somalia'.[3] Usually, however, the delay was a result of nothing more sinister than complicated financial and accounting procedures which meant that disbursing the EU's financial support to AMISOM could take approximately seven months and involved a wide range of often disconnected actors, which could create misunderstanding and delays.[4]

And then, in March 2016, a third controversy arose when the EU Council decided to impose sanctions on the Burundi government related to Article 96 of the Cotonou Agreement.[5] The EU therefore suspended direct financial support to the Burundian administration, causing the AU to search for an alternative payment mechanism or donor.

The public arguments that ensued saw several of the AMISOM contributing countries threaten to leave the mission. In February 2016, for example, President Uhuru Kenyatta threatened to withdraw Kenya's contingent from AMISOM and criticized the EU's decision to place a cap on its allowances payments, saying his country was paying with blood and flesh to stabilize Somalia.[6] In April 2016, the head of Uganda's Defence Forces, General

---

the overall level of financial support it provided to AMISOM through its African Peace Facility. Rather, the monies that were saved by reducing the allowances payments by 20 per cent were reallocated to provide AMISOM with support in other areas, including renting houses for AMISOM in Nairobi, some running costs for the AU headquarters, and supporting AMISOM's training of the Somali National Army in Somalia. The rationale behind the EU's decision was twofold. First, that a reduction in allowances was necessary to ensure the longer term sustainability of its African Peace Facility. And, second, that this reallocation was in line with AMISOM's stated exit strategy and the need to provide more support to developing Somalia's national security forces. See 47th Meeting of the UN General Assembly's Fifth Committee, GA/AB/4116, 3 July 2014, https://www.un.org/press/en/2014/gaab4116.doc.htm

[2] 'Burundi threatens to sue AU, pull out troops from Somalia', *The East African*, 30 December 2016, http://www.theeastafrican.co.ke/news/Burundi-threatens-to-sue-AU-pull-out-troops-from-Somalia/2558-3502180-88bvsw/index.html

[3] Pierre Ngendakumana, 'Towards a lawsuit against AU?', *Iwacu*, 26 December 2016, http://www.iwacu-burundi.org/englishnews/towards-a-lawsuit-against-au/. The Ugandan press, for example, reported that its soldiers had not been paid for nine months during 2015. Risdel Kasasira, 'UPDF in Somalia not paid for nine months', *Daily Monitor* (Uganda), 6 September 2015, http://www.monitor.co.ug/News/National/UPDF-in-Somalia-not-paid-for-nine-months/-/688334/2859660/-/93v1xq/-/index.html

[4] For details on the process see Paul D. Williams, 'Paying for AMISOM', *IPI Global Observatory*, 11 January 2017, https://theglobalobservatory.org/2017/01/amisom-african-union-peacekeeping-financing/

[5] 'Burundi: EU closes consultations under Article 96 of the Cotonou agreement', European Council press release, 115/16, 14 March 2016.

[6] Rawlings Otiemo, 'Don't fund AMISOM, Uhuru tells African States', *Standard Digital*, 29 February 2016, http://www.standardmedia.co.ke/article/2000193286/don-t-fund-amisom-uhuru-tells-african-states

Katumba Wamala, complained about delays in his troops receiving their allowances.[7] Not for the first time, Uganda's government later threatened to withdraw from AMISOM, but said this was because of frustration with the limited progress being made to develop a Somali army and ineffective military advisers from the United States, United Kingdom, and Turkey.[8] In November 2016, the AMISOM Military Operations and Coordination Committee publicly criticized the EU's decisions to reduce the rate of allowances payments and to differentiate its payments to Burundi.[9] The following month, Burundian President Pierre Nkurunziza not only threatened to withdraw more than 5,000 Burundian troops from AMISOM but also to sue the AU.[10]

This chapter analyses the other major challenges AMISOM faced in trying to develop and implement a successful exit strategy. It begins by summarizing the different modes of exit that are usually available to peace operations and discusses how some of these occurred in earlier foreign military operations in Somalia since the early 1990s. It then examines the evolution of AMISOM's exit strategy as articulated in various official documents. Five major challenges to implementing a successful exit strategy are discussed in the third section, while the conclusion briefly summarizes how, by mid-2017, AMISOM was trying to handover the lead security role to Somali security forces.

EXIT STRATEGIES FOR PEACE OPERATIONS

For peace operations, an exit strategy can be defined as *the process of generating the resources needed for the mission to leave the host country*. Successful exit strategies involve a mission leaving its host having achieved all or most of its stated objectives.[11] Ironically, the concept of 'exit strategies' in peace operations is usually traced to US engagement in Somalia in the early 1990s

---

[7] Nicholas Wassajja, 'UPDF receives 1,800 soldiers from Somalia', *New Vision* (Kampala), 24 April 2016, http://www.newvision.co.ug/new_vision/news/1422949/updf-receives-800-soldiers-somalia

[8] 'Uganda to withdraw troops from Somalia's Amisom force', *BBC News*, 23 June 2016, http://www.bbc.com/news/world-africa-36606194 Uganda's government had made what turned out to be idle threats to withdraw from AMISOM several times before, including during the 2011 crisis that led to the Kampala Accord and in 2012 after the UN Group of Experts accused Uganda of supporting the M23 rebels in the DRC.

[9] http://www.peaceau.org/uploads/press-statement-mocc-11.11.2016v2.pdf

[10] Gildas Yihundimpundu, 'Burundi's president issues ultimatum over unpaid AMISOM salaries', *IOL* (South Africa), 30 December 2016, http://www.iol.co.za/news/africa/burundis-president-issues-ultimatum-over-unpaid-amisom-salaries-7299379 and Ngendakumana, 'Towards a lawsuit'.

[11] For good discussions, see William J. Durch, 'Supporting Peace: The End', *Prism*, 2:1 (2010) and William J. Durch, 'Exit and Peace Support Operations' in Richard Caplan (ed.), *Exit Strategies and State Building* (Oxford: Oxford University Press, 2012).

when Washington was concerned about avoiding 'mission creep' and getting bogged down in a longer term state-building operation.[12]

Strategy involves figuring out how to sensibly get from one stage to the next in the conflicted relationship(s) in question. It is a perpetual process of diagnosing the current set of problems faced and how to move beyond them and onto the next set of problems.[13] An 'exit' is therefore best thought of as a process rather than a discrete event that occurs on a particular date. In contemporary peace operations, this has usually revolved around identifying and trying to achieve particular milestones or benchmarks.

When the mandated tasks are difficult, exit is likely to be a long process. This is especially true for missions with state-building components in their mandates. The World Bank, for example, concluded that transitions to just a 'good enough' level of governance in even the most successful developing states emerging from war probably take between ten and forty years, with most countries taking well over twenty years.[14] In this sense, AMISOM's ten years in the field is not excessive given its mandated tasks.

Finally, as an inherently political process, a peace operation's exit strategy will generally encounter fewer challenges the more support it enjoys from local elites. When key elements of an exit strategy are at variance with the interests of local elites, successful withdrawal will be very difficult unless the peace operation can generate considerable leverage over the conflict parties, which is rarely the case. In this sense, AMISOM's exit strategy was always intimately connected to the behaviour of Somalia's political elites.

Understood in this manner, there are at least six ways a peace operation can end (see Table 13.1).[15]

A Designated Timetable: One option is for a peace operation to end at a predetermined point. This might be a specified period of time or it might be a schedule tied to a particular event (the date of which might alter).

Cut and Run: In some cases, the authorities responsible for a peace operation may decide to terminate the mission before it has achieved its stated object-ives. This could happen owing to a reluctance to suffer more sunk costs with the prospect of little forthcoming benefit; a change in conditions which render the stated objectives increasingly difficult to achieve; or recognition that the stated objectives were unrealistic or mistaken in the first place.

Expulsion: Peace operations may sometimes have to exit a theatre because they are legally required to do so after the host state government withdraws

---

[12] Gideon Rose, 'The Exit Strategy Delusion', *Foreign Affairs*, 77:1 (1998), pp. 56–67.

[13] Lawrence Freedman, *Strategy: A History* (New York: Oxford University Press, 2013).

[14] World Development Report, *Conflict, Security and Development* (Washington DC: World Bank, 2011), p. 109.

[15] My list builds upon that provided by Richard Caplan, 'Exit Strategies and State Building' in Caplan (ed.), *Exit Strategies and State Building*, pp. 9–11.

Table 13.1. Summary of potential modes of exit for peace operations

Exit Mechanism	Description
A Designated Timetable	Withdrawal is fixed to a predetermined period of time.
Cut and Run	The mandating authorities decide to terminate the mission before it has achieved its stated objectives.
Expulsion	Exit follows the host state authority's withdrawal of consent for the operation's presence.
Sequencing	Devise withdrawal plan based on predetermined sequenced objectives.
Benchmarking	Devise withdrawal plan based on indicators of progress towards the mission's mandated goals.
Successor Mission(s)	Transition some or all of its forces into a successor operation.

Source: Compiled by author.

its consent for the mission's presence. Interestingly, although no host government has ever expelled an AU peace operation, in 2013 the Somali Federal Government called for the withdrawal of the Kenyan contingent in AMISOM.[16] The Somali Parliament also called for the KDF's withdrawal from Somalia in November 2015.[17]

Sequencing: Peace operations are sometimes designed with sequenced objectives in order to facilitate the mission's departure. For example, a mission with a nation-building mandate might be designed to ensure public security and humanitarian assistance, restore governance, then economic stabilization, followed by democratization, and finally long-term development aid.[18]

Benchmarking: First used by UN peacekeeping operations in the case of UNAMSIL in Sierra Leone from 1999, benchmarks are indicators of progress towards a mission's mandated goals. There is a potentially wide range of benchmarks to inform an operation's exit strategy, from the reduction of organized violence to security sector reform to conducting free and fair elections in the host state.

Successor Mission(s): A peace operation can also exit by transitioning some or all of its forces into a successor operation. Exit thus entails passing on the peacekeeping baton to another actor or placing it in the hands of a different institutional authority. Such successor operations might be authorized and conducted by the same set of stakeholders; for example, the transition from UNOSOM I to the much larger and more ambitious UNOSOM II in Somalia

[16] See Bruton and Williams, *Counterinsurgency in Somalia*, p. 69.
[17] 'Somalia's parliament votes to evict Kenyan troops', *Economist Intelligence Unit*, 23 November 2015, http://country.eiu.com/article.aspx?articleid=253705409&Country=Somalia&topic=Politics&subtopic=Forecast&subsubtopic=International+relations&u=1&pid=695734653&oid=695734653&uid=1
[18] James Dobbins et al., *The Beginner's Guide to Nation-Building* (Arlington, VA: RAND, 2007).

Table 13.2. Modes of exit in major foreign military operations in Somalia, 1992–2015

Operation	Year of Exit	Precipitated By	Mechanism	Success or Failure
UNOSOM I	1993	Changed circumstances	Successor mission	Failure
UNITAF	1993	Avoid quagmire	Successor mission	Partial Success
UNOSOM II	1995	Withdrawal of key TCC	Phased withdrawal	Failure
IGASOM*	2006	N/A—did not deploy	Successor mission	Failure
International Stabilization Force*	2008	N/A—did not deploy	Successor mission	Failure
Ethiopian Intervention 1	2009	Avoid quagmire	Phased withdrawal + successor mission	Partial Success
Kenyan Intervention	2012	Legitimacy & financial costs	Rehatted forces	Partial Success
Ethiopian Intervention 2	2014	Legitimacy & financial costs	Rehatted forces	Partial Success
Ethiopian Intervention 3	Mostly 2016/17	Lack of international finance	None	Too soon to tell

* Operation did not deploy but conceptualized an exit strategy nevertheless.

in 1993. Alternatively, there could be a transfer of authority from one set of stakeholders to another; for example, transitioning an African-led mission into a UN peacekeeping operation. As discussed below, this approach was evident in Somalia and was the exit strategy initially envisaged for AMISOM.

In order to provide some country-specific historical context for the analysis of AMISOM, Table 13.2 summarizes how nine previous foreign military operations in Somalia managed their exit process between 1992 and 2015.

The most relevant missions for AMISOM were arguably IGAD Peace Support Mission to Somalia (IGASOM) and several of the unilateral Kenyan and Ethiopian interventions. As discussed in Chapter 1, although IGASOM did not deploy, its envisaged exit strategy was clear: a form of institutional transfer wherein IGASOM would transition into an AU-led operation. As discussed in Chapter 2, for Ethiopia's initial intervention in 2006, AMISOM's deployment was a way to withdraw its troops while leaving behind a security presence to defend the TFG in Mogadishu. The original plan was that AMISOM would be transitioned into a UN peacekeeping operation by August 2007. The problem was that AMSIOM's failure to generate sufficient numbers of troops and contributing countries meant that Ethiopian forces became stuck in Somalia without an alternative security force to cover its withdrawal. By late 2008, Meles Zenawi was facing increasing domestic pressure to leave Somalia because of the growing financial burden and criticism from within the EPRDF.[19] To save a partial success (installing the TFG), the ENDF was forced to wait over eighteen months longer than it wanted for AMISOM troops to arrive in sufficient strength to facilitate its exit.

AMISOM was also the way out for Kenya's unilateral Operation *Linda Nchi* (2011–12) (analysed in Chapter 5). Kenya's exit strategy was to rehat the majority of its forces into a successor mission, namely, AMISOM. Kenyan authorities would subsequently supplement their forces in AMISOM with additional air and maritime assets that were not put under AU command and control.

When Ethiopian forces returned to Somalia in unilateral operations in December 2011, most of them too were eventually rehatted into AMISOM in January 2014. As discussed in Chapter 6, this was made possible by the UN Security Council authorizing a temporary 'surge' in AMISOM's authorized strength up to 22,126 uniformed personnel. For Ethiopia, financial concerns were arguably the most important factor that led to over 4,000 ENDF soldiers joining AMISOM. Like Kenya, Ethiopia continued to conduct unilateral operations in Somalia in support of its AMISOM contingent.

These earlier examples illustrate just how much political pressure was absorbed by AMISOM in terms of providing the exit strategy for four different military operations in Somalia. This suggests that despite all the problems these military operations generated, foreign powers were reluctant to completely remove their forces and disengage from Somalia. Instead, what started as unilateral operations by Kenya and Ethiopia that were intended to create buffer zones or neutralize the perceived threat within Somalia were largely (if not completely) integrated into AMISOM. The original plan for both Ethiopia and Kenya was to increase their influence at the local level in Somalia, and by extension increase their leverage over the Federal Government. For AMISOM this created a major challenge: how to ensure the national interests of these frontline states did not override the mission's mandate to support the Federal Government?

THE EVOLUTION OF AMISOM'S EXIT STRATEGY

AMISOM had a theory of its exit strategy since day one. In the AU's original conception of the mission, AMISOM was supposed to last only six months before its responsibilities were taken over by the UN. This exit strategy was based on the recommendation of the AU Technical Assessment Mission, which had visited Mogadishu on 13–15 January 2007. Specifically, the AU stated that: 'AMISOM shall be deployed for a period of 6 months, aimed essentially at contributing to the initial stabilization phase in Somalia, with a clear understanding that the mission will evolve into a United Nations

---

[19] Wikileak Cable 08ADDISABABA3393, 19 December 2008.

operation that will support the long term stabilization and post-conflict reconstruction of Somalia'.[20] This decision was taken without also being authorized by the UN Security Council.[21] This approach was reflected in AMISOM's original concept of operations, which envisaged the mission unfolding in four phases.[22] Phase IV, titled, 'Redeployment / Exit Phase', was to coincide with a foreseen handover to a UN peacekeeping operation.

In AMISOM's next Strategic Directive of May 2008, the mission's overall objective was to 'create a safe and secure environment in preparation for the transition to the UN'.[23] AMISOM's 'End State' was defined in the following terms: 'the consolidation of the TFG's authority in Somalia will have been established to allow for continuation and transition of the AMISOM responsibilities to follow-on UN Peacekeeping authorities'.[24] To achieve this goal, AMISOM was conceptualized as having four phases: an Initial Deployment phase; an Expansion of Deployment phase; a Consolidation phase; and, finally, a Redeployment/Exit Phase. In what was presumably an uncorrected error, the directive envisaged a handover 'to the advance contingent of a UN led peacekeeping mission within six months'.[25] Importantly, one of the assumptions built into the directive was that 'The TFG will agree to the envisaged transition of peacekeeping authority in Somalia from AMISOM to the UN'.[26]

As discussed in Chapter 2, in late 2008, the concept of a UN-authorized ISF was briefly floated by the AU and the George W. Bush administration in the United States as an interim mechanism to withdraw AMISOM and eventually replace it with a UN peacekeeping operation. However, the Stabilization Force concept failed to gain traction with any potential TCCs and thus quickly disappeared.[27] From that point on, the UN Secretary-General explored other options to support AMISOM, which would eventually produce UNSOA in 2009 (as analysed in Chapters 3 and 8). Ever since UN Security Council resolution 1863 (16 January 2009), the UN kept open the possibility that it might take over from AMISOM given the right conditions on the ground in Somalia.

Between early 2009 and August 2011 when AMISOM forces succeeded in driving the main *al-Shabaab* force out of Mogadishu, very little changed in the way AMISOM thought about its exit strategy. The only issue that received

---

[20] Cited in PSC/PR/2(LXIX), 19 January 2007, §33d and then PSC/PR/Comm(LXIX), 19 January 2007, §9.

[21] UN Security Council resolution 1744 (20 February 2007) noted the AU's decision (preamble) and requested the Secretary-General to assess, within sixty days, the possibility of deploying a UN peacekeeping operation to Somalia following AMISOM's deployment (§9).

[22] The document was available at AMISOM's webpages at http://au.int/RO/AMISOM/about/military/concept-operation-conops [accessed 14 April 2012] but was subsequently removed.

[23] *Strategic Directive for the African Union Mission in Somalia (AMISOM)* (AU internal document, 20 May 2008), §22.

[24] *Ibid.*, §27.　　　[25] *Ibid.*, §24f.　　　[26] *Ibid.*, §23c.

[27] *Report of the Secretary-General on the Situation in Somalia* (S/2008/709, 17 November 2008), §31–43.

increased attention was the growing realization that AMISOM would have to work harder to build a capable set of Somali security forces. Consequently, AMISOM's 2010 revised operational plan noted that 'the ultimate security of Mogadishu and an eventual exit strategy of AMSIOM will largely depend on a well trained, disciplined and cohesive TFG force that is well resourced and motivated'.[28] But little was done in practice to build such a TFG force.

AMISOM's Mission Implementation Plan for 2011 continued in much the same vein, defining the mission's 'vision' as being 'to stabilize the security situation in Somalia and to create a safe and secure environment in preparation for the deployment of a United Nations Mission through the re-hatting of AMISOM'.[29] AMISOM's 'desired political end state' involved the 'immediate term' objective of creating 'an enabling environment for the effective implementation of the stipulated tasks as enshrined in the Transitional Federal Charter'. This was to be achieved 'through both military and institutional building means'.[30] The plan also noted some technical aspects of AMISOM's exit strategy, namely that the transition to a UN peacekeeping operation would be preceded by a joint AU–UN technical assessment mission in Somalia and that when the UN Security Council decided to authorize a UN peacekeeping operation, the 'UN will re-hat AMISOM in line with a set UN criteria and policy'.[31] At this stage, the mission's concept of operations envisaged a UN peacekeeping force of 20,000 personnel.[32] (This figure reflected the AU's desire to increase AMISOM to 20,000. But as discussed in Chapter 4, the UN Security Council rejected that number, instead proposing an increase to 12,000 personnel in resolution 1964 on 22 December 2010.)

In AMISOM's 2012 Mission Implementation Plan the strategic end state was once again defined as 'the consolidation of security and established TFG authority in Somalia that allow for gradual transition of AMISOM responsibilities to UN peacekeeping mission'.[33] Once again, emphasis was placed on empowering Somali security forces to 'gradually take over from over from AMISOM forces as part of the exit strategy'.[34] The January 2012 CONOPS reiterated the same point: that AMISOM's 'eventual exit strategy ... will largely depend on a well trained, disciplined and cohesive TFG force that is well trained, well resourced and motivated under a coordinated command and control'.[35] These points were repeated by AMISOM in May 2012 when the mission noted it 'must be focused on capacity building rather than simply

---

[28] *AMISOM Modified Strategic Plan* (AU internal document, October 2010), p. 64.

[29] *Mission Implementation Plan, March-December 2011* (AU internal document, no date), §5.

[30] *Ibid.*, §30.   [31] *Ibid.*, Annex E.   [32] *Ibid.*, Annex B-7.

[33] *Mission Implementation Plan, January–December 2012* (AU internal document, January 2012), §11.

[34] *Ibid.*, §30. The plan also expanded the mission's objectives to include creating a Somali state 'where democratic freedoms, law and order thrives'.

[35] *Ibid.*, Annex B-8.

sustaining current forces'.[36] Specifically, a successful exit required the mission to plug three gaps: support for the Somali National Security Forces; enhanced capabilities for AMISOM; and a well-resourced and coherent UN role in AMISOM's exit strategy.[37]

In early 2013, the AU Commission's Strategic Review of AMISOM, envisaged the mission as unfolding in three further phases: Phase 1, territorial recovery and consolidation (2013–17); Phase 2, handover and drawdown (2016–18); and Phase 3, drawdown and withdrawal (2017–20).[38] These phases assumed AMISOM would 'facilitate the conduct of general elections by 2016'.[39]

This was followed in mid-2013 by the joint AU–UN benchmarking review. It was this report, completed in October 2013, which first made use of a list of benchmarks for assessing whether the UN should deploy a peacekeeping operation to Somalia to take over from AMISOM. As discussed in Chapter 6, the report listed eight benchmarks that should guide this decision.[40] With these benchmarks still far off, the emphasis was put on enhancing AMISOM and building the capacity of Somalia's own security forces. As noted in Chapters 6 and 7, the major enhancement to AMISOM came in the form of a temporary 'surge' of reinforcements authorized in UN Security Council resolution 2124 in November 2013.[41]

The surge did not change AMISOM's exit strategy but did boost its ability to conduct offensive operations against *al-Shabaab*. It also led to a new concept of operations for AMISOM that included a short section on the mission's exit strategy.[42] This emphasized the need to improve the capacity of the Somali army and police so that they could maintain effective security and thereby eventually 'enable a safer environment for the political process including reconciliation and elections'. The document also envisaged 'a reduction in the tempo of combat operations a few months after holding of the general elections planned for 2016'. This would allow 'for draw down of AMISOM military operations with the possibility of transition to a UN Peacekeeping Operation'. But this would depend on 'the deployment of agreed local administrations to govern and provide services in newly recovered areas in a timely manner, and to coordinate the military, political, governance and service delivery expansion envisaged'. The revised concept of operations used the same three phases for AMISOM's subsequent operations as outlined in the AU

---

[36] Communique of the Joint Security Committee, Mogadishu, 8 May 2012, p. 2.

[37] UNSOM SRSG Nicholas Kay, S/PV.7030, 12 September 2013, p. 5.

[38] *AUC Strategic Review of AMISOM* (2013), p. 9.   [39] *Ibid.*, p. 8.

[40] *Joint Benchmarking Report 2013*, §17.

[41] This resolution built on the earlier communiqué of the AU Peace and Security Council, PSC/PR/COMM.(CCCXCIX), 10 October 2013. The surge was extended by the UN Security Council in S/RES/2232, 28 July 2015, §3.

[42] *Revised Concept of Operations for AMISOM* (AU internal document, January 2014), §21–2.

Commission's Strategic Review of 2013, namely, Phase 1, territorial recovery and consolidation (2013–17); Phase 2, handover and drawdown (2016–18); and Phase 3, drawdown and withdrawal (2017–20).

After conducting Operations Eagle, Indian Ocean, Ocean Build, and planning for the shaping phase of Operation Juba Corridor, in mid-2015, the AU and UN conducted another benchmarking review. As detailed in Chapter 7, this set out a revised list of the eight benchmarks for a transition from AMISOM to a UN peacekeeping operation previously identified in the 2013 joint review.[43]

Several notable conclusions emerge from even this short overview of AMISOM's official discourse on its exit strategy. First, for roughly ten years, there was consistent tactical evolution in the way AMISOM conceptualized its exit strategy while retaining roughly the same strategic objective. Second, AMISOM evolved with little prospect of the UN deploying a peacekeeping operation and little appetite (at least on the UN side) for a joint AU–UN mission as recommended by the 2013 AU Strategic Review team. This necessitated greater attention on how to enhance AMISOM and prepare it for a longer haul rather than focus on the modalities of a transition to a UN or a joint AU–UN operation. Third, over time, increasing emphasis was given to building effective local security capabilities, particularly the SNA and to a lesser extent the SPF. Fourth, AMISOM identified the need for two interrelated transitions: first, a transition from operations led by foreign forces to Somali-led operations;[44] and, second, a transition from military-led operations to police-led operations, especially in the newly recovered settlements and Somalia's regions more generally.[45]

PRACTICAL CHALLENGES TO AMISOM'S EXIT

As can be seen from the preceding discussion of AMISOM's plans, a successful exit would require the mission to achieve its three strategic objectives, namely, to help facilitate a political settlement that clarified the federal structures that would govern relations between Somalia's centre and its regions; to degrade *al-Shabaab*; and enable stabilization efforts in the recovered areas by supporting local authorities to deliver a genuine peace dividend to local

---

[43] *Joint Benchmarking Review 2015*, §42.

[44] This would likely unfold in four phases: 1) AMISOM leads operations with SNA support; 2) joint AMISOM/SNA operations; 3) SNA leads operations with AMISOM support; and 4) SNA conducting operations alone.

[45] Eventually, there must be an additional transition from policing focused on counter-insurgency against *al-Shabaab* towards more general community policing.

populations. In order to make progress on these three goals AMISOM had to overcome five major practical challenges.

Challenge 1: The Lack of a Political Settlement

AMISOM's most fundamental problem was that the process of constructing a federal state in Somalia not only failed to make sufficient progress but sometimes actively generated conflict between the subsequent centres of power across the south-central part of the country. AMISOM was mandated to support the Federal Government but had to operate without an overarching political settlement setting out how Somalia should be governed and by whom. The underlying problem, as the UN Monitoring Group on Somalia put it, was the inability of 'Somalia's political elite to prioritize the long-term goals of State-building over the short-term capture of State resources'.[46]

The subsequent lack of national elite consensus about the political vision that should guide security sector reform generated several practical challenges for AMISOM's desired exit strategy. First, it led to considerable delays over how to interpret the country's provincial constitution, which was finally adopted in 2012, and choosing the next Federal Government. Originally, the Federal Government's 'Vision 2016' envisaged one-person one-vote elections would establish a new administration by August 2016. In July 2015, however, the Federal Government publicly gave up on this idea and instead opted for a process of intra-elite consultations and selection aimed at enhancing the legitimacy of whatever government emerged from that process.[47] As discussed in Chapter 7, the new President was hence not chosen until January 2017. The numerous rounds of infighting amongst Somalia's political elites distracted them from building a genuinely national army and police force and taking the fight to *al-Shabaab*. As the arguments over the formation of the Interim Jubaland Administration in 2013 illustrated, the Federal Government's central problem was that its sovereign authority was recognized internationally, but this did not automatically translate into its decisions being accepted domestically by Somali power brokers outside the Banadir region (see Chapter 6).

For AMISOM, the fractured politics generated an additional set of tasks related to providing security and logistical support at the numerous regional conferences and meetings across south-central Somalia that took place in the process of establishing the interim regional administrations. Since most of the influential players in the process of establishing the regional administrations derived their power from clan affiliations rather than political parties or religious

---

[46] *SEMG Report*, 19 October 2015, p. 6.
[47] See The Somalia National Consultative Forum on the Electoral Process in 2016, *Facilitation Guide* (no date), https://www.scribd.com/doc/287843236/Facilitation-Guide

movements, it highlighted that *al-Shabaab* was not the only security threat facing the Federal Government and AMISOM. Among the most important were clan conflicts over the newly recovered towns, inter-communal clashes, and fighting over land and water resources.[48]

The second major problem for AMISOM (and its international partners) was that Somalia was left without a national security strategy setting out the vision for and roles of its security forces. Without such a document there could be no clarity on how to build truly national and inclusive security forces and what form they should take. As analysed in Chapter 9, the *Guulwade* ('Victory') and *Heegan* ('Readiness') plans that emerged in 2015 were poor substitutes. It was not until July 2017 that Somalia developed its first national defence strategy, which among other things provided some indication of the force structure that international partners could help build.

Challenge 2: The Threat of al-Shabaab

Although *al-Shabaab* had been weakened significantly since its 'golden age' (2009–10), it still posed a deadly threat to AMISOM, the Somali security forces and government officials, and civilians.[49] As discussed in Chapter 7, AMISOM's expansion and consolidation operations since 2014 did not deal a major blow to *al-Shabaab*'s combat capabilities. Nor did they stop *al-Shabaab* benefiting from the illicit trades in charcoal and sugar. In this sense, AMISOM continued to face an adaptable enemy that was down but not out.

First of all, *al-Shabaab* continued to wage an effective war of destabilization and harassment using a flexible range of tactics. It proved able to disrupt AMISOM's main supply routes, which also generated problems for delivering humanitarian relief supplies that could reduce local reliance on *al-Shabaab*. It was also able to establish enough roadblocks and taxation points to generate significant revenue and continue exerting influence over the local population. The militants also evolved their use of IEDs and suicide attacks. And when waging a war of destabilization, *al-Shabaab* needed only to survive and launch reasonably regular attacks to be deemed effective.

Second, AMISOM's operations prompted some members of *al-Shabaab* to relocate north into Puntland and south into Kenya, perhaps most notably in the Boni forest.[50] Since these were both outside AMISOM's area of operations,

---

[48] See *SEMG Report*, 19 October 2015, p. 6.

[49] The phrase is from Hansen, *Al-Shabaab in Somalia*, Chapter 6.

[50] One of *al-Shabaab*'s recent propaganda videos even extolled the virtues of jihadi life in Kenya's Boni forest where its fighters could feast on giraffe and other local wildlife. 'The Tourism of my Ummah is Jihad' (Al-Kataib Foundation, 2015).

the AU mission was limited to addressing only one geographic portion of an increasingly transnational organization.[51]

Third, *al-Shabaab* still retained its ability to blend with the local population, and hence enjoy relative freedom of movement, and also to infiltrate the Somali security forces, including on 25 December 2014 gaining access to AMISOM's main base at Mogadishu International Airport. As well as enabling surprise attacks, this made it difficult for AMISOM to assess the extent to which it was actually degrading *al-Shabaab*. And as analysed in Chapter 7, *al-Shabaab*'s ability to launch larger-scale conventional attacks against AMISOM and SNA forward bases kept its propaganda machine running.

In sum, *al-Shabaab* lost the political significance and numerous settlements it once held in Somalia, but it remained a deadly foe, able to conduct operations cheaply and effectively, in part because of its ability to infiltrate government forces, and in part because its freedom of movement enabled it to choose the time and place of its attacks against overstretched AMISOM and SNA forces.[52]

Challenge 3: AMISOM's Internal Problems

A third set of challenges jeopardizing AMISOM's effective exit was problems and limitations within the mission itself. Recall that the AMISOM that existed on paper in UN Security Council resolutions and AU communiqués was not the same as the AMISOM that existed on the ground. In the field, AMISOM suffered from several major internal problems that hindered its ability to achieve its mandated tasks.

AMISOM's first internal challenge was its persistent lack of military enablers. Perhaps most notably, AMISOM was forced to conduct its offensive operations without sufficient military helicopters, armoured vehicles, ISR capabilities, and a quick reaction strike force (ideally comprising air mobile troops) that could operate across AMISOM's sectors. All these capabilities had been authorized in previous UN Security Council resolutions, some more than five years ago. Yet AU member states and external partners consistently failed to deliver them to the commanders in the field.

As noted in Chapter 5, the lack of military helicopters in particular left AMISOM without the ability to strike *al-Shabaab* in depth and enabled the militants to simply retreat before AMISOM's greater firepower, while

---

[51] See Anderson and McKnight, 'Kenya at war', and *Al-Shabaab as a Transnational Security Threat* (IGAD and Sahan Foundation, March 2016).

[52] The extent to which there was ongoing collusion between some members of the Somali political elite, including Members of Parliament, and *al-Shabaab* remained an open but important question.

retaining the luxury of freedom of movement across large parts of Somalia. Although both Ethiopia and Kenya deployed their own air assets inside Somalia, they were not part of AMISOM and hence were not able to deliver sustained or coordinated cross-sector operations. It was only in December 2016 that AMISOM acquired three military utility helicopters from Kenya. Helicopters would also have been useful to provide rapid response and protection of AMISOM's supply routes and bases. Logistical issues were analysed at length in Chapter 8, but they also impinged on AMISOM's ability to implement an effective exit strategy. Another important gap was in the area of civil affairs, which hindered AMISOM's ability to roll out effective stabilization programmes in the liberated settlements, either on its own or in tandem with Somali authorities (see Chapter 12).

A second challenge stemmed from problems in AMISOM's command and control structures. While the lack of centralized control over the operation's contingents had the benefit of ensuring autonomy and flexibility of action for the TCCs, it also made internal cohesion and cross-sector operations difficult. Some *al-Shabaab* fighters were thus able to hide in the areas between AMISOM's sector boundaries.[53] Finally, there also appear to have been some significant lapses in the command of particular bases, most notably perhaps the Ugandan FOB at Janaale in September 2015 (see Chapter 7).

A third problem, as discussed in Chapter 10, was misconduct by some AMISOM personnel. Arguably the most egregious examples were the killing of local civilians and allegations of sexual exploitation and abuse. Such actions tarnished AMISOM's relations with the local population and gave a boost to *al-Shabaab*'s propaganda.

Finally, as noted at the start of this chapter, some AMISOM TCCs also complained of their troops suffering from reduced morale because of the lack or reduced amounts of allowances payments. This reduced their willingness to conduct risky operations.

Challenge 4: Problems in the Somali National Army

AMISOM's limitations in the field were amplified by the failings of its principal military partner, the SNA. Effective operations against *al-Shabaab* clearly required good coordination between AMISOM and the SNA. However, this was not always possible because of the dire state of many SNA units, which suffered from shortfalls in equipment, infrastructure, organization, and morale. In short, as one senior AMISOM official put it, 'it would be

---

[53] Interviews, AU and US officials, Nairobi, 9 April 2015; US officials, Djibouti, 2 March 2016.

irresponsible for AMISOM to leave Somalia without leaving behind a set of local security forces that could contain *al-Shabaab*'.[54]

Like AMISOM, and as discussed in Chapter 9, the SNA lacked capabilities in almost every area, including mobility (especially armoured vehicles); all types of ammunition;[55] heavy weapons; communications equipment; field defences; as well as specialist vehicles such as ambulances and water trucks. The SNA also suffered major shortages and problems related to training, logistics capacity, vehicle maintenance facilities, arms and ammunition storage facilities, medical support (medical facilities and ambulances), and barracks for its troops. To make matters worse, it also suffered from a missing generation of junior officers and non-commissioned officers, which would take considerable time to develop and train.

There were more political problems too. For AMISOM's entire duration, the SNA also remained largely a collection of militias that owed their principal allegiance to individual commanders and clans and regional formations rather than the Federal Government. Without genuine loyalty to the Somali state there could be no effective command and control structure for the SNA as a whole.

Command and control was also undermined by corruption. Some of the SNA's senior military leaders proved time and again they were corrupt, which undermined the ability of outsiders to build a professional military force.[56] For example, the inability or unwillingness to address the endemic corruption among senior officials connected to the SNA made some external donors reluctant to provide it with the tools to lead the fight against *al-Shabaab*. The British government, for instance, would not provide lethal equipment to the SNA out of concerns about lack of oversight and the potential for the diversion of arms and ammunition.[57] Similarly, the UN Security Council granted only a partial lifting of the arms embargo on Somalia, which still prevents the SNA from purchasing heavy weapons (although it received considerable amounts of small arms and ammunition). This left the SNA in the rather odd position of having fewer heavy weapons than several clan militias.[58] The Federal Government also regularly failed to pay salaries to its soldiers, which did not help earn their loyalty or boost their morale.

---

[54] Communication, senior AMISOM official, 7 November 2015.

[55] Although note that the UN Monitoring Group on Somalia concluded the SNA should have received about 9 million rounds of ammunition. *SEMG Report*, 19 October 2015, §136.

[56] On misappropriation and corruption in the Somali security sector see *ibid.*, §67–9.

[57] See the comments of the UK Ambassador to Somalia on Twitter, 4 November 2015, https://twitter.com/harrietlmathews/status/661903179311878145

[58] For example, the SNA did not own a single tank whereas several clan militias possessed multiple tanks, mostly acquired after the collapse of Siad Barre's regime in 1991. Communication, Federal Government official, 2 November 2015.

In sum, the Somali authorities faced the very difficult challenge of simultaneously building a new army and fight a war with it. But this considerably reduced AMISOM's ability to implement an effective exit strategy.

Challenge 5: Negative Local Perceptions of AMISOM

Generally speaking, the longer a peace operation remains in its host country, the harder it has to work to avoid local criticism.[59] Although some AMISOM survey data suggests that after a bad start, Somali perceptions of the mission improved especially after *al-Shabaab* was forced out of Mogadishu in 2011, the AU force struggled to consistently win the trust and support of the Somali populace, its security forces, and even some of the country's political elites.[60] As noted in Chapter 11, AMISOM suffered a significant drop in its popularity with local citizens between 2014 and 2016.

Negative perceptions of AMISOM stemmed from several sources including views that AMISOM had become a vehicle for Somalia's neighbours to pursue their own selfish agendas, a money-making enterprise for its contributing countries which had reduced the incentive to defeat *al-Shabaab*, and a source of harm to Somali civilians as well as a distraction from the more important job of building effective Somali security forces.[61]

Within the SNA, there was at times significant resentment towards AMISOM, evident within both the leadership and rank and file. For the aging professional SNA commanders who where part of Somalia's army before 1990, reliance on foreign troops was a constant reminder of Somali weakness. That Ethiopia and Kenya played leading roles in AMISOM just added to the discontent. Some senior officers went as far as describing the current situation as the effective occupation of Somalia by Ethiopian and Kenyan troops.[62] The goal of these outside powers was often thought to be keeping Somalia weak and manipulating the formation of regional administrations in areas under their influence in order to increase their leverage over

[59] This section draws on Paul D. Williams with Abdirashid Hashi, *Exit Strategy Challenges for the AU Mission in Somalia* (Mogadishu: Heritage Institute for Policy Studies, February 2016), pp. 34–5.

[60] Polling of just over 1,031 adults carried out during March and April 2013 in Mogadishu for the AU–UN Information Support Team suggested that 59 per cent felt that AMISOM had been 'very' or 'fairly' effective in providing security for the local community. Communication, AU–UN IST official, 10 October 2013.

[61] For a flavour of some of these criticisms see '*They Say They're Not Here to Protect Us*'. *Civilian perspectives on the African Union Mission in Somalia* (International Refugee Rights Initiative, May 2017).

[62] Communication, senior SNA officer, 10 December 2015; interview Somali government official, Djibouti, 27 February 2016.

the Somali Federal Government. Such perceptions were reflected in 2016 opinion polling which found that only 10 per cent of respondents thought Kenyan troops were in Somalia for the benefit of the Somalia people. The figure for Ethiopia was just 9 per cent. In contrast, 52 per cent of respondents answered in the affirmative about Djibouti.[63]

Arguments arose between the Somali federal authorities and Kenya over accusations that Kenyan troops were involved in the illicit trade in charcoal and sugar that was indirectly benefiting *al-Shabaab*.[64] But there were also tensions when Nairobi began issuing concessions in the oil-rich Indian Ocean maritime border that Somalia claimed as its own. In mid-2014, this prompted Somalia to ask the International Court of Justice in The Hague to determine the maritime boundary between the two countries.

Rank and file SNA troops are also well aware of their inferior status to AMISOM in terms of power, money and influence, despite often fighting alongside AU forces since 2009 without the luxury of sophisticated weapons, armoured vehicles, good communications equipment, regular salaries, dedicated medical care, or even barracks. Their AMISOM counterparts generally remained better armed, better fed, better protected, better supplied, better cared for when wounded, and better paid. This led Somali commanders to criticize the proportion of external resources allocated to AMISOM in comparison to the Somali army and police. As one senior officer put it in 2011, 'the principle [*sic*] motive of the international community has been the defeat of Alshabaab [*sic*], and not the creation of a Somali national army'.[65] That is an important distinction.

AMISOM also received criticism for not sufficiently securing Mogadishu after *al-Shabaab* withdrew its main forces.[66] It also came in for criticisms for failing to protect Somali parliamentarians, especially when they were outside legislature sessions. Between 2012 and 2015, for instance, more than 4 per cent of Somali parliamentarians were killed. This and other forms of violence led some Somali parliamentarians to openly criticize AMISOM's presence, question its performance, and raise doubts about the mission's long-term prospects.[67] Civil society and diaspora groups also regularly voiced critical opinions, including that AMISOM absorbed resources that would be better

---

[63] *Citizens Perception of Peace and Stabilization Initiative in Somalia: Mid-line Survey Report* (Ipsos unpublished document, July 2016).

[64] See, for example, the reports of the UN Monitoring Group on Somalia since 2012 and Journalists for Justice, *Black and White*.

[65] [Name withheld. Senior TFG military commander.] *Brief Report on the Situation of Somalia's Security Forces* (Unpublished document, October 2011), p. 9.

[66] For example, Faisal A. Roble, 'Challenges and Opportunities and the Firing of Prime Minister Saacid', *Waardheernews*, 11 November 2013, at http://www.wardheernews.com/challenges-opportunities-firing-prime-minister-saacid/

[67] Faisal Roble, 'The town hall meeting that shook Somalia', *WardheerNews*, 17 October 2015, http://www.wardheernews.com/the-town-hall-meeting-that-shook-somalia/

given to local organizations, and that the mission was trying to tackle too wide a range of non-peacekeeping issues, including holding workshops on leadership, citizenship, and even female genital mutilation.

AMISOM was also criticized by Somali civilians, perhaps most notably by the famous cartoons published by Amin Arts. Most ordinary Somalis in towns with an AMISOM presence had limited interactions with the peacekeepers or saw little direct benefit from the AU mission, which focused its protection efforts on top government officials and around vital strategic facilitates such as Mogadishu's seaport and airport. Misconduct by AMISOM personnel was also a major source of complaints, as discussed in Chapter 10. Civilians living in some of the newly recovered settlements also criticized AMISOM's inability to prevent *al-Shabaab* forces blockading their towns.[68] The abrupt withdrawal of AMISOM forces from some of the newly liberated towns and forward positions also generated anger for exposing Somali security forces, civilian administrators, and ordinary citizens to grave risks, especially those who publicly welcomed the arrival of AU contingents. AMISOM's decision to commandeer various private and public properties and convert them into military bases—including the University of Kismayo and Stadium Mogadishu—also became a source of public debate and sometimes criticism. Nor was it lost on Somalis that most of AMISOM's major contributing countries were poor role models for good governance for the Federal Government or IRAs to follow.

Overall, by June 2016, there was a 'a high level of disillusionment about AMISOM' with 48 per cent of surveyed Somali citizens wanting to see AMISOM leave immediately (the figure was 55 per cent among Mogadishu residents); 18 per cent wanted the AU mission to stay for just six more months, 12 per cent for another six months to two years, and only 12 per cent wanted the AU mission to stay for more than two years. In contrast, in 2014, only 15 per cent of respondents had wanted AMISOM to leave immediately.[69]

THE BEGINNING OF THE END

How AMISOM will cope with these five challenges remains to be seen, but the outcome will significantly affect its exit from Somalia. In light of the AU's ten-year lessons learned exercise on AMISOM conducted in early 2017, and

[68] See, for example, 'Somalia: Humanitarian situation in besieged town sours', *Horseed Media*, 15 July 2015, https://horseedmedia.net/2015/07/15/somalia-humanitarian-situation-in-besieged-town-sours/

[69] Ipsos, *Citizens Perception of Peace*.

the AU–UN Joint Review of AMISOM conducted in mid-2017, AMISOM's partners set out their transition plan. Its key elements were as follows.[70]

The first, and arguably most crucial point was the commitment of the Somali Federal Government to assume the lead in security responsibilities based on 'a responsible, viable and realistic transition plan'. For its part, AMISOM should therefore follow a realistic time frame for transition linked to conditions on the ground rather than set timetables. This was intended to avoid the risk of a premature AMISOM drawdown generating a security vacuum that could advantage *al-Shabaab* and other opposition groups and the opposite scenario where withdrawing too slowly provided a counterproductive crutch for the Somali security forces that reduced their willingness to assume the lead in providing domestic security.

Second, as the transition to Somali-led operations took place, AMISOM would need to be reconfigured to support the next phase of state building in Somalia. The AU therefore offered yet another revised mandate for AMISOM based around six tasks and the reconfiguration of its forces, notably a reduction of about 2,000 soldiers and an increase of about 500 police.[71] One thousand troops were supposed to be withdrawn by 31 December 2017 while 500 police would be added (comprising two additional FPUs, 120 IPOs, and sixty additional personnel to bring AMISOM's three existing FPUs up to the standard number of 160 personnel). Depending on the conditions in Somalia, a further 1,000 troops would be withdrawn by October 2018. The transition would also require coordinating more joint operations, and therefore increasingly co-locating AMISOM and Somali forces to facilitate the handover of bases.

Third, for co-location and the transition to run smoothly, there was a recognition that a comprehensive assessment of the operational readiness of the Somali security forces was required to catalogue and clarify basic but still unclear issues such as identities of personnel, their locations, weapons, and equipment. This assessment commenced in September 2017. To complicate matters further, there would also need to be a transition from military-led operations to police-led operations and hence a reduction of the size of Somalia's army and an increase in the number of officers in its police forces.

Finally, the whole transition plan rested on the assumption that the AU and its partners could secure predictable funding for AMISOM, the UN missions (UNSOS and UNSOM), and the Somali security forces. So it was that AMISOM ended its first ten years much as it had started: entering an uncertain future and wondering who would pay the bills.

---

[70] PSC/PR/COM.(DCC), 12 July 2017.   [71] See S/RES/2372, 30 August 2017.

Conclusion

This book's two principal aims were to analyse AMISOM's evolution and to understand how the mission and its key partners tried to overcome its major operational challenges. In keeping with the practical purpose of peacekeeping, it also sought to identify lessons from AMISOM's experiences that might improve the mission's effectiveness as well as the design and conduct of peace operations beyond Somalia. Rather than repeating the lessons and conclusions identified in Part II of this book relating to logistics, security sector reform, civilian protection, strategic communications, stabilization, and exit strategy, this concluding chapter reflects on how to assess AMISOM's first ten years and what this means for whether the AMISOM model should be replicated elsewhere.

ASSESSING AMISOM

AMISOM was the AU's longest, largest, most expensive, and most deadly peace operation. Indeed, by mid-2017 it was the largest deployment of uniformed peacekeepers anywhere in the world and in a category all of its own in terms of casualties. But how should we assess the mission overall?

One place to start is with AMISOM's self-assessments. Neither AMISOM nor the AU Commission possessed a dedicated capacity for learning lessons. Unsurprisingly, therefore, AMISOM's own attempts to identify and learn lessons were usually dependent on ad hoc support from some of its partners. As a result, they were usually held outside Somalia, inconsistent in terms of methodology, suffered from limited participation and attendance by key players, and had no means of ensuring that lessons identified were actually learned and acted upon. Between February 2012 and March 2014, for instance, AMISOM held four lessons learned conferences, three of which were supported by the British Peace Support Team in Kenya. All of them were held outside Somalia. Although they proved useful in identifying lessons (sometimes the same ones consistently) there was inconsistent attendance of key personnel and limited follow-up, which produced little consistent implementation to act on them.[1] Other sources of learning came from After Action Reviews conducted by individual AMISOM TCCs. But these were also inconsistent in frequency and methodology and the results not consistently disseminated.

Nevertheless, some of AMISOM's planning documents were clear about what needed to happen for the mission to successfully implement its mandate. The mission's 2013 Strategic Directive, for example, noted that the prospects for success hinged on making progress in several areas. They included progress on achieving national reconciliation and the institutions envisioned under Somalia's provisional Constitution; the development of a professional, non-partisan police, military, intelligence, and civil service to serve all citizens of Somalia; the Federal Government being in a position to assert its authority throughout the country; Somali security forces increasingly able to take the lead role in, and responsibility for, the security of the state of Somalia and the civilian population; essential service delivery is prioritized and essential services restored in the AMISOM Area of Operation; IDPs and refugees continue to return home or a new place of settlement; all key mission personnel and functions are operating from Mogadishu and in all mission sectors; and the security and political situation in Somalia continues to improve. AMISOM's leadership was well aware that if such benchmarks were not met or progress was extremely slow, then the mission would struggle to achieve its goals.

It was not until late 2016 that the AU PSC called upon the Commission to undertake a lessons learned process.[2] This was done to mark the occasion of ten years of AMISOM operations. Concluded in March 2017, this exercise made several recommendations, many of which echo themes discussed at length in this book.[3] At the political level, the AU recognized the uncertainty that had developed regarding AMISOM's role beyond military enforcement, especially what roles its small and understaffed civilian component should play given the presence of UNSOM. There was also recognition that AMISOM needed to devote more emphasis to developing the Somali security forces and more effective strategic communications. At the strategic level, the AU Commission recognized the need to improve its human resources, administrative, and financial procedures to enable better mission support, including through better information sharing and knowledge management. Operationally, the

---

[1] The March 2014 conference, for example, generated lessons related to pre-deployment and in-mission training; joint operations with Somali forces; indirect-fire policy and protection of civilians; interoperability of forces (cultural and doctrinal variances); legal constraints on peace enforcement operations; civil–military cooperation; roles of civilian and police components; media operations; post-traumatic stress disorder management; welfare matters (rest and relaxation, sports amenities); logistics; and troop rotations.

[2] PSC/PR/COMM(DCXXII), 6 September 2016, §11.

[3] *Report on AMISOM Lessons Learned Conference, Nairobi, Kenya, 9–10 March 2017* (AU Commission, 2017), especially pp. 5–7, http://www.peaceau.org/uploads/ll-eng-1.pdf

AU called for more unified command and control within AMISOM and for its capabilities to be aligned with its key tasks related to counterinsurgency, such as mobility, better intelligence gathering, effective logistical support, and counter-IED activities. It was also noted that AMISOM needed a more effective measure of the extent to which it was actually degrading *al-Shabaab*. Consensus also emerged on the need for AMISOM's exit strategy to be conditions based and anchored on the performance of 'an inclusive politically agreed set of Somali security institutions' to enable a transition from AU-led to Somali-led operations. To that end, the document called for greater co-location of SNA and AMISOM units as well as more joint operations and mentoring. Rather ominously, it noted that the mission's 'continued presence in Somalia will be significantly influenced by the availability of predictable and sustainable resources' (see Chapter 13).

The ad hoc nature of these attempts to derive lessons from AMISOM's operations highlights the AU Commission's need for a dedicated lessons learned capacity that is agile enough to inform training, doctrine, and structure. It was therefore a positive, if belated, step when the Commission began to develop a Lessons Learned and Best Practices Cell in late 2016.

From an external perspective, and based on the preceding analysis in Parts I and II of this book, what does AMISOM's balance sheet look like from the vantage point of mid-2017?

The starting point should be recognition that Somalia since early 2007 represented an extremely complex and insecure strategic environment, which fundamentally shaped how AMISOM and its partners operated. Particularly during the first four years, the intense insecurity fuelled international pessimism about the mission, limited the number of TCCs, left the mission under-resourced and hence with no option but to remain on the defensive, and kept AMISOM a military-heavy mission that was unable to deploy significant police and civilian components until 2012. The insecurity in Somalia stemmed from the civil war in the late 1980s and subsequent lack of a functional central government since 1991. This generated a situation where armed groups proliferated in AMISOM's area of operations. Beyond various militant organizations like *al-Ittihad al-Islamiya*, *al-Shabaab*, and *Hizbul Islam*, these included clan militias, clan paramilitaries, district commissioners' militias, business security guards, personal protection units, local private security firms, international private security firms, and neighbourhood watch groups.[4] Any assessment of AMISOM should therefore begin by acknowledging that it faced an extremely difficult strategic environment. It is also worth speculating what Somalia would look like today if AMISOM had

---

[4] Menkhaus, *Non-State Security Providers*, pp. 21–31.

not deployed. My view is that it is highly likely *al-Shabaab* would have toppled the TFG soon after Ethiopia withdrew its forces.[5]

In that sense, AMISOM's first and most important success was its ability to protect the TFG. This was the crucial foundation upon which all other developments in Somalia were based. AMISOM went on to successfully protect the second iteration of the TFG and secure the two electoral processes that produced new Somali Federal Governments in September 2012 and January 2017.

In the process, AMISOM was also able to degrade *al-Shabaab*, certainly from the period of the movement's 'golden age' during 2009 and 2010. Most notably, AMISOM won the battle for Mogadishu during 2010 and 2011, which led *al-Shabaab* to withdraw the majority of its forces from the city. As previously discussed, this was initially made possible by *al-Shabaab*'s counterproductive terrorist attack on Kampala in June 2010 and its failed Ramadan offensive in Mogadishu in August and September 2010. As discussed in Chapter 4, AMISOM was able to sustain an effective offensive because of shifts in its pre-deployment training regimes, the innovative use of urban warfare tactics such as sniper teams, 'mouse holes', and breaching operations, and the sheer resilience of the mission's rank-and-file troops. Importantly, AMISOM was never in a position to defeat *al-Shabaab*, which is a task only Somalis can accomplish. Nor was AMISOM designed and configured to stop *al-Shabaab* waging its subsequent transnational war of destabilization, principally through asymmetric and terror tactics. The ability of *al-Shabaab* fighters to blend with the local population and retain considerable freedom of movement raised regular problems for AMISOM. There was also a persistent and significant risk of the militants infiltrating Somali forces. Nevertheless, *al-Shabaab* in mid-2017 was a weaker organization than it was when the Ethiopians withdrew from Mogadishu in January 2009.

There followed from these strategic successes other positive impacts. For example, AMISOM helped extend humanitarian access and itself provided various forms of humanitarian and medical assistance to significant numbers of Somalis. Its engineering works to rehabilitate some of the country's road network and repair infrastructure were also significant and will probably be its most visible legacy after the mission leaves. AMISOM also succeeded in giving the UN a relatively secure foothold in Somalia, which enabled UNSOM's deployment and expansion from 2013. The same could be said for most of the international embassies that were set up in Mogadishu that relied, in part, on AMISOM's security blanket.

On the other hand, there were also areas that clearly did not go according to the mission plan. Arguably the most damaging of AMISOM's early failures

---

[5] Of course, without AMISOM, it is unclear how long Ethiopian troops would have remained in Mogadishu.

was its inability to stop harming local civilians, either through indirect fire, accidental shootings, traffic accidents, or SEA. As discussed in Chapter 10, AMISOM did not receive a civilian protection mandate because it was focused on protecting the Somali authorities and degrading *al-Shabaab* and neither the AU nor its various partners were willing to provide AMISOM with the additional resources that such a mandate would require. Recall also that the mission's small CCTARC—recommended by the UN Security Council in February 2012—did not become operational until June 2015. AMISOM's reputation was also damaged by allegations of corruption when some of its personnel engaged in the illicit sale of various commodities. This became most politically controversial in relation to the role of Kenyan forces in Sector 2 and Kismayo with regard to the illicit export of charcoal in breach of a UN embargo.

But the most fundamental challenge was aligning AMISOM's military and political tracks. And hence the most important political obstacle was that AMISOM and its partners failed to get Somalia's elites to reconcile, agree on the nature of the new federal state, and genuinely prioritize *al-Shabaab*'s defeat. Ultimately, there was no military solution to Somalia's problems, most of which are fundamentally about issues of governance. In addition, it is Somalis, not foreign peacekeepers, who hold the key to peace. AMISOM therefore found itself in a difficult position because no matter what military successes it achieved, stabilization and sustainable peace in Somalia depended on political progress being made on the fundamental questions of national, regional, and local governance. And on these issues, for most of AMISOM's first ten years, Somalia's political elites failed to reconcile and unite around a shared agenda to defeat *al-Shabaab*. The lack of effective Somali institutions had a particularly important negative impact on AMISOM's ability to pursue its stabilization agenda from 2013. Specifically, after recovering numerous towns, the mission was unable to consistently carry out the 'clear', 'hold', and 'build' phases of its operations because of the lack of governance capacity possessed by the Somali authorities. Hence, in some cases, AMISOM eventually withdrew from recovered towns only for *al-Shabaab* to regain control largely unopposed. For example, six years after expelling *al-Shabaab* from Mogadishu and its environs, at the time of writing (mid-2017), the insurgents were able to hold towns such as Bariire within 60 km of the capital city.

The AU did not always help itself, however, making some errors of its own. Most notable here was the rather distant and disengaged political leadership demonstrated by early heads of the mission who were based outside Somalia. This forced successive AMISOM force commanders to become the default interlocutor with most local stakeholders, a task that they met—through no fault of their own—with inconsistent success. This only intensified AMISOM's problem of aligning the mission's progress on both the military and political tracks. While AMISOM managed at various times to make significant military progress, political processes usually lagged behind and although not solely responsible, the lack of effective AU political leadership in Mogadishu was a contributing factor.

There was also a major political failure with regard to force generation. As a result, AMISOM was left to endure severe capability gaps in two senses. First, the capabilities authorized by the AU and UN for the mission were insufficient to achieve its stated objectives, especially once it expanded beyond Mogadishu. This was in large part due to the faulty assumption that the SNA would be able to field over 15,000 effective troops. Second, the AU and its partners failed to deploy some of the capabilities they had authorized for AMISOM. Put simply, the AU's political leaders and their international partners failed to generate AMISOM's authorized resources. The result was large and persistent vacancy rates, a lack of critical enablers such as aviation, engineering, medical, special forces, mine action and unexploded ordinance disposal, heavy transportation, ISR units, and night-fighting capabilities, as well as a woefully short-staffed civilian component, which struggled to hire and retain sufficient numbers of personnel. There was a related failure to secure predictable, sustainable, and flexible financing for the mission. This resulted in the allowances for AMISOM's peacekeepers being regularly delayed and not always aligned with the rates available to UN peacekeepers (see Figure 13.1).[6] It is difficult to assess precisely what impact this had on morale and the overall effectiveness of the mission, but its effect was not positive.

Finally, the mission failed to establish a unified system of command and control. As discussed in earlier chapters, there were sometimes technical limitations and challenges that led to the breakdown of the chain of command such as the lack of a dedicated mission signal unit and of signalmen to staff existing communications nets. But the more fundamental issues were political. When the mission's contingents suffered from various interoperability issues it was not surprising that the national contingents usually listened to their national commanders and capitals before the AMISOM force commander. Nevertheless, the fact that in February 2016, after nearly nine years of operations, the AU Commissioner for Peace and Security had to make a strong public appeal for the TCCs to follow the force commander's orders revealed much about how the real chain of command worked in the mission.[7] This had several negative consequences, but probably the most obvious was the mission's subsequent inability to launch and coordinate cross-sector operations, which allowed *al-Shabaab* to seek relative safety in the borders between AMISOM's sectors.

---

[6] For details on the bureaucratic reasons for some of the delays see Williams, 'Paying for AMISOM'.

[7] Djibouti Declaration, Djibouti, 28 February 2016, at https://www.un.int/djibouti/news/summit-troop-and-police-contributing-countries-african-union-mission-somalia-amisom

THE AMISOM 'MODEL' REVISITED

Where does this leave the AMISOM model as a form of international conflict management? This is, of course, an important question for the AU as it develops revised doctrine for its peace operations. It will also affect how the UN and AU should best strengthen their partnership on peace and security issues, including whether the AU should always look to quickly transition its peace operations into UN missions.[8] It is also relevant to deciding whether the AU and its international partners should embrace the growing tendency of establishing ad hoc coalitions authorized by the AU to fight non-state enemies such as the Lord's Resistance Army, Boko Haram, and various rebel and criminal groups in Mali and across the Sahel.[9]

Based on the preceding analysis, I submit that the AMISOM model that developed from late 2009 could not and should not be reassembled as the basis for conducting sustained peace enforcement tasks. AMISOM is thus likely to represent more the exception than the rule as a means of organizing robust peace enforcement operations. There are several reasons for reaching this conclusion related to the model's three elements concerning political authority, finance, and operations.

Political Authority

With regard to political authority, the sheer complexity of the AMISOM model would make it incredibly difficult to replicate, even if the desire to do so existed. Despite being an AU operation, AMISOM depended on assembling and coordinating a range of external partners, in both official, formal partnerships (e.g., with UNSOA/UNSOS, the EU, and key states) and parallel operations that took place within the mission's area of responsibility but supported some of the same objectives (e.g. unilateral operations conducted by Kenya, Ethiopia, and the United States).

The model also generated confusion about which organization should really call the shots on AMISOM. At times, political differences emerged and unhelpful political competition developed. For many years the mission was

---

[8] See S/2016/809, 28 September 2016 and 'Joint United Nations-African Union Framework for Enhanced Partnership in Peace and Security'. (UN–AU internal document, 19 April 2017), https://unoau.unmissions.org/sites/default/files/signed_joint_framework.pdf

[9] The three AU-authorized coalitions were the Regional Coalition Initiative against the Lord's Resistance Army (2011), the Multinational Joint Task Force against Boko Haram (2015), and the G5 Sahel Joint Force against various rebel groups in the Sahel (2017). The International Conference of the Great Lakes Region proposed an ad hoc intervention brigade against the M-23 rebels in the Democratic Republic of the Congo (2012), but this subsequently deployed as part of the UN stabilization mission there (MONUSCO) in 2013.

given two different mandates: one written by the UN Security Council and one by the AU PSC. Competition also flared between the AU, UN, and Somali authorities over which actor should influence the direction of civilian operations in south-central Somalia. And when AMISOM entered its stabilization phase after 2012, its partners did not always share the same vision of what to prioritize. Sometimes the lack of a shared vision wasted time and resources. On other occasions, it also undermined the legitimacy and effectiveness of the mission.

The model also generated additional problems because of the legitimate differences that emerged from the distinct organizational cultures at the UN, AU, and EU. Each of these organizations had different rules, frameworks, and procedures for dealing with aspects of crisis response and they were not always in synch. AMISOM–UNSOA relations became at times particularly fraught because the UN's rules and procedures were based on expectations of supporting a fairly standard UN peacekeeping operation. AMISOM, however, was never a standard peacekeeping mission and instead found that despite the efforts of UNSOA personnel, the UN was not able to consistently meet the logistical demands of conducting manoeuvre warfare across an area as large as south-central Somalia.

Finally, the range of partnerships required to make AMISOM function also added an additional layer of bureaucratic complexity to already complicated issues of strategic coordination and cooperation. As the number of partners increased, so the mission's coordination structures had to expand. But it was not clear that the increasing decision-making layers and sophistication of the various coordination structures delivered greater effectiveness in the field.

Finance

The second element of the AMISOM model concerned financial support. On the positive side, AMISOM's partners did generate considerable amounts of funding for the mission, which by 2014 was costing approximately US $1 billion per year. But overall AMISOM's finances were not predictable, sustainable, or sufficiently flexible. They too had to rely on a range of international partners. While the EU was able to pay the monthly allowances to AMISOM's peacekeepers, unlike, for instance, the United States, which would supply equipment, including lethal materiel, but not allowances, the EU could not sustain its commitments indefinitely. By early 2017, the EU had signalled it would reduce its funding stream to AMISOM from 2018. From January 2016, it also allocated less of its financial support to paying AMISOM's monthly allowances, which were reduced by 20 per cent. Hence, ten years after the mission first deployed, AMISOM peacekeepers were receiving monthly allowances of approximately $800 while the standard rate for UN peacekeepers was approximately $1,400. Despite the problem this caused for the morale of AMISOM's peacekeepers, the AU failed to find other donors to take the EU's place. Similarly, when the UN had resorted to the use of trust funds to support the mission, the allocated money was not consistent and often came with caveats that meant it was difficult to spend on what the mission really needed.

The model also revealed how fickle partners can potentially undermine the mission. To give just one example, in late 2008, the George W. Bush administration strongly pushed for a UN peacekeeping operation to take over from the AU, but this was stopped by the incoming Obama administration, which instead supported the UNSOA mechanism to finance AMISOM's logistical needs. Then, from early 2017, the new Trump administration adopted a different approach to its predecessor by announcing its desire to cut $1 billion from US funding to the UN, most of which would have to come from cuts to the UN's assessed peacekeeping contributions, the source of the UNSOS budget. The model was also susceptible to other forms of shifting partner priorities that affected AMISOM's financial arrangements. In 2016, for instance, both the United States and EU suspended various forms of aid and security cooperation with Burundi following the internal unrest that had broken out across the country in 2015. This led to another delay in payments to the Burundian contingent and, once again, generated problems for the mission that distracted from its mandated tasks.

Operations

As noted above, this model consistently failed to generate AMISOM's authorized force requirements, thereby undermining morale and reducing the operation's ability to achieve its mandated tasks. This was partly because AMISOM was based on optimistic assumptions about the potential for reconciliation among Somalia's political elites and their ability to develop an effective set of Somali security forces. But there were other problems as well. Chapter 8 in particular discussed how AMISOM's logistics support mechanism was based on rules and expectations calibrated for UN peacekeeping but which were not suited to the mission's war-fighting needs. Unfortunately, this model of logistical support also broke one of the cardinal rules of warfare: not to separate a commander from control of their logistics. The resulting 'push' model could work reasonably well with the right planning, coordination, and preparation, but it was ill-suited to respond rapidly and flexibly to unpredictable needs. Nor was the model well-suited to ensuring oversight of, and accountability for, non-UN security forces. These issues became even more acute after the UN adopted its HRDDP in July 2011. The challenge was exacerbated by the fact that the AU embarked on AMISOM before it had developed internal guidelines and standard operating procedures on a range of relevant issues from civilian protection and SEA to medical policy and risk assessments. Taken together, the limitations of the AMISOM model with regard to political authority, financing, and operational effectiveness suggest it would be unwise to try and replicate for other operations that might need to fight for peace.

*   *   *

This book has told only the first ten years of AMISOM's story. But the mission continues to pursue its three strategic objectives: to reduce the threat posed by *al-Shabaab* and other armed opposition groups; to provide security in order to enable the political process, reconciliation, and peacebuilding in Somalia; and to enable the gradual handing over of security responsibilities from AMISOM to the Somali security forces contingent on their abilities.[10] In the foreseeable future, reducing the threat posed by *al-Shabaab* will hinge on building capable, legitimate, inclusive, and affordable Somali security forces based on a shared political vision for governance arrangements in the security sector. Moreover, while *al-Shabaab* remains a transnational insurgency utilizing asymmetric tactics, degrading the group will rely more on policing, law enforcement, and intelligence capabilities than military operations. It will also require widespread popular rejection of *al-Shabaab*'s ideology and propaganda and the active education and participation of local Somalis in countering such extremist organizations.[11] This will probably be the focus of the next chapter in AMISOM's story.

[10] S/RES/2297, 7 July 2016, §5.
[11] On which, see *Countering Al-Shabaab propaganda and Recruitment Mechanisms in South Central Somalia* (UNSOM, 2017).

A Note on Major Somali Non-State Armed Groups

The Islamic Courts: Having begun operating in Somalia in early 1994, the primary function of the Islamic Courts was to provide law and order as well as a degree of security for commerce. Initially established in northern Mogadishu, they subsequently spread south and ceased to operate in the north of the city from early 1998. The Courts became more prominent from 2003 under the leadership of Sheikh Sharif Sheikh Ahmed. Politically, the Courts represented a 'broad mosque', bringing together individuals from the moderate and fundamentalist ends of the Islamic spectrum.

Harakat Al-Shabaab: Al-Shabaab was formed in 2005 by a group of about thirty former members of the Somali *al-Ittihad al-Islamiya* militant organization who had fought against the Soviets in Afghanistan, and some of whom had ties to *al-Qa'ida*. *Al-Shabaab*'s radicals emerged as a key military faction partnering with the Islamic Courts in the fight against the warlords. They quickly gained a fashionable reputation among many youngsters in Mogadishu, in part because of their focus on discipline and order. By mid-2007, *al-Shabaab* had come to symbolize a new populist and militarized movement targeting Ethiopian and TFG forces inside Somalia.

Supreme Council of Islamic Courts (SCIC): The SCIC was formed in June 2006 to act as the governing coalition of the Islamic Courts that took control of Mogadishu from the various warlords. Hassan Dahir Aweys, was the head of its shura, and Sheikh Sharif Sheikh Ahmed was its administrative head. It included *al-Shabaab* fighters as part of its militia and was widely believed to have colluded with elements of *al-Qa'ida*.

Alliance for the Re-Liberation of Somalia (ARS): Following a failed attempt to organize a national reconciliation conference by the TFG in July and August 2007, the SCIC's leaders refused to participate and instead held their own version in Asmara, Eritrea in September. This ended with the formation of the Alliance for the Re-Liberation of Somalia (ARS). However, consensus did not last long within this alliance and it soon split into two factions: a more moderate wing led by Sheikh Sharif Sheikh Ahmed and Sharif Hassan moved to Djibouti (ARS-Djibouti), while a more hardline group led by Hassan Dahir Aweys remained in Eritrea (ARS-Asmara). The two factions were deeply divided over whether or not to engage with the TFG. Following the 2008 Djibouti peace agreement, ARS-Djibouti merged its forces with the TFG and its leader Sheik Sharif Shekh Ahmed became president of the TFG in January 2009.

Ahlu Sunna Wal Jamaa (ASWJ): ASWJ was a religious group formed in the early 1990s that had focused on providing free education in the mosques in response to radical anti-Sufi armed groups. In late 2008, however, it became involved with armed attempts to resist *al-Shabaab*'s efforts to capture the central Somali towns of Dusamareb, Gelinsor, and Guricel. Worried about the extreme Islamist agenda being peddled by *al-Shabaab*, ASWJ allowed militia fighters raised by a group of Habir-Gedr businessmen to operate under its official banner in order to resist. It received money and arms from Ethiopia, was involved in various deals with the TFG (though these often collapsed), and also fought other radical groups including Hizbul Islam.

Ras Kamboni: Ras Kamboni mujahidiin were mainly Ogaden clan militia that operated primarily in Jubaland and took their name from a small coastal town in southern Somalia that had reportedly served as a training camp for *al-Qa'ida* and fighters from the Islamic Courts. The group first came to prominence in August 2008 when it fought alongside *al-Shabaab* during the battle for Kismayo. In early 2009 it joined with three other organizations to form Hizbul Islam (see below). But by late 2009 the Ras Kamboni fighters suffered internal disagreements and split into two factions. One was led by the original leader Hassan Abdullah Hersi al-Turki and aligned with *al-Shabaab* and *al-Qa'ida*. The other was led by Ahmed Mohamed Islam ('Madobe') who abandoned his allegiance to *al-Qa'ida* and *al-Shabaab* and formed the Ras Kamboni Movement. Madobe's Movement subsequently became Kenya's preferred local ally in Jubaland: in October 2011, his fighters fought with Kenyan and TFG troops to dislodge *al-Shabaab* from locations in Gedo and Lower Juba and in September 2012 they helped to secure Kismayo with AMISOM forces.

Hizbul Islam: This group was established in early 2009 by the formation of a four-party coalition comprising the Alliance for the Re-liberation of Somalia (ARS), the Ras Kamboni militia, *Jabhatul Islamiya* (Islamic Front), and Anole, also called the Anoole Forces. The coalition did not hold long and its first leader, Omar Imam Abubakar, was replaced in May 2009 by Hassan Dahir Aweys, formerly leader of the SCIC and subsequently the ARS–Asmara faction. Hizbul Islam refused to join the ARS–Djibouti faction that had formed the new TFG administration in January 2009 and instead partnered with *al-Shabaab*. However, its relationship with *al-Shabaab* broke down and by late 2009 and 2010 it had lost most of its territory to *al-Shabaab*. By the end of 2010, Hizbul Islam effectively ceased to exist and its remnants merged into *al-Shabaab*.

AMISOM's Senior Leadership, March 2007–January 2018

Special Representatives of the Chairperson of the AU Commission	Force Commanders	Police Commissioners
Amb. Nicolas Bwakira (Burundi, Mar. 2007–Nov. 2009)	Maj. General Levi Karuhanga (Uganda, Mar. 2007–Feb. 2008) Maj. General Francis Okello (Uganda, Feb. 2008–July 2009)	Dr Charles Makono (Zimbabwe, Nov. 2011–May 2013)
Amb. Boubacar G. Diarra (Mali, Nov. 2009–Oct. 2012)	Lt General Nathan Mugisha (Uganda, July 2009–Aug. 2011) Maj. General Fred Mugisha (Uganda, Aug. 2011–May 2012)	
Amb. Mahamat S. Annadif (Chad, Nov. 2012–July 2014)	Lt General Andrew Gutti (Uganda, May 2012–Dec. 2013)	[Acting] Ben Oyo Nyeko (May 2013–May 2014)
Amb. Maman S. Sidikou (Niger, Aug. 2014–Oct. 2015)	Lt General Silas Ntigurirwa (Burundi, Dec. 2013–Dec. 2014)	Anand Pillay (South Africa, May 2014–Nov. 2017) [Acting] Daniel Ali Gwambal (Nigeria, Dec. 2017–present)
Amb. Francisco C.J. Madeira (Mozambique, Oct. 2015–present)	Lt General Jonathan K. Rono (Kenya, Dec. 2014–Dec. 2015) [Acting] Maj. Gen Nakibus Lakara (Ethiopia, Jan.–July 2016) Lt General Osman Noor Soubagleh (Djibouti, July 2016–Jan. 2018)	

Source: compiled by author.

A Note on AMISOM Fatality Estimates

The number of AMISOM personnel killed during their deployment in Somalia has become the source of considerable controversy. For AU peace operations generally there are standard operating procedures for reporting deaths and disabilities suffered on missions, including following a formal process of receiving a notification of casualties and constituting a Board of Inquiry to assess medical documents such as death certificates or injury reports. It would be highly unusual for compensation payments to be made to the next of kin for cases that have not been properly documented.

For AMISOM, the AU decided not to publicly release official numbers of fatalities because it said that responsibility and decision should lie with the TCCs that suffered the losses. However, throughout the mission, the governments of the TCCs consistently decided not to publicly release the names of all their fallen peacekeepers. The most frequent justifications for this approach were that there was little to gain by releasing full information about AMISOM fatalities and it would reduce morale and embolden the mission's enemies.

On the other hand, the AU's policy on this issue generated several controversies and considerable criticism. One criticism was that peacekeepers who died while carrying out their duties should be publicly honoured for their sacrifice. The UN, for example, publicly recognizes all its fallen peacekeepers and the AU had announced official fatality numbers for some of its other operations, such as its mission in the Central African Republic. Interestingly, in January 2015, the Chairperson of the AU Commission, Nkosazana Dlamini Zuma, stated 'We should have a monument for our AU peacekeepers who have lost their lives in the duty of the peoples of the continent'.[1] The AU's policy on AMISOM would likely mean that any such monument would have to include 'unknown' peacekeepers.

A second criticism was that the TCC governments did not all publicly clarify their policy on reporting casualty figures and hence there was inconsistency in the release of relevant information. Public information thus emerged about AU fatalities suffered during numerous specific incidents but no official overall total was released for the number suffered by AMISOM as a whole. This led to other organizations publishing partial information about certain periods of time. For example, in July 2011, the UN Monitoring Group on Somalia estimated that between April 2010 and April 2011, AMISOM suffered ninety-nine casualties.[2]

A third argument was that the AU policy led to considerable unhelpful speculation about the issue. At various times, journalists, analysts, and even government officials

---

[1] 'Statement to the 26th Ordinary Session of the AU Executive Council', Addis Ababa, 26 January 2015, p.8, https://au.int/sites/default/files/speeches/29496-sp-statement_en_0.pdf

[2] *Report of the Monitoring Group on Somalia and Eritrea pursuant to Security Council resolution 1916 (2010)* (S/2011/433, 18 July 2011), Annex 1.1.d, pp. 123–6.

and representatives of international organizations decided to try to fill the information gap. To give just a few illustrative examples:

- In October 2012 in a public forum on Somalia, Richard Onyonka, Kenya's Deputy Minister of Foreign Affairs, said that Uganda had lost more than 2,700 troops in AMISOM since 2007.[3] This prompted UPDF spokesperson Col. Felix Kulayigye to counter: 'That's not correct because both Burundi and Uganda have lost less than 500, including the injured. . . . His remarks should be treated with the contempt they deserve'.[4]

- On 9 May 2013, the UN Deputy-Secretary-General Jan Eliasson stated: 'You would be shocked to learn that maybe it is up to 3,000 AMISOM soldiers that have been killed during these years that AMISOM has been there [Somalia]'.[5] Shortly thereafter, the UN released a retraction of Eliasson's statement saying that it was based on 'information from informal sources' and should not be taken as accurate.[6]

- In January 2015, one analysis by the head of a South African think tank and a retired British General claimed that AMISOM had lost 'perhaps over 4,000 troops'.[7] The analysis provided no evidence to support their claim.

- On 20 July 2017, in a speech to the UN Security Council, the AU's Commissioner for Peace and Security stated 'the number of casualties by African troops in peace support operations in the last decade exceeds the combined casualties experienced in UN peacekeeping missions over the last 70 years'.[8] The vast majority of this number was from AMISOM.

A fourth criticism argued that the AU policy bred confusion and undermined AMISOM's credibility as a source of accurate information. As the AU/UN Information Support Team put it in November 2011,

---

[3] 'Morning Headlines', *AMISOM Daily Media Monitoring*, 1 November 2012, http://somaliamediamonitoring.org/november-1-2012-morning-headlines/

[4] Risdel Kasasira, 'Uganda, Burundi lost 500 soldiers in Somalia', *Daily Monitor* (Kampala), 2 November 2012, http://www.monitor.co.ug/News/National/Uganda++Burundi+lost+500+soldiers+in+Somalia+/-/688334/1609430/-/476x5dz/-/index.html

[5] Press Conference transcript, 9 May 2013, http://www.un.org/press/en/2013/dsgsm668.doc.htm

[6] 'Note to Correspondents', Office of the UN Secretary-General, 10 May 2013, https://www.un.org/sg/en/content/sg/note-correspondents/2013-05-10/note-correspondents-response-questions-concerning-number

[7] Greg Mills and Dickie Davis, 'Somalia: A case for (very) cautious optimism', *Daily Maverick*, 27 January 2015, https://www.dailymaverick.co.za/article/2015-01-27-somalia-a-case-for-very-cautious-optimism/#.WYMv4a2ZM2J

[8] Cited in UN document S/PV.8006, 19 July 2017, p. 4. As of 30 June 2017, 3,599 UN peacekeepers had died. At https://www.un.org/en/peacekeeping/fatalities/documents/stats_1jun.pdf. The same statistic and the AU's confusion about this issue had been noted five years earlier in Linnéa Gelot, Ludwig Gelot, and Cedric de Coning, 'Challenges, Key Issues and Future Directions' in Linnea Gelot, Ludwig Gelot, and Cedric de Coning (eds.), *Supporting African Peace Operations* (Nordic Africa Institute, Dag Hammarskjöld Foundation and Norwegian Institute of International Affairs, 2012), pp. 101, 104.

Table A.1. Estimates of cumulative AMISOM fatalities

Date	Estimated Fatalities (Additional Injured)	Source
10 Dec. 2008	12 (25 injured)	AMISOM Full Brief Presentation (AMISOM internal document, 25 Feb. 2009)
Feb. 2011	205 (798 injured)	AMISOM Medical records
25 Dec. 2011	237 + 84 MIA (985 injured)	*AMISOM Annual Report 2011* (AU internal document, no date), §63
5 July 2012	491 + 36 MIA (1,500 injured)	Briefing by AU PSOD to the AU Partners' Group, Addis Ababa, 5 July 2012.
Aug. 2009–Sept. 2012	439 (803 injured)	*AMISOM Financial and Narrative Reports* (AU internal documents, Aug. 2009–Sept. 2012).
1 Jan. 2009–31 Dec. 2014*	1,108	SIPRI Multilateral Peace Operations Database https://www.sipri.org/databases/pko
2017 (up to 19 Nov.)	281	'Amisom begins to withdraw troops from Somalia', *Daily Nation* (Kenya), 19 November 2017

* The figure supplied to SIPRI by the AU for 2014 of sixty-nine fatalities suffered covered only those due to hostile action. The AU has not supplied SIPRI with any data about fatalities beyond 31 December 2014.

Currently, AMISOM's mechanism for reporting troop casualties in Somalia is unclear. Following a fatal incident, different personnel, occupying various roles within AMISOM, the TCCs, and the African Union, brief a range of casualty figures to the media, with no central coordination. This leads to confusion and exposes AMISOM to charges of either incompetence or lying. There is a growing perception in the media that AMISOM's official casualty figures are inaccurate and that AMISOM is purposefully concealing the extent of their casualties. This leads to a loss of trust in AMISOM and moves media attention away from the mission's achievements in Somalia'[9]

Finally, the lack of a rapid and consistent AU response to allegations that AMISOM had sustained casualties provided *al-Shabaab* and other critics of the mission with an opportunity to bolster their propaganda, especially when *al-Shabaab* released photos and videos depicting AMISOM casualties.

   With these points in mind, Table A.1 provides data that has emerged in the course of my research that is relevant for anyone trying to estimate the overall number of AMISOM fatalities. It should be emphasized that I have no way of verifying this data. As discussed in Chapter 7, approximately 370 fatalities could plausibly be estimated from reports about the battles involving AMISOM troops at Jame'ada (2015), Leego (2015), Janaale (2015), El Adde (2016), Halgan (2016), Kulbiyow (2017), and Golweyn (2017).

[9] 'Memo to AMISOM Force Commander from AU/UN Information Support Team' (AU internal document, 1 November 2011), §1 and §2.

Index